World Economic Situation and Prospects

United Nations
New York, 2021

The *World Economic Situation and Prospects 2021* is a report produced by the United Nations Department of Economic and Social Affairs (UN DESA), in partnership with the United Nations Conference on Trade and Development (UNCTAD) and the five United Nations regional commissions: Economic Commission for Africa (UNECA), Economic Commission for Europe (UNECE), Economic Commission for Latin America and the Caribbean (UNECLAC), Economic and Social Commission for Asia and the Pacific (UNESCAP) and Economic and Social Commission for Western Asia (UNESCWA). The United Nations World Tourism Organization (UNWTO) and the UN Office of the High Representative for the Least Developed Countries, Landlocked Developing Countries and Small Island Developing States (UN-OHRLLS) also contributed to the report.

For further information, visit https://www.un.org/en/desa or contact:

UN DESA
Mr. Liu Zhenmin, Under-Secretary-General
Department of Economic and Social Affairs
Room S-2922
United Nations
New York, NY 10017
USA
☎ +1-212-9635958
✉ undesa@un.org

UNCTAD
Dr. Mukhisa Kituyi, Secretary-General
United Nations Conference on Trade and Development
Room E-9042
Palais de Nations, 8–14
1211 Geneva 10
Switzerland
☎ +41-22-9175806
✉ sgo@unctad.org

UNECA
Ms. Vera Songwe, Executive Secretary
United Nations Economic Commission for Africa
Menelik II Avenue
P.O. Box 3001
Addis Ababa
Ethiopia
☎ +251-11-5511231
✉ ecainfo@uneca.org

UNECE
Ms. Olga Algayerova, Executive Secretary
United Nations Economic Commission for Europe
Palais des Nations
CH-1211 Geneva 10
Switzerland
☎ +41-22-9174444
✉ unece_info@un.org

UNECLAC
Ms. Alicia Bárcena, Executive Secretary
Economic Commission for Latin America and the Caribbean
Av. Dag Hammarskjöld 3477
Vitacura
Santiago, Chile
Chile
☎ +56-2-22102000
✉ secepal@cepal.org

UNESCAP
Ms. Armida Salsiah Alisjahbana, Executive Secretary
Economic and Social Commission for Asia and the Pacific
United Nations Building
Rajadamnern Nok Avenue
Bangkok 10200
Thailand
☎ +66-2-2881234
✉ escap-scas@un.org

UNESCWA
Ms. Rola Dashti, Executive Secretary
Economic and Social Commission for Western Asia
P.O. Box 11-8575
Riad el-Solh Square, Beirut
Lebanon
☎ +961-1-981301
@ https://www.unescwa.org/contact

ISBN: 978-92-1-109182-3
eISBN: 978-92-1-005498-0
Print ISSN: 1995-2074
Online ISSN: 2411-8370
United Nations publication
Sales No. E.21.II.C.1

Sustainable Development Goals

Goal 1. End poverty in all its forms everywhere

Goal 2. End hunger, achieve food security and improved nutrition and promote sustainable agriculture

Goal 3. Ensure healthy lives and promote well-being for all at all ages

Goal 4. Ensure inclusive and equitable quality education and promote lifelong learning opportunities for all

Goal 5. Achieve gender equality and empower all women and girls

Goal 6. Ensure availability and sustainable management of water and sanitation for all

Goal 7. Ensure access to affordable, reliable, sustainable and modern energy for all

Goal 8. Promote sustained, inclusive and sustainable economic growth, full and productive employment and decent work for all

Goal 9. Build resilient infrastructure, promote inclusive and sustainable industrialization and foster innovation

Goal 10. Reduce inequality within and among countries

Goal 11. Make cities and human settlements inclusive, safe, resilient and sustainable

Goal 12. Ensure sustainable consumption and production patterns

Goal 13. Take urgent action to combat climate change and its impacts

Goal 14. Conserve and sustainably use the oceans, seas and marine resources for sustainable development

Goal 15. Protect, restore and promote sustainable use of terrestrial ecosystems, sustainably manage forests, combat desertification, and halt and reverse land degradation and halt biodiversity loss

Goal 16. Promote peaceful and inclusive societies for sustainable development, provide access to justice for all and build effective, accountable and inclusive institutions at all levels

Goal 17. Strengthen the means of implementation and revitalize the Global Partnership for Sustainable Development

Explanatory notes

The following symbols have been used in the tables throughout the report:

... **Three dots** indicate that data are not available or are not separately reported.

– **A dash** indicates that the amount is nil or negligible.

- **A hyphen** indicates that the item is not applicable.

- **A minus sign** indicates deficit or decrease, except as indicated.

. **A full stop** is used to indicate decimals.

/ **A slash** between years indicates a crop year or financial year, for example, 2020/21.

- **Use of a hyphen between years**, for example, 2020–2021, signifies the full period involved, including the beginning and end years.

Reference to "dollars" ($) indicates United States dollars, unless otherwise stated.

Reference to "billions" indicates one thousand million.

Reference to "tons" indicates metric tons, unless otherwise stated.

Annual rates of growth or change, unless otherwise stated, refer to annual compound rates.

Details and percentages in tables do not necessarily add to totals, because of rounding.

Project LINK is an international collaborative research group for econometric modelling, coordinated jointly by the Economic Analysis and Policy Division of UN DESA and the University of Toronto.

For **country classifications**, see Statistical annex.

Data presented in this publication incorporate information available as at **30 November 2020.**

The following abbreviations have been used:

AfCFTA	African Continental Free Trade Area
BIS	Bank for International Settlements
CIS	Commonwealth of Independent States
ECA	United Nations Economic Commission for Africa
ECB	European Central Bank
ECE	United Nations Economic Commission for Europe
ECLAC	United Nations Economic Commission for Latin America and the Caribbean
ESCAP	United Nations Economic and Social Commission for Asia and the Pacific
ESCWA	United Nations Economic and Social Commission for Western Asia
EU	European Union
FAO	Food and Agriculture Organization of the United Nations
FDI	foreign direct investment
G20	Group of Twenty
GCC	Cooperation Council for the Arab States of the Gulf
GDP	gross domestic product
GVC/s	global value chain/s
ICT	information and communication technology
ILO	International Labour Organization
IMF	International Monetary Fund
LDCs	least developed countries
LLDCs	landlocked developing countries
MSME/s	micro-, small and medium-sized enterprise/s
ODA	official development assistance
OECD	Organization for Economic Cooperation and Development
PPE	personal protective equipment
SAR	Special Administrative Region
SDG/s	Sustainable Development Goal/s
SDRs	special drawing rights
SDT	special and differential treatment
SIDS	small island developing States
UBI	universal basic income
UN DESA	Department of Economic and Social Affairs of the United Nations Secretariat
UNCTAD	United Nations Conference on Trade and Development
UNICEF	United Nations Children's Fund
UNIDO	United Nations Industrial Development Organization
UN-OHRLLS	United Nations Office of the High Representative for the Least Developed Countries, Landlocked Developing Countries and Small Island Developing States
UNWTO	United Nations World Tourism Organization
VAT	value-added tax
WEFM	World Economic Forecasting Model
WGP	world gross product
WTO	World Trade Organization

Acknowledgements

The *World Economic Situation and Prospects 2021* is a report produced by the United Nations Department of Economic and Social Affairs (**UN DESA**), in partnership with the United Nations Conference on Trade and Development (**UNCTAD**) and Economic Commission for Africa (**UNECA**), Economic Commission for Europe (**UNECE**), Economic Commission for Latin America and the Caribbean (**UNECLAC**), Economic and Social Commission for Asia and the Pacific (**UNESCAP**) and Economic and Social Commission for Western Asia (**UNESCWA**).

The United Nations World Tourism Organization (**UNWTO**) and the UN Office of the High Representative for the Least Developed Countries, Landlocked Developing Countries and Small Island Developing States (**UN-OHRLLS**) also contributed to the report. The forecasts presented in the report draw on the World Economic Forecasting Model (WEFM) of UN DESA as well as inputs from the United Nations regional commissions.

Under the general guidance of Liu Zhenmin, Under-Secretary-General for Economic and Social Affairs, and Elliott Harris, United Nations Chief Economist, Assistant-Secretary-General for Economic Development, and Officer-in-Charge of the Economic Analysis and Policy Division (EAPD), Hamid Rashid, Chief of the Global Economic Monitoring Branch of EAPD, led and coordinated the writing of the report with a core team of authors from **UN DESA**, comprising: Helena Afonso, Grigor Agabekian, Ian Cox, Andrea Grozdanic, Matthias Kempf, Poh Lynn Ng, Lennart Claas Niermann, Ingo Pitterle, Hamid Rashid, Julian Rodrick Slotman, Sebastian Vergara and Yasuhisa Yamamoto.

The contributions of Hoi Wai Jackie Cheng, Kristinn Sv. Helgason, Nicole Hunt, Mario Huzel, Nazrul Islam, Alex Julca, Cornelia Kaldewei, Hiroshi Kawamura, Leah C. Kennedy, Marcelo Lafleur, Gabe Scelta, Oliver Schwank, Nancy Settecasi, Shari Spiegel from **UN DESA;** Rachid Amui, Bruno Antunes, Jeronim Capaldo, Chantal Line Carpentier, Cambiz Daneshvar, Marco Fugazza, Taisuke Ito, Richard Kozul-Wright, Wei Li, Nicolas Maystre, Janvier Nkurunziza, Ralf Peters, Mesut Saygili, Miho Shirotori, Dong Wu from **UNCTAD**; Bartholomew Armah, Joseph Atta-Mensah, Christine Achieng Awiti, Yesuf Mohammednur Awel, Jean Paul Boketsu Bofili, Hopestone Kayiska Chavula, Amandine Nakumuryango from **UNECA;** José Palacín Lucio from **UNECE**; Michael Hanni, Noel Pérez, Daniel Titelman, Cecilia Vera from **UNECLAC**; Witada Anukoonwattaka, Shuvojit Banerjee, Zheng Jian, Jeong-Dae Lee, Mia Mikic, Sweta Saxena, Vatcharin Sirimaneetham from **UNESCAP**; Mohamed Bchir, Jan Gaska, Mohamed El Moctar Mohamed El Hacene, Ahmed Moummi, Souraya Zein from **UNESCWA**; Sandra Carvão, Michel Julian and Javier Ruescas from **UNWTO;** and Susanna Wolf from **UN-OHRLLS** are duly acknowledged.

Bernard Hoekman and Ben Shepherd contributed a background paper for chapter II of the report.

The report was edited by Michael Brodsky.

Executive summary

A once-in-a-century crisis—a Great Disruption unleashed by a viral pandemic—hit the world economy in 2020. The pandemic spread like a forest fire, reaching every corner of the world, infecting more than 90 million and killing close to 2 million people worldwide. For several months, uncertainties and panic paralysed most economic activities in both developed and developing economies. Trade and tourism came to a grinding halt, while job and output losses exceeded levels seen in any previous crisis. In a matter of months, the number of people living in poverty increased sharply, while income and wealth inequality trended towards new highs.

The pandemic has killed close to 2 million people and counting

Governments around the world responded rapidly—and boldly—to stem the health and economic contagion of the crisis. Fiscal and monetary stimulus packages were quickly rolled out to save the economy. The crisis responses, however, entailed difficult choices between saving lives and saving livelihoods, between speed of delivery and efficiency, and between short-term costs and long-term impacts. Limited fiscal space and high levels of public debt constrained the ability of many developing countries to roll out sufficiently large stimulus packages.

The Great Disruption

The short-term economic costs of the Great Disruption do not fully account for its long-term impacts on employment, productivity and potential output. While large-scale fiscal stimulus prevented total economic collapse and supported the incomes of millions of households, there is little sign that these measures will boost long-term investments and create new jobs. Unless investments in physical and human capital pick up, the world economy will likely adjust to a lower growth trajectory. Slow and protracted recovery of growth will in turn impact the realization of the 2030 Agenda for Sustainable Development.

The long-term impacts of the current crisis will be equally severe

The pandemic has exposed the systemic vulnerability of the world economy. It has also shown that sustainable development—promoting inclusive and equitable growth, reducing inequality and enhancing environmental sustainability—can provide safeguards and resilience against future crisis. There is clearly no sustainable development without resilience and there is no resilience without sustainable development. Building economic, social and environmental resilience must guide the recovery from the crisis. Economic resilience with new fiscal and debt sustainability frameworks, societal resilience with universal social protection schemes and climate resilience with greater investments in the green economy must be the building blocks of a resilient recovery. This will also require a stronger and more effective multilateral system which can complement and reinforce—not undermine—national efforts to put the world firmly on the trajectory of sustainable development.

There is no sustainable development without resilience and there is no resilience without sustainable development

Economic growth tumbled worldwide

The pandemic hit the developed countries the hardest...

World gross product fell by an estimated 4.3 per cent in 2020—the sharpest contraction of global output since the Great Depression. In contrast, world output had shrunk by 1.7 per cent during the Great Recession in 2009. The pandemic clearly hit the developed economies the hardest, given the strict lockdown measures that many countries in Europe and several states of the United States of America imposed early on during the outbreak. Output in developed economies is estimated to have shrunk by 5.6 per cent in 2020, with growth projected to recover to 4.0 per cent in 2021. A renewed outbreak, however, set off new lockdown measures in the third quarter of 2020 in many countries in Europe, making a quick recovery more unlikely.

...and developing countries have not escaped the wrath of the current crisis

The developing countries experienced a relatively less severe contraction, with output shrinking by 2.5 per cent in 2020. Their economies are projected to grow by 5.7 per cent in 2021. The least developed countries (LDCs) saw their gross domestic product (GDP) shrink by 1.3 per cent in 2020, with growth expected to reach 4.9 per cent in 2021. The countries in Latin America and the Caribbean and South Asia experienced the sharpest declines. In contrast, the economies in East Asia fared relatively better than those in all other developing regions, with GDP expanding by 1 per cent in 2020. On the back of China's quick - and robust - recovery, the East Asian economies are forecast to grow by 6.4 per cent in 2021.

The economies of the Group of Twenty (G20)—which account for nearly 80 per cent of world output—contracted by 4.1 per cent, mirroring the overall performance of the world economy. Only China, among G20 members, managed to register positive growth in 2020. It will remain critical that the G20 economies return to the trajectory of growth, not only to lift the rest of the world economies but also to make the world economy more resilient to future shocks.

Job losses skyrocketed

The pandemic and shutdowns affected more than four out of five jobs worldwide

The GDP estimates mask the severity of the employment crisis unleashed by the pandemic. By April, full or partial lockdown measures had affected almost 2.7 billion workers, representing about 81 per cent of the world's workforce. The aggregate unemployment rate in the Organization for Economic Cooperation and Development (OECD) reached 8.8 per cent in April 2020, before falling to 6.9 per cent in November. Unemployment rates still remain high relative to pre-crisis levels in all developed countries. The COVID-19 crisis has also wreaked havoc on the labour markets in the developing world. By mid-2020, unemployment rates had quickly escalated to record highs: 27 per cent in Nigeria, 23 per cent in India, 21 per cent in Colombia, 17 per cent in the Philippines and above 13 per cent in Argentina, Brazil, Chile, Saudi Arabia and Turkey.

Women have been particularly hit by the pandemic, as they account for more than 50 per cent jobs in labour-intensive service sectors, such as in retail trade and tourism, where working remotely is often not an option for many workers. While some crimes have registered a decline, women and girls are increasingly becoming victims of violence during the implementation of the lockdown measures. It is also likely child marriages will see a global uptick against the backdrop of falling female labour force participation and rising poverty.

The potential output of the world economy will adjust downward

The long-term consequences of the crisis will be equally severe. The pandemic will likely accelerate the pace of digitalization, automation and robotization, which will further depress labour demand in the medium term. While productivity will experience some growth in economic sectors embracing automation, average productivity growth will falter. Declining investments in fixed capital, low average productivity growth and lower labour-force participation rates will further depress potential output of the world economy.

Massive liquidity and low inflation are fueling a financial bubble

The Great Disruption choked global and domestic supply chains. But the shock to income and consumer demand outweighed the supply-side shocks. Weaker consumption and investment spending during most of the year dampened inflationary pressures around the world. Consumer price inflation is projected to remain low in 2021 as unemployment will likely remain high relative to pre-crisis level in most economies. Corrections in asset prices in financial and real estate markets would likely further dampen inflationary pressures.

While the central banks around the world have been broadly successful in injecting massive amount of liquidity and keeping long-term interest rates low, they have been less successful in meeting their inflation targets, with actual inflation falling below expectations. The environment of excessive liquidity and low inflation has allowed financial markets to underprice risks and create a massive financial bubble, which may exacerbate financial instability. Low inflation will also adversely impact the sustainability of high levels of public and private debt worldwide. As debts are typically contracted in nominal values, a lower-than-expected inflation will keep the real value of debt high. The rising real value of debt and stagnant or falling revenue will likely worsen the risks of debt defaults.

A toxic combination of excessive liquidity and low inflation have triggered a massive financial bubble, potentially threatening financial stability and recovery

Fiscal stimulus measures prevented a Great Depression

Massive and timely fiscal responses prevented a Great Depression-like economic catastrophe worldwide. The fiscal outlays from the developed countries represented nearly 80 per cent of the $12.7 trillion of fiscal stimulus worldwide, with Germany, Japan and the United States accounting for more than 50 per cent of all the fiscal stimulus worldwide. The group of 46 least developed countries (LDCs), for example, collectively managed to increase direct and indirect fiscal support by only 2.6 per cent of their GDP, while the size of the stimulus for the developed countries averaged 15.8 per cent of their GDP.

In dollar terms, stimulus spending per capita averaged nearly $10,000 in the developed countries, while it amounted to less than $20 per capita in the least developed countries. That is, for every additional dollar per capita of stimulus that the LDCs managed to spend, the developed countries spent nearly $580 per capita on stimulus. The disparity in the size of the stimulus between the LDCs and the developed economies dwarfed the income disparity between these two group of countries. The per capita income of the developed countries is only 30 times larger than the per capita GDP of the least developed countries.

The stimulus measures have been highly uneven with the developed countries managing to spend significantly more to support consumption and boost growth

Massive liquidity is not boosting investments

Thanks to massive stimulus spending worldwide, the financial markets are now awash with liquidity. While credit flows stabilized, there has been little growth in fixed investment. In the United States, for example, fixed non-residential investments fell by 7.8 per cent in the second quarter, while money supply increased by 23.2 per cent during the same period. Most of excess liquidity went to acquisition of financial assets. Acquisitions of financial assets clearly do not increase fixed investments, which are critical for creating jobs and boosting economic growth. Against the backdrop of a raging pandemic, the world is witnessing the build-up of a massive financial bubble, with major stock market indices registering record increases during the past 10 months. The S&P 500 index, for example, rose by nearly 40 per cent compared with average annual increases of 10 per cent during the past five years.

Boosting investments will remain critical for accelerating recovery and building resilience to future shocks

Public finance and debt are facing unprecedented risks

Deficits and debt are increasing to record levels, exacerbating the risks of debt distress.

Saving the livelihoods today must not compromise the prosperity of the future generations.

The rolling out of large stimulus packages, and falling government revenues, have strained and stretched public finances worldwide. In almost one in five developing and transition economies, the government deficit is projected to reach double digits as a percentage of GDP in 2020. A slower recovery of growth will only further exacerbate fiscal deficits.

Along with growing fiscal deficits, total public debt worldwide increased by an estimated $9.9 trillion in 2020. This is the largest increase in public debt since the Second World War. Governments around the world borrowed from the future to minimize the impact of the crisis on the current generation. The current generation therefore has the responsibility to make sure that the borrowed money is well invested to ensure that the well-being of the current generation does not come at the expense of the well-being of future generations. The urgency and emergency of the current crisis cannot justify depriving those future generations of their right to enjoy prosperity. The rise in public debt should not in itself be a concern as long as additional debt expands productive capacity and stimulates growth.

Avoiding austerity is a must

Growing concerns for fiscal deficits and debt sustainability should not push Governments towards austerity. Countries with high levels of public debt—and constrained by fiscal rules—may be forced to cut back spending too quickly to balance their budgets. These concerns should rather encourage Governments to ensure that deficits and debt actually promote growth. With a benign inflation outlook, real public debt will remain high relative to real GDP. It will be politically and economically infeasible for many Governments to raise taxes during the recovery period. These constraints may encourage Governments to look to the alternative of making devastating cuts in fiscal spending to reduce deficit and debt.

Austerity measures will inevitably stifle recovery and undermine progress on sustainable development

A premature embrace of austerity will inevitably weaken the speed and quality of the recovery and undermine resilience to future shocks. Austerity measures almost always cut back social sector spending on health and education and public services with far-reaching consequences for many SDGs. The global spillover effects of spending cuts—via trade, investment and official development assistance (ODA) flows—will have dire consequences for sustainable development.

The crisis is worsening poverty and inequality

More than 131 million have fallen into poverty in 2020 and more will likely follow if a robust and inclusive recovery remains elusive

High unemployment and loss of income have pushed millions into destitution during the pandemic. The total number of people living in poverty is expected to increase by 131 million in 2020 alone, representing a sharp rise from the last projections presented in the World Economic Situation and Prospects mid-year update released in June 2020. As many as 797 million people will still be trapped in extreme poverty in 2030, representing a poverty headcount ratio of over 9 per cent. The cardinal Sustainable Development Goal of eradicating extreme poverty by 2030 (Goal 1.1) will likely be missed by a large margin. Poverty will remain pervasive in sub-Saharan Africa and many landlocked countries. Other SDGs will suffer collateral damages as a consequence of rising poverty.

While nearly 8 million people in the United States lost their jobs during the pandemic and the national poverty rate jumped from 9.3 per cent in June to 11.7 per cent in November 2020, the total wealth of 644 United States billionaires increased by 31.6 per cent between March and October 2020, from $2.95 trillion to $3.88 trillion. The richest five among them saw their total wealth increase by 66 per cent, from $358 billion to $596 billion, during the same period. The growing income and wealth divides—reinforced by lingering uncertainties on the health and economic fronts—will breed further discontent, fray social cohesion and potentially undermine recovery efforts. Reining in inequality will remain critical for steering a resilient recovery from the current crisis.

Recovery with resilience

The pandemic—and its uneven economic impact on the poorer segments of the population—is further polarizing societies in both developed and developing countries. While timely and massive fiscal interventions helped to prevent the worst, they did not mitigate the broader discontent that stems from marginalization of the most vulnerable population groups and the stark inequality that divides the haves and the have nots in society. The pandemic responses need to prioritize efforts to reduce inequality not only in income and wealth but also in access and opportunities.

Many developing countries will face growing challenges of accelerating recovery and catching up

Many developing countries buffeted by the pandemic and unable to respond with large fiscal responses will likely see their growth and development path adjust downward relative to the pre-crisis trends. This may reverse or at least delay the long-term trend of convergence in the per capita incomes of the developed and developing countries, thwarting the objectives of reducing inequality between countries as envisaged in the 2030 Agenda for Sustainable Development.

The path to recovery and progress on SDGs will critically hinge on the ability and political commitment of countries to make sure that the crisis response builds resilience against future economic, social and climatic shocks. As noted above, there is no sustainable development without resilience and there is no resilience without sustainable development. The imperatives of strengthening public finance and debt sustainability, expanding social protection and building climate resilience must inform policy choices to put the world firmly on the trajectory of sustainable development.

Future of global trade

The COVID-19 crisis has delivered a significant shock to global trade, restricting cross-border travel, disrupting international production networks and depressing demand worldwide. After trade flows collapsed in the early stages of the pandemic, merchandise trade has been recovering since mid-2020 on the back of strong demand for electric and electronic equipment, pharmaceuticals and, especially, personal protective equipment. The recovery in merchandise trade has been led by China and other East Asian economies, which were relatively successful in containing the spread of the virus and experienced a faster-than-expected rebound in economic activities.

The collapse in global tourism has created an emergency for many developing countries

International travel has been hit particularly hard by the pandemic. As travel restrictions persist across the world, global tourism remains at a fraction of its pre-pandemic level. Worldwide tourist arrivals are estimated to have plunged by 70 per cent in 2020, the largest decline on record; and international tourism receipt losses are estimated to have amounted to US$ 1.1 trillion. This has created an emergency for many developing countries, especially small island developing States, where tourism accounts for up to 80 per cent of total export revenues. Cross-border trade in services sectors that require physical distancing, such as construction, has also fallen sharply, whereas trade in computer services has been boosted by rising demand for digital solutions.

The global trade outlook is clouded by major uncertainties

Lingering trade tensions will impede the recovery of global trade

Overall, global trade in goods and services is estimated to have declined by 7.6 per cent in 2020, a slightly smaller contraction than during the global financial crisis. The UN DESA baseline scenario projects a moderate recovery in global trade over the next two years as countries slowly bring the pandemic under control and ease movement restrictions. Annual growth in global trade is forecast at 6.9 per cent in 2021 and 3.7 per cent in 2022, buoyed by a recovery in international travel. The global trade outlook is clouded, however, by significant uncertainties, including over the future spread of the virus; lasting damage from the crisis—for example, to labour markets and balance sheets; and lingering trade tensions among major trading partners.

The crisis has affected international commodity markets very unevenly

Commodity exporters have taken a hard hit although some commodities did not experience a sharp decline

The COVID-19 pandemic has affected commodity markets very unevenly, in contrast to the global financial crisis, during which commodity prices moved mostly together. Agricultural commodity prices have been resilient as global demand remained robust and supply chain disruptions were generally only short-lived. Since global markets for major food staples are well supplied, agricultural price indexes are projected to remain fairly stable in 2021. After falling sharply during the early stages of the pandemic, the prices of metals have rebounded faster and more strongly than expected. As a result of strong demand from China and supply disruptions, the prices of copper, aluminium and iron ore are now well above their pre-pandemic levels. Meanwhile, the crisis has severely affected the global energy industry, with potentially long-lasting consequences. While the initial collapse in oil prices has been followed by a steady recovery on the back of improving global prospects, oil supply cuts and a weakening dollar, elevated global oil inventory levels and surplus production capacity limit the upward potential of oil prices going forward.

The changing global trade landscape will impact progress on the SDGs

Beyond short-term dynamics, the pandemic has accelerated several structural shifts, which are shaping the future of the global trade landscape. These include the rise of digital technologies, the increasingly significant role of services in the global economy and the evolving configuration of global value chains (GVCs). The changing international trade environment will have a profound impact on countries' growth prospects and their progress towards sustainable development. How global trade patterns and trade policies evolve over the coming decade will be an important determinant of progress towards achievement of all of the goals within the SDG framework.

Digitalization is transforming manufacturing and service delivery worldwide

Across the globe, COVID-19 has created rapidly growing demand for digital services, accelerating ongoing digital transformation. With lockdowns and movement restrictions in place, operating digitally has been the only viable option for many firms to stay in business and government agencies to perform their functions. Digital processes are becoming ever more embedded in production and trade as information and communication technology (ICT) services control business processes and facilitate transactions within networks and between firms and customers. New technologies, such as 3D printing and additive manufacturing, have the potential to fundamentally alter business models and redefine comparative advantage by facilitating scale-independent efficient production and bringing production systems closer to consumers. In the medium term, such developments could support reshoring trends by increasing the competitiveness of previously non-competitive production locations and by encouraging a shift from the traditional model of economies of scale of large plants serving global markets to networks of smaller, more flexible and geographically distributed plants. Moreover, digitalization and emerging technologies, including artificial intelligence and machine learning, are also transforming service delivery worldwide. They will increasingly facilitate the cross-border exchange of health, education and other services, reinforcing the growing importance of services in global trade and development.

New technologies, accelerating the pace of digitalization and automation, are redefining comparative advantages in global trade

The pandemic has highlighted the need for more resilient and flexible supply chains

By exposing the risk presented by complex and geographically dispersed production networks, the COVID-19 crisis may accelerate the reconfiguration and, possibly, the shortening of GVCs. For many developing countries, especially in East Asia, participation in GVCs has contributed to gains in productivity and employment, yielding increases in per capita incomes and reductions in poverty in recent decades. After rising rapidly in the 1990s and 2000s, the expansion of GVCs has visibly slowed since the global financial crisis. The maturing of existing production networks, along with pushback against globalization and adoption of more inward-looking trade policies in many parts of the world, has brought about a shift towards more domestically oriented supply chains. For many firms, the pandemic has reinforced the need to reassess potential trade-offs between efficiency (based on low inventories and just-in-time delivery) and resilience. In the medium term, GVCs could become more flexible and robust through diversification of the supply base and a shortening of the distance between suppliers and the retail base.

The global supply chains are becoming more nimble and flexible, and possibly more resilient

Digitalization and servicification are redefining comparative advantages

Rapid technological change and shifting global trade patterns present developing countries with major challenges but could also be the source of immense opportunities. In the past, many developing countries struggled to replicate East Asia's success in using trade as an engine for development. Often, exports have not become a main vehicle for technological progress and their dynamic effects on productivity growth and structural change have therefore been limited. Against this backdrop, the changing global trade landscape requires developing countries to reassess their development strategies and explore models of the dynamic comparative advantages to be derived from digitalization and the expansion of service-related activities. Unlike in manufacturing, geographical disadvantages are less important in building an export base of services. Moreover, servicification—i.e., the increased use, production and export of services in other sectors—can serve as a tool for the modernization of farming and manufacturing.

The global digital divide will place many developing countries at a competitive disadvantage

Developing countries will need to prioritize service contents in their exports to remain competitive in the emerging trade landscape

The global digital divide will place many developing countries, especially low-income countries that lack digital infrastructure, at a competitive disadvantage in the new trade environment. Development efforts are also hampered by a highly fragmented global regime for regulation of data flows. To harness the opportunities arising from the changes in the international trade environment, national Governments will need to focus on developing as well as upgrading workforce skills, and to establish regulatory and policy frameworks that enable the private sector to set up required ICT infrastructure successfully. In many developing countries, it is vital that national innovation systems are strengthened in order to invigorate firms' capabilities to absorb and utilize knowledge and adjust to changing circumstances.

The rule-based multilateral trading system remains moribund

The COVID-19 pandemic has exposed some of the critical challenges faced by the multilateral trading system as countries around the world initially resorted to unilateral trade measures to protect domestic interests. Rising protectionist tendencies and shifts towards bilateral and regional trade agreements are threatening to further weaken the role of the World Trade Organization (WTO) as the central governing body for global trade. This in turn could lead to an increasingly polarized and fragmented international trade landscape in the coming decades which would be harmful for small and low-income countries, including the least developed countries, landlocked developing countries and the small island developing States.

The pandemic has added yet another challenge to an already weakened World Trade Organization

While creating new challenges, the COVID-19 pandemic can also serve as a catalyst for restoring confidence in the multilateral trading system. The pandemic has underscored that in times of crisis, keeping trade flowing and limiting protectionist and nationalist measures are vital to ensuring the safety of lives and livelihoods. Recognizing that current and future challenges can be met only through global partnerships and strong multilateral frameworks could generate positive momentum for WTO reform. Breaking the existing stalemate will require a rebuilding of trust in WTO based on establishing reaffirmed commitments to multilateralism and the development agenda of trade integration; revisiting some of the organization's long-standing practices; and ensuring constructive engagement by members on controversial and emerging issues such as e-commerce, subsidy policies and climate change-motivated trade policies. This could help create a multilateral trading system that is fit for purpose for a twenty-first century global economy which will be increasingly service-based and digital.

Regional outlook

The pandemic has caused a crisis of historic proportions across the world economy. In many developed countries, economic activity virtually came to a standstill in the second quarter of 2020, triggering the enactment of significant policy measures in both the fiscal and the monetary realm. However, during the subsequent midyear rebound, developed economies failed to attain the pre-crisis level of economic output. The recovery in domestic demand has been fragile, owing to general uncertainty and the paralysing effect of the pandemic on economic activity. Against this background, the growth trajectory remains strongly dependent on policy support measures.

Developed economies took the hardest hit

While developed economies are forecast to see a recovery in 2021, this outlook is subject to great uncertainty. In the United States, as monetary easing continues, consumption of durable goods and residential investments continue to grow. However, other demand components, particularly corporate investments and exports, are forecast to remain weak as long as the uncertainties associated with the COVID-19 pandemic persist. In a context of weak employment prospects and wage growth, the fragile recovery could easily be reversed if fiscal support measures remain inadequate. An indicator of the elevated uncertainty has been the spike in household savings in the United States and other developed economies. In Europe, the risks to the outlook include the further evolution of the pandemic and the lockdown measures taken in the fourth quarter in order to deal with the resurgent case numbers. In addition, the region is also facing challenges that predated the pandemic, including those related to the future relationship between the European Union (EU) and the United Kingdom of Great Britain and Northern Ireland as well as disruptive structural changes in the automotive industry in a number of countries. In developed Asia, the outlook is heavily dependent on the revival of external demand, particularly from East Asia. The stability of shared global supply chains, commodity demand and tourism will be important determinants of economic performance.

Many developed countries are facing the renewed challenges of a second wave of the virus, which will undermine their recovery efforts

Lower commodity prices compounded the challenges for the Commonwealth of Independent States (CIS) and Georgia

The outbreak of the COVID-19 pandemic has unleashed multiple shocks in the Commonwealth of Independent States (CIS) and Georgia. The disruptive effect of the lockdown and quarantine measures introduced in the region was further compounded by lower commodity prices, including for important non-oil commodities exported by the CIS countries. The shocks have been widespread across the region, resulting in declines in output in almost all countries. The magnitude of those declines has depended on a country's economic structure and its capacity to adopt offsetting measures, which was larger for energy-exporting countries. The economic outlook for the region is uncertain, with downside risks predominating, including the further trajectory of the pandemic. While the banking sector has remained stable during the current crisis, the deterioration of asset quality and high levels of dollarization in many countries will constrain lending and increase risks. In addition, geopolitical tensions have mounted and, in some cases, have spiraled into real conflict.

Lower commodity prices and the collapse of tourism are posing significant challenges Commonwealth of Independent States (CIS) and Georgia

South-Eastern Europe has experienced high unemployment and negative fallout from trade linkages

In South-Eastern Europe, the crisis has led to an increase in unemployment from already high levels, reversing some of the improvements seen in previous years. The fallout of the pandemic in the European Union, the main destination for the region's exports and a source of investments and remittances, has depressed external demand and reduced income, while supply chain disruptions have dampened manufacturing production. The effects have varied across the region, depending on policy space and the level of dependency on tourism.

Africa faces the dire risk of the reversal of the development gains of recent decades

The pandemic is quickly reversing the decades of development gains in Africa, as unemployment and poverty rise significantly around the continent

Africa has been experiencing an unprecedented economic downturn with major adverse impacts on the long-term development of the continent. Domestic lockdowns required to control the pandemic, lower external demand combined with lower commodity prices, the collapse of tourism and lower remittances have set off severe economic disruptions. Although many countries in Africa have taken action quickly to counter the spread of the pandemic, most are severely hampered by a lack of the resources needed to support health systems, protect vulnerable population groups and support the recovery. Given its magnitude and unequal effects across population groups, the current crisis is causing a rise in unemployment, poverty and inequality, which threatens to wipe out the development gains of recent decades. In addition, more difficult financing conditions and rising public debt are exposing many African countries to debt distress. The continent is forecast to see a modest recovery in 2021, but this depends on the relaxation of lockdown constraints and an improvement in trade and commodity markets.

East Asian economies fare better than others

Against the backdrop of a relatively quick recovery of aggregate demand in China, the East Asian economies have outperformed other regional economies

East Asia saw a sharp deceleration in economic growth in 2020, marking the region's weakest expansion since the Asian financial crisis. Measures designed to contain domestic outbreaks, including widespread restrictions on mobility and enforced business closures, significantly curtailed household spending and investment activities. The region's investment prospects have been further dampened by heightened uncertainties and risk aversion. Large policy stimulus measures helped to offset some of these negative effects by providing support to domestic demand. However, considerable negative fallout also came from the external front, with export volumes contracting owing to supply chain disruptions and weakened global economic activities. In many parts of the region, the pandemic has caused significant setbacks to social and economic development, with a disproportionate impact on the vulnerable segments of society. The region will see a recovery in 2021, but this will be from a low base and with great uncertainty stemming from the potential for renewed lockdown measures.

The pandemic has ravaged South Asia and progress on many SDGs has been reversed

South Asian economies faced the worst economic declines, with GDP per capita growth contracting by nearly 10 per cent in 2020

The pandemic and the global economic crisis have left deep marks on South Asia, turning this former growth champion into the worst performing region in 2020. Without exception, all economies in the region have been badly hit by the crisis, whose impact has been amplified and accelerated by existing vulnerabilities. These vulnerabilities were aggravated by weak progress on achieving the SDGs before the crisis and, notably, by the weakness of the region's public health infrastructure, with low levels of public health expenditure and few physicians, nurses, midwives and hospital beds per capita, as compared with both the global average and measures for other developing regions. At the same time, poorly organized labour markets and the absence of a reliable social safety net have prevented Governments from implementing the effective restrictions needed to contain the spread of the pandemic, while fiscal constraints and limited economic diversification restricted Governments' manoeuvring space. As a result, the crisis has devastated livelihoods across the region, reversing many years of progress on achieving the SDGs. As the population continued to grow in 2020, GDP per capita fell by nearly

10 per cent, while poverty is rising sharply and existing inequalities are widening. At the same time, it is the most vulnerable that have been hit hardest by the crisis. These include women, children, slum dwellers, migrant workers and the elderly.

Western Asia confronts the challenges of low energy prices and declining tourism revenues

In Western Asia, the pandemic and the subsequent mitigation measures stalled economic activities across the region. The pandemic's impact was felt most acutely in the region's high-performing tourism sector, and that impact led to a significant weakening of accommodation, transport, and wholesale and retail trade services. At the same time, weak energy market conditions stifled revenues for commodity exporters, putting additional constraints on fiscal policy options. Economic recovery in the region will depend on global energy demand, international tourism and the extent of the recovery of domestic demand on the back of fiscal support measures.

Latin America and the Caribbean has been hit severely by the crisis

Monetary and especially fiscal support have helped cushion the impact of the crisis

Latin America and the Caribbean has suffered the devastating consequences of the pandemic, as evidenced by both the heavy human toll exacted and the massive economic damages incurred. The health crisis has been accompanied by an economic downturn of historic proportions, which follows several years of disappointing growth. The downturn was caused by prolonged national lockdowns, weaker merchandise exports and a collapse in tourism, triggering a sharp increase in the number of the poor. Moreover, the crisis has been responsible for further setbacks to achievement of the SDGs by exacerbating deep-rooted structural inequalities, for example, between formal and informal workers, and between women and men. Despite severe fiscal constraints, many of the region's Governments have adopted substantial stimulus packages in response to the pandemic. This support, along with monetary easing, a gradual lifting of restrictions and a pickup in global economic activity, has prompted a modest recovery starting in the second half of 2020. However, aggregate output is expected to reach its pre-crisis level only by the end of 2023. In addition, the recovery will likely remain fragile and uneven, with significant political risks and the possibility of a debt crisis looming in several countries in the region.

Table of contents

Page

Boxes

Figures

Tables

Page

Statistical annex

Country classifications

Annex tables

CHAPTER I

Global Economic Outlook

The Great Disruption

World economy on a cliffhanger

The world economy is still reeling from the COVID-19 pandemic, which brought economic activities to a grinding halt during the second quarter of 2020. Governments around the world introduced social distancing, lockdown and quarantine measures and restricted a wide range of economic activities to tame the spread of the virus. A Great Disruption ensued, which helped to save lives but also disrupted the livelihoods of hundreds of millions of people worldwide. An estimated 420 million full-time equivalent (FTE) jobs were lost on average during the second and third quarters of the year (ILO, 2020).

Governments introduced a wide range of measures to tame the spread of COVID-19...

Figure I.1a
Monthly COVID-19 related deaths

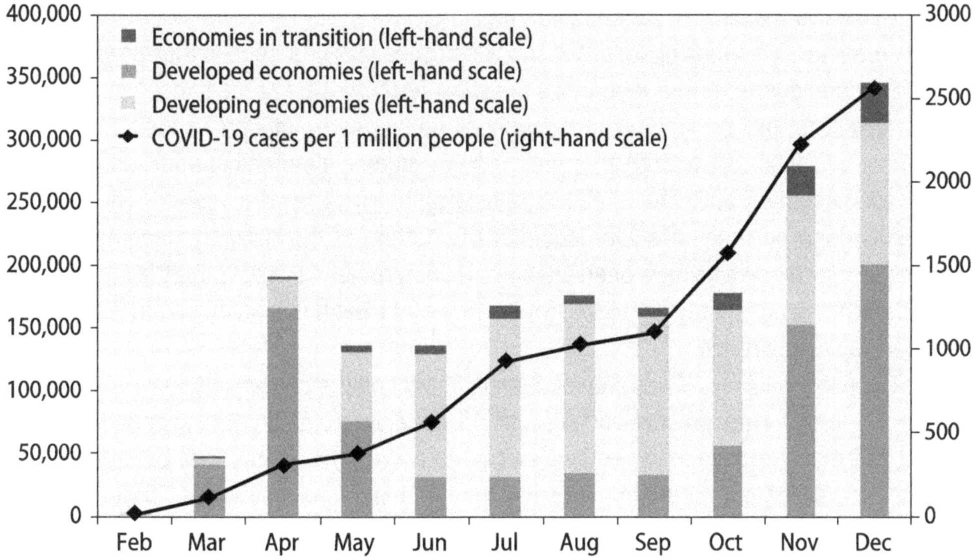

Source: UN DESA, based on data from Johns Hopkins University.
Note: As of 1 January 2021.

Against the backdrop of massive stimulus spending and the possibility of a vaccine roll-out, a quick economic recovery seemed just around the corner in the third quarter of the year. The hope for a quick recovery soon dissipated with the second wave of the pandemic hitting the major economies in October 2020. In November 2020, COVID-19 related deaths worldwide exceeded the previous highest monthly death toll of April by 45 per cent (figure I.1a). Although the survival rate among the confirmed cases has improved through a better understanding, and treatment, of the disease (figure I.1b), the daily death tolls continue to rise, with the total death toll of the pandemic reaching 1.7 million worldwide by mid-December. The number of infections per million people is showing no signs of decline. Economic costs of the pandemic continue to mount, while uncertainties about a next wave keep the world economy on a cliffhanger.

...which saved lives but also disrupted livelihoods

Figure I.1b

Daily COVID-19 survival rate

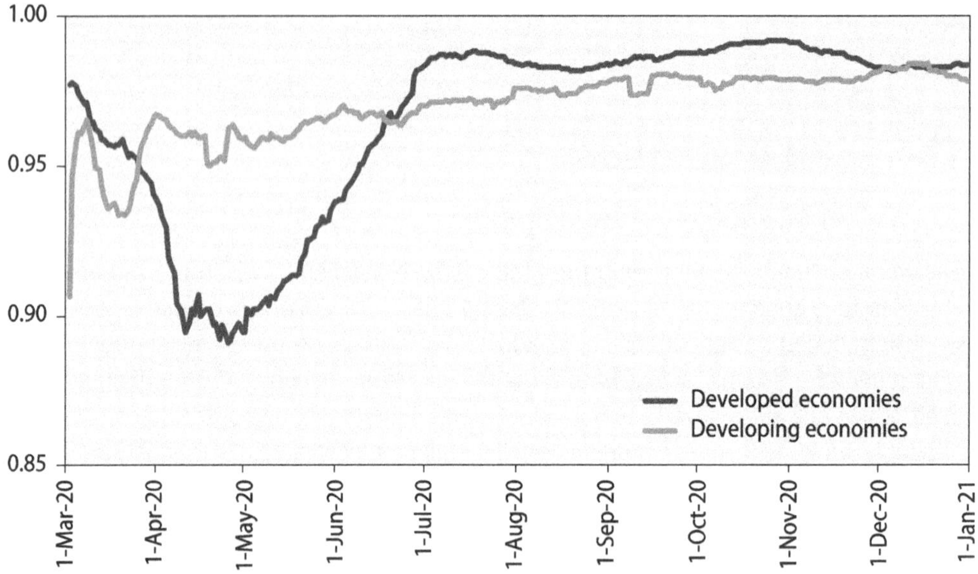

Source: UN DESA, based on data from Johns Hopkins University.

Note: As of 1 January 2021. Survival is calculated as a 7-day moving average of the difference between COVID-19 confirmed cases and COVID-19 related deaths divided by number of COVID-19 confirmed cases.

Thanks to massive fiscal stimulus measures worldwide—as large as 14 per cent of world output in 2020—the impact of the shock has been less pronounced than predicted during the second quarter of the year. While the short-term impacts of the pandemic prompted policymakers to roll out large fiscal responses, the long-term impacts of the pandemic on consumer behaviour, economic structures, growth, income distribution, trade, debt sustainability and financial stability have received less attention in policy discussions. The pandemic has disproportionately affected people at the bottom of the skills and income distribution, especially those who have been unable to work remotely. The asymmetric employment effect is worsening already high levels of income and wealth inequality in many developed and developing countries.

The pandemic's uneven impacts will likely further polarize societies in both developed and developing countries

The pandemic—and its uneven economic impact on the poorer segments of the population—will likely further polarize societies in both developed and developing countries. While timely and massive fiscal interventions helped to prevent the worst, they did not mitigate the broader discontent rooted in marginalization and stark inequality that divide the haves and the have nots in society. The pandemic responses need to prioritize efforts to reduce inequality not only in income and wealth but also in access and opportunities to pave the path for a resilient recovery.

With the crisis accelerating the pace of automation and digitalization, millions of lost jobs will not come back

While the short-term impacts of the pandemic have been devastating, its long-term impacts will be equally severe and will be felt for years to come. Like the 1918 influenza pandemic more than a century ago, the COVID-19 pandemic will also change the world (box I.1). With the crisis accelerating the pace of digitalization, automation and changing economic structures, millions of jobs that were lost in 2020 will not come back. Unemployment rates will remain elevated in the near term. While productivity in some sectors of the economy will rise during the post-crisis period, average productivity growth—along with potential output—will likely remain weak in the near term. Unless massive fiscal and monetary stimulus measures manage to boost investment, economic growth will continue to falter. A toxic

Box I.1
The 1918 pandemic and COVID-19: then and now

COVID-19 is the fifth influenza pandemic[a] to have disrupted human lives on a global scale in the past 100-odd years. Among these, the 1918 influenza pandemic stands out for its severity, which infected nearly one third of the world's population and killed an estimated 20 million-50 million people worldwide. The severity of the current pandemic thus raises the question whether the experience of the 1918 influenza pandemic can offer the world any lesson on how to avoid mistakes and steer recovery.

There are noteworthy differences between the two pandemics. Unlike COVID-19, the 1918 pandemic had an exceptionally high case mortality rate, of 2–3 per cent among young and healthy individuals, which can be attributed in part to the less advanced treatment and therapeutics available at the time. Its detrimental health implications made the 1918 pandemic the deadliest health crisis in recent history. The devastating human losses from the 1918 pandemic—and the First World War—led to a severe shortage in labour supply and rising wages in the United States of America (Garrett, 2009). This stands in stark contrast to the labour-market implications of the COVID-19 outbreak. Further, many countries engaged in the war actively censored information on the 1918 pandemic which, in conjunction with large-scale troop movements, led to a faster spread of the pandemic in its early stages.

Still, the two pandemics are in many ways similar, with the influenza virus being transmitted through respiratory droplets and aerosols in both cases. In both pandemics, similar mitigation strategies—including the use of face masks, social distancing and quarantine measures—were deployed. The fiscal climates at the time the pandemics struck were comparable, with extraordinarily high levels of public debt in many countries. Massive government spending as part of the war effort had significantly increased public debt prior to the 1918 pandemic. Similarly, public external debt since the financial crisis has recently more than doubled, while public external debt owed to private creditors has increased nearly 200 per cent (Stiglitz and Rashid, 2020).

In addition to the looming debt crisis, the stock market has witnessed the build-up of a massive bubble, while stock market confidence indexes reached their lowest levels in many years (Shiller, 2020). The 1918 pandemic marked the beginning of the Roaring Twenties—a decade that witnessed reckless borrowing and spending and the build-up of a massive bubble which culminated in a crash and the Great Depression. The lessons from the 1918 pandemic should guide the fiscal and monetary responses to prevent financial bubbles and direct resources towards investments.

Despite the risks, every disruption can present opportunities. The 1918 pandemic, which exposed the risks to labour supply, became a major driving force for investments in new technology and automation, which unleashed high productivity growth. Similarly, COVID-19 could change the way we live and work for the better. It could boost digitalization, lead to a reduction in greenhouse gas emissions from commuting and business travel, and enable the development of scalable, high-quality online education resources. However, unsustainable debt levels, an increasing risk of market volatility, and growing inequality—exacerbated by the COVID-19 pandemic—must serve as a serious warning signal.

a The other four being the so-called Spanish flu (1918–1919), Asian flu (1957–1958), Hong Kong flu (1968) and swine flu (2009–2010) pandemics.

Author: Lennart Claas Niermann

combination of weak investment, low inflation and low growth will make debt unsustainable for many developed and developing countries.

Many developing countries will see their growth and development path adjust downward

Many developing countries buffeted by the pandemic that are unable to respond with large fiscal responses will likely see their growth and development path adjust downward relative to pre-crisis trends. This may reverse the trends or at least delay the long-term convergence of the per capita incomes of the developed and developing countries, thwarting the objectives of reducing inequality between countries as envisaged under the 2030 Agenda for Sustainable Development.[1] The crisis demands policy responses that strike a delicate

1 General Assembly resolution 70/1.

balance between meeting short-term urgent needs and advancing the long-term sustainable development priorities to build resilience and realize the 2030 Agenda for Sustainable Development.

Economic growth plunged worldwide

Developed countries were the hardest hit...

World gross product fell by an estimated 4.3 per cent in 2020—the sharpest contraction of output since the Great Depression (table I.1). During the Great Recession in 2009, world output contracted by 1.7 per cent. The pandemic clearly hit the developed economies the hardest, with many countries in Europe and several States of the United States of America adopting strict lockdown measures early on during the outbreak. Output in developed economies is estimated to have shrunk by 5.6 per cent in 2020, with growth projected to recover to 4.0 per cent in 2021.

...while developing countries experienced a relatively less severe contraction

The developing countries experienced a relatively less severe contraction, with output shrinking by 2.5 per cent in 2020, owing partly to the delayed outbreak of the pandemic and the generally less restrictive measures taken by Governments to contain its spread. Their economies are projected to grow by 5.7 per cent in 2021. The least developed countries (LDCs) saw their gross domestic product (GDP) shrink by 1.3 per cent in 2020, with growth projected to reach 4.9 per cent in 2021. There are, however, significant differences in the size of the shock among developing countries, with Latin America and the Caribbean and the South Asian economies taking the hardest hits (figure I.2A). In contrast, the economies in East Asia fared relatively better than all other developing regions, with GDP expanding by 1 per cent in 2020. On the back of a quick and robust recovery in China, the East Asian economies are forecast to grow by 6.4 per cent in 2021.

G20 economies need to jump-start recovery and make the world more resilient to future shocks

The Group of Twenty (G20) economies—accounting for nearly 80 per cent of world GDP—contracted by 4.1 per cent, largely mirroring the performance of the world economy and signifying the systemic importance of these major economies. Only China, among the G20 members, managed to register a positive growth rate in 2020 (figure I.2B). It is critical that the G20 economies jump-start their economies, not only to accelerate recovery but also to make the world economy more resilient to future shocks. Among regional economic groups, the economic contraction was most severe in the member States of the European Union and the South Asian Association for Regional Cooperation, while the members of the East African Community experienced the shallowest decline in growth (table I.2).

The baseline scenario of the current forecast assumes that infection rates will slowly begin to decline during the first quarter of 2021 with growing shares of the population in developed countries receiving a vaccination. Businesses and households will further adapt to social distancing and other precautionary measures. Elevated levels of unemployment and underemployment—relative to pre-crisis levels—are expected to depress labour-force participation rates and the labour share in national income, contributing to lower potential output under the baseline scenario.

In contrast, the pessimistic scenario assumes a higher number of new infections in major economies during the first half of 2021—with vaccination drives failing to secure herd immunity and new variants of the virus spreading more quickly—requiring Governments to reintroduce some form of lockdown measures. Under this scenario, global output would grow by just 2.8 per cent in 2021 and remain at about 2.6 per cent per year until 2025 (figure I.3). The optimistic scenario—though unlikely—assumes a more successful containment of

Table I.1
Growth of world output and gross domestic product

Annual percentage change	2019	2020[a]	2021[b]	2022[b]	Change from WESP 2020	
					2020	2021
World	2.5	-4.3	4.7	3.4	-6.8	2.0
Developed economies	1.7	-5.6	4.0	2.5	-7.1	2.3
United States of America	2.2	-3.9	3.4	2.7	-5.6	1.6
Japan	0.7	-5.4	3.0	1.8	-6.3	1.7
European Union	1.5	-7.4	4.8	2.7	-9.0	3.1
Euro area	1.3	-7.9	5.0	2.6	-9.3	3.5
United Kingdom of Great Britian and Northern Ireland	1.5	-9.5	6.8	2.0	-10.7	5.0
Other developed countries	1.6	-4.9	3.6	2.4	-8.6	3.0
Economies in transition	2.2	-3.4	3.4	3.0	-5.7	0.9
South-Eastern Europe	3.5	-3.8	4.0	3.1	-7.2	0.6
Commonwealth of Independent States and Georgia	2.2	-3.4	3.4	3.0	-5.7	1.0
Russian Federation	1.3	-4.0	3.0	2.4	-5.8	1.0
Developing economies	3.6	-2.5	5.7	4.6	-6.5	1.4
Africa[c]	2.8	-3.4	3.4	3.6	-6.6	-0.1
Northern Africa[c]	2.9	-3.3	4.9	4.1	-6.9	1.2
East Africa	6.5	-0.7	3.0	4.1	-6.7	-3.2
Central Africa	1.9	-4.3	2.9	3.6	-7.2	-0.2
West Africa	3.3	-2.7	2.5	3.7	-6.3	-1.3
Southern Africa	-0.2	-6.4	2.9	2.6	-7.3	1.0
East and South Asia	4.9	-0.5	6.5	5.2	-5.7	1.3
East Asia	5.3	1.0	6.4	5.2	-4.2	1.2
China	6.1	2.4	7.2	5.8	-3.6	1.3
South Asia[d]	3.1	-8.6	6.9	5.3	-13.7	1.6
India[d]	4.7	-9.6	7.3	5.9	-12.3	0.7
Western Asia	1.2	-4.8	3.8	3.4	-7.2	1.0
Latin America and the Caribbean	-0.3	-8.0	3.8	2.6	-9.3	1.8
South America	-0.7	-7.9	3.8	2.7	-9.0	1.8
Brazil	1.4	-5.3	3.2	2.2	-7.0	0.9
Mexico and Central America	0.6	-8.3	3.8	2.4	-9.9	1.9
Caribbean	0.4	-7.8	3.8	2.8	-13.5	0.4
Least developed countries	4.8	-1.3	4.9	4.6	-6.4	-0.5
Memorandum items						
World trade[e]	1.0	-7.6	6.9	3.7	-9.9	3.7
World output growth with PPP weights[f]	2.5	-4.4	4.9	3.8	-7.6	1.5

Source: UN DESA.
a Estimated.
b Forecast.
c Excludes Libya.
d Growth rates provided are on a calendar-year basis. For fiscal-year growth figures, please refer to the Statistical annex.
e Includes goods and services.
f Based on 2015 benchmark.

Figure I.2
Growth of gross domestic product

a. World regions

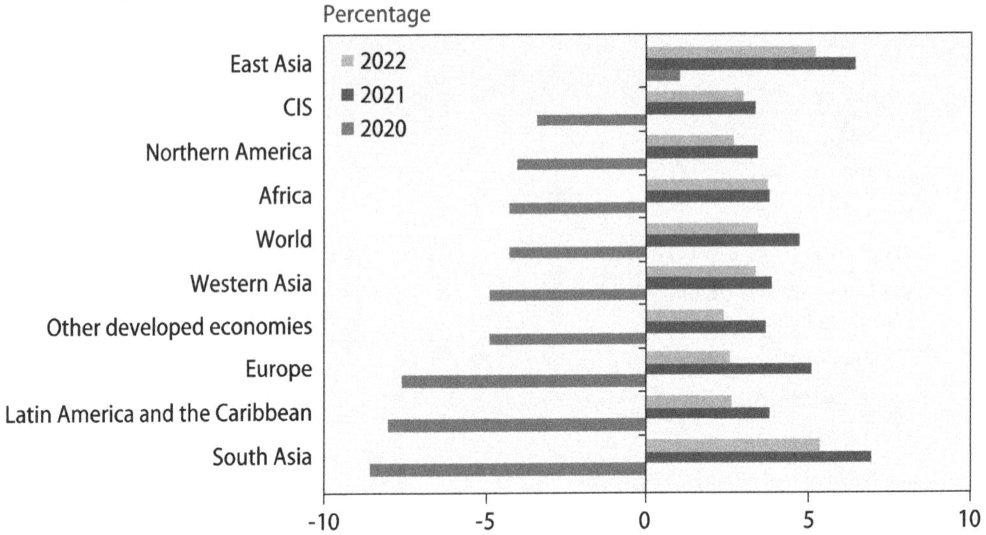

Source: UN DESA, based on projections and scenarios generated by the World Economic Forecasting Model (WEFM).

b. G20 members

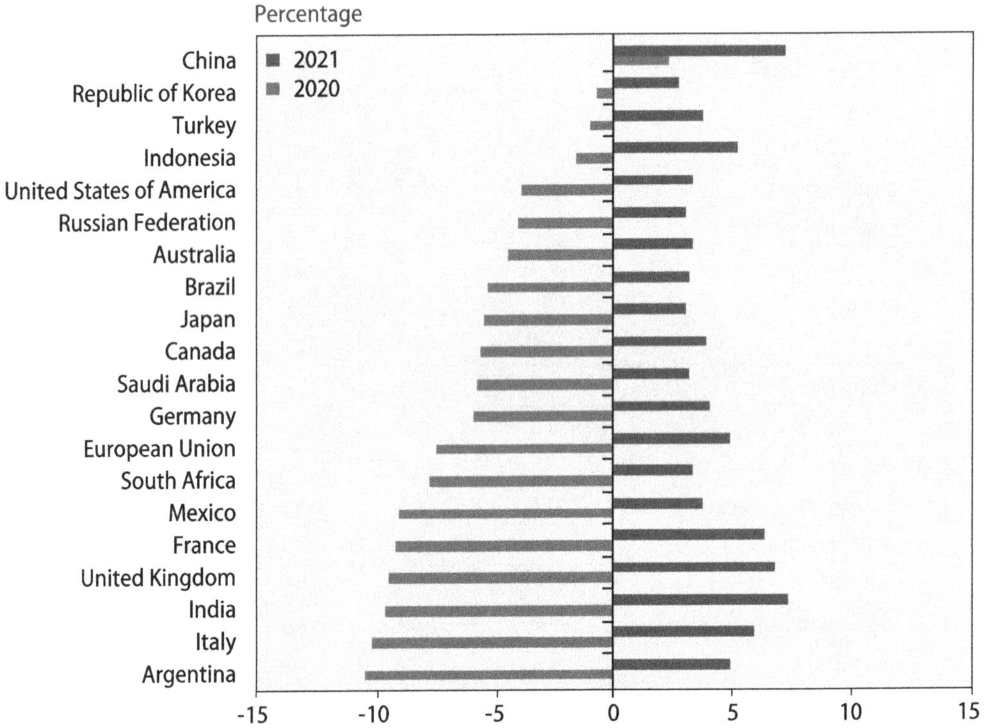

Source: UN DESA, based on projections and scenarios generated by the World Economic Forecasting Model (WEFM).

Note: Growth rates for India are on a calendar year basis.

the virus than is assumed under the baseline, with fast and widespread vaccination and progress in treatments contributing to improved consumer confidence and the return of economic activities to pre-crisis trends during the first half of 2021. Global growth under this scenario will reach 5.8 per cent in 2021, before declining to about 3 per cent by 2025.

Table I.2
Growth of gross domestic product in selected regional economic groups

Annual percentage change	2019	2020	2021	2022
SAARC	4.5	-8.0	7.1	5.5
EU-27	1.5	-7.4	4.8	2.7
SIDS	1.5	-6.8	4.7	3.0
MERCOSUR	0.5	-6.5	3.6	2.3
OECD	1.7	-5.5	4.0	2.6
G7	1.6	-5.5	4.0	2.5
GCC	0.6	-5.4	3.5	2.5
SADC	0.8	-5.1	2.8	2.8
World	2.5	-4.3	4.7	3.4
G20	2.6	-4.1	4.8	3.4
ASEAN	4.3	-3.7	5.6	4.7
CIS	2.2	-3.4	3.4	3.0
ECCAS	0.8	-3.3	2.3	3.2
ECOWAS	3.3	-2.7	2.5	3.7
LLDC	4.3	-2.4	4.1	4.4
G77	4.0	-2.2	6.1	4.9
LDC	4.8	-1.3	4.9	4.6
BRICS	5.1	-0.5	6.5	5.3
EAC	6.4	-0.3	3.2	4.1

Abbreviations: ASEAN, Association of Southeast Asian Nations; BRICS, Brazil, Russian Federation, India, China and South Africa; CIS, Commonwealth of Independent States; EAC, East African Community; ECCAS, Economic Community of Central African States; ECOWAS, Economic Community of West African States; EU, European Union; G7, Group of Seven; G20, Group of Twenty; GCC, Cooperation Council for the Arab States of the Gulf; MERCOSUR, Southern Common Market (Mercado Común del Sur); OECD, Organization for Economic Cooperation and Development; SAARC, South Asian Association for Regional Cooperation; SADC, Southern African Development Community; SIDS, small island developing States.

Source: UN DESA, based on projections and scenarios generated by the World Economic Forecasting Model (WEFM).

Figure I.3
Global growth scenarios

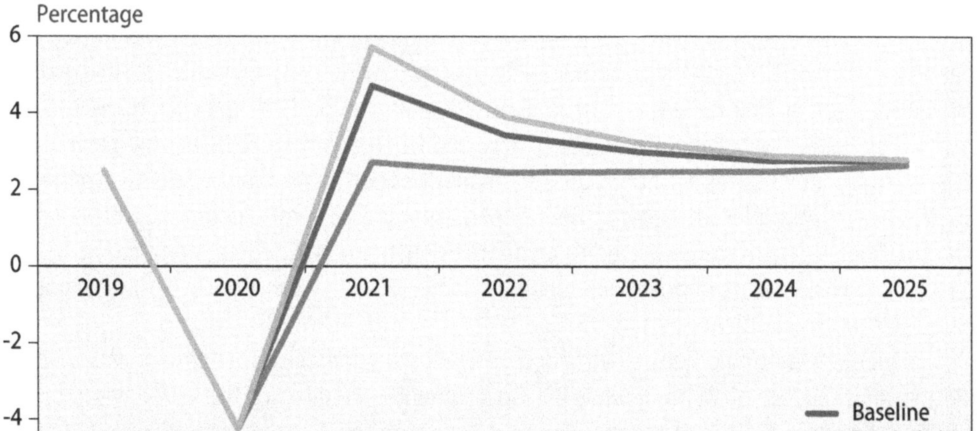

Source: UN DESA, based on projections and scenarios generated by the World Economic Forecasting Model (WEFM).

Not all are in the same boat

The pandemic is not an egalitarian crisis...

The pandemic has affected different countries and population groups differently. While the developed economies received the most severe blow, certain demographics and income groups bore the brunt of the health and economic shocks of the crisis. The most vulnerable population groups exposed to the virus—the elderly, caregivers, first responders and health-care professionals—took the hardest hit. Countries with larger shares of a younger population and populations in better health before the onset of the pandemic, on the other hand, managed to keep both the infection and mortality rates low through timely identification, containment, treatment and post-treatment easing of restrictions.

The pandemic also disproportionately affected low-skilled services sector workers, who are unable to work remotely. While the health response to the pandemic varied across countries, the preparedness of the health-care system, the social protection coverage and the overall timeliness and quality of government initiatives generally determined the health and economic impacts of the pandemic.

...as it disproportionately affected the most vulnerable population groups, including women, and low-skilled services sector workers

Preliminary evidence suggests that the level of inequality partly explains the cross-country differences in the speed and intensity of the spread of the coronavirus (box I.2). A population's vulnerability to diseases is usually income and wealth inequality and COVID-19 is no exception. In the case of COVID-19, inequality additionally impacted social distancing-related choices, linking initial socioeconomic conditions with the spread of the disease. The cost of social distancing is higher for members of poorer households who cannot work remotely and maintain their level of income. For millions of low-income workers, the harsh prospects of losing livelihoods potentially outweighed their concerns for exposure to COVID-19. It was also likely that high levels of inequalities undermined social cohesion and trust in government policies, which affected citizens' willingness to comply with government-mandated lockdowns, social distancing and other preventive measures, enabling the spread of the disease.

Lockdown measures triggered discontent and protests...

Lockdown measures and restrictions on economic activities bred discontent, especially among low-income groups in both the developed and the developing countries, as they disproportionately hurt low-skilled, low-wage workers—including temporary, migrant and informal sector workers—who typically lack social protection or personal saving, cannot work remotely and cannot afford to lose work for a few months. The pandemic exposed how stark inequality affected the ability of people to cope with the economic impact of the crisis.

...with the pandemic exposing how stark inequality determined people's ability to cope with its economic impact

There have been numerous demonstrations against lockdown measures during the pandemic, as those measures affected the lives of millions of people worldwide. In the United States, large-scale protests occurred in April and May in parts of the country where the number of cases of infection was relatively low, and where many workers deemed lockdown measures as unnecessarily undermining personal freedom. Often anti-lockdown protests coalesced with broader anti-government sentiments and general discontent with government policies, which were perceived to favour the rich. In France, protests erupted as social distancing requirements imposed an undue burden on overcrowded poorer neighbourhoods compared with wealthier ones.

Argentina, among other developing countries, witnessed several demonstrations during the third quarter of 2020 against the Government's handling of the coronavirus crisis and the economic effects of the lockdown. In Brazil, protests flared up against lockdowns imposed by State governors. Despite the massive spread of the virus and one of the highest

Box I.2
The spread and intensity of COVID-19: did inequality matter?

The COVID-19 pandemic has spread with varying speed and intensity across the world. Several factors may explain the disparities in infections and deaths between countries, including population age structure, level of preparedness of health systems, political commitment, effectiveness of government response, and public confidence in official sources of information. Socioeconomic inequalities potentially played an important role in explaining the cross-country differences in COVID-19 infections and mortality rates, acting as a catalyst for a faster and more widespread transmission of the virus.

Inequalities influenced the spread of the virus through several channels. Inequalities are associated with worse health conditions of populations and poverty (Pickett and Wilkinson, 2015). Poverty, in turn, often limits access to sanitation, housing and health care which are essential for preventing infectious diseases. Moreover, socioeconomic inequalities combined with behavioural risk factors affect chronic disease outcomes (Nordahl, 2014) and impose an unequal burden of morbidity and mortality on the poor. Elevated socioeconomic inequalities may also hinder some forms of social capital, such as confidence in State institutions and civic engagement, which has been an important factor in combating this epidemic (Elgar, Stefaniak and Wohl, 2020). Moreover, inequalities influence social distancing choices (Weill and others, 2020), as the cost of greater social distancing is higher for members of poorer families who cannot isolate and still maintain their incomes and levels of consumption. Previous studies have shown that inequalities actually play a crucial role in the spread of infectious diseases (Rutter and others, 2012).

Data show that countries with higher levels of inequality have had higher levels of COVID-19 cases and deaths (figure I.2.1). While this does not control for other important dimensions at the coun-

Figure I.2.1
Cases and deaths per 100,000 population and Gini coefficient by country

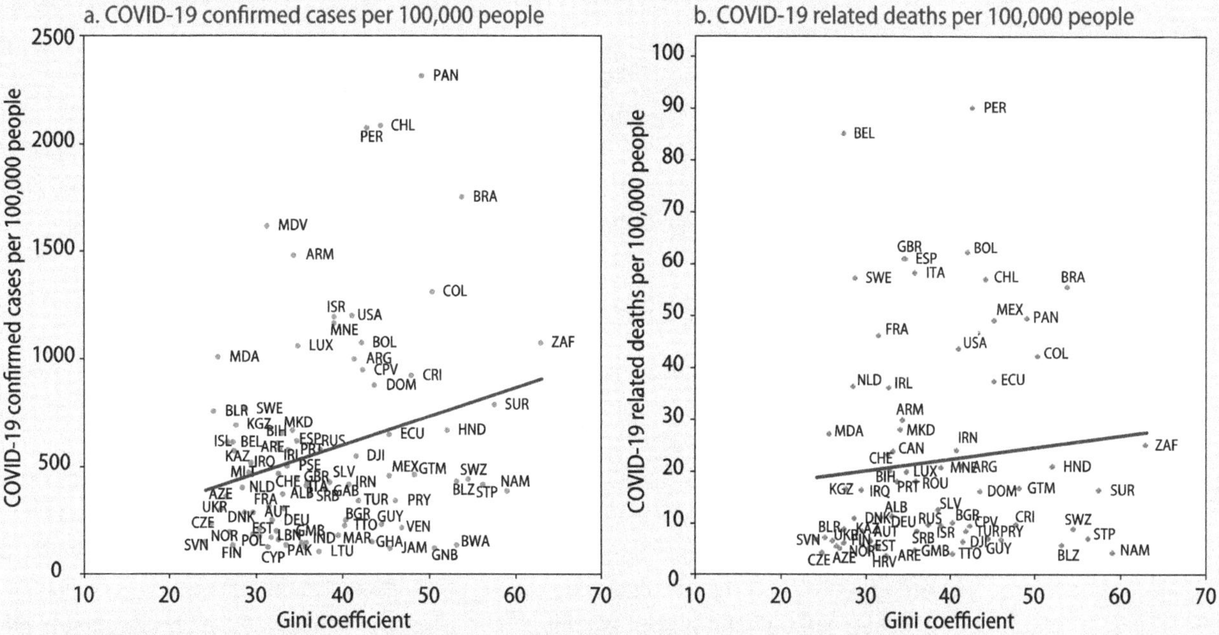

Source: UN DESA, based on data from John Hopkins University and World Development Indicators (World Bank).

Note: Cumulative number of cases and deaths at the sixth month of the epidemic for each country. Charts display countries with at least 100 cases per 100,000 people and 3.5 deaths per 100,000 people.

(continued)

Box I.2 (*continued*)

try level, it is indicative that there is a link between inequality and how fast the virus can spread. In fact, some large countries with relatively high levels of income inequality, such as Brazil, Mexico, South Africa and the United States of America, have been battered by the pandemic. As of 10 December, these four countries accounted for almost 40 per cent of the global death toll from the pandemic, while accounting for only 9.5 per cent of the world's population.

How inequality correlates with cases and mortality rates across countries raises an important question, while controlling for levels of development, stringency of measures to control the pandemic, poverty, share of urban population, share of population over age 65, and quality of institutions, among other variables (Afonso and Vergara, 2021, forthcoming). A preliminary empirical analysis, based on monthly data for cumulative cases and deaths since the first recorded case in each of 154 countries, confirms that a country's share of urban population has a positive and significant correlation with COVID-19 cases and deaths, while the share of population above age 65 is positively correlated to mortality rates but not to cases. The results also show that poverty is not correlated either to cases or to deaths.

The preliminary empirical results exhibit a positive and significant correlation between the different inequality measures—the Gini coefficient, the Palma ratio and the income share held by the highest 10 per cent of earners—and the number of COVID-19 cases across countries. A positive but weaker correlation with mortality rates was also found. This suggests that inequalities accelerate the transmission of the virus and thus contribute to a higher number of cases, which indirectly increases mortality. The statistical insignificance of poverty suggests that inequality possibly impacts COVID-19 cases mainly through differences in labour-market conditions, such as contact intensity of jobs and teleworking possibilities. In sum, preliminary research confirms that high levels of inequality mattered in the spread of the COVID-19 pandemic, and that fighting inequality will remain critical for reducing vulnerability to health shocks and enhancing resilience of societies.

Authors: Helena Afonso and Sebastian Vergara

death tolls in the world, the message that the economy must stay open at all costs resonated with millions of poor Brazilians. In May, violent protests erupted in India, when the Government extended lockdown measures and suspended all inter-city travel, which left millions of migrant workers stranded. In Indonesia, public discontent with government policies in support of jobs and incomes found broader expression as massive protests erupted against the implementation of new labour laws and other planned unpopular economic reforms.

Low inflation, new worries

Income and consumer demand fell sharply, dampening inflationary pressures

The Great Disruption choked global supply chains during the second quarter. But the supply-side shocks were less pronounced than the shock to income and consumer demand, dampening inflationary pressures throughout the world. The abrupt decline in aggregate demand also drove down energy prices, while the prices of agricultural commodities remained relatively stable and metal prices rebounded strongly.[2]

Consumer price inflation is projected to remain low in 2021 as unemployment rates are expected to remain higher than the pre-crisis level in most economies, diminishing the prospects of demand-pull inflation in the near term. On an annual basis, commodity prices are projected to see mild gains in 2021. The expected recovery of demand for consumer durables and housing is expected to create moderate inflationary pressures. In several developed economies, there has been a surge in the demand for housing in the second half

2 See www.macrotrends.net/1476/copper-prices-historical-chart-data.

of 2020, which may continue into 2021 against the backdrop of strong stock market performances and asset price bubbles. A correction in financial and real estate markets will likely further dampen inflationary pressures.

In developed economies, the broad money supply grew rapidly in 2020, but the impact of monetary expansion on the real economy will likely remain limited. The rapid credit expansion in 2020—part of stimulus packages—provided liquidity. These credits mostly filled revenue shortfalls but did not go towards new investments, which could boost aggregate demand and output.

Massive liquidity did not go into investments

The prospects for large-scale depreciation of exchange rates, and the attendant likelihood of imported inflation, also remain weak for most developing and emerging economies. Expected slow recovery in import demand will prevent sharp increases in current account deficits. But the risks of a looming debt crisis can add downward pressure on exchange rates and increase inflation expectations. It will be critical for many commodity exporters in Africa and Latin America—with large external debt servicing burdens—to proactively manage capital flows and exchange rates so as to prevent unexpected inflation.

Paradoxically, the crisis has created a massive financial bubble...

Despite the massive injection of liquidity and historically low interest rates, low inflation expectations will likely persist, posing two policy challenges: the risk of a financial bubble and consequent financial instability, and the risk of rising real public and private debt. As debts are typically contracted in nominal values, lower-than-expected inflation tends to increase the real value of debt. The rising real value of debt and stagnant public revenues will likely undermine public, corporate and household debt sustainability. While central banks around the world have been broadly successful in pursuing unconventional monetary policy, injecting liquidity and keeping long-term interest rates low, they have been less successful in meeting their explicit and implicit inflation targets, with actual inflation falling below expectations. The environment of excessive-liquidity and low inflation has allowed firms to underprice risks and increase the acquisition of financial assets, as evidenced in the surge of asset prices in most stock exchanges around the world. The crisis has paradoxically created a massive financial bubble, diverting financial resources away from real investments, while rising unemployment and loss of income are hurting millions of people worldwide.

Global employment has taken a big hit

...while rising unemployment and loss of income hurt millions worldwide

The GDP growth numbers in 2020 mask the severity of the employment crisis unleashed by the pandemic. By April, full or partial lockdown measures affected almost 2.7 billion workers, representing about 81 per cent of the world's workforce. According to the International Labour Organization (ILO) (2020), total working-hour losses averaged 10.7 per cent during the first three quarters of 2020, representing $3.5 trillion in lost labour income, which is equivalent to about 5.5 per cent of global output in 2019. The aggregate unemployment rate among the Organization for Economic Cooperation and Development (OECD) member states reached 8.8 per cent in April, before falling to 6.9 per cent in November 2020. Unemployment rates may still climb back to about 8 per cent or higher in early 2021, as France, Germany and the United Kingdom reintroduced lockdown measures in late 2020.

Job protection strategies prevented further increases in unemployment in most developed economies...

Various job protection strategies prevented further job losses in most developed economies. Australia, the Baltic States, Canada, Denmark, Germany, Hungary, the Netherlands, New Zealand and the United Kingdom of Great Britain and Northern Ireland introduced new schemes or expanded the coverage of existing short-time work schemes (subsidizing hours not worked), or provided wage subsidies (in the case of full-time employment)[3] to protect jobs, especially in small and medium-sized enterprises. Denmark, for example, implemented an employee furlough scheme, paying 75-90 per cent of wages, as well as a compensation scheme to assist self-employed workers who recorded significant losses of revenue.

...while the COVID-19 crisis battered labour markets in the developing world

The COVID-19 crisis has wreaked havoc on labour markets in the developing world. By mid-2020, unemployment rates had quickly escalated to record highs: 27 per cent in Nigeria, 23 per cent in India, 21 per cent in Colombia, 17 per cent in the Philippines and above 13 per cent in Argentina, Brazil, Chile, Saudi Arabia and Turkey. As the number of discouraged workers rose, labour-force participation fell. Pre-existing inequalities along educational, gender, age, racial and migration divides largely explained the employment impacts of the crisis. The livelihood and income impacts have been particularly harsh for about 2 billion informal workers with limited social protection, especially those self-employed in the informal economy. The informal sector accounts for more than 60 per cent of jobs in a number of large developing countries, including India, Indonesia and Mexico.

The pandemic has disproportionately affected labour-intensive services sectors in both developed and developing countries. Commercial air travel, tourism, catering, leisure, personal care and retail industries, manufacturing, trade and transportation—which typically employ large numbers of low-skilled workers—faced the largest job losses. Many of the jobs in these sectors cannot be performed remotely, making them vulnerable to lockdown and quarantine measures. The pandemic has also adversely affected female labour-force participation in labour-intensive sectors, as more than 50 per cent of workers in those sectors are women, and they are often the entry point into work for women, youth, migrant workers and the rural population.

The capacity to work remotely varies sharply across educational and income divides...

The ability to work remotely varies significantly across educational and income divides. For example, nearly 75 per cent of employees in the top income quintile in the European Union (EU) are able to work remotely—which makes them less susceptible to the risks of infection—compared with less than 5 per cent of the workers in the lowest quintile who can do the same (figure I.4). In the United Kingdom, women were one third more likely than men to work in a shut-down sector. These jobs will remain vulnerable until the pandemic is brought completely under control (Scudellari, 2020). Workers holding jobs in these sectors have faced disproportionately high health risks because of their physical proximity to the customers they serve. Those who are more educated, skilled and economically secure have faced fewer financial and health risks from the pandemic—a harsh reality that will profoundly impact both the supply of, and demand for, labour in the future.

Short-term pain, long-term scars

...and those who are able to work remotely face fewer pandemic-related health and financial risks

The pandemic will likely transform consumer behaviour and economic structures. It is unlikely that in-person interactions will quickly return to pre-crisis levels even if millions are inoculated against COVID-19. Remote work will likely become the new norm for many service sector jobs. Meetings and conferences may remain largely digital, reducing demand for business travel-related services. Consumer spending will increasingly move online. Leisure and entertainment will also become increasingly digital, replacing brick-and-mortar venues

3 For further details on job retention policies, see OECD (2020c); and United Nations, Department of Economic and Social Affairs (2020).

Figure I.4
Employees in teleworkable occupations, by workers' characteristics, EU-27

Percentage

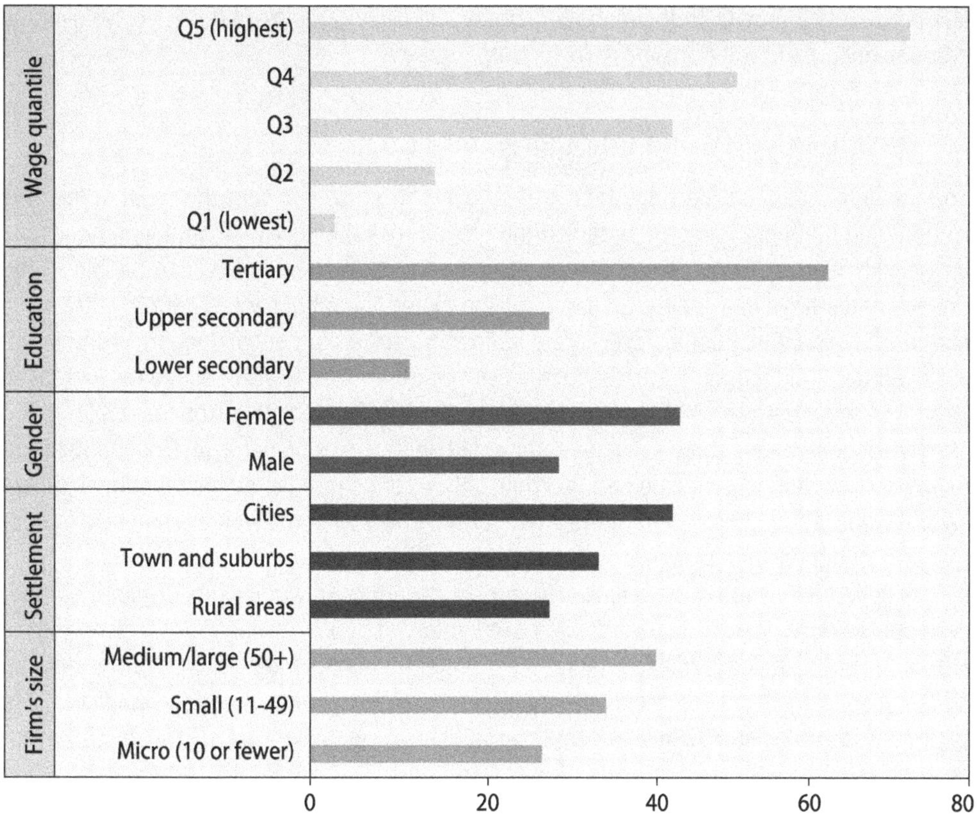

Source: Calculations by Sostero and others (2020), based upon EU Labour Force Survey and Structure of Earnings Survey.

for retail and entertainment. These shifts will likely reduce local government revenues and adversely impact the delivery of basic services—health, sanitation, education, transportation and public safety—in urban centres worldwide. These shifts, already under way before the pandemic, will profoundly impact the trajectory of sustainable development.

The temporary underutilization of capital and labour due to pandemic-related restrictions on economic activities will likely increase the level of risk aversion and precautionary savings among households and businesses and depress investment in the long run. Private investments in fixed capital never fully recovered from the global financial crisis, which pushed the world economy onto a lower growth path during the past decade. The current shock to aggregate demand—and the hysteresis effects of the crisis—will likely reduce the potential output of the world economy. Some research suggests that a one percentage point decline in actual output in Europe could lead to a 0.6 per cent loss in potential output in the long run (Heimberger, 2020).

Furthermore, the pace of digitalization, automation and robotization will likely accelerate during the post-pandemic period, as businesses will pursue resilience and safeguards against shocks to labour supply. Accelerated and more widespread automation and digitalization will likely make many job losses permanent. While automation and innovation typically increase the productivity of workers and firms that can embrace new technologies, they also displace less productive workers and firms. In a post COVID-19 world, firms and sectors that can quickly adapt digital technologies will likely fare better, while making many existing jobs redundant. This will likely widen wage and income inequality both within and across sectors. While there will be increases in marginal productivity in those sectors, average productivity growth in the global economy will likely remain subdued. Lower average productivity growth will translate to lower output growth.

Rising poverty and inequality: adding insult to injury

Massive job and income losses are quickly pushing millions into poverty

The pandemic has laid bare the cost of inequality in societies, with the most vulnerable income and demographic groups facing the gravest risks. Massive job and income losses are quickly leading to massive increases in poverty. While nearly 8 million people in the United States have lost their jobs and 4 million exited the labour force permanently since March 2020 and the national poverty rate jumped from 9.3 per cent in June to 11.7 per cent in November 2020 (Long, 2020), the total wealth of 644 United States billionaires increased by 31.6 per cent between 18 March and 13 October 2020, from $2.95 trillion to $3.88 trillion.[4] The five richest among them saw their total wealth increase by 66 per cent, from $358 billion to $596 billion, during the same period. While only 4 per cent of the highest-income workers had lost jobs, about 20 per cent of the jobs that the lowest-income workers had held in February no longer existed in June.

The impact of the crisis on poverty is more pronounced worldwide. The total number of people living in poverty is expected to have increased by 131 million in 2020 alone (figure I.5), representing a sharp rise from the earlier projections presented in the *World Economic Situation and Prospects 2020* mid-year update, released last June. Given the current shock to poverty, as many as 797 million people will still be living in extreme poverty in 2030, representing a poverty headcount ratio of over 9 per cent. Even under the best-case scenario of a vigorous and universal economic recovery combined with declining inequality in all developing countries, the overall eradication of extreme poverty by 2030 will remain beyond reach (Slotman, 2020).

COVID-19 is making inequality worse both within and across countries

The pandemic is worsening inequality both within and across countries. As millions fall below the poverty lines at the national levels and the income of the top quintiles rise or even remain unchanged, income inequality will inevitably increase. The combination of low growth and high job losses will disproportionately affect people in the lowest income group. Analysing five previous pandemics, Furceri and others (2020) found that after a pandemic event, the shares of incomes going to the top deciles increased and those going to the bottom deciles fell. They expect that, given the magnitude of the current pandemic, the inequality impact will be significantly larger. Rising income inequality will likely further reinforce structural inequalities in access and opportunities, often determined by age, gender, race, disability, rural/urban divides and other dynamics of inequality.

Digital divides will worsen inequality between and among countries

The existing digital divides within and between countries will contribute to a further worsening of inequality. Even in the most developed countries, the lack of access to broadband Internet during the pandemic has been disproportionately undermining the learning opportunities for children from low-income households. A study undertaken by the RAND Corporation showed that only 30 per cent of teachers in high-poverty schools in the United

4 https://americansfortaxfairness.org/billionaires/.

Figure I.5
Poverty projections before and after COVID-19

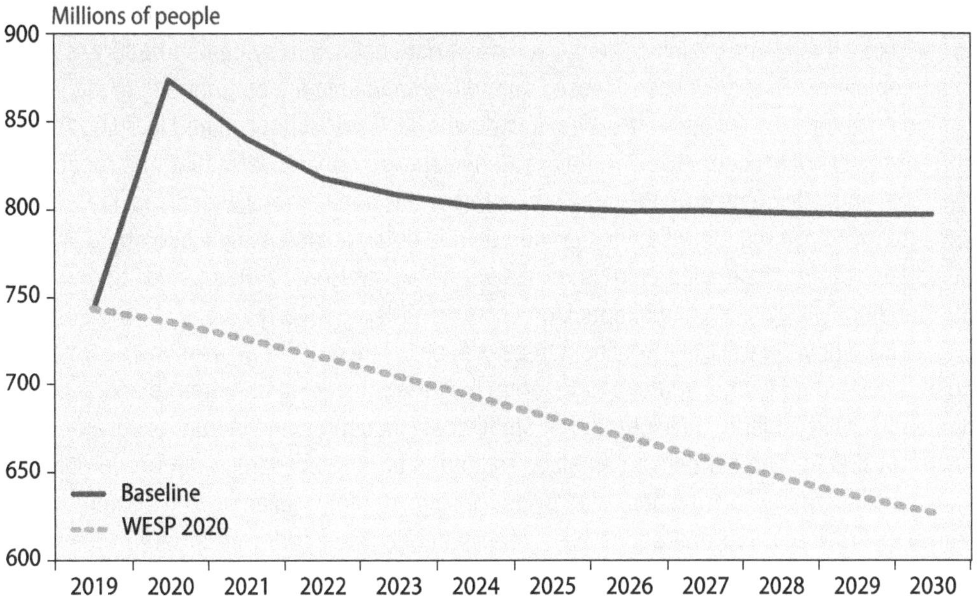

Source: UN DESA, based on projections and scenarios generated by the World Economic Forecasting Model (WEFM).

States reported that all or nearly all of their students had access to the Internet at home, compared with 83 per cent of teachers in low-poverty schools (Stelitano and others, 2020). UNICEF has reported that one third of the world's schoolchildren (463 million) and nearly half of the schoolchildren in Africa have no access to remote learning (UNICEF, 2020). Seventy-two per cent of schoolchildren who are unable to access remote learning live in their country's poorest households. These structural impediments related to learning opportunities during the pandemic will impact the lifelong income potential of the children affected and further exacerbate income and wealth inequality.

Inequality among countries is also expected to worsen through growth, trade and debt channels. Developing countries falling behind in recovery will likely see a greater divergence in per capita income growth during the post-pandemic period. Weak recovery of exports and the likelihood of a debt crisis—depressing investment growth—will further accentuate the divergences in per capita income growth and worsen inequality between countries.

Many Sustainable Development Goals are suffering collateral damages

The pandemic is quickly turning into a hunger crisis. An estimated 270 million people worldwide are now facing the prospect of crisis-level hunger, a majority of them in conflict countries. The number of people facing hunger has increased by 82 per cent since the outbreak of the pandemic (World Food Programme, 2020; Oxfam International, 2020). Latin America has seen an almost 300 per cent increase in the number of people requiring food assistance, with job and income losses driving millions into destitution. The hunger crisis is also rapidly unfolding in West and Central Africa, with nearly a 135 per cent jump in the number of food-insecure people since the onset of the pandemic.

The pandemic is exacerbating health outcomes

Beyond directly affecting the health of populations (covered under SDG 3), the pandemic is also exacerbating health outcomes and contributing to an increase, to an increase in death due to AIDS, malaria and tuberculosis and in neonatal mortality, as the response to the pandemic is constraining the capacities of national health systems to address other health concerns. Rising livelihood losses during the pandemic are contributing to increases in alcohol abuse and suicide rates. With lockdowns, levels of schooling and learning for the current cohort of students (SDG 4) have fallen, disproportionately affecting the most marginalized and vulnerable groups—girls, ethnic minorities and persons with disabilities. While some crimes have registered a decline, women and girls are increasingly becoming victims of violence during the implementation of stay-at-home measures (SDGs 5 and 16) and child marriages will likely see a global uptick on account of rising poverty.

Rising poverty will likely lead to increases in child labour (SDG 8), as many poor households will need additional sources of income. Lingering financing constraints and subdued demand will likely hinder development of small-scale industries and industrial development at large (SDG 9). The pandemic has also resulted in an unprecedented decline in demand and revenue for public transport worldwide, posing a great challenge to its future in cities (SDG 11). Recycling operations have reportedly declined owing to safety precautions and, in some countries, all municipal waste has been treated as non-recyclable and sent for incineration or to a sanitary landfill during the outbreak (SDG 12), potentially exacerbating environmental degradation. Commitments to fight climate change have taken a back seat as the fight against the pandemic has become the fiscal priority (SDG 13), diverting resources away from mitigation and adaptation efforts. The consumption of single-use plastics as a consequence of the pandemic is increasing plastic pollution and environmental degradation worldwide (SDG 14). Wildlife conservation efforts are also suffering setbacks, as a result of reduced funding, restrictions on the operations of conservation agencies, and elevated human threats to nature (SDG 15). Moreover, with government revenues, foreign direct investment (FDI) flows and remittances plummeting and debt servicing rising, most developing countries will face significant challenges to mobilize resources for sustainable development (SDG 17).

A few SDGs have seen some progress during the outbreak; but without sustained action the progress will be fleeting

A few of the Goals have seen some progress but without sustained action this progress will be fleeting. As a result of lockdowns, a significant number of deaths were averted through a reduction in both road traffic injuries and ambient air pollution (SDGs 3 and 11). In some countries, lockdowns saved more lives by restraining ambient air pollution than by preventing COVID infection (Burke, 2020; Giani and others, 2020; Khomsi and others, 2020). Water and sanitation efforts gained renewed importance as access to clean water and frequent hand washing became imperative for stopping the spread of the virus (SDG 6). Ambient water quality improved during lockdowns, for example, in the Yamuna River (Patel, Mondal and Ghosh, 2020) and Sabarmati River in India (Aman, Salman and Yunus, 2020), as did water-use efficiency in Europe (Roidt and others, 2020). The share of renewable energy in total energy increased during the pandemic, an effect that should last into 2021 (International Energy Agency, 2020) (SDG 7). These unintended consequences can be leveraged and built upon with appropriate policy measures to sustain current progress. Otherwise, these improvements will quickly return to business as usual. The pre-pandemic progress in SDG achievement has helped some countries cope better with COVID-19 and limit SDGs-related damages, demonstrating that sustainable development can strengthen resilience to unanticipated health and economic shocks.

Extraordinary crisis, extraordinary responses

Governments and central banks around the world responded to the pandemic with massive stimulus measures aimed at mitigating its health, humanitarian and economic fallouts. The global fiscal response amounts to $12.7 trillion, including $5.9 trillion for additional spending and $5.8 trillion in liquidity support (figure I.6a). At 15.8 per cent of world gross output in 2020, this is the largest fiscal response since the Second World War.

Fiscal responses to the pandemic reached a staggering $12.7 trillion...

Fiscal stimulus has saved the day

Assuming an average fiscal multiplier of 1.6—with every dollar of additional fiscal outlays generating 60 cents of additional output—then $5.9 trillion of pandemic-related fiscal spending and tax cuts generated an additional output of about $3.6 trillion in the world economy (Blanchard and Leigh, 2013). This is equivalent to about 4.5 per cent of world output in 2020. Without massive fiscal stimulus measures, world output would have contracted by double digits in 2020, instead of experiencing the estimated 4.3 per cent decline. The impacts on employment, household income and poverty would have been significantly more catastrophic. The unprecedented fiscal stimulus interventions helped the world avert an even worse catastrophe.

Figure I.6

a. Global fiscal response

Trillions of US dollars

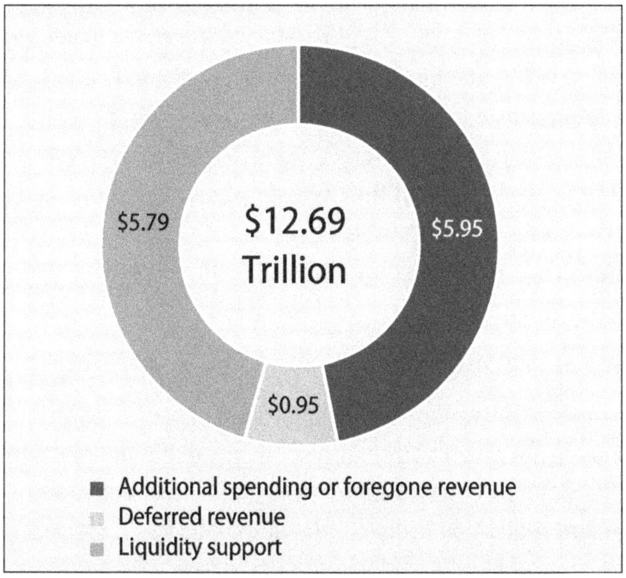

b. Fiscal response as a share of GDP

Percentage

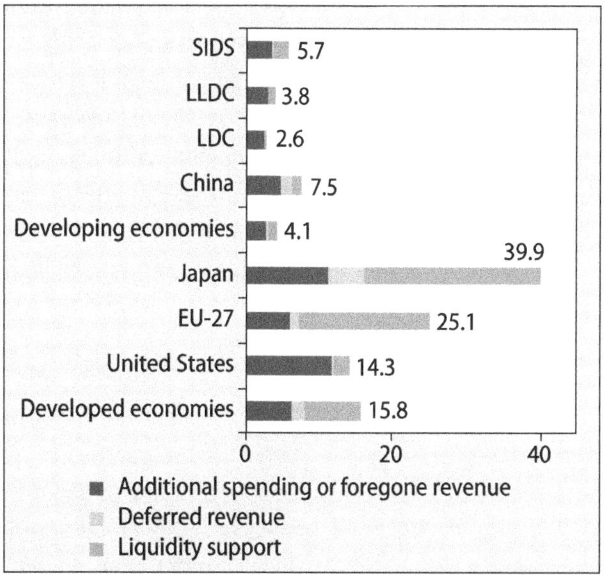

Source: IMF Fiscal Monitor Database of Country Fiscal Measures in Response to the COVID-19 Pandemic, available at https://www.imf.org/en/Topics/imf-and-covid19/Fiscal-Policies-Database-in-Response-to-COVID-19.

Note: Fiscal response as a share of GDP represents unweighted averages for the countries and country groups.

...which helped avert Great Depression-scale suffering

The fiscal support included additional spending, tax cuts and tax deferrals, all of which had direct budgetary impacts and increased fiscal deficits. The fiscal measures also included "below the budget line" support measures—equity injections, loans, asset purchases and guarantees—with long-term budgetary implications. As a result, most Governments face significantly higher levels of deficits and debt, which will increase even further should the recovery falter. A robust recovery of the world economy—and a return to a path of sustainable development—will depend not only on the effectiveness of the vaccines but also on the efficacy of the stimulus measures.

The developed countries' outlays accounted for almost four fifths of fiscal stimulus worldwide

The fiscal outlays of the developed countries represented nearly 80 per cent of all fiscal stimulus worldwide, with the United States, Germany and Japan accounting for more than half of the worldwide fiscal stimulus. In contrast, the responses from the developing countries have been modest relative to the magnitude of the shock. The COVID-19 crisis hit many developing countries—especially in Africa and Latin America and the Caribbean—when their public finances were already under strain. The group of 46 least developed countries, for example, collectively managed to increase direct and indirect fiscal support by only 2.6 per cent of their GDP, while the size of the stimulus for the developed countries averaged 15.8 per cent of their GDP.

In dollar terms, stimulus spending per capita averaged $9,836 in the developed countries, while it amounted to only $17 per capita in the least developed countries. That is, for every additional dollar per capita of stimulus rolled out by the LDCs, the developed countries spent nearly $580. The disparity in the size of the stimulus between the LDCs and the developed economies dwarfed the income disparity between these two groups of countries. The per capita income of the developed countries is only 30 times larger than the per capita GDP of the least developed countries.

The disparities in the size of the stimulus reflect the stark reality of the differing financing constraints faced by the developed and the developing countries, with significant consequences not only for the pace of their recovery from the crisis but also for their long-term growth and development trajectory. Many developing countries buffeted by the pandemic and unable to respond with large fiscal responses will likely see their growth and development path adjust downward relative to the pre-crisis trends. This may reverse the trends or at least delay the long-term convergence of the per capita incomes of the developed and developing countries, thwarting the objectives of reducing inequality between countries as envisaged in the 2030 Agenda for Sustainable Development, as noted above.

Not only the quantity but also the quality of stimulus matters

The large fiscal stimulus measures—protecting jobs and supporting household consumption—differed greatly across countries, not only in size but also in scope and priorities, reflecting differences in governance structures, political preferences and the levels of commitment to social protection. The welfare protection systems and automatic fiscal stabilizers allowed most countries in Europe to protect jobs and income immediately (Fatas, 2019). The United States, the United Kingdom and Canada, among others, as well as Japan, relied more on discretionary fiscal policy measures in pursuing similar objectives of protecting jobs and income.[5] In the EU and Japan, fiscal responses provided largely liquidity support, while in the United States direct income support to households helped to sustain consumption. In contrast, China's stimulus measures largely promoted new investments to support job growth and recovery. How these types of emergency spending will shape recovery and growth remains an open question. However, if these measures do not stimulate investment and growth, public debt will likely become unsustainable and force Governments to cut back spending, undermining the prospects of recovery.

Governments faced hard choices in addressing urgency on the one hand...

While the size of stimulus packages matters, the quality of fiscal spending matters equally, if not more. There are growing concerns about the distributional impacts and effectiveness of these emergency fiscal spending. Governments clearly faced difficult trade-offs in addressing urgency on one hand and exercising due diligence on the other to prevent misallocation, mis-targeting, corruption and fraud in the use of public resources. Under an ideal scenario, Governments should be able to target additional fiscal spending to households and businesses that are facing the gravest economic risks from the pandemic. If a stimulus measure is too broad in scope, it may stretch resources too thin to help anyone. On the other hand, if the stimulus is targeted too narrowly, it may exclude many businesses and households that deserve to receive government support. In the United States, for example, a mere 1 per cent of firms—many deemed as not facing any significant pandemic related risks—received 25 per cent of the disbursements from the $523 billion Paycheck Protection Program that was rolled out to support small and medium-sized businesses (Cowley and Koeze, 2020), raising concerns about misuse and mis-targeting of scarce fiscal resources. Striking a delicate balance among the imperatives of timeliness, scope, reach and effectiveness of stimulus measures required a deliberative vetting process, but the urgency of the response made such due diligence politically untenable.

...and exercising due diligence on the other to prevent mis-targeting and fraud

In many developing countries, citizens concerned about corruption and fraud in the deployment of stimulus packages. In South Africa, allegations of corruption related to overpricing and potential fraud in the procurement of personal protective equipment (PPE) and the distribution of social grants and food parcels, have provoked a public outcry and prompted investigations. There are calls in Argentina for an investigation of irregularities in the use of COVID-19 related funds. In Indonesia, concerns arose that a new stimulus package contained measures that could undermine workers' protections and cause widespread environmental damage.

The crisis response also raises the broader question of how Governments should assist businesses during a crisis and what risks they should assume while averting moral hazards. In Germany, for example, the Government's decision to take a significant ownership stake in Lufthansa, partially nationalizing the country's biggest airline, sparked debates over whether the Government should assume downside risks of a business entity or simply extend a loan to save the flagship carrier. Fiscal stimulus also provided an opportunity for Governments to shift the behaviour of firms towards creating public goods. In France, the government assistance package for Air France-KLM came with expectations that the airline group would promote environmental sustainability.

5 By activating the general escape clause of the Stability and Growth Pact, the European Commission has allowed Governments to take the budgetary action necessary to fight the pandemic. However, internal disagreements and the lack of a meaningful central fiscal capacity within the European Monetary Union have constrained the discretionary fiscal response.

Austerity cannot be an option

The fiscal responses will have differing long-term consequences for the sustainability of public debt, as most of the additional spending, tax cuts and deferrals have been funded in many countries with additional borrowing by their Governments. Countries saddled with high levels of public debt—and constrained by fiscal rules—may be forced to cut back spending too quickly to balance their budgets. Many developing countries are already facing significant debt distress and additional debt will only further weaken their debt sustainability. With a benign inflation outlook, real public debt will remain high relative to real GDP. It will be politically and economically infeasible for many Governments to raise taxes during the recovery phase. These constraints may encourage Governments to look to the devastating alternative of cutting fiscal spending to reduce deficits and debt.

Premature austerity will stifle recovery

A premature path to austerity will inevitably weaken the speed and quality of the recovery (UNCTAD, 2020) and undermine resilience to future shocks, as the experience of the last global financial crisis amply demonstrated. Austerity measures almost always cut back social sector spending on health and education and public services with far- reaching consequences for many SDGs. The developed countries pursuing austerity will also likely reduce their official development assistance (ODA), limiting the availability of development finance for the many developing countries that partly rely on ODA for budgetary support. The global spillover effects of spending cuts will have devastating consequences for sustainable development.

Robust monetary responses to complement fiscal measures

Central banks have rolled out unprecedented monetary measures...

The impact of COVID-19 on financial markets prompted central banks across the world to roll out monetary measures on an unprecedented scale. Since March 2020, 92 central banks have cut policy rates 241 times. Many central banks implemented additional monetary and prudential measures to boost liquidity and ensure financial stability. China, Indonesia, Malaysia and the United Arab Emirates, for example, lowered bank reserve requirements to inject liquidity. Argentina, Brazil, Sri Lanka, Taiwan Province of China and the United Kingdom launched or expanded special credit facilities for small and medium-sized enterprises. Brazil, Mexico, the Republic of Korea and Singapore, among others, established temporary United States dollar swap lines with the Federal Reserve. Hong Kong SAR, Norway, South Africa and the United Kingdom relaxed macroprudential regulations—suspending countercyclical capital or liquidity buffers—to enhance credit flows.

Responding to the pandemic, several central banks have also announced changes in their monetary policy frameworks to enhance policy flexibility and improve monetary transmission. The Fed announced a shift to "average inflation targeting" (Powell, 2020), which allows for inflation to overshoot its target for some time, in order to support a sustained recovery in labour markets. The European Central Bank has also hinted that it will commit to allowing inflation to overshoot its target following a period of weak price growth.

The Bank of England, the Bank of Canada and the Reserve Bank of New Zealand are exploring the possibility of introducing negative interest rates. Currently, the European Central Bank, and the central banks of Denmark, Japan and Switzerland, have a negative policy rate. Evidence on the effectiveness of negative interest rates in stimulating economic growth is somewhat mixed, and there are growing concerns over adverse side effects, including the potential for under-pricing risk. An extended period of negative interest rates could also erode bank profitability, leading to weaker balance sheets and reduced lending capability. In several countries, negative yields have dampened investment returns for insurance companies and pension funds, making it harder for them to meet their obligations. In December 2019, Sweden ended its negative interest rates policy, citing concerns over unintended side effects. Andersson and Jonung (2020) concluded that the Riksbank's negative policy rate from 2015 to 2019 had not contributed to significantly higher inflation, while creating major imbalances in the process.

In many countries, household saving rates have increased substantially since the outbreak of the pandemic. In normal times, this could be considered good news. But during these extraordinary times, it reflects a higher degree of risk aversion. Given elevated uncertainties over future income and employment conditions, precautionary savings will remain high. Low interest rates are unlikely to stimulate spending and investment, particularly in countries with weak social protection. Dossche and Zlatanos (2020) report that households in the euro area expect to spend less on major purchases over the next year, notwithstanding their accumulated savings. Amid a weak demand outlook and elevated debt, firms are more likely to postpone or cancel new capital spending plans, regardless of financing costs.

Lenders of last resort are becoming buyers of last resort

In times of financial turmoil, demand for equity and fixed income assets plummets, which can quickly dry up liquidity, push up yields and increase rollover and borrowing costs. The global financial crisis in 2008 prompted the United States Federal Reserve to engage in purchase of fixed assets directly from the financial market—the unconventional monetary policy tool that came to be known as quantitative easing—to increase liquidity and reduce long-term interest rates, which are critical for investments.

...and many are engaged in direct asset purchases

As many as 30 central banks are now engaged in direct asset purchases (Central Bank News, 2020). Developing country central banks have also started their own asset purchase programmes. The central banks of Chile, the Philippines, the Republic of Korea, Turkey and South Africa launched asset purchase programmes for the first time, buying mostly government bonds to signal their willingness to assume the role of buyer of last resort (Arslan, Drehmann and Hofmann, 2020).

Both the Federal Reserve and the Bank of Japan announced the unlimited purchase of government-backed debt and also started to buy corporate bonds for the first time, while the European Central Bank launched a €750 billion emergency bond-buying programme, with the amount later increased to €1.85 trillion. The balance sheets of the three largest central banks have increased by nearly $7.5 trillion—nearly 8 per cent of world gross product—since March 2020 (table I.3). Early evidence suggests that the monetary policy measures in major developed and emerging economies helped to ease liquidity constraints, while fueling a sharp rebound in financial markets (see, for example, Altavilla and others (2020)).

Table I.3
Asset purchases by major central banks

Central Bank	Asset purchases between March–November 2020 (billions of US dollars)
United States Federal Reserve	3,021
European Central Bank	3,028
Bank of Japan	1,405

Sources: United States Federal Reserve Board, European Central Bank and Bank of Japan.

Liquidity is not stimulating investments

The onset of the pandemic in March 2020 set off a rush to safety and a scramble for liquidity. Reminiscent of the panic at the beginning of the global financial crisis in September 2008, corporate and financial sector entities scrambled for cash, selling off bonds and pulling back from commercial paper markets and money market funds. Even the demand for United States Treasuries—the safest and most liquid financial asset—fell as financial markets panicked. The large-scale liquidity support from central banks, especially the United States Federal Reserve, eased the liquidity constraints and calmed the financial markets. By the end of April, central banks' bold actions had successfully mitigated the liquidity crisis (BIS, 2020). The unprecedented level of actions of central banks, at times in coordination with fiscal authorities, averted a financial meltdown and stabilized credit flows (IMF, 2020c).

Ten months into the pandemic, the financial markets are now awash with liquidity. While credit flows stabilized, there has been little growth in fixed investment. In the United States, fixed non-residential investments fell by 7.8 per cent in the second quarter, while money supply increased by 23.2 per cent during the same period (table I.4). The pandemic and the associated persistent uncertainties have further weakened the correlations among liquidity, credit and fixed investment. Acquisition of financial assets do not increase fixed investments, which are critical for boosting growth and employment.

While M2 in the United States has increased by $1.4 trillion since March, the excess reserves of the banks also increased, by about $1.0 trillion during the same period, having very little effect on credit creation. Evidence suggests that macroprudential tools—providing incentives for banks to lend to priority sectors and discouraging credit flows to speculative sectors—can be far more effective in stimulating credit growth and investment. This explains why the increase in the monetary base through quantitative easing (QE) itself does not usually have a multiplier effect unless it changes banks' lending behaviour.

But a surge in global liquidity poses a threat to financial stability

The surge in global liquidity has contributed to the under-pricing of risk in financial markets, posing a threat to longer-term financial stability. There has also been a growing disconnect between the performance of financial markets and the real economy. Igan, Kirti and Martinez Peria (2020) concluded that unprecedented central bank support in mid-March 2020 directly resulted in a significant decline in both risk premiums and risk-free discount rates, driving up asset prices to record levels. The world is witnessing the build-up of a massive financial bubble with major stock market indices registering record increases during the past 10 months. The S&P 500 index, for example, rose by nearly 40 per cent compared with average annual increases of 10 per cent during the past five years (figure I.7). There is a clear

Table I.4
Money supply and gross fixed capital formation

Percentage change	Money supply		Gross fixed capital formation	
	2019	Q1–Q2 2020	2019	Q1–Q2 2020
United States	6.0	23.2	0.7	-7.8
Euro area	5.4	8.9	7.3	-20.5
Japan	2.6	7.9	-2.0	-7.3

Source: United States Federal Reserve Board; European Central Bank; Bank of Japan; United States Department of Commerce, Bureau of Economic Analysis; Eurostat; and Japan, Cabinet Office.

Figure I.7
Change in major stock market indices

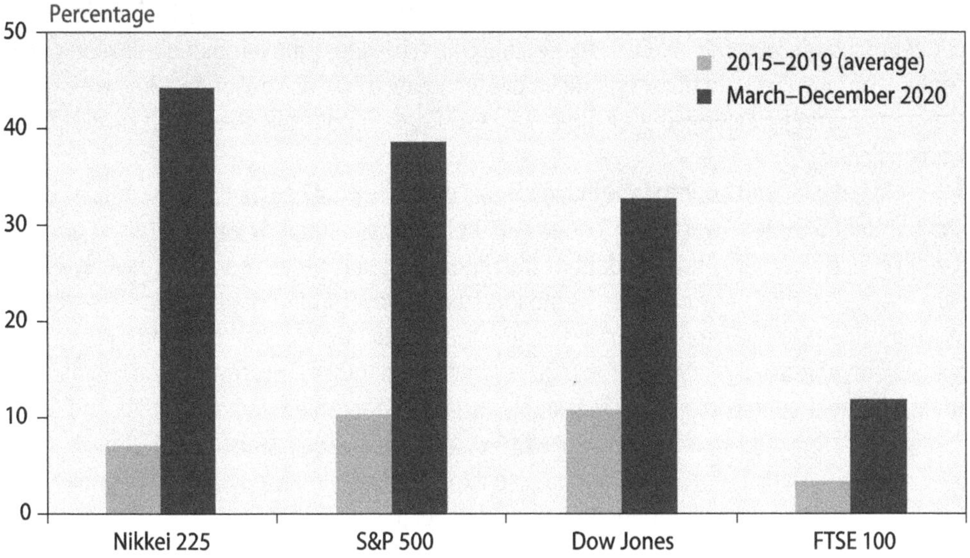

Abbreviations: FTSE, Financial Times Stock Exchange.

Source: UN DESA, based on data from stock exchanges in New York, London and Tokyo.

Note: The variation for March-December 2020 was calculated using monthly averages. Data extend until 15 December 2020.

need for central banks to deploy macro- and micro-prudential tools to ensure that massive liquidity boosts investments in the sectors that present significant potential for growth, such as digital and physical infrastructure, health and climate mitigation and adaptation.

A combination of ultra-low interest rates, high uncertainty and excessive liquidity have weakened monetary policy transmission. Not only are overburdened monetary policies less effective in stimulating economic growth, but they also entail significant costs, including distorting markets and exacerbating financial stability risks. The further lowering of borrowing costs in the current context is unlikely to stimulate real investment materially. Instead macroprudential tools and more nuanced and more targeted policies, such as those specifically intended to limit housing credit in countries experiencing a real estate bubble, can positively impact both credit growth and financial stability (Araujo and others, 2020; Akinci and Olmsted-Rumsey, 2015; Lee, Asuncion and Kim, 2015).

Borrowing from the future

Public finance is facing steeper challenges than during the 2008 financial crisis...

The crisis has created a perfect storm for public finances, undermining economic activities and affecting both the revenue and expenditure sides of the budget. Public finance is facing steeper challenges now than during the global financial crisis in 2008-2009. In almost one in five developing and transition economies, the government deficit is projected to reach double digits as a percentage of GDP in 2020. Losses in fiscal revenues contribute significantly more than increases in expenditures to explain projected deficits.

On a GDP-weighted basis, the global public debt-to-GDP ratio is projected to have increased from 106 per cent in 2019 to 127 per cent in 2020. While borrowing costs have declined for most Governments because of extraordinary monetary responses to the crisis (interest rate cuts, expansion of large-scale asset purchase programmes, provision of unprecedented amounts of liquidity), reduced borrowing costs will not be sufficient to bridge large financing gaps and improve fiscal balances. In an environment of low inflation, interest rates and borrowing costs will likely remain low in the foreseeable future, as central banks have pledged to keep interest rates at current levels for some time.

...with government gross debt projected to have increased globally by $9.9 trillion in 2020

Globally, government gross debt is projected to have increased by $9.9 trillion—12.3 per cent of world output—in 2020 (figure I.8). This represents the largest increase in public debt in any given year. In contrast, public debt increased by $4.2 trillion in 2009, when Governments hurriedly deployed their financial resources to confront the fallout of the global financial crisis.

Most developed countries with high levels of public debt—particularly Germany, Japan and the United States—were able to increase their debt significantly without facing any borrowing constraints. Government debt of the United States is projected to increase by 17 per cent in 2020, without any commensurate increase in government bond yields. The yield on 10-year United States Treasuries remains at a record low. Germany and Japan will see their public debt increase by 8 per cent and 20 per cent, respectively. Borrowing constraints—the limits on fiscal space—clearly do not apply to large economies with the ability to borrow domestically and internationally in their own currencies. A large number of developing countries in Latin America and Western Asia also experienced massive increases in public debt relative to increases in debt during the global financial crisis (figure I.9).

The borrowing constraint is, however, binding for many developing countries, even those with low levels of public debt before the crisis. Cambodia, the Democratic Republic of the Congo and Guatemala (figure I.10), for example, will see little increase in their debt. Despite significantly low levels of public debt, many of these countries will find it difficult to borrow during an economic crisis. Credit and debt often flow uphill, especially during an economic crisis. Liquidity dries up quickly in domestic and international capital markets at the first sign of a crisis, which makes it extremely difficult for many developing countries to roll over their existing debt and undertake new debt to mitigate the effects of the crisis. There is a clear need for expanding access to credit for developing countries, especially those with thin domestic capital markets. Support from the IMF emergency credit facilities has been timely but will fall short of what is required to support the recovery efforts of many developing countries.

There is a pressing need to expand the access of developing countries to credit...

Financing constraints are compounded by elevated risks of debt distress and default. As of 30 September 2020, 35 low-income countries were either in debt distress or at a high risk thereof according to the IMF/World Bank debt sustainability analysis (IMF, 2020d). But the situation has also become more difficult for many middle-income countries. Sovereign debt downgrades by the major credit-rating agencies have soared in 2020, reaching the highest level in 40 years (Bulow and others, 2020). Argentina, Ecuador, Lebanon, Suriname and Zambia have defaulted on their sovereign debt and are at different stages of restructuring their debt. Even if the dire scenario of widespread debt distress and disorderly defaults does not materialize, protracted fiscal paralysis could severely undermine countries' prospects of achieving the Sustainable Development Goals by 2030. A large number of developing economies are at risk of becoming trapped in a vicious cycle of high debt and low growth. Currently, the threat of higher future debt burdens already limits policy responses to Covid-19.

...with many developing countries at risk of getting stuck in a vicious cycle of high debt and low growth

Governments across the world have borrowed nearly $10 trillion from the future to minimize the impact of the crisis on the current generation. The current generation in turn has the responsibility to make sure that the money borrowed is well spent and invested to ensure that its well-being does not jeopardize the well-being of future generations. The urgency and emergency of the current crisis cannot justify depriving future generations of their right to enjoy prosperity. The rise in public debt should not in itself be a concern as long

Figure I.8
Increase in general government debt during recent crises

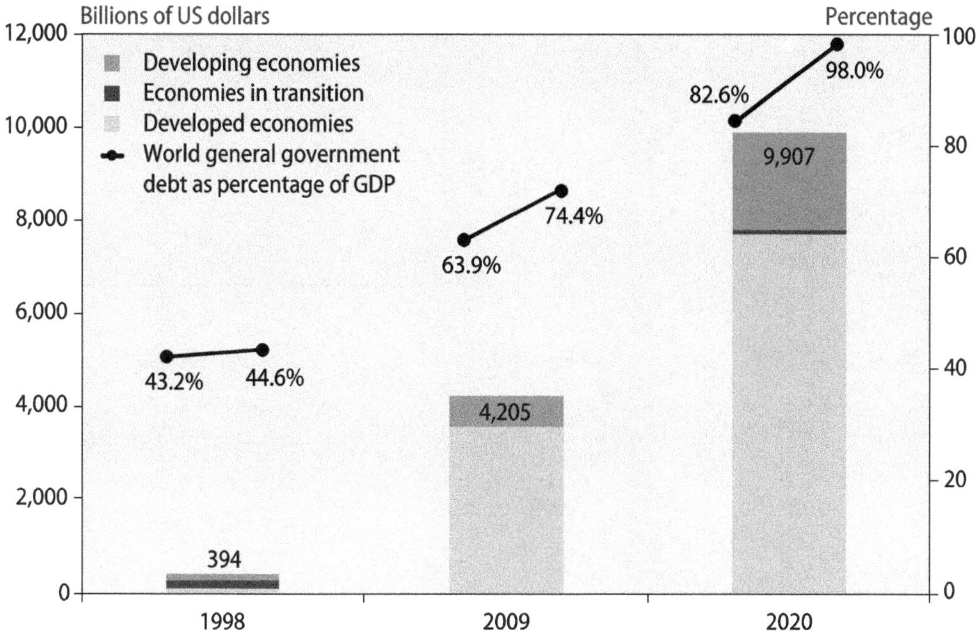

Source: UN DESA, based on IMF (2020g).

Figure I.9
General government gross debt, 2009 and 2020

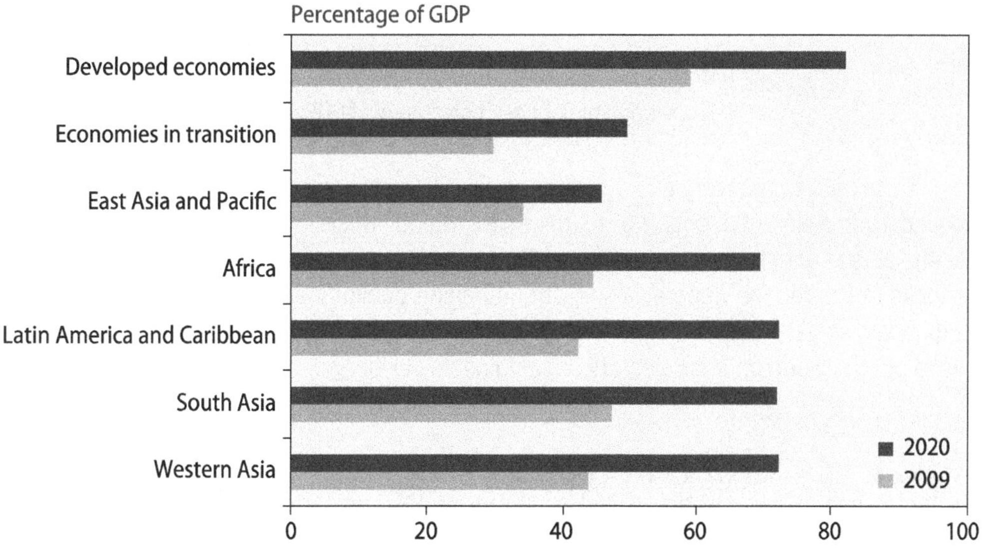

Source: UN DESA, based on IMF (2020g).
Note: 2020 values are estimated.

as additional debt boosts economic growth and generates sufficient additional government revenues to pay for additional debt services. Revenue growth, however, is often inelastic relative to growth in public debt. Even when revenue increases, there can be time inconsistencies between increases in debt service payments and new revenue generated, adding strains on government budgets. There are also risks that contingent liabilities of stimulus measures—loans, equity injection and guarantees—will go sour if firms and financial institutions receiving government support fail to recover from the crisis.

Figure I.10
Changes in government debt in 2020

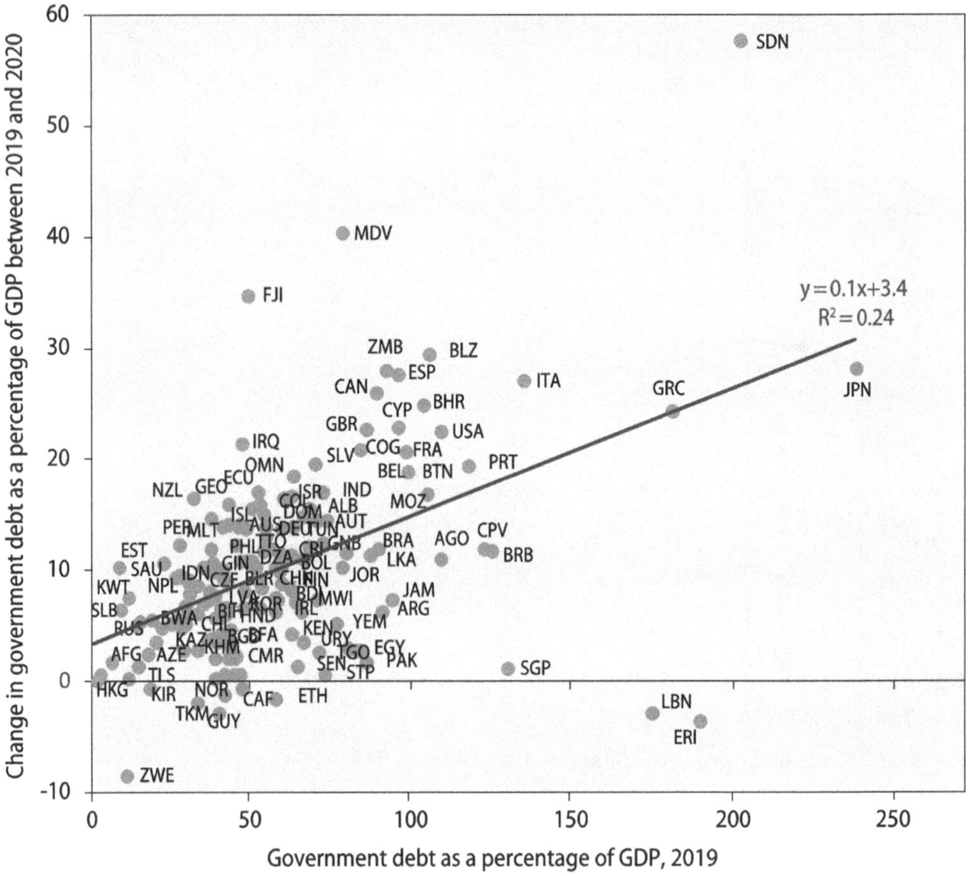

Source: UN DESA, based on IMF (2020g).

Note: Government debt is general government gross debt. 2020 values are estimated. Some country labels have been removed to ensure better visibility.

The current generation should ensure that its borrowings do not risk the prosperity of future generations

The path to recovery and progress on the SDGs will critically hinge on the ability and political commitment of countries to make sure that the crisis response ensures equity within and across generations and builds resilience against economic, social and environmental shocks in future. The imperatives of strengthening public finance and debt sustainability, expanding social protection and building climate resilience must inform today's policy choices to put the world on the trajectory of sustainable development.

Recovery with resilience

The pandemic has laid bare the fragility of the world economy. What began as a health crisis quickly devastated the world economy, plunging production and consumption, destroying jobs and throwing millions into poverty. The economic crisis is still unfolding amid a high degree of uncertainties, despite significant breakthroughs in medical treatment and vaccine development (Box I.3). COVID-19 killed more people in December 2020 than it did during its last peak in April.

The extreme and collective nature of the vulnerability to the pandemic—and its rapid transformation into a catastrophic economic crisis—is a wake-up call for policymakers. The crisis has exposed and exacerbated the weaknesses that persist because of the lack of

Box I.3
COVID-19 vaccines: the race to save lives

With the global economy on a cliff-hanger and COVID-19 still killing tens of thousands daily, breakthroughs in vaccine development are delivering some hope to the world. Globally, over 50 different vaccine candidates are in clinical trials on humans, with more than 100 additional preclinical vaccines under active development. At the time of finalization of the present report, 14 vaccines had reached the last stage of large-scale efficacy testing (Zimmer, Corum and Wee, 2021).

Pfizer and BioNTech confirmed the development of their COVID-19 vaccine in early November, with a confirmed 95 per cent efficacy, demonstrating an unprecedented success in vaccine testing and development. In early December 2020, the United Kingdom of Great Britain and Northern Ireland became the first country to authorize emergency use. The United States of America followed in mid-December. A growing number of other coronavirus vaccines are advancing through clinical trials. By the end of 2020, seven vaccine candidates had been locally approved for limited or early use. Similar to Pfizer and BioNTech, Moderna has had its emergency use application approved in the United States and the European Union; together, they expect to produce up to 2.3 billion doses in 2021. AstraZeneca-Oxford, whose vaccine has been cleared in the United Kingdom and India, expect to supply up to 3 billion doses of their easy-to-make COVID-19 vaccine, and developers of other final-stage vaccine candidates will likely produce comparable quantities once they receive the necessary authorization.

Despite successful clinical trials and approvals, manufacturing capacities will remain limited in the near term. The ultra-low temperature requirements of some vaccines will complicate their delivery, particularly in the global south. Production constraints and logistical challenges are compounded by the fact that many developed countries have ordered millions of doses of the vaccines to hedge against the risks of not obtaining them in time. The race to pre-order millions of doses not only reflects coordination failures but also lays bare the inequities in access to vaccines. High-income countries have currently secured their claim to 3.9 billion doses, which would allow some of them to vaccinate their entire population six times over (Duke Global Health Innovation Center, 2020). Although not all of these vaccines will necessarily receive approval, the imbalance is also at play in the context of procurement of the most promising vaccine candidates.[a] Given that low-income countries have not been able to make any public deals, it is likely that they will rely on vaccine coverage for 20 per cent of their population in 2021 through the COVID-19 Vaccines Global Access (COVAX) Facility, co-led by Gavi, the Vaccine Alliance; the Coalition for Epidemic Preparedness Innovations; and the World Health Organization. Leveraging their own drug-manufacturing strengths may be key for developing countries' efforts in securing advance market commitments. A world divided along the lines of those who have vaccines and those who have not would only reinforce the pains inflicted by inequality within and between countries.

While the vaccine outlook for most of the developing countries remains bleak, the end of the pandemic by the third or fourth quarter of 2021 looks increasingly likely for many developed countries. Pairing vaccines with more effective health measures, treatments and diagnostics, together with the benefits of seasonality, could lead to an even earlier transition towards normalcy, in the second quarter (Charumilind, 2020).

There are, however, still many unknowns and uncertainties. The degree of efficacy of the vaccines for children under 18 years of age is still largely undetermined. If only adults receive the vaccine, the coverage ratio for reaching herd immunity would be very high, particularly in regions with younger demographics. It is also unclear how long the vaccines' protection will last and how effective they would be against mutations of the coronavirus. New evidence is emerging that the virus may mutate and become more lethal or transmit faster, which will make it an increasingly treacherous adversary and vaccine development an increasingly wild goose chase.

These risks and uncertainties underscore the necessity of fair and equal access and greater global coordination to ensure that the people most at risk—regardless of where they live—are the first to receive the vaccine. People living in developed countries will not be safe if the pandemic continues to infect the vast populations of developing countries. More effective multilateral cooperation and coordination will remain key to ensuring that the vaccine reaches—and protects—those most vulnerable worldwide.

a The United States purchased 200 million doses from Pfizer-BioNTech and Moderna with an option to purchase up to 900 million more. The EU has purchased 360 million doses from Pfizer-BioNTech and Moderna with an option to purchase up to 100 million more. Japan, Canada and the United Kingdom have similar, albeit smaller-scale agreements in place.

progress in the implementation of the 2030 Agenda for Sustainable Development. Policies have not changed fundamentally to drive structural transformations needed for sustainable development—to eradicate poverty and hunger; to rein in rising inequalities, including the flagrant injustice of gender inequality; to accelerate energy transformation and take decisive and effective action against climate change; to halt biodiversity losses and environmental degradation; and to reinvigorate and revitalize the spirit of multilateralism.

This crisis is indeed universal, affecting all, but its impact is not even. Economic activities in some sectors came to a virtual standstill (e.g., tourism and travel, hospitality), with a massive loss of income and employment. Employees in some (mostly higher-skilled) sectors have been able to work remotely from the relative safety of their homes, while others in occupations requiring personal contact with customers have either lost their jobs or have been compelled to expose themselves to potential infection to earn any income. Women have been disproportionately affected by these predicaments, and many have left workforce to care for children amid school closures. While some schoolchildren have been able to continue their schooling online, for others that possibility is out of reach. The COVID-19 pandemic has exposed and widened existing inequalities in access and opportunities across the board, highlighting in particular, the depth of the digital divide between groups in all societies and between countries.

It will be too costly for the world to view the health crisis as an isolated, once-in-a-century event and ignore its long-term impacts on jobs, income and sustainable development, as outlined earlier in the chapter. The world witnessed three major economic crises during the past decade: the global financial crisis in 2008–2009, the European debt crisis in 2011–2012 and the commodity price collapse in 2014–2016. The global financial crisis greatly undermined progress on the Millennium Development Goals and reversed years of development gains. Absent bold and radical policy changes at national, regional and global levels to resuscitate and intensify the implementation of the 2030 Agenda as the foundation of the recovery, the current crisis will have far more devastating long-term impacts and will derail the realization of the Sustainable Development Goals.

There is no sustainable development without resilience

The world made little progress towards sustainable development before it faced the catastrophic pandemic. Meaningful progress in sustainable development—especially progress in health and educational opportunities—would have offered greater resilience against the pandemic. The current crisis demonstrates that there is no sustainable development without resilience and there is no resilience without sustainable development. The world was clearly not prepared to face the calamity. The 2030 Agenda for Sustainable Development provides a universal, cohesive and integrated framework for a sustainable, just and equitable recovery.

The path out of the current crisis presents a unique opportunity to build back better and put in place new foundations for resilience against future shocks, taking into account health, environmental and climate risks, all of which will likely become more frequent and more intense in the future. The efforts to build resilience must entail a holistic approach, with inclusive and sustainable development as its overriding objective.

The economic recovery from the crisis must go well beyond restoring GDP growth. High GDP growth is a means to an end, not an end goal. Economic growth must deliver not only decent green jobs, improved living standards and prosperity and greater equality, including gender equality, but also greater resilience against future shocks. It must do so while improving the environmental and social sustainability of our economic activities. To achieve the objectives of inclusive and sustainable growth and resilience, recovery efforts must strengthen fiscal and debt sustainability frameworks to ensure that Governments worldwide can deliver the public goods of health, education, a clean environment and social protection for all. The failure to deliver these essential elements of the sustainable development agenda can no longer be an option.

A fair and inclusive recovery must not undermine inter-generational equity. Protecting the well-being of the current generation should not unfairly burden future generations with unsustainable levels of debt, debt overhang and recurrent fiscal crises. Recovery efforts—and the trillions of dollars in stimulus money—must prioritize fights against inequality and climate change to make societies more cohesive, united and resilient.

Understanding resilience

Vulnerability and resilience are flip sides of the same coin. Several indicators highlight levels of vulnerability on a global scale. As much as 55 per cent of the world's population—more than 4 billion people—lack any form of social protection benefits, which makes them extremely vulnerable to an economic or a health shock. In addition, many people worldwide—even those who are not income-poor—are highly vulnerable to economic shocks. On average, about 40 per cent of the total population of an OECD member country do not have enough financial wealth to live at the income poverty line for three months—a much more widespread phenomenon than income poverty (Hacker, 2018). Social protection schemes can act as automatic stabilizers, smooth household consumption and minimize the impact of a shock, while reducing income and consumption inequality.

People deal with shocks and uncertainties through social insurance, market insurance, self-insurance (such as precautionary saving) and self-protection (such as investment in human capital and migration). Building systemic resilience requires an integrated risk management system, which covers ex ante risk adaptation, risk shifting and spreading, and ex post risk coping mechanisms.

Building resilience requires an integrated ex ante and ex post risk management system

Social and market insurances that spread risk across a pool of people are often sufficient for dealing with idiosyncratic risks faced by individuals such as an illness or an accident, but they are less effective in dealing with the kind of adverse systemic events that impact a large number of people simultaneously, such as a major financial crisis or a pandemic. In such situations, ex ante forms of adaptation, such as saving schemes that encourage the accumulation of assets to help households sustain themselves during difficult times, and ex post risk coping mechanisms, such as emergency loan programmes, can be helpful. Resilience to economic shocks at the macro level, however, critically depends on the effectiveness and efficacy of fiscal policy and good governance—and the availability of necessary fiscal space—for supporting both ex ante and ex post risk adaptation and mitigation measures.

While insurances spreading risk across a pool of people may be sufficient for idiosyncratic risk...

Rethinking fiscal and debt sustainability

Governments worldwide face daunting challenges in managing their finances during this crisis. Globally, public debt increased by over 15 per cent in 2020, as governments struggled to respond effectively to the twin health and economic crises amid collapsing public revenues, and many developing countries are facing debt distress—if not an outright debt crisis—amid stagnant exports and slow recovery. There will be economic and political pressures—in de-

...resilience to aggregate shocks will require robust fiscal and debt sustainability frameworks

veloped and developing countries alike—to quickly balance budgets, reduce public debt and restore fiscal discipline during the post-pandemic period. However, the experience during the last global financial crisis demonstrates clearly that cutting back spending indiscriminately and shifting to austerity prematurely will slow the recovery and make resilience elusive. More importantly, any significant cuts in social spending, which are often the target of austerity measures, will exacerbate inequalities, undermine resilience and further weaken solidarity and social cohesion.

The challenge of resisting the pressure for a rapid return to a less accommodative fiscal stance is further complicated by the uncertain trajectory of the pandemic. Even with the successful roll-out of vaccines and the increasing possibility of putting the virus on the retreat by the first half of 2021, economic and policy uncertainties—which have risen significantly in recent months[6]—will remain high amid increased political polarization and rising discontent within and across countries, and will further constrain countries' recovery efforts.

Governments will need to rethink fiscal frameworks, prioritizing fights against poverty, inequality and climate change

To respond to this challenge, governments in both developed and developing countries will need to rethink and redesign fiscal frameworks, making the fight against poverty, inequality and climate change the overarching priorities for accelerating recovery and building resilience. Not only the size of the stimulus but also the quality and effectiveness of stimulus and other spending will determine the recovery of growth and the sustainability of public finance. Most Governments will be unable to raise domestic revenues sufficiently in the near term to meet their current obligations. Given the high levels of public debt many Governments, particularly those in developing countries, will face the prospects of debt overhangs, which will constrain their ability to accelerate their sustainable development efforts. International support will remain critical to enable these countries to restructure and reduce their public debt so that they have necessary fiscal space to finance sustainable development.

Universal social protection schemes are the foundation of societal resilience

The pandemic has laid bare the weaknesses in existing fiscal frameworks: the procyclical nature of the present patterns of borrowing and spending, and the lack of fiscal buffers for responding to an extraordinary crisis. Countries with larger fiscal space have been able to respond to the crisis with large fiscal stimulus packages and are therefore weathering the current shocks better. Building and maintaining fiscal space during good economic times will remain key to building economic resilience. Amid persistent uncertainties and growing risks of crisis, an optimal fiscal policy framework would need built-in flexibility in its crisis response mechanisms. Expanded and universal social protection schemes—which can act as automatic stabilizers and offer built-in and flexible crisis response mechanisms—must serve as the foundation for fighting inequality and building economic resilience.

Social protection programmes such as unemployment insurance—which can kick in at a given threshold, independent of political considerations—could help minimize the impact of an economic crisis. But for a large-scale, long-lasting crisis like the current one, standard automatic stabilizers—based on a strict rules-based fiscal framework—will remain insufficient. Brazil and the EU, for example, suspended their fiscal rules to roll out large stimulus measures, while Mexico was unable to increase spending because of a constitutionally mandated policy on new debt issuance (IMF, 2020b). New fiscal frameworks would need to incorporate objective criteria for defining a crisis—such as the level of GDP contraction or

6 As illustrated by the Economic Policy Uncertainty Index (available at https://www.policyuncertainty.com/index.htm).

the level of increase in aggregate unemployment rates—which would trigger an escape from the rules-based fiscal framework and allow Governments to quickly increase discretionary spending, while avoiding costly political debates and delays.

New fiscal and monetary frameworks will also need to incorporate strategies for dealing with, and mitigating, the unintended consequences of increased liquidity stemming from large stimulus packages worldwide. As discussed earlier, macro- and micro-prudential policies must be part of the toolbox for preventing financial market volatility and the formation of big speculative asset price bubbles, as witnessed after the global financial crisis. The financial bubbles, and their subsequent burst, have significant macroeconomic consequences. The current stimulus spending, especially in the form of loans, guarantees and liquidity support given to businesses, must be well targeted for specific sectors and must meet specific investment objectives to ensure that the additional liquidity does not fuel an ever larger speculative bubble, as has been observed since March 2020.

New fiscal frameworks will need strategies for dealing with increased liquidity...

There is no fiscal sustainability without debt sustainability. Since the global financial crisis, most developing countries have seen a sharp increase in their external debt (box I.4). The global debt-to-GDP ratio reached a record 331 per cent in Q1 2020, with private debt accounting for more than two thirds of all debt worldwide (Institute of International Finance, 2020). Public external debt of developing and emerging countries rose from $1.5 trillion in 2009 to $3.0 trillion in 2019, with the African countries registering the sharpest increase (figure I.11). The external debt of the private sector increased from $2.2 trillion to $5.8 trillion during the same period. Average debt servicing costs on external debt—as a percentage of exports of goods and services—rose from about 16 per cent in 2010 to over 30 per cent in 2019. The massive amounts of the fiscal stimulus and quantitative easing in the aftermath of the global financial crisis drove interest rates down even further, which allowed both the private and public sectors in developing countries to borrow extensively. An increasing share of their external debt came from foreign private creditors.

Figure I.11
External debt stock and debt servicing burden in developing countries

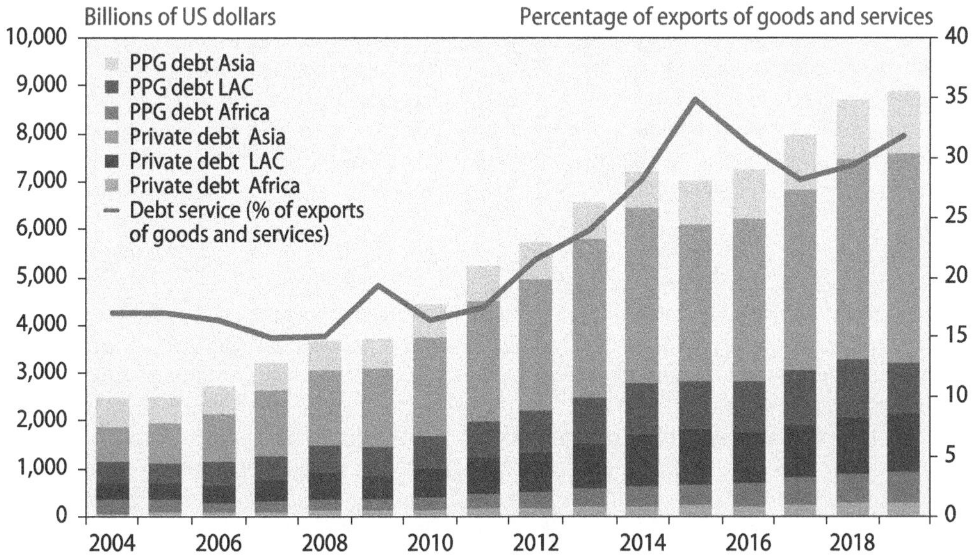

Source: International Monetary Fund, Inter-Agency Task Force on Finance Statistics (IATF) database (2020).

Note: PPG, public and publicly guaranteed.

Box I.4

External debt of the developing countries: the need for comprehensive restructuring

The COVID-19 shock has exacerbated debt trends around the world. Global debt across all sectors reached $255 trillion in April 2020, 40 percentage points higher than at the start of the 2008 financial crisis (Institute of International Finance, 2020). While debt growth was fuelled mainly by private sector debt in developed economies, developing countries experienced an increase in both public and private borrowing (United Nations, Inter-agency Task Force on Financing for Development, 2020). Lending from private creditors was the fastest-growing component of the external debt of developing countries, up fivefold since 2010 (World Bank, 2020). Before the onset of the pandemic, 36 of 70 least developed and other low-income countries and some middle-income countries were already at high risk of—or already in—debt distress.

The pandemic has exerted further pressure on countries' public finances owing to both additional financing needs and dwindling revenues. As of September 2020, many countries had announced unprecedented discretionary fiscal support measures. Debt-financed discretionary fiscal policy measures have helped advanced economies address the health crisis and contain the economic consequences of the pandemic. But unlike advanced economies, many developing countries face tight financing constraints which will likely inhibit necessary fiscal responses. While there has been a global easing in financial conditions since the spread of the coronavirus, more than half of emerging market economies still experienced outflows in the first half of 2020 and saw an increase in the cost of their borrowing.

To help the most vulnerable countries, international financial institutions have responded with emergency measures. As of October 2020, the International Monetary Fund (IMF) had disbursed roughly US$ 30 billion in non-concessional funds for pandemic-related financing through its Rapid Financing Instrument, doubled access to its Rapid Financing Instrument and granted debt service relief of US$ 260 million through its Catastrophe Containment and Relief Trust. The World Bank Group has announced its intention to have provided up to US$ 160 billion, including US$ 50 billion of International Development Association (IDA) resources on grant and highly concessional terms, by the end of 2021. However, while these emergency measures are vital, they do not address the scale of the problem.

G20 responded to the crisis with the Debt Service Suspension Initiative (DSSI), which allows 73 low-income developing countries to temporarily suspend payments of debt service to their bilateral official creditors. As of August 2020, 43 countries had received a temporary debt service suspension of US$ 5 billion, out of more than US$ 11.5 billion initially projected. The initiative, which was extended in October 2020 by another six months,[a] encourages multilateral development banks (MDBs) and private creditors to participate on comparable terms. Multilateral development banks have declined to participate in the DSSI, out of fear that a debt service suspension would impact MDB credit ratings, and instead have agreed to net positive flows to IDA countries. No private creditors have joined the Debt Service Suspension Initiative and borrowing countries have been reluctant to approach their private sector creditors for fear of credit-rating downgrades, along with consequences for longer-term market access.

While the DSSI provides much needed liquidity support, it fails to address solvency concerns in many developing countries. Many of those countries will be confronted with a decision on whether to default on debt service obligations to address the economic fallout from the COVID-19 pandemic. In October 2020, the members of G20 and the Paris Club acknowledged the significant debt vulnerabilities of many low-income countries and agreed in principle on a Common Framework for Debt Treatments beyond the Debt Service Suspension Initiative to deal with solvency issues on a case-by-case basis.

Debt relief discussed within the context of the Common Framework should be part of a broader strategy which takes Sustainable Development Goal (SDG)-related investment needs into consideration. Depending on countries' specific circumstances, official creditors and/or donors could either write down bilateral debt or fund debt buybacks of commercial debt, with recipient Governments com-

a The Debt Service Suspension Initiative will be extended to 30 June 2021, subject to renewal for another six months if the economic and financial situation so requires.

(*continued*)

Box I.4 (*continued*)

mitting to use freed resources for crisis- and SDG- related investments. Debt swaps (including the development of standardized term sheets) and regional resilience funds could channel debt service payments into crisis response expenditures or SDG- and climate-related investments. Moreover, there is a pressing need to address the gaps in the current international sovereign debt architecture. This could include improving market-based approaches to debt restructuring, for example, by developing and encouraging the adoption of model majority restructuring clauses on payment terms for loans and other forms of sovereign debt. Targeted domestic and international law options could help undermine the litigation tactics employed by uncooperative and hold-out creditors and prevent them from blocking agreements on the restructuring of already existing debt stocks. The scale of the current challenges clearly underlines the need for a systematic and timely approach to sovereign debt crisis resolutions.

Figure I.12
Public and publicly guaranteed external debt, by creditor

a. International Development Association (IDA) countries **b. Middle-income countries**

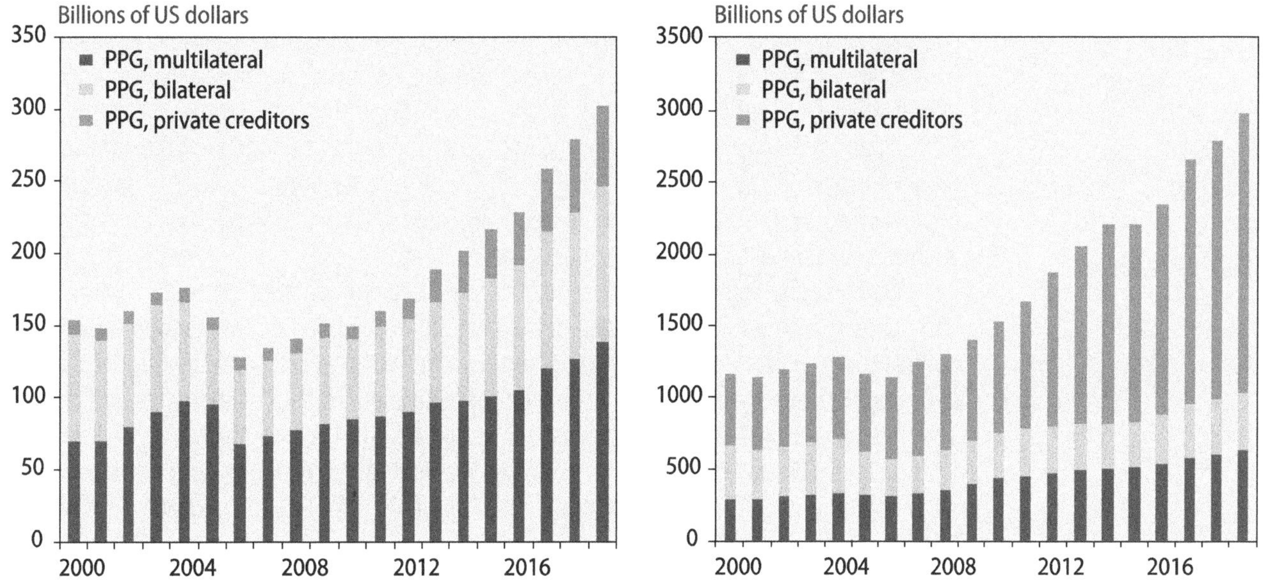

Source: World Bank, International Debt Statistics, October 2020.
Note: PPG, public and publicly guaranteed.

exchange rate depreciates. Exchange rate depreciation increases demand for its exports, which restores the balance-of-payments equilibrium. But the demand for foreign exchange remains high with high debt servicing burdens, which prevents the exchange rate depreciation that can stimulate exports.

The United Nations and the G20 have called for debt relief for the world's poorest countries. The G20 Debt Service Suspension Initiative, which took effect on 1 May 2020 and was extended through June 2021, has so far delivered approximately $5 billion in debt service deferrals for about 40 countries.[7] Meanwhile, as of 15 December, the IMF had provided debt relief via the Catastrophe Containment and Relief Trust to 29 countries, totaling $488.7

7 See IMF, "Questions and answers on sovereign debt issues", available at www.imf.org/en/About/FAQ/sovereign-debt.

million.[8] Through its various lending facilities, the IMF has provided total financial assistance of $102 billion to 83 countries.

These are timely initiatives, but they are only a drop in the ocean. They exclude the majority of the indebted middle-income countries, and they do not provide relief on debt to multilateral development banks, often major creditors of developing countries.

There is a pressing need for a comprehensive restructuring of external debt, with significant and meaningful reduction of the current debt stock, to ease the debt burden of the developing countries and to help build their resilience to external shocks. Unless the current debt level is reduced significantly, the accumulation of new and additional debt will only make their debt even more unsustainable and further constrain their limited fiscal space. It is critical that the international community comes together urgently to address and mitigate the risks of a looming debt crisis. A debt crisis on the heels of a devastating economic crisis will derail recovery efforts by years. Comprehensive debt standstills, debt swaps, replacing current bonds with green bonds to support climate action while reducing debt burden, and debt buybacks are on the table and merit serious consideration as initiatives for easing the debt burden of developing countries (Stiglitz and Rashid, 2020) and improving their debt sustainability. Without such an improvement, there is little prospect of accelerating recovery with resilience, and the continued weakness of these indebted countries will be a drag on the overall global recovery.

These options must be built into globally agreed permanent mechanisms for debt restructuring and reduction as a matter of the utmost urgency, in order to eliminate the uncertainties of the ad hoc arrangements in force today. Such mechanisms must also include private creditors.

Such mechanisms must be based on a redefined concept of debt sustainability, taking into account both public and private debts owed to official and private creditors. New debt contracts will need to ensure greater responsibilities for creditors and their participation in debt restructuring mechanisms, while safeguarding the interests of the sovereign debtors. These new debt sustainability frameworks should reflect the principles for a rules-based, fair and equitable sovereign debt workout mechanism—as envisaged under General Assembly resolution 69/319 of 10 September 2015 containing the Basic Principles on Sovereign Debt Restructuring Processes.

Ensuring universal social protection

Universal protection against economic, health and environmental shocks is a moral imperative...

The increasing vulnerability of hundreds of millions of people to economic, health and environmental shocks underscores the need for universal social protection. Stagnant wages and income—constraining levels of consumption and access to basic services—have made vulnerability an existential reality for millions in both developed and developing countries. Ubiquitous income and wealth inequality, with people at the top of the distribution enjoying unprecedented prosperity—while the bottom 40 per cent of the world's population lack access to basic food, shelter and health care—makes universal social protection not only a moral issue, but also an economic imperative.

8 See IMF, "COVID-19 financial assistance and debt service relief", available at https://www.imf.org/en/Topics/imf-and-covid19/COVID-Lending-Tracker#CCRT.

...which can boost aggregate demand during both crisis and normal times

Universal social protection will help preserve aggregate demand in the global economy not only during a crisis but also during normal times. As was seen during the global financial crisis, social protection enhances resilience and can act as an automatic economic stabilizer in cases of shock.9 Yet social protection is far from universal. In Africa, for example, 80 per cent of the population has no social protection coverage (ILO, 2017).

Countries have been encouraged by the pandemic to roll out some type of universal basic income (UBI) plan

Given the difficulties in designing and implementing effective social protection schemes, there is growing interest in providing universal basic income (UBI) to all adults, without exclusion or any type of means- testing (Hasdell, 2020) (see box I.5). The pandemic has encouraged a number of countries to roll out some form of UBI, without necessarily defining these interventions as such. These countries include the United States, with its $1,200 monthly payout (Ståhl and MacEachen, 2020); Canada, with its Emergency Response Benefit of $500 per week (ibid.); and Spain, with its UBI experiment providing 850,000 low-income households with unconditional monthly payments of up to €1,015 (Arnold, 2020).

But financing constraints will limit the feasibility of an effective and sizeable UBI during normal times. In the United States, for example, a UBI of $12,000 per year for an estimated 236 million adult citizens would cost $2.8 trillion (Clifford, 2020). Even though a distributionally favorable UBI could replace and rationalize current social protection expenditure in part, its implementation would likely still require an increase in taxation, or a cut in other areas of public spending, including spending cuts in public health, education or environment, which could face strong political opposition. Globally, the cost of a UBI could be as high as 15 per cent of GDP. Many developing countries simply do not have the means to fund a UBI, especially when their total tax-to-GDP ratio is often less than 10 per cent. The smaller the

Box I.5

Universal basic income: Pros and cons

For all its apparent advantages, the concept of universal basic income (UBI) does not enjoy universal support. There are concerns that unconditional cash transfers to all adults could generate worse outcomes than today's targeted and means-tested social protection programmes. Some are concerned that individuals could use the income for consumption of items such as alcohol or tobacco, which could increase the health and social costs of such a programme. Others are worried that a UBI could disincentivize work, especially work that is deemed unattractive or dangerous. But studies find no evidence that a UBI encourages suboptimal consumption or discourages work. Evidence from a Stanford Basic Income Lab meta-analysis of 16 review reports on UBI-type programmes worldwide indicates that diverse interventions in low-, middle- and high-income countries had a minimal impact on aggregate measures of labour-market participation (Hasdell, 2020, p. 16 and table 1). When reductions in work occur, time is channeled into other valued activities such as caregiving.

Some also argue that UBI may have unfavourable distributional implications. Means-tested schemes favour families with children, the elderly and the disabled. If a budget neutral UBI replaces current targeted social protection schemes, it could direct a larger share of income to less vulnerable groups and potentially reduce disposable incomes for the bottom of the income distribution. However, if UBI is substantially supplemented by existing and more targeted social protection schemes, its implementation will cause a large downward redistribution of income towards those most vulnerable (Hoynes and Rothstein, 2020).

9 See https://www.social-protection.org/gimi/ShowMainPage.action.

fiscal space of a country and the weaker its governance, the more difficult the challenges it will face in funding an UBI.

While a comprehensive implementation of UBI might currently be out of reach for many developing countries, policymakers should proceed immediately to implement a universal social protection floor,[10] supplemented where possible by means-tested and well-targeted social protection programmes to build resilience for the most vulnerable segment of their population. However, the ultimate objective should remain the introduction of a robust universal social protection system, though this will require considerably more financing.

While the limits of fiscal space are a constraint, there are opportunities to raise revenues that could be used for social protection, including: reallocating public expenditures that are inconsistent with the 2030 Agenda; increasing certain types of taxes; drawing on official development assistance, where available; utilizing the fiscal space created by eventual debt restructuring and debt relief; and global action to reduce and eventually eliminate illicit financial flows. Some of these measures can have important co-benefits in terms of sustainable development. For example, an environmental tax on carbon and the elimination of perverse subsidies on fossil fuels can potentially fund social protection schemes, be it a UBI or other forms of social protection, while also disincentivizing carbon-intensive consumption and associated externalities.

Building climate resilience

Building resilience against climate shocks must include considering differences in vulnerability and exposure

Efforts aimed at enhancing resilience must encompass climate-related shocks, which will likely become increasingly frequent and intense and affect millions of vulnerable people in both developed and developing countries. The impacts of shocks, on one hand, and structural inequalities, on another, are mutually reinforcing. Vulnerability and exposure to shocks are closely linked to existing underlying inequalities: differences in access to physical and financial assets; unequal opportunities to access quality health services, education and employment; and inequality with respect to voice and political representation. When hit by shocks, people afflicted with poverty and social exclusion suffer relatively greater losses in terms of lives and livelihoods than those in more secure circumstances. Such disproportionate impacts further aggravate existing inequalities and may actually undermine the capacities of people to cope and adapt. Exposure to growing climate risks will likely exacerbate existing inequalities within and across countries.

Building resilience against climate shocks must take into account different levels of vulnerability and exposure. The level of exposure to climate risk and the financing and institutional capacities of a country to cope with and mitigate those risks must match. But most developing countries lack the necessary fiscal capacities for dealing with climate risks. A continuum of well-integrated economic, social and environmental policies for building climate resilience would help to build public support for effective and harmonized adaptation and mitigation efforts. No-regret and low-regret policies constitute a good starting point, as they can address immediate vulnerabilities and structural inequalities, without compromising the foundations of future resilience.

The desirable strategy for increasing resilience to climate shocks encompasses both preventive and remedial elements. The preventive measures should include increasing

10 The ILO estimates that introducing a comprehensive social protection floor would cost on average just over 4 per cent of GDP, based on a sample of 57 low-income and lower middle-income countries. See Ortiz and others (2020).

investments in sustainable and climate-resilient physical infrastructure and boosting fiscal reserves. Risk pooling, which includes private and public insurance mechanisms, can be another major strand of such measures. But it will also require greater international and multilateral coordination (Catalano, Forni and Pezzolla, 2020). Building resilience against climate shocks must also balance inter-temporal equities. The protection of, and benefits for, the current generation must not inflict harm on future generations. In terms of resource allocation across time, preventive actions against climate change taken early are preferable to remedial measures taken later. Waiting comes at an increasing cost, and spending earlier, before damages to capital stock have occurred, increases resilience.

Revitalizing multilateralism: United We Stand, Divided We Fall

The crisis is a missed opportunity for bold multilateral action

The pandemic unleashed itself on the world at a low point in multilateral cooperation. Lack of effective cooperation, pervasive mistrust and blame games constrained the multilateral response to the pandemic. In the initial response to the crisis, many countries increased trade protection, and restricted exports of PPE and other medical supplies, which weakened collective responses to the crisis. Despite the efforts of the G20, IMF and a few multilateral institutions (see box I.6), the overall global economic responses to the crisis remained inadequate. Most developing countries—many with severe financing constraints and huge debt—have been left on their own to face the worst crisis in a century.

Regional initiatives cannot be a substitute for an open, inclusive and rules-based multilateral system...

While these bold regional initiatives of the development finance institutions have helped countries fight the pandemic and finance recovery efforts, they cannot be a substitute for an open, inclusive and rules-based multilateral system. In the absence of a comprehensive debt restructuring and debt relief initiative, the financing support from the regional development banks will also increase the overall debt burden of many developing countries.

The crisis and the inadequate collective actions in response also present the multilateral system with a lesson learned. It is clear that the world stands strong only if it remains

Box I.6
Regional economic responses to the crisis

There has been concerted and coordinated economic responses at the regional level. The Asian Infrastructure Investment Bank (AIIB), for example, launched the COVID-19 Crisis Recovery Facility, a $13 billion fund which will extend emergency loans to support public and private entities that have been impacted by the pandemic.[a] Financial resources will be channelled towards supporting public health-care needs, and closing budgetary and liquidity gaps, as well as supporting investments in infrastructure, economic and social protection. Similarly, the Asian Development Bank (ADB) created a $20 billion COVID-19 response package, consisting of grants, concessional loans and guarantees. The African Development Bank (AFDB) established a $10 billion COVID-19 Rapid Response Facility (African Development Bank Group, 2020). Its funds are providing flexible and rapid support to African countries to finance public health interventions, social protection programmes and the injection of liquidity to stabilize and support their economies. The Inter-American Development Bank (IDB) approved a record $21.6 billion in new financing in 2020 to assist its 26 member countries in addressing the ongoing health emergency and the socioeconomic fallout from the crisis (Inter-American Development Bank, 2020). Among other measures, the IDB has mobilized $1 billion to help members acquire and distribute COVID-19 vaccines. Similarly, the European Bank for Reconstruction and Development (EBRD) has launched a €21 billion solidarity package to support the recovery efforts of its member States.

a See COVID-19 Crisis Recovery Facility Toolkit, available at www.aiib.org/en/policies-strategies/COVID-19-Crisis-Recovery-Facility/_download/CRF-Toolkit-Final-1.pdf.

united. Divisions are costly, not only during the pandemic but more so during recovery. Stronger multilateral cooperation must underpin global recovery efforts. As discussed in chapter II, the multilateral trading system must receive a new impetus to revitalize global trade, support growth objectives and enhance resilience of the global economy. Effective climate action, halting biodiversity loss, combatting illicit financing flows, overcoming the digital technological divide and taming inequality are sustainable development imperatives that s cannot be achieved in the absence of multilateral cooperation and renewed solidarity among countries.

...but the multilateral system must reinvent and revitalize itself to confront the challenges of recovery and resilience

The pandemic has exposed the weaknesses and inadequacies of the current practice of multilateralism by consensus. It is often hard to reach consensus in multilateral processes when confronted with high degrees of uncertainty and divergent national interests and priorities. The global efforts towards steering a resilient recovery will need new and binding rules in the areas of climate mitigation and adaptation, debt restructuring and meaningful debt reduction, the exploitation and use of natural resources, illicit financial flows and sustainable finance, and universal social protection, among other pressing issues. Decisions by majority—while safeguarding minority positions and letting countries join the majority decisions when they are in a position to do so—may help reinvigorate the current multilateral system and make it fit for purpose in taking up the challenges of accelerating recovery with resilience. The multilateral system—in its many forms and manifestations—must reinvent, reboot and revitalize itself to accelerate recovery and strengthen resilience for people, the planet and prosperity.

CHAPTER II

The future of global trade[1]

The COVID-19 pandemic resulted in a contraction in international trade in 2020, as widespread lockdowns triggered a collapse in demand and significant disruptions to global production networks. As global economic activity recovers, global trade activity will improve but, until 2022, it is projected to remain below pre-pandemic levels. Beyond these short-term dynamics, the pandemic shock is likely to accelerate ongoing structural trends—including the evolving configuration of global value chains (GVCs), the rise of the digital economy, and the increasingly significant role of trade in services—which are shaping the future of the global trade landscape. In addition, the rules-based multilateral trading system is facing unprecedented challenges amid ongoing disputes at the World Trade Organization (WTO) and rising protectionism in parts of the world.

The pandemic delivered a massive shock to global trade

The changing international trade environment is having a profound impact on global growth and development prospects, reinforcing the need for many developing economies to assess export-oriented growth strategies. While rapid digitalization and the servicification of the manufacturing and agricultural sectors present countries with major challenges, they could also be the source of immense opportunities.[2] In order to harness such potential, national trade policy strategies would need to be comprehensive; centred around technology, infrastructure and human capital; and supported by a reformed and revitalized multilateral trading system.

How global trade evolves over the coming decade will be a crucial determinant of the achievement of the Sustainable Development Goals (SDGs) worldwide. Indeed, global trade patterns and trade policy developments will shape progress towards all of the goals within the SDG framework.[3] Most important, trade can serve as a powerful engine of growth and development and thus help lift people out of poverty (SDG 1). Ending hunger, achieving food security and improved nutrition, and promoting sustainable agriculture (SDG 2) depend strongly on the character of agricultural trade policies. In this regard, the pandemic has served as a stark reminder that an open and predictable trading environment is vital to preventing disruptions in food supply chains and ensuring cross-border flows of the medical supplies needed to support healthy lives (SDG 3).[4] By promoting sustainable development, trade can also help facilitate the building and maintaining of peaceful societies (SDG 16).[5]

The future global trade landscape will significantly impact progress on the SDGs

1 The present chapter is based in part on a background paper prepared by Hoekman and Shepherd (2020).

2 Servicification refers to the increased use, production and export of services in other sectors. Sect. 3 of this chapter examines the trends of growing servicification and digitalization.

3 Four Sustainable Development Goal indicators are explicitly linked to trade: the proportion of tariff lines applied to imports from least developed countries (LDCs) and developing countries with zero-tariff (10.a.1); the worldwide weighted tariff-average (17.10.1); the average tariffs faced by developing countries, LDCs and small island developing States (17.12.1); and developing countries' and LDCs' share of global exports (17.11.1).

4 To facilitate the access of developing countries to life-saving vaccines, India and South Africa have called for the World Trade Organization (WTO) to grant a temporary waiver from certain provisions of the WTO Agreement on Trade-Related Aspects of Intellectual Property Rights (TRIPS Agreement) (Usher, 2020).

5 The first edition of the Trade for Peace Week, hosted by the WTO from 30 November to 4 December 2020, focused on the role of trade in fragile and conflict-affected countries (WTO, 2020d).

While international trade has brought immense benefits, it is also creating significant challenges for some areas of sustainable development. Experiences of the past few decades have illustrated that trade policies and developments strongly impact global inequality (SDG 10). While trade has supported income growth in many developing countries, thus helping to reduce between-country inequalities, it has often contributed to widening gaps within countries (UNCTAD, 2019). Furthermore, trade is closely connected with environmental sustainability (covered under SDGs 12–15), with trade-related activities having strongly contributed to the surge in greenhouse gases, pollution and biodiversity loss. At the same time, climate change is increasingly affecting global patterns of trade in goods and services, through, for example, its impact on crop productivity (Gouel and Laborde, 2018) and its disruption of trade infrastructure (Dellink and others, 2017). Enhanced recognition of these linkages has led to new initiatives aimed at intensifying discussions on trade and the environment at the multilateral level.[6]

New and emerging challenges faced by global trade

Short-term trends: impact of COVID-19 on global trade

After a strong decline in 2020, global trade is set to recover

International trade contracted in 2020 for the first time since the global financial crisis, as the COVID-19 crisis triggered widespread lockdowns, severely impacted factory output, disrupted travel and depressed demand worldwide. According to UN DESA estimates, the volume of global trade in goods and services fell by 7.6 per cent in 2020. Following a massive contraction in March and April, trade recovered in the second half of the year driven by a rebound in economic activities in East Asia (figure II.1).

Figure II.1
Volume of merchandise exports, January 2005–September 2020

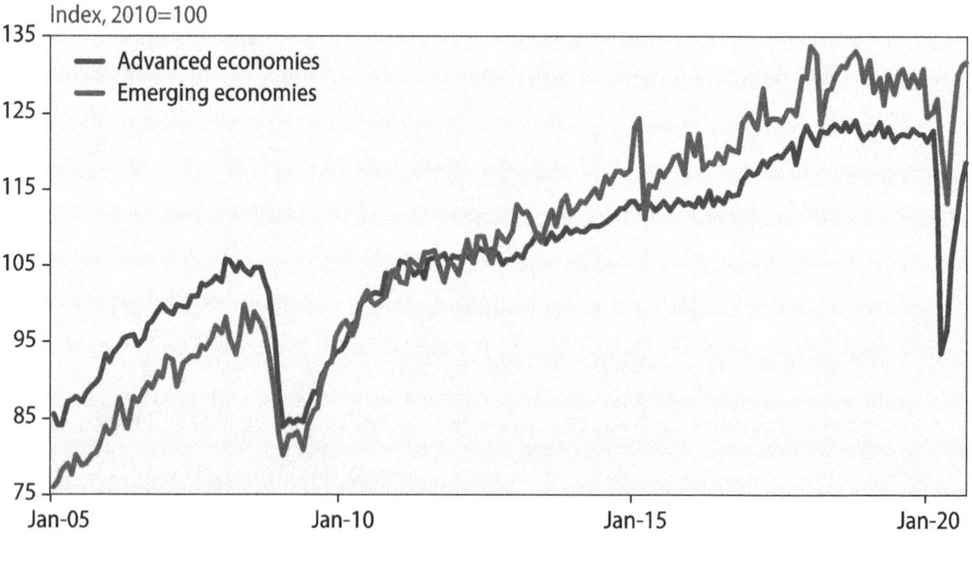

Source: UN DESA, based on data from CPB Netherlands Bureau for Economic Policy Analysis.

Note: Regional groupings are not strictly comparable with those used in *World Economic Situation and Prospects 2021*, but rather are illustrative of regional tendencies.

6 Under the WTO initiatives, structured discussions on trade and environmental sustainability are being established and an informal dialogue has been launched on plastics pollution and environmentally sustainable plastics trade (WTO, 2020c).

The recovery in trade is expected to continue over the next two years. The UN DESA baseline scenario projects that global trade in goods and services will grow by 6.9 per cent in 2021 and 3.7 per cent in 2022. There are both upside and downside risks to this forecast. If vaccines help bring the pandemic under control, the trade recovery, especially in tourism services, could be stronger than expected thanks to pent-up demand. On the other hand, if movement restrictions remain in place and uncertainties over the pandemic persist, cross-border trade activities will remain subdued in 2021.

Economies of East Asia are driving the recovery in trade

Regional trade performances differed considerably in 2020 (figure II.2). Trade activities in East Asia recovered more quickly than in other parts of the world as most of the region's economies managed to control the spread of the virus. Indeed, several economies, including China, Taiwan Province of China and Viet Nam, returned to positive year-on-year trade growth in the third quarter of 2020, when other regions were still experiencing significant contractions. While Africa, Europe and Northern America saw very large declines in export volumes in 2020, a rebound is expected for 2021.

Figure II.2
Volume of exports of goods and services in selected regions

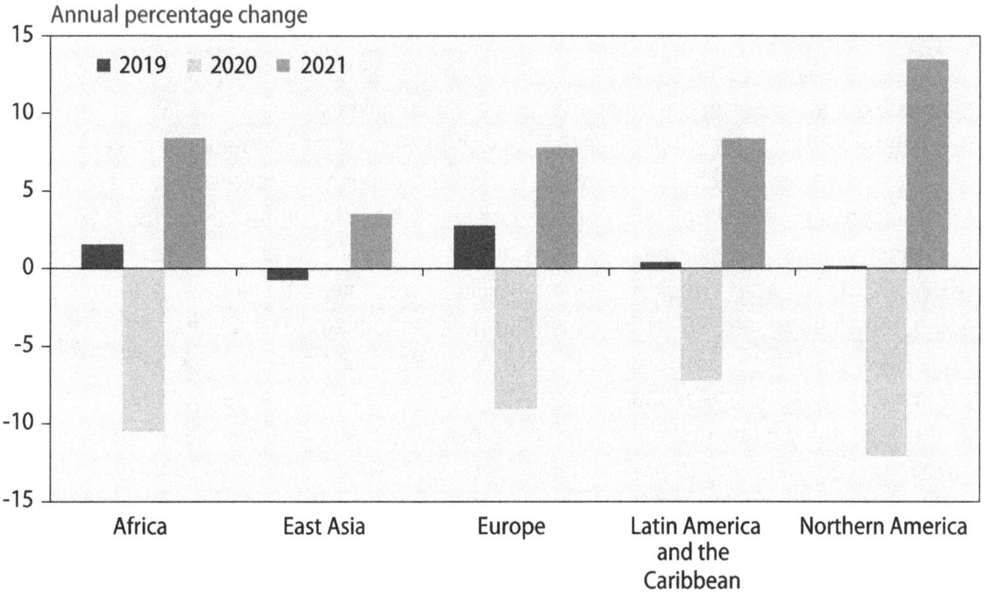

Source: UN DESA, based on projections produced with the World Economic Forecasting Model (WEFM).

East Asia's trade recovery can be attributed partly to growth in a number of sectors that benefited from the pandemic (figure II.3). For example, international trade in communication equipment and office machinery expanded substantially in 2020. As households, businesses and Governments upgraded their information and communication technology (ICT) infrastructure to improve remote working conditions, producers in China, the Republic of Korea and Taiwan Province of China benefited from the increase in demand for electric and electronic equipment. At the same time, trade in pharmaceuticals and personal protective equipment (PPE) soared. By contrast, trade contracted in many other manufacturing sectors, especially in the automotive sector, owing to supply disruptions and weaker demand; trade in travel products, handbags and footwear also fell sharply.

Figure II.3
World trade by sector

Year-on-year percentage change

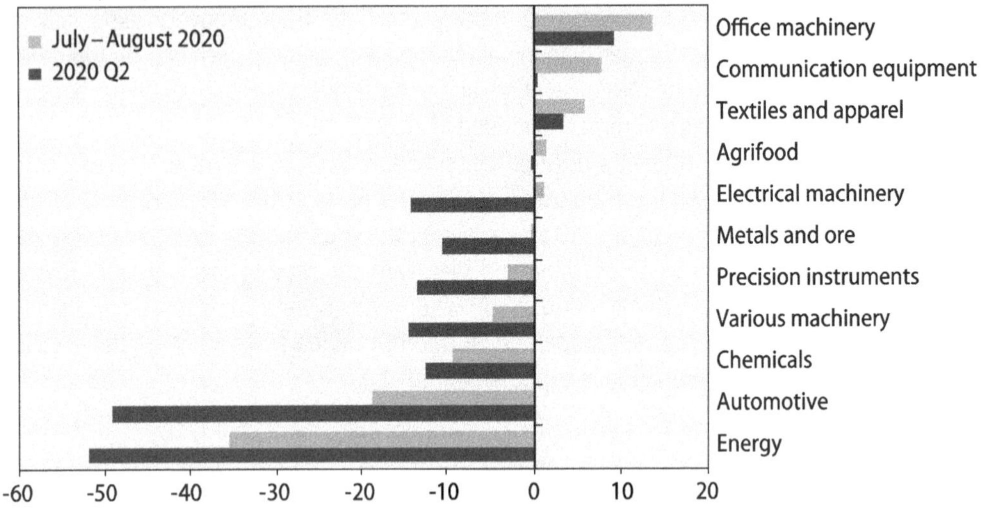

Source: UNCTAD estimates, based on national statistics of China, the European Union and the United States of America.

Note: Data excludes intra-EU trade.

Global tourism industry has taken an unprecedented hit

Global trade in commercial services is estimated to have contracted by about 14 per cent in 2020, a steeper decline than during the global financial crisis. The tourism industry has been the hardest-hit services sector, as COVID-19 brought international travel to a virtual standstill from March 2020 onward. Before the pandemic, travel services accounted for almost one third of developing countries' services exports.[7] International tourist arrivals (overnight visitors) are estimated to have plunged by about 70 per cent globally in 2020 (UNWTO, 2020e), which would represent 1 billion fewer international arrivals than in 2019 and a potential loss of US$ 1.1 trillion in international tourism receipts, the largest decline ever. The shock has put 100 million to 120 million direct tourism jobs at risk, with large spillovers into other sectors. A rebound in tourism is expected in 2021, assuming that by the end of the year, many travel restrictions will have been lifted and that traveller confidence will have improved. Recovery to pre-pandemic levels is, however, estimated to take two and a half to four years. (see box II.1).

The COVID-19 crisis has affected international commodity markets very unevenly

The global pandemic has affected international commodity markets very unevenly (World Bank, 2020b). For example, there was a much smaller decrease in trade in agricultural products than in overall merchandise trade. Agricultural commodity prices remained broadly steady, though food prices spiked in several countries, especially in Africa, Latin America and South Asia.[8] Since global markets for major food staples are well supplied, agricultural price indexes are projected to remain fairly stable in 2021. The impact on energy markets, by contrast, has been severe, and the consequences could be experienced for several years. As consumer and industry demand faltered, energy prices declined sharply. In April 2020, collapsing demand and lack of storage capacity sent crude oil futures, temporarily, into negative territory. This unprecedented episode was followed, however, by a steady recovery in oil prices in the second half of the year, which was driven by improving global prospects,

7 World Bank, World Development Indicators, based on IMF, Balance of Payments Statistics.

8 In Nigeria, for example, wholesale prices of white maize doubled from March to September 2020 (FAO, 2020).

significant reductions in oil supply and a weakening dollar. Brent oil averaged about $43 per barrel in 2020, a price that was about one third below the 2019 average of $64 per barrel; but for 2021, a moderate increase to about $50 per barrel is projected as economic activities pick up and travel demand returns. However, even in the medium term, oil prices are likely to remain below the pre-pandemic level; and higher global oil inventory levels and surplus production capacity in key oil producers will limit the upward pressure on prices. Lower prices, coupled with uncertainty about the pandemic's long-term effect on demand structures and the accelerating energy transition, will in turn continue to weigh on investment in the oil sector. Meanwhile, metal prices rebounded much faster than expected in the course of 2020 as stimulus measures in China boosted demand and prolonged lockdowns in South America caused significant supply disruptions. The price of copper, which is used predominantly in electrical applications and telecommunications, hit a seven-year high in December, as the global 5G network roll-out continues and demand for comprehensive ICT infrastructure is on the rise. The prices of iron ore, aluminium, nickel, tin and zinc also recovered strongly in the second half of the year. Going forward, metal prices will likely be supported by continuing rapid growth in China and a more broad-based recovery in global demand.

Box II.1
Promoting a sustainable recovery of tourism

Tourism is one of the sectors hardest hit by the COVID-19 pandemic

The pandemic has caused an unprecedented disruption to tourism as Governments implemented lockdowns and travel restrictions to contain the spread of coronavirus disease. This has generated huge economic and social impacts, placing over 100 million direct tourism jobs at risk, especially in micro-, small and medium-sized enterprises (MSMEs), which represent 80 per cent of the sector and employ a high share of women and young people. Women, who make up 54 per cent of the tourism workforce as compared with 39 per cent of the overall economy (UNWTO, 2019), as well as youth and migrant workers with limited or no access to social protection, have been among those most severely affected by the collapse in tourism.

The pandemic represents a major shock for developed economies and an emergency for many developing countries, especially small island developing States (SIDS). Tourism accounts for over 30 per cent of total exports in most SIDS and for as much as 80 per cent of total exports in some cases (UNWTO, 2020b).

A wide range of policy measures have been implemented to support the recovery of tourism

Support for the millions of livelihoods that depend upon a sector that has been affected by months of inactivity is key to accelerating the recovery of tourism, as well as to designing a responsible and sustainable travel experience—one that ensures the safety of host communities, workers and travellers. As demonstrated by the UNWTO policy tracker, there have been swift and strong responses by Governments around the world aimed at minimizing the impacts of COVID-19 (UNWTO, 2020a). Overall, the immediate response consisted of cross-cutting fiscal and financial measures to mitigate the economic impact of the crisis on tourism, with a special focus on MSME liquidity and the protection of jobs, reflecting a recognition of the labour-intensive nature of tourism. In addition to short-term work schemes and expansion of unemployment benefits, measures have included support for training and skills development, talent retention, assistance with digital transformation of businesses, and access to innovative tools.

(*continued*)

Box II.1 (*continued*)

The most recent measures announced indicate that an increasing number of countries are moving forward with initiatives to restart tourism, particularly by promoting domestic tourism, which is over six times the size of international tourism (UNWTO, 2020c). Tourism in rural areas offers important opportunities for recovery, as tourists are searching for destinations that are less populated, open-air activities, and experiences that are more authentic (UNWTO, 2020d).

The pandemic has provided an opportunity to make tourism more sustainable and inclusive

Owing to continued uncertainty and the rapid evolution of the situation, the capacity of consumers, businesses and the industry at large to adapt will be crucial in the near term. Mitigating the economic impact and ensuring a coordinated response with regard to travel restrictions and harmonized safety protocols, while protecting tourists and workers, should be key priorities for a safe restart of tourism.

While considerable challenges lie ahead, the crisis also provides an unprecedented opportunity for transformation. It offers the possibility of rethinking tourism so as to leverage its impact on destinations and build more resilient communities and businesses through innovation, digitalization, sustainability and partnerships. Innovation and sustainability will be two key pillars of a recovery focused on building tourism back better and stronger. In a sector that employs 1 in 10 people globally, the goals of harnessing innovation and digitalization, embracing local values, fostering accessibility and creating decent jobs for all, especially for youth, women and the most vulnerable groups, should be at the forefront of that recovery. The present crisis presents the opportunity to transform the relationship of tourism with nature, climate and the economy; to rethink how the sector impacts natural resources and ecosystems; to empower local communities; to improve the measurement and management of tourism through data and research; to ensure a fair distribution of its benefits; and to advance the transition towards a tourism economy that is carbon-neutral and resilient (United Nations, 2020a).

Authors: Sandra Carvão, Michel Julian and Javier Ruescas (UNWTO)

Shift in global trade towards developing countries

Global trade has increasingly shifted towards developing countries

Global trade has undergone profound transformations in recent decades. Since the 1980s, trade has increasingly shifted from developed to developing countries, as many developing countries adopted manufacturing export-led growth strategies which have helped raise living standards. These strategies have been most successful among East Asian economies, with Hong Kong SAR, the Republic of Korea, Singapore and Taiwan Province of China having undergone rapid industrialization early on.

Multinationals have driven changes in trade patterns

This shift was reinforced by the surge of bilateral trade agreements, the reduction in trade costs, the rising role of China, the expansion of multinational firms, the ICT revolution and the establishment of GVCs. Amid significant trade liberalization worldwide, the changes in the trade landscape were also driven by foreign direct investment (FDI), with multinational firms playing a catalytic role in fostering globalization. As a result, a greater share of FDI went to developing countries, and multinational firms implemented aggressive internationalization strategies to expand their systems of production and gain access to world markets.

East Asian economies benefited from participation in GVCs...

The shift gained momentum in the 2000s, with the accession of China to the WTO and its consolidation as the "world factory". Global value chains expanded rapidly, especially in the automotive, electronics and garment industries. Intermediate goods and services as part of such chains—in which trade and investment linkages across countries support complex multi-country production platforms—accounted for an increasing share of trade in those industries. Through their active participation in emerging GVCs, East Asian economies, including Indonesia, Malaysia, the Philippines, Thailand and Viet Nam, increased their relevance in global trade.

...and exports became a major source of productivity growth

While developed countries still account for the bulk of global merchandise trade, there has been a visible shift towards East Asia, whose share in total merchandise exports rose from 16 per cent in 1993 to 25 per cent in 2010 and to 28 per cent in 2019 (figure II.4). This shift was driven mainly by China, which accounted for 13 per cent of global exports in 2019 compared with less than 3 per cent in 1993. In addition, the composition of international trade also changed. Many East Asian economies were able to move away from low value added natural resources and low-technology products to higher value added manufactures, and higher-technology products; and integration into GVCs enabled them to build productive capacities and diversify their export matrix. Exports became a major source of productivity growth as the result of a significant reallocation of resources, the accumulation of technological capabilities and "learning by exporting", which encouraged productivity gains across domestic activities (figure II.5).

Figure II.4
Share of global merchandise exports

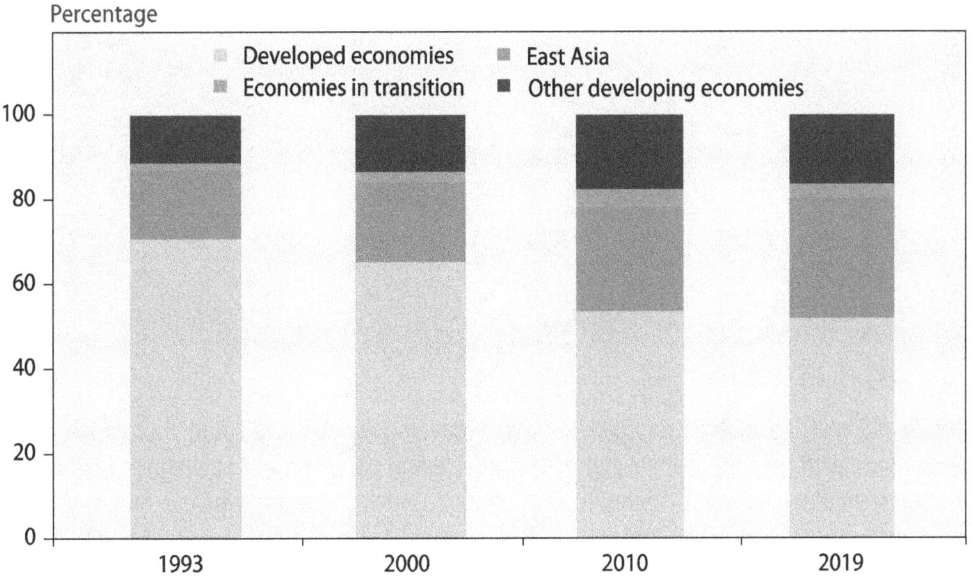

Source: UN DESA, based on data from UNCTADstat.

Many developing countries struggled to transform trade into an engine for development

Developing countries in other regions have generally been less successful in leveraging trade opportunities and upgrading to higher value added activities. Notably, the least developed countries (LDCs) have remained marginalized: their share in world merchandise exports stood at 1 per cent in 2019, remaining virtually unchanged from a decade ago.[9] While most developing regions and the economies in transition saw their shares in global trade rise during the 2000s, this was primarily a result of the commodity boom. In Africa, Latin America and the Caribbean, and Western Asia, export-led strategies often failed to replicate East Asia's success. In countries such as Chile, Colombia, Ethiopia and Rwanda, exports have played a critical role in promoting short-term growth, with positive effects on living standards. However, exports have often not become a main vehicle for technological progress and their dynamic effects on productivity growth and structural change have there-

9 UNCTADstat database, available at https://unctadstat.unctad.org/.

fore been limited. Furthermore, the majority of countries in these regions are still heavily dependent on commodities. Even in countries that actively participate in GVCs—especially Mexico and, to a large extent, Brazil and South Africa as well—exports of high-technology products take the form, mainly, of assembling activities with little local content and weak domestic linkages. Indeed, in most countries, participation in GVCs is incipient or in its early stages, and concentrated in low-tech sectors.

Figure II.5
Labour productivity in developing regions

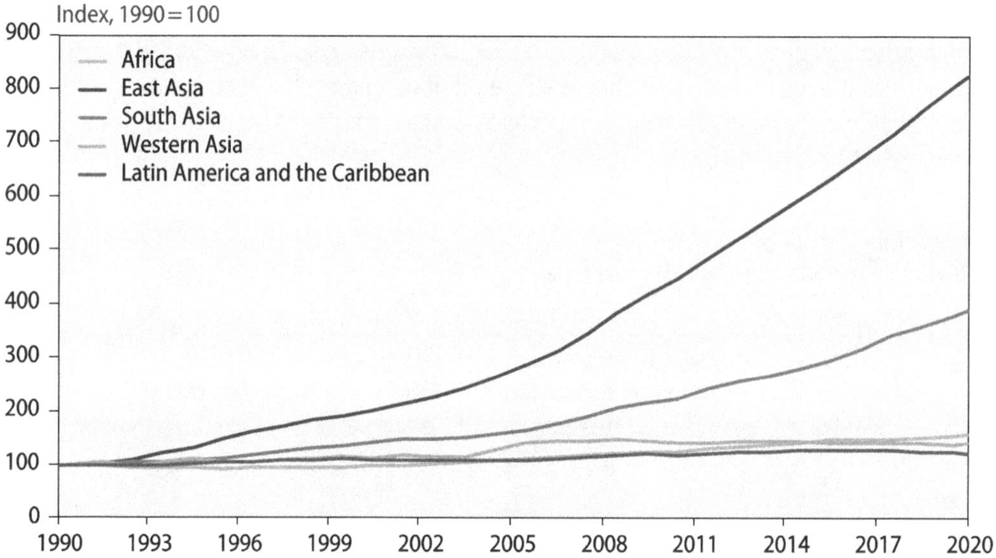

Source: UN DESA, based on data from The Conference Board Total Economy Database, July 2020.

Note: Regional averages are represented by country-level labour productivity data weighted by the number of persons employed.

New development strategies: the end of manufacturing export-led growth?

Shifting trade patterns and technological changes pose challenges for export-led growth

Within the shifting global trade environment, developing countries find themselves at a crossroads with respect to their export-led growth and development strategies. Rising protectionist tendencies, rapid technological change and the maturing of existing GVCs are among the factors that will impact the international trade outlook going forward. At the same time, the digitalization trend will continue to accelerate, reflecting the convergence of fixed, mobile and broadcast networks, the increasing connectedness of devices and objects, and the resulting changes in social interactions. This will boost trade in services by reducing trade costs, increasing productivity of services sectors and blurring the differences between goods and services-related activities. There will be rising demand for high-skilled services going forward and services will become increasingly important owing to, among other things, changes in demographics and a reduction in the importance of face-to-face interactions (WTO, 2019b). Development strategies over the coming decades will therefore need to strike a balance, in terms of focus, between manufacturing and services.

Services offer significant opportunities for developing countries

The growing importance of trade in services and digitalization presents opportunities and challenges that need to be confronted by developing countries. In fact, services increasingly exhibit pro-development features like tradability, scale, innovation and learning-by-doing, which were once characteristic only of the manufacturing sector (Baldwin and Forslid, 2020). Indeed, growing service-related activities offer significant opportunities for job creation in the medium term. Moreover, new technologies like robotics, artificial intelligence and 3D printing can also reduce costs and generate significant gains such as the creation of more environmentally sustainable production plants. Automation and robotics, for example, have shaped the automotive, rubber and plastics, and electronic industries in recent decades. New technologies can facilitate scale-independent efficient production and bring production systems closer to consumption markets. In the medium term, such developments could support reshoring trends by reducing production costs and thus increasing the competitiveness of previously non-competitive production locations, and by encouraging a shift from the traditional model of economies of scale of large plants serving global markets to a model underpinned by a network of smaller, more flexible and geographically distributed plants (Shih, 2020).

The COVID-19 crisis may accelerate the reconfiguration of GVCs

The pandemic has been responsible for significant disruptions to global and regional value chains (see box II.2). For example, lockdowns in the countries of overseas suppliers and disruptions of logistics services impacted electronic value chains in Viet Nam, seriously interfering with the shipping of electronic components and the delivery of final products to consumers. In addition, the pandemic exposed the fragility of food systems that depend on long GVCs. The world is in fact increasingly prone to recurrent disruptions, including climate

Box II.2

Enhancing the resilience of value chains in least developed countries

Although most least developed countries (LDCs) export mainly raw materials with very limited value addition, the integration of several LDCs in global value chains (GVCs) has grown over the past years. This has enabled them to access foreign markets indirectly through ties to global firms that control access to consumers. Such upstream participation in GVCs, characterized by forward linkages to retailers, has made those countries more vulnerable to demand and price shocks and thus to the disruptions caused by COVID-19 (Frederick and Daly, 2020).

According to the World Trade Organization (WTO), merchandise exports of LDCs contracted by 16 per cent in the first half of 2020, within an export structure that consists mainly of primary products (accounting for 53 per cent of LDC exports in 2019) and simple manufactures (29 per cent in 2019), especially textiles and clothing (figure II.2.1). This trade downturn will likely further reduce the share of LDCs in world exports, which in 2019 stood at 0.96 per cent, well below 2 per cent as called for under SDG target 17.11 (WTO, 2020b).

COVID-19 has disrupted many LDC value chains, as the group's top destinations include countries worst affected by the outbreak. For example, in the garment sector of Bangladesh, orders from major retailers worth about $3 billion have been cancelled. This has affected more than a thousand factories and some retailers have filed for bankruptcy. In addition, the supply of crucial inputs was disrupted. By the third quarter of 2020, export earnings exceeded those of 2019 as government support for firms and wages kept factories in business. However, there are indications that retailers are reducing prices and slowing the payment of orders delivered, depressing wages of the mainly female workforce (Bangladesh, Ministry of Finance, Economic Relations Division, 2020; Anner, 2020).

Exports by Ethiopia of cut flowers and garments as well as the country's tourism sector have been severely affected by the decline in demand. The country lost 80 per cent of the (mainly European) demand for its cut flowers at the beginning of the pandemic. The Government has provided support to firms, thereby keeping workers on payroll. Ethiopian Airlines has shifted most of its operations to cargo, benefiting from the designation of Addis Ababa as a distribution hub for medical supplies across Africa and enabling the recovery of flower exports. The garment sector, which is often located in indus-

(*continued*)

Box II.2 (*continued*)

Figure II.2.1
Merchandise exports of least developed countries

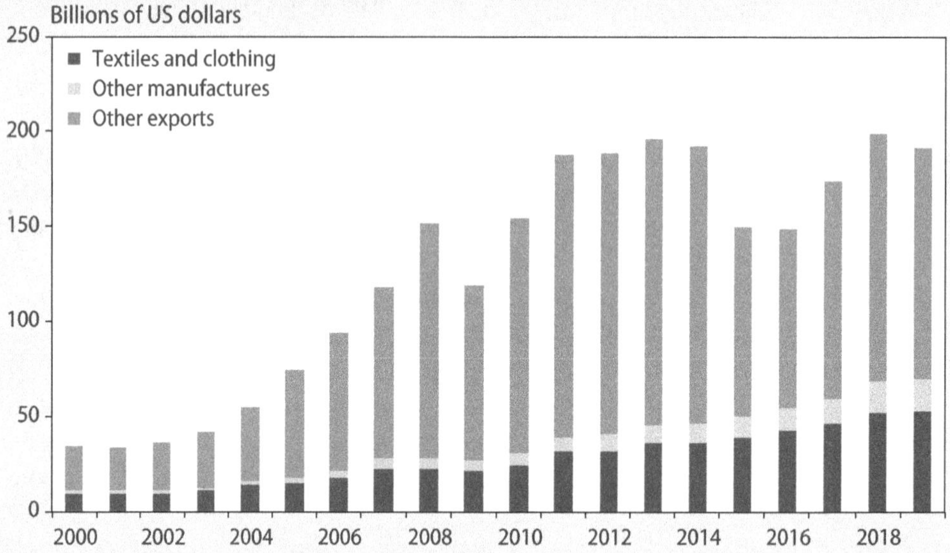

Source: UN-OHRLLS calculations, based on UNCTADstat data.

trial parks, has shifted the focus of some of its production to personal protective equipment (PPE) for the domestic market (Banga and others, 2020).

In addition, many LDCs depend on tourism, which has been at a virtual standstill since the onset of the pandemic. Before the pandemic, the share of commercial services in total exports of LDCs grew steadily, reaching 17 per cent in 2018. The travel exports of LDCs dropped by about 60 per cent in the first half of 2020 (WTO, Subcommittee on Least Developed Countries, 2019).

In the present context of subdued global trade performance, it becomes more important for LDCs to diversify not only their export products so as to enhance value addition but also their markets and participate in regional value chains. The African Continental Free Trade Area can play an important role in this regard by reducing the production costs associated with tariffs, non-tariff barriers and trade facilitation issues (World Bank, 2020a).

Digitalization is one factor that enables participation in value chains, as demonstrated by several LDCs that have created e-commerce platforms, which helped to stabilize demand during the pandemic. Least developed countries also need to support cooperation across value chains by identifying horizontal linkages between industries which could include, for example, strengthening ties with local food producers in the tourism industry.

Several LDCs could benefit from joining tourism-related GVCs in order to consolidate their position as regional and international tourist destinations, once travel resumes. This could include adapting products that appeal to local and regional customers, and upgrading processes, through, for example, improving the relationships between domestic distribution intermediaries and global tour operators.

The further extension of effective duty- and quota-free market access for all products originating from LDCs, including through developing simple and transparent rules of origin, would facilitate the integration of LDC producers in GVCs. Continued application of LDC-specific special and differential treatment support and flexibilities enjoyed under the WTO Agreement on Trade-Related Aspects of Intellectual Property Rights (TRIPS Agreement) after graduation will help them achieve a meaningful integration into global and regional value chains.

In addition, enhanced aid for trade would allow LDCs to take measures to enhance competitiveness and overcome obstacles to exporters, including through diversification and capacity-building in the field of trade-related administration. In the context of an estimated sharp drop in foreign direct investment to LDCs in 2020, investment promotion measures implemented by host countries would foster linkages with foreign firms and allow LDCs to enter new markets.

Author: Susanna Wolf (UN-OHRLLS)

change-related shocks, trade disputes, geopolitical uncertainties and other challenges whose frequency and magnitude continue to grow. According to some estimates, supply chain disruptions "lasting a month or longer now occur every 3.7 years on average" (McKinsey, 2020). By laying bare existing vulnerabilities, the COVID-19 crisis may accelerate the reconfiguration—and possibly the shortening—of GVCs, especially as the use of new technologies and digitalization intensifies. Large firms will need to reassess trade-offs between efficiency and resilience in the context of their strategies; and "just in time" and "lean manufacturing" strategies—emphasizing efficiency, low inventories and on-time deliveries—might need to evolve towards placing a greater emphasis on reliability, resilience and regionalization.

Amid increasing digitalization, more widespread use of new technologies and the growing importance of supply chain resilience, the current crisis may reshape export-led growth strategies, especially if its economic and political legacies result in trade policy changes. While the debate over resilience of supply chains is not new, the scale of the COVID-19 crisis, together with recent technological advances, might serve as a major force for change. Global value chains could become more agile and flexible through diversification of the supply base and a shortening of the distance between suppliers and the retail base. The trade-related tensions between China and the United States of America have led some firms to adopt a "China plus one strategy", which entails spreading production between China and countries such as Indonesia, Thailand and Viet Nam.

Developing countries must reassess export-led development strategies

Manufacturing exports will continue to play an important role in countries' growth and development strategies. Yet, the shifting trade landscape is forcing developing countries to redefine their development strategies and explore models of dynamic comparative advantages to be derived from digitalization and the data economy. Countries in the early stages of manufacturing-led growth are particularly at risk, as it may be difficult to repeat the success stories of the previous decades. While manufacturing will likely remain a high value added sector, its impact on job creation and development will be less pronounced in the medium term than it was in the 1980s and 1990s for the emerging Asian economies.

Pushback against multilateralism and rising protectionism

Benefits and costs from trade liberalization have been unevenly distributed

Trade liberalization and rapid export growth since the 1990s have created millions of relatively well-paying manufacturing jobs, particularly in the East Asian economies, which has helped lift large numbers of people out of poverty.[10] At the same time, many economies experienced massive job losses in manufacturing sectors as the effects of automation were exacerbated by a shift in production to low-wage, low-cost destinations. A growing body of empirical studies have documented the uneven distribution of the benefits and costs from global trade integration both within and across countries. In fact, the adjustment costs associated with trade liberalization—including higher unemployment, lower labour-force participation and downward pressure on wages in affected sectors—have been found to be larger and more persistent, in both developed and developing countries, than was previously expected.[11] Relatively unskilled workers in the manufacturing sector have borne the brunt of the adjustment burden, whereas high-skilled workers reaped most of the benefits. Given a

10 According to World Bank data (see the World Development Indicators database), between 1990 and 2017, an estimated 1.2 billion people, of whom 740 million were in China, were lifted out of poverty.

11 Autor, Dorn and Hanson (2013) have found higher unemployment, lower labour-force participation and reduced wages in manufacturing industries in the United States owing to rising import competition from China. Based on a sample of developing countries, Hollweg and others (2014) have concluded that adjustment periods associated with trade liberalization can be very long and that not all affected sectors recover.

lack of mitigating social policies, displaced workers were often not adequately compensated for their losses. Hence, trade liberalization has not only contributed to a rising skill premium, pushing up overall income inequality, but also made some groups worse off in absolute terms.[12]

The rules-based multilateral trading system has faced growing challenges

The failure to address adverse distributional effects has triggered a backlash against globalization and free trade in some parts of the world. In this regard, de Bolle and Zettelmeyer (2019) have documented a broad-based rise since the mid-2000s in economic nationalism in the G20 countries, encompassing both developed and emerging economies.[13] This shift has posed significant challenges for the rules-based multilateral trading system operating under the auspices of the WTO. The Doha Development Round, launched in 2001 with the aim of further reducing trade barriers and revising trade rules, has reached an impasse. In lieu of forging a global trade deal, policymakers have turned increasingly to bilateral and plurilateral trade agreements. The number of regional trade agreements in force has increased, from 82 in 2000 to 306 in September 2020. At the same time, the WTO is facing the deepest crisis since its inception in 1995, with the dispute settlement system remaining paralysed since December 2019.

The COVID-19 crisis has reinforced the rise in subsidies

Meanwhile, protectionism has been on the rise. While, recently, much of the spotlight's focus has been on trade disputes (especially those between the United States and China and between the United States and the European Union (EU)) and the associated tariff increases, the move towards protectionism has in fact been a more widespread phenomenon, with non-tariff measures accounting for almost all trade interventions. The share of global merchandise imports, for example, affected by import restrictions has been steadily growing since the global financial crisis (figure II.6); but those restrictions are only part of the story. Export subsidies and other types of subsidies account for a growing share of trade-related support measures introduced over the past decade (figure II.7), a trend that has been further accelerated by the COVID-19 pandemic, with Governments stepping in to support domestic firms and workers. Kozul-Wright (2020) underscores that the massive production and export subsidies provided by developed countries cannot be matched by developing countries, which generally have more limited fiscal space. In the medium run, these subsidies threaten to distort competition, constraining trade opportunities for smaller developing economies and exacerbating inequities (Evenett, 2020). Warning that a broad-based shift towards higher subsidies could worsen existing trade tensions, Hoekman and Nelson (2020) have called for enhanced international cooperation in addressing potential conflicts in this area.

Retreat from multilateralism weighs on trade prospects of many developing countries

The retreat from multilateralism has brought about significant challenges for many developing countries, particularly LDCs, landlocked developing countries and small island developing States; and the impact has been compounded by the sharp rise in trade policy uncertainties in recent years, which have dampened global trade flows and commodity prices. The shift towards the more discriminatory and exclusionary rule making associated with bilateral and regional trade agreements has introduced further complications into the global trade landscape.

12 See, for example, Di Comite, Nocco and Orefice (2018) and UNCTAD (2019).

13 De Bolle and Zettelmeyer (2019, p. 7) define "economic nationalism" in terms of "policies designed to further domestic economic interests...at the expense of foreign economic interests, at least in the short run".

Figure II.6
Cumulative trade coverage of import-restrictive measures in force since 2009

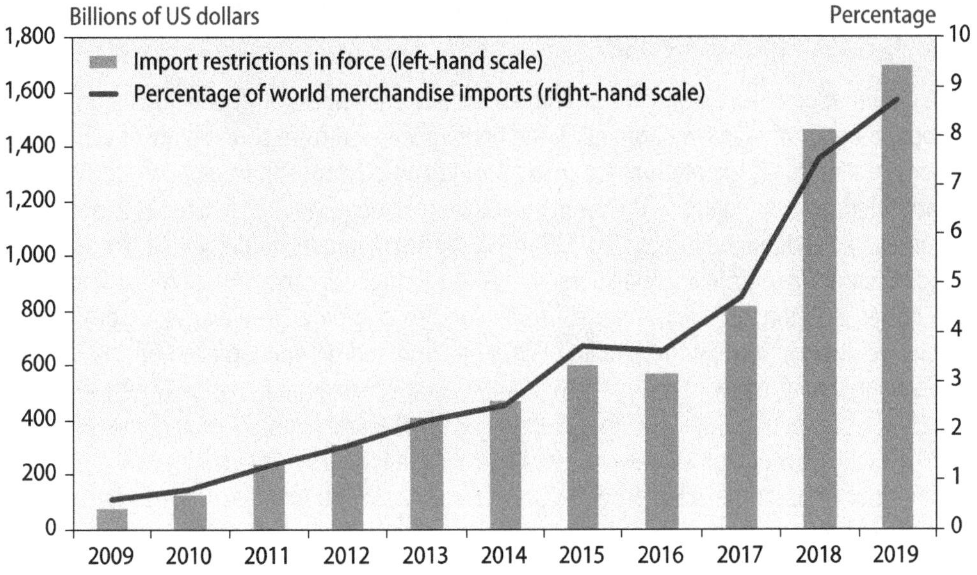

Source: WTO secretariat.

Note: Figures do not include trade remedy measures.

Figure II.7
Discriminatory commercial policy interventions

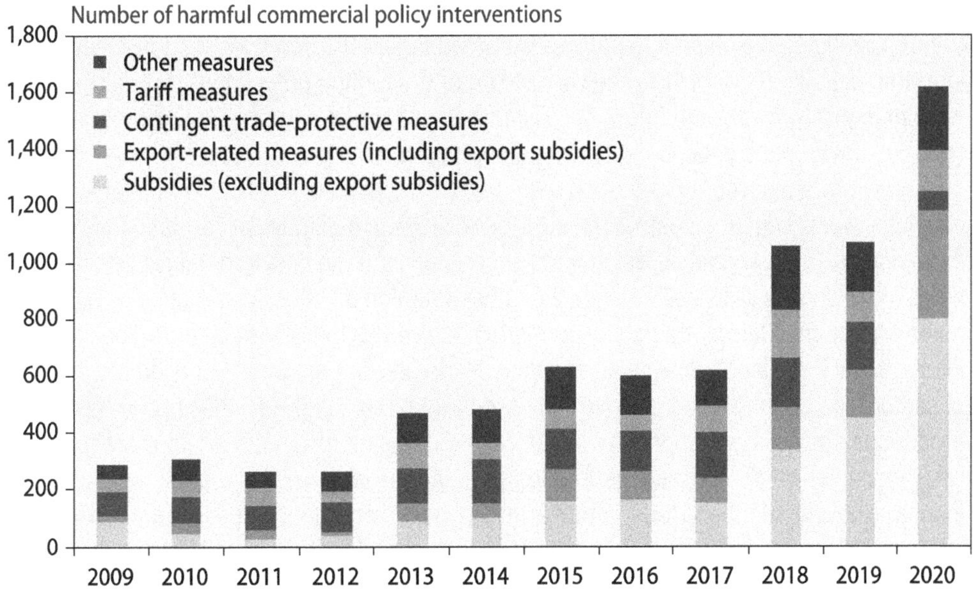

Source: Global Trade Alert (accessed on 13 November 2020).

Note: The figure incorporates only the policy changes implemented and documented between 1 January and 12 November of each year, which ensures comparability across years. For details, see www.globaltradealert.org/global_dynamics/day-to_1211.

Global value chains at a crossroads

Drivers of global value chain growth prior to the global financial crisis

The proliferation of GVCs over the past three decades has had a profound impact on the development path of many economies.[14] The findings derived from a vast body of work in the empirical literature indicate that for many developing countries, participation in GVCs has contributed to strong gains in productivity and employment, yielding increases in per capita incomes and reductions in poverty.[15] The GVC business model, under which the stages of production are geographically dispersed, has led to higher production efficiency, as firms are better able through this approach to exploit the comparative advantages of different countries. Importantly, integration into GVCs has boosted production and exports of many developing countries by enabling them to practise specialization in narrowly defined tasks, which is less resource-intensive than the setting up of entire supply chains domestically.

Major global trends will impact the future of GVCs

Global value chains are nevertheless currently reaching a turning point. Since the global financial crisis, the expansion of GVCs has visibly slowed owing to several factors. For one thing, the maturing of existing production networks has limited the opportunities for further specialization. Moreover, unlike in the 1990s and 2000s, there has been a lack of major breakthroughs in trade liberalization capable of spurring a more rapid spread of GVCs. Instead, many parts of the world are today witnessing a backlash against globalization and the adoption of inward-looking trade policies. In addition, anecdotal evidence points to the emergence of a trend towards reshoring of manufacturing activities.

Alongside the evolution of the trade policy landscape, there are other major global trends—including digitalization, process automation and the servicification of manufacturing—that are also transforming the very nature of production processes. This will have significant implications for the future of global trade and the structure of GVCs; but it remains to be seen whether trends in digitalization and automation processes will ultimately result in shorter GVCs and more production reshoring as the comparative advantage of locations offering lower production costs is reduced, or will instead facilitate the formation of new and more complex supply chains. Heightened uncertainty and the desire to reduce potential vulnerability to shocks will also influence the future direction of GVCs, in particular if challenges related to the multilateral trading system are perceived as unlikely to be met. The changing international trade landscape could exert a considerable impact on the economic prospects of sectors and countries that are currently deeply integrated into GVCs. As firms realign their production strategies, changes in the nature and direction of foreign direct investment will likely occur, which could translate into less capital formation. This would undermine local industrial development and jobs, in turn affecting poverty reduction and income distribution. Against this backdrop, policymakers in developing countries are understandably concerned over whether GVC participation can still offer large development gains.

14 Global value chains refer to the international sharing of the production process, a phenomenon where production is broken into activities and tasks carried out in different countries (Seric and Tong, 2019).

15 *World Development Report 2020* (World Bank, 2020d) summarizes much of the content of the literature, including recent empirical evidence, on the drivers of GVCs and the impact of GVC participation on developing countries.

GVC participation rates increased prior to the global financial crisis

Figure II.8 illustrates the changes in GVC participation rates of countries over time. A country's GVC participation rate is estimated based on the share of exports that are imported intermediate inputs (indicating backward linkages) and the share of exports that are used by another country in the production of its exports (indicating forward linkages). The figure shows that between 1990 and 2008, GVC participation rates visibly increased across developed and developing regions. However, there is considerable variation in the degree of participation among countries and regions. For example, most of the developed countries are characterized by deep participation in GVCs, while in the developing regions, economies of the Latin America and the Caribbean region exhibit relatively lower GVC participation rates. Since the global financial crisis, however, there has been a broad-based decline in GVC participation rates, as illustrated in the second panel of the figure. The implications of this phenomenon will be further discussed below.

Rapid GVC growth was catalysed by several major trends

In tandem with strong growth in intraregional trade, there was rapid growth in regional GVCs in the 1990s and 2000s, which was driven by several catalytic factors. First, the ICT revolution, by significantly reducing the cost of managing and coordinating production across country borders, promoted the dispersion of production-related tasks and activities. Second, major trade liberalization initiatives during this period led to the lowering of tariffs and regulatory barriers across many regions of the world, providing an impetus to the expansion of GVCs. The formation of the WTO in 1995 put in place a global rules-based multilateral trading system, which supported smoother and freer trade flows. In the 1990s, there was also a global wave of efforts towards deepening regional integration, which included the formation of the EU. The creation of this single market contributed to an increase in intra-EU trade intensity from 12 to 22 per cent of GDP between 1992 and 2012 (European Parliamentary Research Service, 2017).

Figure II.8
Global value chain participation by country and region

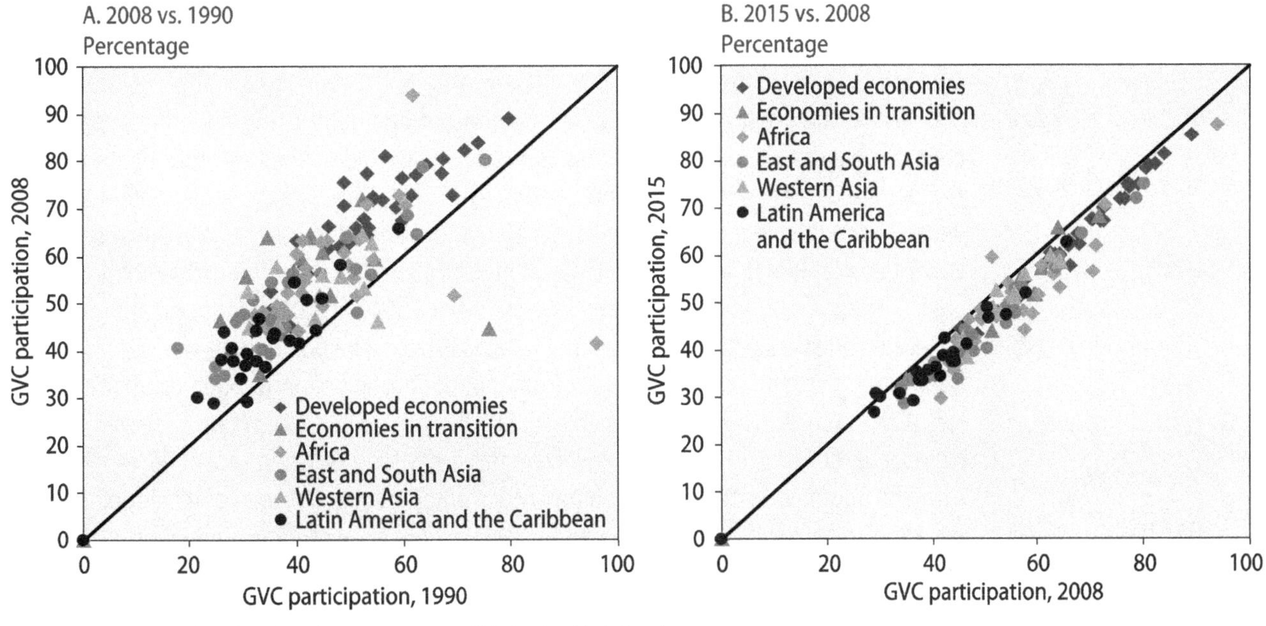

Source: UN DESA, based on data from the UNCTAD–Eora Global Value Chain Database.

Note: A country's GVC participation rate is estimated based on the share of exports that are imported intermediate inputs and the share of exports that are used by another country in the production of its exports.

Third, China's accession to the WTO in 2001 marked a significant shift in the international trade landscape. The opening up of China—a developing country with a very large and relatively skilled workforce earning low wages—facilitated the formation of new and more dispersed production networks, amid a rapid expansion of the manufacturing sector. China is now the largest supplier of components in manufacturing sector GVCs, surpassing other manufacturing powerhouses, including Germany, Japan and the United States (Neumann and Bhaumik, 2020).

The expansion of GVC-linked production has been accompanied by a marked increase in FDI flows over the past few decades. Indeed, GVCs have strengthened the linkages between international trade and FDI, with multinational enterprises playing an important role in driving cross-border investment as they seek to increase cost efficiency while expanding market access across countries. Between 1990 and 2006, the global value of annual FDI inflows increased about twelvefold, peaking at over $3 trillion in 2006. Prior to the global financial crisis, 80–90 per cent of inward FDI was channelled towards developed economies. Since then, however, this share has fallen visibly as a greater proportion of FDI has been directed to developing economies and economies in transition. In fact, by 2019, developed countries' share of FDI worldwide had fallen to about 65 per cent. At the same time, overall growth in FDI inflows slowed, in tandem with the deceleration of GVC expansion and international trade.

Emerging trends are redefining global value chains

Participation in GVCs has yielded significant economic benefits for many developing economies. Ignatenko, Raei and Mircheva (2019) found that participation in GVCs has a stronger positive effect on a country's income per capita and productivity than conventional trade, although the gains vary across countries. In addition, not only do GVC-related FDI inflows generate employment and support domestic industries through backward linkages, but recipient countries also gain technological know-how, management skills and access to global markets.

GVCs play a big role in the agrifood sector and various services sectors

While the presence of GVCs has been most apparent in the manufacturing sector, they also play an important role in the agrifood sector and various services sectors. These sectors are garnering increased interest from policymakers based on their potential to produce value added in the economy. In the agriculture and food sectors, the enhancement of GVCs can play an important role in boosting productivity growth and rural incomes, with possible positive effects on food security. Between 2004 and 2014, trade and agrifood GVCs generated on average 20–26 per cent of total agricultural labour income, derived from countries' direct participation in trade and from indirect participation through downstream sectors (Greenville, Kawasaki and Jouanjean, 2019). The OECD (2020b) has observed a strong increase in developing countries' involvement in agrifood GVCs in recent years, notably in Asia and South America. In sub-Saharan Africa, international linkages of the agriculture sector are also growing, but they remain limited mainly to upstream production stages (Del Prete and others, 2016). Looking ahead, GVCs in the agrifood sector are likely to gain in importance, given the ongoing modernization of the agriculture sector and the rising importance of food security issues.

Rising servicification and digitalization will redefine GVCs

The servicification of manufacturing industries is another important trend that is likely to redefine GVCs. Currently, the manufacturing sector is increasingly involved in purchasing, producing, selling and exporting various types of services. Thangavelu, Wang and Oum (2018) found that Asian countries with a higher level of participation as well as a lower position in manufacturing GVCs tend to have a higher level of foreign servicification (i.e., use of foreign services as input) compared with domestic servicification, owing in part to better access to overseas markets. Besides using productivity and efficiency enhancing services such as logistics and management, manufacturing firms are also adding services to their product offers, in an effort to differentiate their goods (Lodefalk, 2015). Some of the implications of servicification for developing countries are discussed in box II.3.

The rising trend towards servicification is accelerated by growing digitalization and automation in production processes. Digital platforms bolster the production of most business-to-business and business-to-consumer goods and services through GVCs, by allowing different activities to be sourced from the most competitive suppliers no matter where they are physically located. However, increased digitalization and automation could also incentivize the onshoring of production, amid a reduced need for physical presence in other coun-

Box II.3

Servicification as a tool for promoting development

Servicification refers to the increased use, production and export of services in other sectors, namely, manufacturing and agriculture. This is unlike tertiarization, which refers to the increasing share of services in direct output, employment, investment and trade. Servicification includes the provision of services as intermediary inputs to a sector, for example, provision of automated crop monitoring services to agriculture; software services to the automotive industry; and telecommunication services for digital financial services.

The significance of servicification is apparent in the contribution of services to the value added of exports. In developing economies, services accounted for 19 per cent of total direct exports and 33 per cent of total value added exports in 2014.[a] In Brazil, the difference was even larger, with services accounting for 17 per cent of direct exports and 48 per cent of value added exports in 2015 (UNCTAD, forthcoming a). Two thirds of the growth in the value added of services in exports came from the contribution of services to the production of merchandise exports, instead of from direct services exports, such as tourism receipts.

The performance of agriculture and manufacturing is becoming linked more and more to the effectiveness of services inputs. In developing countries, services account for two thirds of total productivity growth (UNCTAD, 2017). The development of services—acting as a catalyst to promote agriculture and manufacturing—is a key element in any balanced growth strategy. Servicification can therefore serve as a tool for the modernization of farming and industrialization. The SDGs reflect the importance of services in this regard by placing transport, increased access to information and communication technology (ICT) and access to financial services as preconditions for achieving Goal 9, which is to build resilient infrastructure, promote inclusive and sustainable industrialization and foster innovation.

To enhance the contribution of services to the economy, the policy mix must be coherent and reflect the cross-cutting nature of services. For example, the digital transformation strategy for Africa highlights the need to align services negotiations and regulatory cooperation frameworks (UNCTAD, Trade and Development Board, 2020, para. 6). Trade policies should aim at improving access to foreign

(continued)

a See World Bank, Export Value Added Database.

Box II.3 (*continued*)

services and inputs that enable domestic services; improving access to foreign markets that support economies of scale in services; and inviting competition to boost productivity growth. There is also a need to ensure consistency between trade and tax policies. For example, authorities in Brazil are currently revisiting their drawback regime which grants tax relief for goods inputs in merchandise exports but not (yet) for services inputs so as to avoid "taxing" services exports (UNCTAD, forthcoming a).

Improving the impact of servicification also requires the development of relevant skills and the collection of reliable data for evidence-based policymaking. The United Nations Conference on Trade and Development, working with authorities and experts in Brazil and the European Commission, has developed a guidebook on a methodology for the measurement of services value added in exports (UNCTAD, forthcoming b).

Moreover, industrial policies need to be developed in tandem with trade policies so as to promote the diversification and upgrading of services. This is especially important given the relatively high dependence of developing economies on traditional services, such as travel and transport. Some of these services are less effective in enhancing the broader supply and export capacity than knowledge-intensive services such as ICT and financial services. Developing economies should therefore aim at broadening the spectrum of services, which would include fostering knowledge-intensive services so as to increase competitiveness in higher value added merchandise exports. Pertinent in this regard is the Centre for Research and Assistance in Technology and Design (Centro de Investigación y Asistencia en Tecnología y Diseño del Estado de Jalisco (CIATEJ)), a public research centre in Mexico that provides the R&D services and training needed to boost the competitiveness of the agroindustry.[b]

The economic crisis triggered by the COVID-19 pandemic makes the call for the use of servicification to promote export diversification and a robust economic recovery only more urgent. This is particularly important for those countries that have been hit the hardest, such as small island developing States and commodity-dependent economies. The recovery of tourism services in the wake of the pandemic would, for example, be facilitated by more effective inputs from health and sanitary safety certification services and ICT services that enable travel agencies to better connect with clients. At the same time, improving financial and logistics services, along with e-commerce infrastructure, could help these countries benefit more fruitfully from the creative economy, which includes such industries as advertising, arts and crafts, design, fashion, film and music.

b Further details are available at www.conacyt.gob.mx/index.php/el-conacyt/sistema-de-centros-de-investigacion/directorio-de-centros-de-investigacion-conacyt/item/ciatej.

Authors: Bruno Antunes and Mesut Saygili (UNCTAD)

tries in order to benefit from cost advantages and market access. Foster and Azmeh (2020) and Lee, Malerba and Primi (2020) note that digitalization and process automation may also drive greater inequality across countries, in part because of technology and skills gaps.

Many countries are struggling to move up the value chain

Not all developing countries have managed, however, to successfully integrate into regional and global production networks. When deciding on the appropriate geographical location for establishing its production network, a firm takes into account many factors, including a country's physical and digital connectivity, the size and skills of its labour force, the quality of its infrastructure, its trade and investment policies, the quality of its institutions, and its political stability. Ahmad and Primi (2017) have found that the presence of strong domestic supply chains in a country provides the foundation for its integration at a more global level. Many countries that are currently plugged into GVCs are struggling to move up the value chain, and have been unable to capture a higher share of value added in the production process. Some studies have shown that for developing countries, GVC integration has in fact discouraged export diversification and has also been associated with the lowering of domestic value added, and the widening of within-country income inequality (UNCTAD, 2015; 2018).

The ability of countries to adapt to changing global trade structures and to harness the opportunities arising from the changing configuration of GVCs depends on many factors. If firms are to participate in digitalization and benefit from its trends, national Governments will need to focus on developing as well as upgrading workforce skills, and to establish regulatory and policy frameworks that enable the private sector to set up required ICT infrastructure successfully. Some Governments may choose to expand beyond horizontal policies and pursue industrial-digital approaches that support local firms through active regulation of dominant foreign firms' market access, including to digital platforms and online marketplaces. However, a multiplicity of different regulatory norms across countries implies increased costs for international business. Moreover, the existing digital divide will place many developing countries at a competitive disadvantage in the new trade environment; and trade and investment agreements have often contributed to a reduction of policy space, limiting the ability of countries to implement the specific reforms needed to boost development prospects. Regardless of the direction taken by countries' industrial and development policy choices, those choices will influence global trade patterns.

ICT infrastructure and enabling policy frameworks play a critical role

Challenges to further expansion of global value chains

Since the global financial crisis, there has been a clear deceleration in the pace of GVC expansion. The WTO (2019a) found that while GVCs have continued to grow, they have done so at a pace slower than that of the growth of total trade, especially in the middle-income countries. The average GVC participation rate, measured as countries' GVC-related trade as a share of total trade, has declined at an annual rate of 1.6 per cent since 2012. At the same time, Miroudot and Nordström (2020) have observed that, over the past eight years, there has been a gradual shift towards more domestically oriented supply chains. As existing supply chains matured, subdued global GVC growth and investment since the financial crisis have dampened the proliferation of new GVCs. Looking ahead, critical transitions in the global economy could significantly alter trade patterns and the nature of existing GVCs. This in turn would pose challenges for developing countries, while raising concerns over whether GVCs can still offer them opportunities for further development progress.

The pace of GVC expansion has slowed over the past decade

In addition, the COVID-19 pandemic has exposed the risk posed by complex and geographically dispersed production networks. Lockdown measures have had a strong impact on the manufacturing sector in many countries, amid the closures of production facilities and shortages of intermediate inputs. Baldwin and Freeman (2020) have noted that as the coronavirus disease outbreak hits major GVC hubs sequentially, the initial supply chain contagion is working in reverse through "reinfection", as trade-linked contagion ripples through to countries that depend on each other's manufacturing inputs.

The pandemic may accelerate the trend towards onshoring of production

The backlash against globalization in many parts of the world and economic and political pressures for reshoring could undermine the future of GVCs that largely depend on cost efficiency. Furthermore, concerns over labour and environmental standards are increasingly challenging the cost-efficiency rationales for establishing GVCs. The trade dispute between China and the United States as well as the withdrawal of the United Kingdom of Great Britain and Northern Ireland from the EU pose additional challenges for GVCs. These developments have highlighted the vulnerability of GVCs to policy shocks in host countries. Indeed, populists in many countries have been pushing for the reshoring of economic activities in order to reduce the share of foreign value added in production and exports, which would result in shorter and less dispersed supply chains. However, it is unclear whether domestic supply chains offer a national economy greater resilience. A country-level shock would tend to have a greater impact on domestic production networks compared with one with international sourcing, which effectively diversifies risks when shocks are uncorrelated across countries. Against this backdrop, a question that is key for the future of global trade concerns the extent to which GVCs can be unravelled through trade policy actions.

GVCs have remained resilient to China-United States trade tensions

In the case of the China-United States trade tensions, the shock to bilateral tariffs between these two economies has been large in both absolute and relative terms. The costs of the prolonged trade dispute have been substantial at an aggregate level, amounting to estimated GDP losses of 0.32 per cent for China and 0.05 per cent for the United States. Using a quantitative trade model to delve beyond the aggregate impacts, Shepherd (2020) analysed changes to GVCs resulting from the trade dispute. The model demonstrated, through application of the decomposition approach of Wang, Wei and Zhu (2013), that in proportional terms, China and the United States had experienced only a modest reduction in dependency on GVC linkages compared with the pre-shocks period. While there were some disruptions to production networks, GVCs exhibited a significant degree of resilience in the face of the trade dispute. Neumann and Bhaumik (2020) found that trade tensions between China and the United States appeared to have raised, not lowered, the reliance of third markets on inputs from China, with China gaining global export market share. China has managed to compensate for its direct loss of market share in the United States through an increase in market share elsewhere, either directly or through the sale of intermediate inputs ultimately bound for the United States. While it remains unclear whether further protectionist measures will induce a large-scale shift towards the reshoring of existing GVCs, the heightened global uncertainty associated with unpredictable changes in trade and investment policies will continue to weigh on the expansion of GVCs. Public policy may struggle to strike the right balance between efficiency and resiliency, given the bluntness of available trade policy instruments, such as tariffs and import quotas. At the firm level, there will no doubt be some reassessment of network fragilities and strengths, taking stock of experiences during the COVID-19 pandemic.

Digitalization and servicification: redefining comparative advantages

Digitalization and new technologies

Digital services are increasingly embedded in production and trade

The digital economy is increasingly shaping competitiveness, production, trade and economic outcomes. The concept of the digital economy is focused on the convergence of fixed, mobile and broadcast networks, the increasing connection of devices and objects to form the Internet of Things, and the resulting changes in social interactions and personal relationships (OECD, 2015). The use of ICT by firms has expanded rapidly, with digital processes becoming more embedded in production and trade. ICT services are now used consistently to measure and control businesses processes and facilitate transactions within networks and between firms and customers. In 2019, ICT services accounted for a record 10 per cent of total global trade in services (figure II.9).

Figure II.9
Global ICT services exports

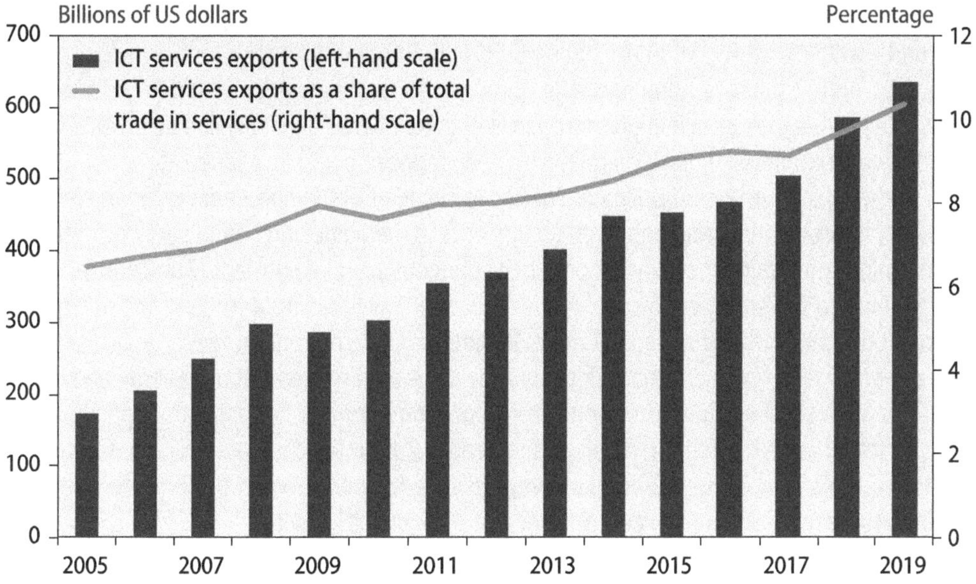

Source: UN DESA, based on data from UNCTADstat.

Technological developments allow for new consumer experiences

These technological developments will underpin new business models that impact the volume and direction of trade. A wide range of products and services, such as travel reservations, translations, support and customer services, telemedicine and e-learning, are already being delivered remotely with relative ease. Consumers' shopping experiences can be analysed abroad by digital platforms that intermediate local demand and supply, leveraging the power of artificial intelligence, big data and fast web connections to gather detailed data on personal preferences and customize product offerings and advertisements. Digital technologies, such as 3D printing, allow mass customization of goods and services for the buyers worldwide who prefer personalized products. Technology has also reduced transaction costs between owners and renters regardless of location, since the sharing of surplus or idle assets (e.g., a spare room or car) is now easier than ever. Social networks allow people to communicate and global positioning system (GPS) services enable them to locate and compare goods, while online payment systems handle the billing. Importantly, the new technologies enable a more efficient use of existing resources. This allows reductions in energy and water use, greenhouse gas emissions and waste generation, provided that efficiency gains are not offset by increased consumption.

New technologies shape manufacturing and merchandise trade

Digitalization of both manufacturing and services activities will continue its rapid advance. Machine vision, automation and additive manufacturing have the potential to bring about fundamental changes in the organization and distribution of manufacturing activities, reducing resource intensity and generating increasing returns to scale for investment and production. These types of technologies can support reshoring of manufacturing by enabling scale-independent efficient production, although to date the use of such technologies is still relatively limited. Their use will be accompanied by greater digitalization, with trade entailing the cross-border flow of digital design files, printers and feedstock. The composition of trade in tangibles will change, with a shift away from trade in parts, components and finalized products towards trade in material inputs and equipment.

Technology is transforming service delivery

Services will become more automatized as robotic processes and artificial intelligence are increasingly used in interactions with clients, for example, in customer service and marketing. Business decision-making will be increasingly informed by high-frequency monitoring and feedback from customers based on product usage. Software tools to support data analytics and regulatory compliance (e.g., corporate tax obligations across jurisdictions) will further drive the digitalization of trade-related services. There will also be an associated expansion along the extensive margin, with new services being developed.[16]

Digitalization of services creates both opportunities and challenges

At the same time, the application of ICT services offers the prospect of significant productivity improvements and improved quality care in medicine and health services, reducing commuting and wait times and improving diagnostics and treatment. The reduced need for patients to travel to health-care provider locations will facilitate trade of those services across borders. There is already some evidence that international trade in health services has grown. So far, however, this reflects mainly increased movement of patients and health workers, with a rising number of countries importing services to deal with capacity shortfalls in their health systems (Hanefeld and Smith, 2019). Process automation and related software tools may generate competitive pressure for some types of services that have been outsourced, such as call centre work and back office activities.

The value of cross-border data flows is difficult to capture

Cross-border movements of data are central to the economic activities described above, but there is no commonly agreed methodology for collecting or valuing them. An estimate by McKinsey (2016) suggests that global data flows contributed $7.8 trillion to global GDP in 2014. It was estimated that in developing economies, the Internet of Things — which refers to the sensors, actuators and data communication technology built into physical objects that are used to enable those objects to be tracked, coordinated or controlled across a data network or the Internet—could have an economic impact of $0.81 trillion to $1.86 trillion per year by 2025 (UNIDO, 2015, box 2.1). It was also estimated that by 2025 in developing economies, advanced robotics—that is, robots with greater dexterity, flexibility and adaptability, as well as the ability to learn from, and interact with, humans—could have an economic impact of $0.3 trillion to $0.9 trillion (ibid.).

The global regime for data flows is highly fragmented

Access to consumer data by producers, distributors and retailers is regulated at the national level, with national data privacy and security standards determining the price of data. Firms that are able to collect, collate and analyse consumer data nationally and across countries are poised to gain advantages over their competitors. Accordingly, access to consumer data will strongly affect the dynamic comparative advantage of a country in international trade. Measuring the flow of data across countries and determining their true market value pose significant challenges for government authorities, particularly in developing countries where data governance is still at a nascent stage. The current global regime for regulation of data flows is highly fragmented, with laissez-faire approaches in some countries and more tightly regulated environments in others. Regulation can be motivated by such factors as a commitment to protection of privacy and citizens' rights, perceived security imperatives or concerns about market power and abuse of dominant positions by leading firms.

Trade agreements are beginning to include specific obligations on cross-border data flows, and some jurisdictions are establishing "equivalence regimes," which determine whether foreign providers will be treated in the same way as domestic firms with respect to

16 In this context, extensive margin refers to the development of new (different) services, as opposed to intensive margin which refers to the development of existing services.

accessing and processing of data. The welfare consequences of the possible emergence of data trading blocs are still poorly understood.

The rise of the services economy

Services have gained in importance as inputs and as final products

The rise of services has been a key feature of the world economy in recent decades and—driven by digitalization and the increased use of machine learning and artificial intelligence to process vast quantities of consumer data services—services will become even more important in the future. The evolution of economic processes has extended from mostly agrarian activities to industrial production and, increasingly, to data product development. Services (e.g., financial and legal services, logistics and advertising) have, in tandem, gained prominence both as intermediate inputs to the production process and as final products, for example, in the fields of education, entertainment and health care.

Countries are becoming increasingly service-based

The share of services in total value added has risen steadily, from 60 per cent of GDP in 2000 to 65 per cent in 2017. The transformation was especially rapid in some developing economies. In China, for example, the share of the services sector in GDP more than doubled in the last 40 years; and services now account for a larger share of GDP than manufacturing. The importance of the services sector has also risen sharply in other large developing economies, such as Brazil and India. Some developing countries, especially geographically disadvantaged economies, have moved directly to services, bypassing traditional industrialization.

Employment in certain services is expected to decline over the next decade

Currently, services provide over 60 per cent of the jobs in developing countries and 80 per cent of the jobs in developed countries (WTO, 2019b, p. 14). The coming decades will see major shifts in the composition of services sector employment owing mostly to automation. Functions that are likely to see a net job decline by 2030 include some customer interaction jobs (e.g., hotel workers, travel agents, cafeteria workers), office support jobs (e.g., information clerks, payroll processors, administrative assistants) and jobs carried out in predictable settings (e.g., factory workers, transportation workers, installation and repair workers) (McKinsey Global Institute, 2017). By contrast, positive job growth is expected in categories such as health-care providers, professionals (e.g., engineers, scientists), technology professionals, managers and executives, and educators. While these trends are currently most relevant for developed economies, they will be affecting developing countries more and more. The consequences of automation of services will be compounded by enhanced cross-border trade in services. As technology reduces the need for face-to-face contact, many services sector functions are becoming tradable and will move increasingly from higher- to lower-cost locations (Baldwin, 2019).

Current data understate the true level of services content in international trade

Trade in services across countries can be classified under four Modes of supply, depending on where the supplier and consumer are located at the time of the transaction: Mode 1—cross-border transaction, which occurs when a service is supplied across borders, most likely digitally via email or through an online platform; Mode 2—consumption abroad, which occurs when a consumer moves to a foreign country to receive the service (e.g., tourism and medical treatment); Mode 3—commercial presence abroad, which occurs when a service is supplied through commercial presence, e.g., by a branch or subsidiary of a foreign bank or by a foreign-owned hospital or in connection with FDI; Mode 4—presence of natural persons, which occurs when a service is provided by a person through temporary cross-border movement (e.g., a software engineer or a consultant on a temporary visa engaged in work on a project overseas).

Data on trade in services—especially trade in services between a parent firm and its cross-border subsidiaries or affiliates—are less comprehensive and reliable than merchandise trade statistics. Most countries collect only a limited quantity of data on cross-border services trade. In many developing countries, services trade data are limited to pure cross-border transactions and movement of the consumer to a foreign country, with little information available on disaggregated categories of services. Even in developed countries, collection of data on the supply of services across borders is not systematic. The absence of a single or harmonized data source for trade in services, particularly intrafirm activities, has important impacts on trade invoicing, affecting financial flows and taxation.

Prior to COVID-19, trade in services grew faster than trade in goods

A new data set compiled by the WTO documents the rapidly growing role of international trade in services in the global economy.[17] Global trade in commercial services is estimated to have increased from about $7 trillion in 2005 to about $13.3 trillion in 2017, which is close to the level of total merchandise exports, estimated at $17 trillion. Trade in services has grown faster than trade in goods in recent decades. Since 2005, trade in services has expanded by 5.4 per cent per year on average, while trade in goods has expanded at a rate of 4.6 per cent annually. Although both the global financial crisis of 2008–2009 and the COVID-19 pandemic triggered sharp declines in the global services trade, the value of global services exports is expected to continue rising in the future.

Developing countries account for a growing share of services trade...

The participation of developing countries in international trade in services has been on the rise. Between 2005 and 2017, developing economies' share of global trade in services (excluding the LDCs) grew by more than 10 percentage points, reaching 25 per cent ($3.4 trillion) for exports and 34 per cent ($4.5 trillion) for imports. This large increase was driven by structural transformation and successful trade diversification entailing a shift from goods to services, especially in Asia, as well as by the advent of novel means of trading in services.

... owing largely to the success of five economies

Among the developing economies, services trade is, however, highly concentrated. Just five economies (China, Hong Kong SAR, India, the Republic of Korea and Singapore) accounted for more than 50 per cent of services exports from developing countries in 2017. Services exports in these countries have increased at a faster rate than among the developed economies. Moreover, high value added services, such as research and development (R&D), ICT and financial services, account for a growing share of their trade in services. These five economies have invested in services trade by establishing branches and subsidiaries both in other developing regions and in developed economies.

For the LDCs, progress in trade in services has been slow. In 2017, LDCs accounted for 0.3 per cent of world services exports ($38.3 billion) and 0.9 per cent of world services imports ($124.1 billion). These shares were only slightly higher than in 2005, when they stood at 0.2 per cent and 0.5 per cent, respectively. Services exports growth has been led by tourism, an important source of revenue for many LDCs and the only services sector where the group's participation in global exports exceeded 1 per cent.

Cross-border services are provided mainly by foreign affiliates

Commercial presence abroad accounts for the largest share of global services trade (59 per cent), half of which are financial and distribution services, involving banks, wholesalers and retailers (figure II.10). Yet, in some developed countries, such as the United

17 See WTO, Trade in Services data by Mode of Supply (TiSMoS) database, available at https://www.wto.org/english/res_e/statis_e/trade_datasets_e.htm#TISMOS

Figure II.10
World exports of services, by Mode of supply

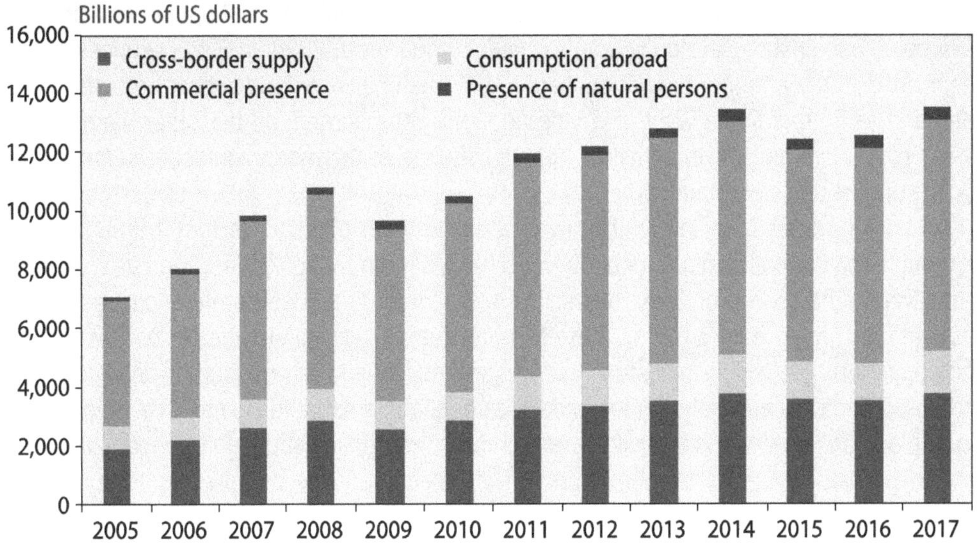

Source: UN DESA, based on the WTO Trade in Services data by Mode of Supply (TiSMoS) data set.

States and countries in Europe, the share of services provided by affiliates is declining, in favour of online cross-border transactions made possible by digitalization. At 28 per cent, cross-border transactions are the second largest category of services. Technological developments that facilitate trade in digital products and cross-border provision of services, such as mobile banking and online sales, can be expected to increase the share of cross-border transactions in total trade in the future. Much will depend, however, on government policy and the ability of suppliers to meet a range of regulatory requirements in importing countries. Consumer purchases abroad constitute the third largest category of trade in services (10 per cent), driven mainly by tourism activities. The services of persons abroad constitute only 3 per cent of all traded services, a share that has remained relatively unchanged during the past two decades.

Service value added is also embodied in manufacturing exports

The four Modes of supply do not give a full picture of the extent of services trade since other sectors of the economy make large use of services inputs. Exports of tangible products embody a significant amount of services value added. For example, the OECD Trade in Value Added database reports that services value added accounts for over 23 per cent of the gross value of Indonesia's manufacturing exports.[18] A similar observation applies to tasks performed within firms. Most manufacturing firms employ substantial numbers of people who engage in services activities. They range from engineers to back office specialists and providers of sales and support, custodial and security services. Accounting for the total services content of exports is impeded by the fact that these transactions are carried out not in markets but within firms and might therefore give rise to problems such as trade mis-invoicing.

The pandemic has accelerated online trade...

The COVID-19 pandemic has created an even higher demand for digital services, many of which are provided by firms across borders. Online sales of physical goods have experi-

18 See OECD, Trade in Value Added, available at https://www.oecd.org/sti/ind/measuring-trade-in-value-added.htm#access.

enced a surge in demand during the pandemic and numerous brick-and-mortar businesses shifted to e-commerce as consumers flocked to digital services amid stay-at-home measures and social distancing requirements. Profits in Amazon's international operations, for example, rose sharply year on year in the second quarter of 2020. In 2020, services of foreign firms in the areas of education, health and media also reported robust growth, while demand for international voice and video call services surged; on the other hand, online sales of tourism and travel activities—previously one of the most significant segments of online purchasing—plummeted.

...but further digitalization of services faces obstacles

Looking ahead, certain shifts in the consumption of services may be permanent, although some developments could be short-lived and may not outlast the current crisis. However, in the course of numerous shifts in customer habits and preferences, businesses and consumers have become more familiarized with online services in both work and personal settings, which indicates that longer-term changes to consumer behaviour and cross-border trade are likely. For instance, the pandemic is expected to have a lasting impact on the demand for e-working facilities and cross-border online education transactions.

The path ahead for services trade nevertheless depends on how countries manage the challenges. For example, consumer protection will need to be strengthened to prevent online fraud and deception. Direct shipments to consumers of large volumes of small parcels present several types of challenges related, for example, to compliance with health and safety regulations in importing countries; protection of the health of workers involved with the handling and inspection of goods; and environmental sustainability. Many consumers and businesses in developing countries are struggling to secure reliable Internet access and electricity connections, acquire affordable computers and telecommunication devices, set up online payment solutions and establish online visibility. Digital divides within and across countries are likely to have been reinforced by the crisis.

Climate change disrupts trade in services

The effects of climate change will be a key determinant of services trade in the future. Extreme weather events are already affecting tourism and port closures, while global warming affects shipping lanes. Climate change also affects trade indirectly, impacting labour productivity, inputs (such as energy and water supply), risk-return matrices and investment decisions. Climate change policies may affect services trade through more stringent regulation of the carbon content of imported goods and services. Countries with stringent decarbonization requirements will seek to restrict access to their markets by producers that operate under less stringent standards.

Fostering participation in the services and digital economy

Several developing countries have built competitive service industries

Tradable services offer immense opportunities for developing countries in the medium term. Unlike in the manufacturing sector, the disadvantages of geography will play a less relevant role in building an export base of services. Creating an enabling environment for technology, infrastructure, human capital and regulatory policy is critical for developing internationally competitive service industries. While India stands out in terms of building competitive services exports, there are also other cases that are worth highlighting. Mauritius and Senegal, for example, have established a presence in the ICT sector and in business process outsourcing, focusing on cost savings and specific language skills. In the last two decades, Mauritius has emerged as an exporter of ICT services, with the share of services in GDP (mainly travel and tourism, financial services, transportation and ICT) having increased from

55 per cent in 2000 to 67 per cent in 2019. In Chile, services exports are less dominated by large firms and tend to be more skill-intensive than manufacturing exports. At the same time, services firms are as innovative as manufacturing firms, illustrating the role that services can play as a driver of trade and innovation (Zahler, Iacovone and Mattoo, 2014).

Trade policy has played a crucial role in promoting services exports

The success stories in service exports across developing countries highlight the important role of trade policy (Balchin and others, 2016). In Kenya, for example, regional integration, together with the establishment of diversified financial hubs and advances in mobile technology, has been key to promoting the rapid expansion of financial services exports, creating both high- and low-skilled jobs. ICT exports, on the other hand, depend critically on access to export markets through digital infrastructure and regulatory standards. At the same time, agreement on mutual recognition of services sector qualifications can help reduce trade costs. The members of the Association of Southeast Asian Nations (ASEAN) have, for example, concluded mutual recognition agreements (MRAs) that facilitate cross-border provision of a range of professional services. The EU–CARIFORUM Economic Partnership Agreement permits professionals from EPA members in 29 categories to enter the EU without quotas.

Global cooperation is needed to improve services trade regulation

In recent decades, developing countries have reduced barriers to services trade through WTO and regional trade agreements, with the exception of temporary cross-border movement of people, for which barriers remain high. Notwithstanding such progress, there is a strong case to be made for increased global cooperation in particular areas to deal with cross-border spillovers. Multilateral approaches are needed to ensure that regulatory outcomes in the areas presenting new challenges do not reflect only the standards of major countries or country blocs. Thus, while building their services sectors and expanding digital capabilities, developing countries should proactively engage with the emerging global regulatory agenda in these areas. Indeed, lack of engagement may leave them in the position of rule takers, rather than rule makers. While for many small and low-income countries, active engagement would require developing technical capacities and reducing the digital divide, a strong case can be made that at least the larger developing countries should get involved in rule making of services sectors. This is the only pathway towards ensuring that the global regulatory advances in these areas take the needs of developing countries into account.

Connectivity and digital infrastructure are priorities for small and low-income countries

As Governments attempt to address the adjustment costs associated with the shift to a services economy and the repercussions of efforts to decarbonize production and consumption, they will need to identify national priorities and align their policy frameworks accordingly. Given that many countries still concentrate on manufacturing, there are important policy issues that need to be considered. Trade policy must be embedded in a broader development strategy which recognizes trade-offs and synergies between objectives. The issue of digitalization is of particular importance for developing countries, as it will alter business models, redefine comparative advantages and accentuate the shift towards services. Notably, countries need to assess how to leverage data and digitalization to foster productivity growth. Small and low-income countries need to prioritize the development of connectivity and digital infrastructure so as to reduce the risk of exclusion from global trends. The regulation of trade in digital services will, to a large extent, determine how countries can benefit from these emerging opportunities in the coming decades.

Education and training policies play a key role in developing the services economy

Developing country Governments have a wide range of instruments at their disposal—including tax incentives, subsidies, local content requirements and FDI incentives—for building human and physical infrastructure, strengthening domestic capabilities and fostering participation in global and regional value chains. The participation in the services economy calls for stronger emphasis on education and training to improve labour-force skills. Policy approaches must be guided by countries' dynamic and evolving comparative advantages in the medium to long term. For example, creating a business environment and a trade policy regime conducive to relationship-specific investments by multinational firms can offer significant opportunities for developing countries. This can include more specific and targeted efforts to attract multinational firms in areas compatible with national development priorities. Maintaining sufficient policy space is crucial for developing countries in this context. In the past, trade and investment agreements have been widely criticized for constraining Governments' policy options (Gallagher, 2010; McNeill and others, 2017).

Strengthening innovation systems is vital for developing countries

Developing countries need to strengthen national innovation systems in order to invigorate firms' capabilities to absorb and utilize knowledge and adjust to and benefit from the changing trade environment (United Nations, 2018). Knowledge—as a firm's most significant resource—promotes the development of new and more advanced products and services, enables the use of new processes and technologies, and facilitates the creation and discovery of new markets. Innovation is, however, often concentrated in low-tech sectors with limited spillovers, and manufacturing innovation tends to be highly informal. Amid weak institutional frameworks, the levels of private investments in R&D are usually low, and the partnerships and linkages among the private sector, universities and research institutions are limited. Many developing countries also face educational mismatches and a critical shortage of high-skilled labour.

Technological capabilities can help drive export growth

In recent decades, more formal approaches to promoting innovation and the accumulation of technological capabilities have gained relevance in the policy agendas of many developing countries, often involving major changes in institutional frameworks. These approaches need to be comprehensive, taking into account the systemic nature of innovation activities and how they enhance a country's dynamic comparative advantages. This being the case, an expansion of R&D investments must be complemented by the tackling of existing barriers to physical and human capital accumulation, including deficits in managerial capabilities and technological infrastructure. Amid the rise of digitalization and new technologies, stiffer international competition and a growing role of labour and environmental standards and trade regulations, many developing countries will find it increasingly difficult to compete on the basis of low labour costs alone and participate in global or regional value chains.

The multilateral trading system: facing a crisis of confidence

There is a pressing need to revitalize multilateral trade cooperation

The COVID-19 pandemic has exacerbated some of the critical challenges currently faced by the multilateral trading system. The imposition of export restrictions on medical supplies by a significant number of countries has demonstrated their preference, during a global health crisis, for using unilateral trade measures to protect domestic interests. In addition, ongoing structural trends, including rising protectionist tendencies and shifts towards bilateral and regional trade agreements, are threatening to further weaken the role of the WTO as the central governing body for global trade. This in turn could lead to an increasingly polarized and fragmented international trade landscape in the coming decades. The need to reform and revitalize multilateral trade cooperation is thus more pressing than ever. While the COVID-19 crisis has added yet another challenge to an already weakened WTO, it may also create an opportunity to strengthen multilateralism. By raising the stakes and demonstrating the benefits of global cooperation, the pandemic could serve as a catalyst for achieving progress on WTO reforms so as to create a global trade governance framework that can effectively address new and emerging challenges within the international trade landscape (Evenett and Baldwin, 2020).

Challenges for the multilateral trading system

The pandemic has exposed weaknesses of the current multilateral trading system

The pandemic has further exposed the weaknesses of the current multilateral trading system. Amid a sharp increase in global demand for medical equipment, a large number of Governments imposed export restrictions on medical supplies and other essential products, leading to an acute shortage of these goods in some countries. Between January and November 2020, 98 countries worldwide are reported to have introduced export restrictions on products such as face masks, gloves, disinfectants, medical devices and foodstuffs.[19] While some of the measures introduced in the early stages of the pandemic were later lifted, many have remained in place—potentially in violation of WTO regulations which allow only temporary emergency use of restrictions (WTO, 2020a). In addition, there has been a lack of transparency at the multilateral level, with members failing to notify export restrictions to the WTO.

Furthermore, in the first 10 months of 2020, Governments implemented a record 1,477 policy interventions which are estimated to negatively affect the commercial interests of their trading partners (Evenett and Fritz, 2020). Government subsidies—including bailouts for airlines and large-scale support for the automotive industry—accounted for almost three quarters of those interventions. While these measures have played a vital role in protecting jobs and stabilizing national economies, they have also created significant cross-border spillover effects which could trigger tit-for-tat moves and have a long-lasting negative impact on competition (Hoekman and Nelson, 2020).

The WTO is facing significant operational challenges

The global pandemic emerged on the heels of already heightened trade tensions amid a weakened multilateral trading system. Over the past two decades, WTO member countries have increasingly struggled to resolve long-standing differences and to negotiate new rules in response to an evolving global trade environment. Special and differential treatment (SDT) is one example of an issue that has recently stoked contention. Some developed countries have sought to terminate the current practice of self-declaration of developing country status, requesting greater reciprocity in liberalization commitments. Developing countries remain generally opposed to such proposals, noting the prevalence of still large divides and highlighting the vital role of SDT provisions in creating policy space for the promotion of sustainable development.

As a result of these differences, the WTO has been unable to fulfil its core functions, which are to support multilateral market opening and rule making; resolve trade disputes; and ensure transparency. With the exception of the WTO Agreement on Trade Facilitation (2013), the first global trade accord to be negotiated since the 1990s, there have been few meaningful outcomes of multilateral trade negotiations in recent years. At the same

19 See the International Trade Centre (ITC) Market Access Map, available at www.macmap.org/en/covid19.

time, trade conflicts between major economies have intensified. In defiance of the rules-based multilateral trading system, there has been an increase in the use of unilateral trade-distorting measures in recent years. Although China and the United States signed an interim bilateral agreement in January 2020, trade tensions between the two countries remain elevated. Moreover, disagreement over procedures and mandates of the dispute settlement mechanism has caused a paralysis of the Appellate Body, the WTO's highest court. Since December 2019, the Appellate Body has been unable to function, which includes an inability to hear new cases, owing to lack of consensus on the appointment of new judges. This is of particular concern for small countries, which, given an incapacity to enforce compliance with negotiated agreements, rely most heavily on the WTO.

Trade governance architecture has become more fragmented

In the absence of meaningful global progress, many countries have turned to bilateral and regional free trade agreements. Most new rule making has occurred under preferential trade agreements and not within the WTO.[20] The past few years have seen a proliferation of regional trade and investment agreements. Several of these new agreements have broad membership and cover a significant share of world trade.[21] The most prominent are the Agreement Establishing the African Continental Free Trade Area (AfCFTA), which entered into force on 30 May 2019; the Comprehensive and Progressive Agreement for Trans-Pacific Partnership (CPTPP), agreed by 11 countries on 8 March 2018; and, most recently, the Regional Comprehensive Economic Partnership (RCEP) Agreement, which was signed on 15 November 2020 by 15 countries of East Asia and Oceania.[22]

There has been a long-standing debate on how the move towards preferential trade agreements affects the WTO and the multilateral trading system. Since these agreements discriminate against third parties, they give rise to trade diversion and potentially marginalize non-participating countries. More important, there has been a rise in concerns that the adoption of new rules, regulations and standards through regional trade agreements could result in a more fragmented global trading system featuring competing regional blocs. Bhagwati, Krishna and Panagariya (2014, p. 25) argue that preferential trade agreements could "undermine not only the trade liberalization function of the WTO, but also its rule-making role".[23]

Revitalizing and reforming the multilateral trading system

COVID-19 can help restore confidence in the multilateral trading system

Revitalizing the multilateral trading system will hinge on Governments' ability to reform the WTO and create an effective global trade governance framework. The impasse in the WTO can be attributed to differences in priorities across member States, an erosion of mutual trust and working practices that have impeded efforts to agree on changes to the rule book. While creating new challenges, the COVID-19 pandemic can also serve as a catalyst for

20 Preferential trade agreements—which may be bi- or plurilateral in composition—are treaties between States by which they give preferential market access to each other's domestic markets and set rules for international commerce between the parties.

21 These new agreements differ substantially in respect of the depth of their regulatory commitment.

22 In 2019, the combined GDP of signatory countries to the AfCFTA agreement represented 3 per cent of world gross product (WGP); the combined GDP of signatory countries to CPTPP represented 13 per cent of WGP; and the combined GDP of signatory countries to the RCEP Agreement represented 30 per cent of WGP.

23 Trommer (2017) notes that "the network of preferential agreements ... benefits those with the technical and political capacity to successfully navigate the fragmented governance architecture".

restoring confidence in the multilateral trading system. The pandemic has underscored that in times of crisis, keeping trade flowing and limiting protectionist and nationalist measures are vital to ensuring the safety of lives and livelihoods. Recognizing that current and future challenges can be met only through global partnerships and strong multilateral frameworks could generate positive momentum for WTO reform. Breaking the existing stalemate will require a rebuilding of trust in the WTO based on establishing reaffirmed commitments to multilateralism and the development agenda of trade integration; revisiting some of the organization's long-standing practices; and ensuring constructive engagement by members on controversial and emerging issues.

Two key WTO operational modalities are consensus-based decision-making and the "single undertaking" approach to negotiation of agreements. The term "consensus-based" signifies that all members have to agree on matters of both process and substance; "single undertaking" signifies that during a negotiation round, all issues are up for negotiation until every item is agreed. These practices, which ensure ownership and legitimacy, serve in particular to protect the interests of countries with weak bargaining power. However, with WTO membership having become increasingly heterogeneous over decades, they have also contributed to the stalled negotiations of the Doha Development Round. The drawbacks associated with these approaches to negotiation have prompted calls—especially from developed country groups—for more flexible multilateral approaches.[24]

Joint statement initiatives facilitate WTO discussions on key policy areas

Since the Eleventh Ministerial Conference of the WTO, held in Buenos Aires from 11 to 13 December 2017, subsets of WTO members have adopted so-called joint statement initiatives (JSIs) as a means of discussing possible cooperation in key policy areas. Participation in these initiatives is open to all members but no member is required to join. The groups currently focus on four areas: e-commerce; investment facilitation; domestic regulation of services; and micro-, small and medium-sized enterprises (MSMEs). In all of these areas, there are potential gains to be derived from addressing coordination failures and identifying good regulatory practices (Hoekman and Shepherd, 2020).

Data-related issues and the digital divide pose challenges in e-commerce negotiations

The growing importance and complexity of e-commerce presents one of the most difficult challenges faced in multilateral negotiations. In order to create an enabling environment for cross-border digital trade going forward, there is a need to address transaction costs that arise from the heterogeneity of international regulatory frameworks, to prevent abuse of a dominant position and to safeguard competition.[25] The global value of e-commerce is estimated to have reached almost $26 trillion in 2018, equivalent to about 30 per cent of world gross product (UNCTAD, 2020a). The COVID-19 pandemic has further accelerated the shift away from physical to digital stores.

As the negotiations between member countries have progressed, three main challenges have emerged (Ismail, 2020). First, there is a lack of clarity on the matter of scope when trade-related aspects of e-commerce are being addressed. Second, large differences exist between members as regards their views on data-related issues, including data flows, data localization, invasions of privacy by data collectors, Internet taxes and Internet censorship. Third, the global digital divide, which remains significant, represents a major obstacle. Many developing countries still lack adequate capabilities, skill sets and infrastructure as the

24 In this regard, see, for example, European Commission (2018).

25 There is also a pressing need to reach an international agreement on digital services taxation. This, however, is, outside the scope of the discussion of e-commerce within the WTO.

basis for taking full advantage of e-commerce. They have also yet to develop national regulatory frameworks, such as e-transaction laws, consumer protection, data protection and privacy laws.

Views on open plurilateral agreements differ significantly

Hoekman and Sabel (2019) propose open plurilateral agreements as a novel vehicle for possibly avoiding some of the pitfalls of preferential trade agreements. These agreements may offer an alternative to discriminatory trade agreements and a pathway towards sustaining multilateral cooperation without requiring the agreement or participation of all WTO members. Open and non-discriminatory by design, they permit participants to come to a common understanding of good practices in regulatory areas and of means for attenuating negative policy spillover effects. However, potential integration of plurilateral approaches into the framework of the WTO is viewed by some observers as clashing with the spirit of multilateralism. Several developing countries are opposed to new plurilateral negotiation initiatives.

Global discussions on emerging issues can help revitalize the multilateral trading system

Some observers argue that integration of open plurilateral agreements into the WTO framework could also open up the possibility of addressing the important systemic issues that are at the core of trade tensions (Hoekman and Shepherd, 2020). One area of contention spans industrial, technology and innovation policies, including subsidies. These are policies that directly affect competition and can influence the location of GVC activities. Another important area is that of climate change-motivated trade policies. It is unclear how measures such as border carbon adjustment mechanisms, for example, which are at the centre of policy debates, could be structured to comply with WTO rules.[26] In response to growing demands in this area, Structured Discussions on Trade and Environmental Sustainability were launched at the WTO in November 2020. The question of how OPAs can contribute to the discussions on such issues needs to be carefully examined, including in the light of the future WTO reform debate.

Encouraging participation of developing countries and addressing their concerns and capacity constraints in all of these areas is critical. Engagement by all member countries could help sustain an open multilateral trading system—one fit for purpose for a twenty-first century global economy that will be increasingly service-based and digital. The Twelfth Ministerial Conference of the WTO, to have been held in Nur-Sultan, Kazakhstan, in June 2020, was postponed owing to the outbreak of COVID-19. Yet, with the global pandemic adding a new dimension to the WTO reform debate, there is still an opportunity to create fresh momentum for revitalizing the rules-based multilateral trading system.

26 See, for example, European Parliament (2020).

Developed economies

GDP Growth

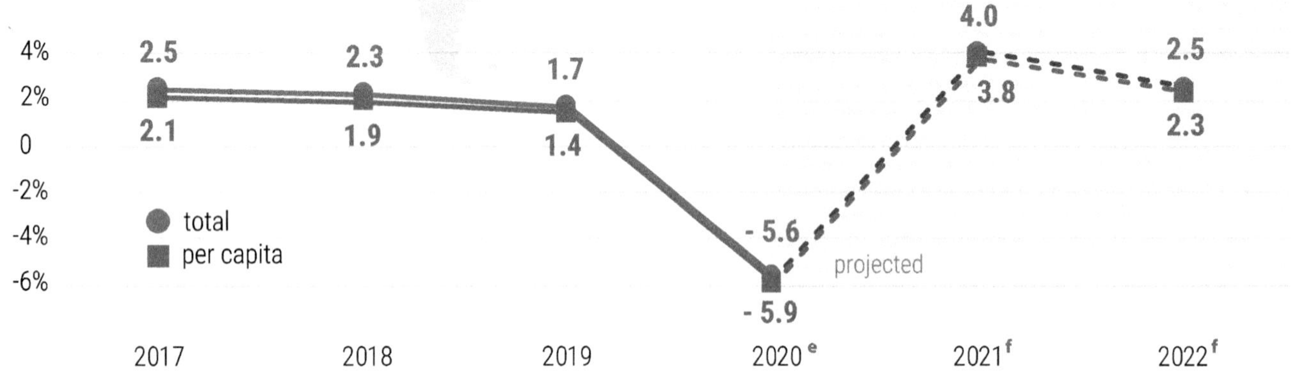

COVID-19 Cases per 100,000 people

by 1 January 2021

GDP per capita

2020

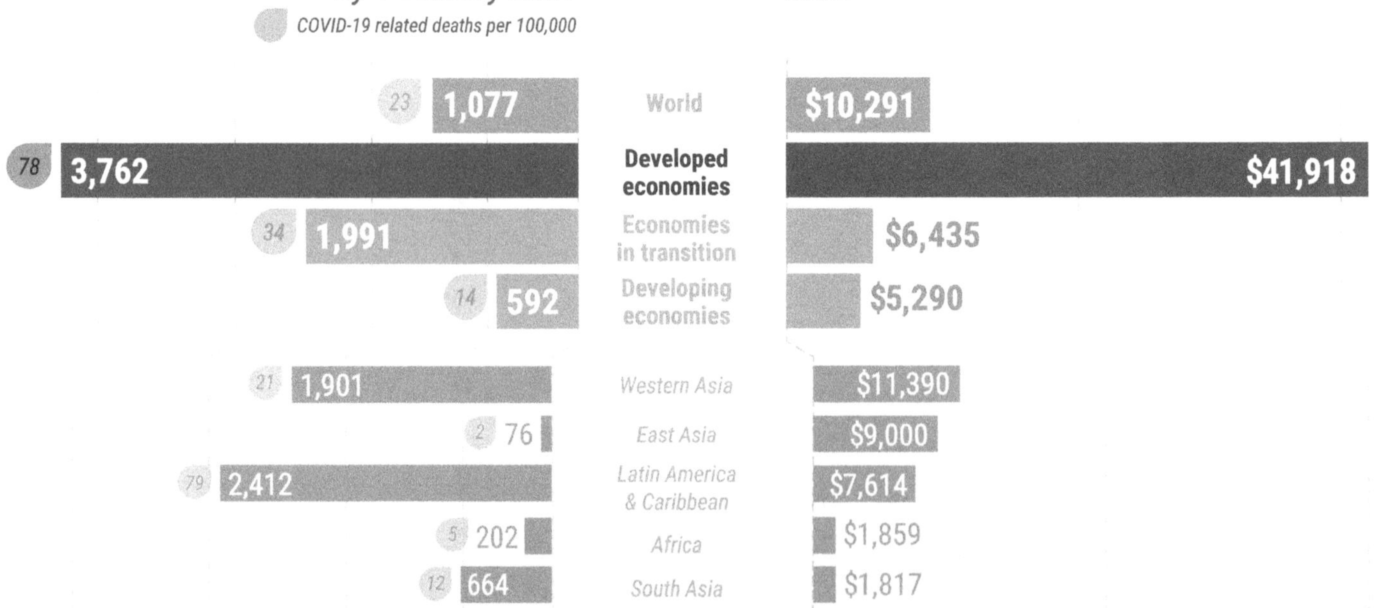

Note: The boundaries and names shown and the designations used on this map do not imply official endorsement or acceptance by the United Nations. The map represents countries and/or territories or parts thereof for which data is available and/or analysed in *World Economic Situation and Prospects 2021*. The shaded areas therefore do not necessarily overlap entirely with the delimitation of their frontiers or boundaries.

Aggregate data for Africa, excluding Libya.

e: 2020 estimates, **f:** 2021-22 forecasts.

Source for COVID-19 data: UNDESA calculations, based on data from Johns Hopkins University.

CHAPTER III

Regional developments and outlook

Developed economies

- In their midyear rebound, developed economies failed to attain the pre-crisis level of economic output
- Domestic demand recovery has been fragile and could easily be reversed if fiscal support measures weaken
- Economies with larger exposure to tourism were hit hard

Northern America: the strong midyear economic rebound nevertheless fell short of the pre-crisis level of output

United States of America: while GDP plunged, aggregate personal income grew owing to stimulus measures

In the United States of America, real gross domestic product (GDP) is estimated to have contracted by 3.9 per cent in 2020. The economy came to a standstill in mid-March owing to lockdown measures taken to combat the coronavirus disease (COVID-19) pandemic; and the unemployment rate jumped to 14.7 per cent in April from 3.5 per cent in February. The Government promptly responded with an unprecedented stimulus package (the Coronavirus Aid, Relief, and Economic Security (CARES) Act), whose size cumulatively totalled 12 per cent of GDP by the end of October. This measure, which expanded income transfers to households and provided emergency loans to businesses, sustained growth in aggregate disposable personal income in the second quarter (figure III.1). Nevertheless, domestic demand imploded.

Figure III.1

Disposable personal income, employee compensation and personal consumption in the United States

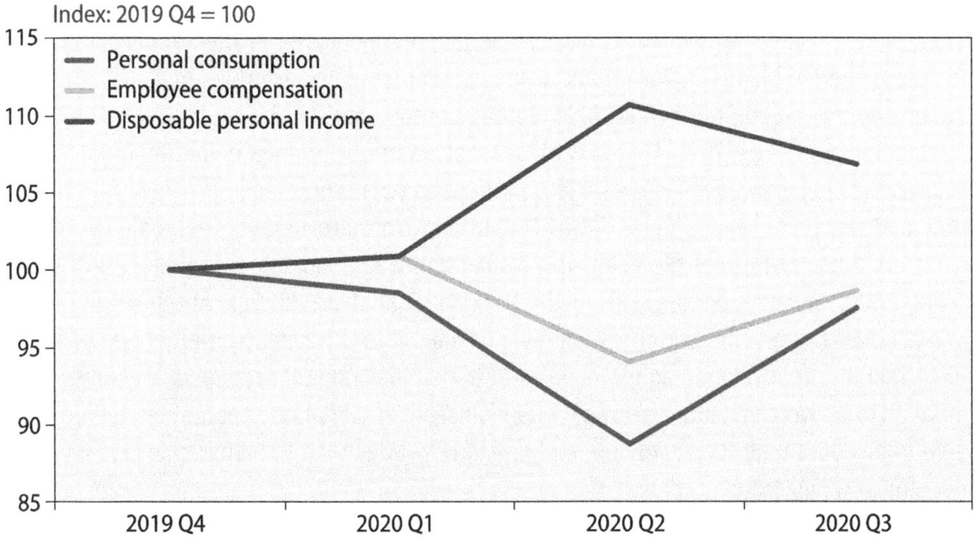

Source: The Bureau of Economic Analysis of the United States Department of Commerce, "Gross Domestic Product, Third Quarter 2020 (Advance Estimate)", October 29, 2020, available at https://www.bea.gov/sites/default/files/2020-10/gdp3q20_adv.pdf.

Note: Calculation based on seasonally adjusted annural rates.

Household savings rates spiked in the United States and other developed economies

In the United States, while the impact of the stimulus packages has been waning, the household savings rate has remained high, at 13.6 per cent in October, significantly higher than the pre-crisis yearly average of 8.0 per cent. There are several explanations for the pattern of such increases in savings rates which emerged across the developed economies (figure III.2).

Figure III.2
Household savings rate, selected developed economies

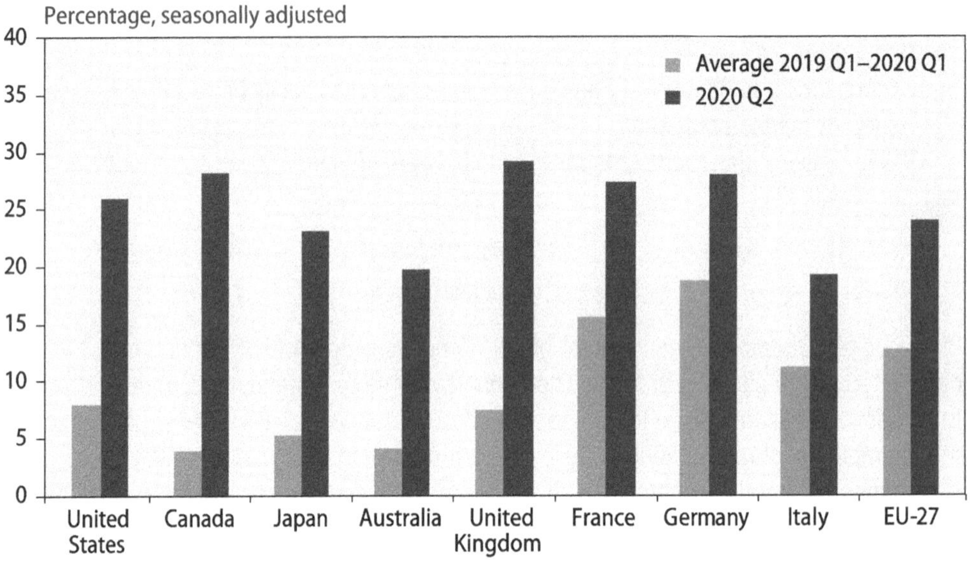

Sources: Australian Bureau of Statistics (2020); Statistics Canada (2020); Japan, Cabinet Office (2020); United Kingdom, Office for National Statistics (2020b); United States Department of Commerce, Bureau of Economic Analysis (2020); Eurostat (2020) (France, Germany, Italy and EU-27).

The main driver of the spikes has been a massive decline in household consumption and large increases in temporary government transfers. However, as lockdown measures prevented households from spending on non-essential items, the decline in spending does not necessarily represent a fundamental shift in savings behaviour. According to the permanent income hypothesis (PIH), households do not change their patterns of consumption expenditure in response to a temporal change in income if they perceive no change in their permanent income. The PIH can therefore partially explain household behaviour in countries where the household disposable income increased in the second quarter of 2020 despite the plunge in wages and wage supplements, for example, Australia, Canada, Japan and the United States (Australian Bureau of Statistics, 2020; Statistics Canada, 2020; Japan, Cabinet Office, 2020; United States Department of Commerce, Bureau of Economic Analysis, 2020;). However, in several large European economies, such as France, Germany, Italy and the United Kingdom of Great Britain and Northern Ireland, the scale of income transfers could not offset the decline in wages and wage supplements (European Central Bank, 2020; United Kingdom, Office for National Statistics, 2020a). Another factor that can account for the spikes in the household savings rate is household perception of future uncertainties. In developed economies, as both nominal interest rates and consumer price inflation rates were at historical lows, households, absent inflation expectation, felt no pressure to discount their future income and spend now, which led to historically high levels of precautionary savings.

In the United States, the financial sector absorbed the initial shock, limiting the second-round shock inflicted by the crisis

During the second quarter of 2020, growth of household debt in the United States was curbed as the outstanding amount decreased from $14.30 trillion in the first quarter to $14.27 trillion, which represented the first quarterly decline since 2014. Households refrained from taking up new loans to purchase durable goods. In the same period, the amount of non-financial corporate debt exhibited an increase as total liabilities grew from $16.9 trillion to $17.6 trillion, reflecting the utilization of the special credit facilities made available by the stimulus package. Despite the accelerating financial hardship, the delinquency rate of commercial bank loans remained low, at 1.54 per cent. At its last peak, which occurred in the first quarter of 2010, the delinquency rate had stood at 7.4 per cent. Although the magnitude of the negative shock on economic activities was unprecedented, the United States banking sector—which had accumulated a sufficient level of liquidity and capital owing to the prudential regulations adopted after the global financial crisis of 2008—was able to absorb that shock. This regulatory buffer prevented the amplification of the economic shock throughout the financial sector, thereby limiting the second-round economic impact of the COVID-19 pandemic crisis.

During the third quarter of 2020, the United States economy rebounded as lockdown measures were relaxed. The consumption of goods and residential investments exceeded the pre-crisis level, while the personal savings rate decreased to 14.1 per cent in August from 33.6 per cent in April. As economic activities partially recovered, the unemployment rate decreased to 7.9 per cent in September. However, the midyear rebound fell short of the pre-crisis levels of both consumption of services and corporate investments, which remained weak. Moreover, hopes for the realization of a straightforward recovery scenario were dashed by accelerating COVID-19 outbreaks in many parts of the United States as some business restrictions were reimposed.

The fragile recovery could falter if the fiscal stimulus wanes

The United States economy is forecast to grow by 3.4 per cent in 2021. As monetary easing continues, consumption of durable goods and residential investments continue to grow. However, other demand components, particularly corporate investments and exports, are forecast to remain weak as long as the uncertainties associated with the COVID-19 pandemic persist. While loans to the household sector, particularly through mortgages, are projected to grow, the banking sector is expected to be more cautious in issuing new corporate loans. In a context of weak employment prospects and wage growth, the fragile recovery could easily be reversed if fiscal support measures, including income transfers and loan guarantees, remain inadequate.

Canada: the energy sector remains weak amid the midyear recovery

In Canada, the economy is estimated to have contracted by 5.6 per cent in 2020 and is forecast to grow by 3.8 per cent in 2021. To alleviate the economic impact of the COVID-19 outbreak, an unprecedented fiscal stimulus package (amounting to 16 per cent of GDP), which included income support, loan guarantees and liquidity assistance, was implemented. The fiscal measures supported the growth of aggregate personal income in the second quarter, while production activities plunged. The economy broadly rebounded in the third quarter, led by strong residential investments and housing sales, as a result in part of monetary easing. The unemployment rate, which had jumped to 13.7 per cent in May, fell gradually to 8.9 per cent in October; it remained, however, far above the pre-crisis level, in January, of 5.5 per cent. The energy sector remained weak, reflecting subdued global energy demand, which is likely to constrain the country's growth prospects in the near term.

Europe: fallout from the pandemic is compressing economic activities

Europe has been experiencing an economic crisis of historic proportions, with the region expected to have seen an economic contraction of 7.8 per cent in 2020 (for EU-27) as a consequence of the pandemic. At the end of the first quarter, with rising case numbers and fatalities, a large number of countries implemented widespread and rigorous lockdown measures in order to contain the spread of the pandemic. This led to a virtual standstill in large parts of the economy, which set off a cascade of negative effects. Businesses—especially small businesses with fewer financial reserves—were thrown into a liquidity crisis, as revenues fell off the cliff while costs remained unchanged. After a respite during the summer and signs of economic revival, the pandemic outbreak started again to worsen at the end of October, with many countries, including France, Germany, Italy and the United Kingdom, reintroducing various lockdown measures.

Great uncertainty is associated with the growth forecast for 2021

While it is forecast that the region will experience a return to positive growth of 5.2 per cent in 2021 and 2.6 per cent in 2022, this needs to be put in context. First, base effects would account for the greatest part of the rebound; and second, the baseline forecast is predicated on the assumption that the lockdown measures renewed in the fourth quarter will improve the public health situation. Consequently, an exceptional degree of uncertainty is tied to this forecast. The major risks include a longer-lasting wave of pandemic infections, leading to a continued contraction of economic activities. By contrast, in case of the approval and introduction of a vaccine, sectors such as tourism could see a faster recovery, with actual growth exceeding the recovery's forecasted trajectory. Besides the aforementioned risks, the region is also facing challenges that predated the pandemic, including those related to the future relationship between the European Union (EU) and the United Kingdom as well as disruptive structural changes in the automotive industry in a number of countries, where the shift to alternative technologies would entail the revamping of entire supply sectors.

Countries with larger exposure to tourism have been hit hard

There has been some variation in the fallout from the pandemic across the region. Belgium, France, Italy and Spain have been hit especially hard, in terms of case numbers and fatalities or the magnitude of their economic contraction. In Germany, on the other hand, the fallout and resulting economic contraction, while still significant, have been more limited. The length of the instituted lockdowns and the role and share of the service sector in the economy largely account for the differences in economic contraction across countries. The economies of Southern Europe generally rely to a greater extent on services, in particular tourism. In consequence, large swaths of economic activities were shut down when, in a matter of days, the travel industry, including hotels, restaurants and airlines, suffered a complete collapse (figure III.3). By contrast, over the summer, countries such as Germany, with larger manufacturing sectors and greater exposure to global trade, experienced a quicker rebound. The pandemic has also contributed to the widening of already existing differences across the euro region, inasmuch as several countries with higher pre-existing debt and unemployment levels have been hit especially hard.

While unemployment increased, short-time work measures helped cushion the impact

Under short-time work measures, many employees in the region accepted some reduction in income to avoid unemployment, at least in the first instance. Nevertheless, unemployment increased in the region to 7.5 per cent in September 2020, compared with 6.6 per cent in 2019, with Greece and Spain registering the highest unemployment rates:

Figure III.3
Hotel occupancy rate in selected European countries

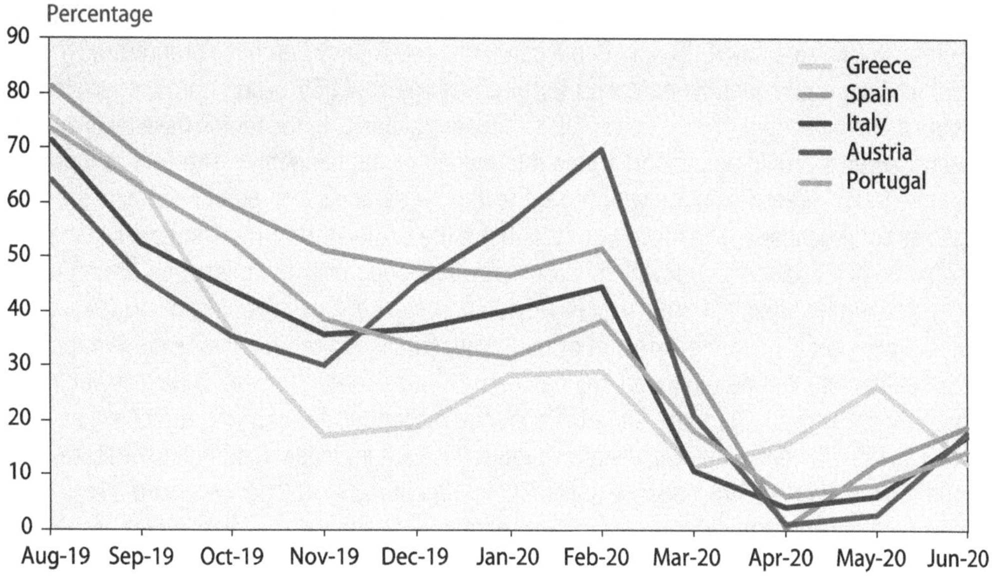

Sources: Eurostat.
Note: Estimates for Greece cover January, February, March, May and June 2020.

16.8 per cent (July) and 16.5 per cent, respectively. Moreover, youth unemployment, which remains a serious challenge across the European Union, increased by more than 2 percentage points year-on-year to 17.1 per cent in September.

Fiscal policy measures included unprecedented steps taken at the EU level

The need to address the pandemic and its fallout triggered the enactment of significant fiscal policy measures, although there were differences among individual countries in terms of the extent and level of their efforts and the limitations they confronted. At the outbreak of the pandemic, the immediate aim was to ramp up spending on health-care capacities and to increase testing and tracing capabilities, within a context where policymakers had only a limited time-window for preventing both the freezing-up of entire economies and further stress in financial markets. This generated a range of fiscal policy measures across countries, which included, among others, wage support schemes, liquidity assistance and tax deferrals. The size and impact of those measures depended, however, on the individual country's fiscal position at the onset of the crisis. Italy, for example, was already facing relatively high levels of public debt and consequently experienced constraints in rolling out a sufficiently large fiscal response to the pandemic. Germany, in contrast, was able, given relatively low public debt, to use its available policy space to initiate a significant fiscal stimulus. The pandemic also led the European Union to take unprecedented fiscal policy-related steps. For example, it activated the escape clause of the Stability and Growth Pact (SGP), which normally limits national fiscal deficits to 3 per cent of GDP and public debt to 60 per cent of GDP. The Pact still remains in force under the escape clause but countries now have the increased flexibility with respect to budgetary rules that they need to support their health-care systems, firms and employees. In addition, the EU has loosened State-aid rules, thereby giving national Governments more leeway in providing support to firms. In recognition of the severity of the policy challenges, the EU also agreed for the first time on joint-debt issuance. This will serve as the means of financing a recovery plan in the amount of

750 billion euros. Under the plan, which will prioritize ecologically sustainable development, digitalization, support for companies and strengthening of health-care systems, loans and grants will be made available to the neediest and hardest- hit economies in the region.

The European Central Bank initiated significant monetary stimulus measures

The pandemic also led to a wide range of monetary policy actions. In March 2020, the European Central Bank (ECB) initiated a pandemic emergency purchase programme (PEPP) and in June subsequently increased its total volume to 1,850 billion euros, equivalent to more than 10 per cent of euro zone GDP. Other central banks in the region have taken similar steps towards providing support within the context of the pandemic. The ECB programme features significant flexibility with regard to the types of assets purchased and the time frames for purchases. The exercise of that flexibility will lead to further increases in the size of the Bank's balance sheet, which has already ballooned over the past years owing to the implementation of similar programmes. In addition, the Bank has kept its policy interest rate at -0.5 per cent. The immediate aim of these measures is to reduce the negative impact of the health crisis on the real economy and to prevent the emergence of a financial crisis. In accordance with its mandate, the ECB continues to target an inflation rate of below—but close to—2 per cent. However, even with the significant increase in stimulus measures, the inflation rate has become negative and in September stood at -0.3 per cent for the euro area. Lower energy prices have been a major contributing factor, but even when energy and unprocessed food are excluded, inflation stood at only 0.4 per cent, well below the policy target. This sets the stage for an increasingly serious policy predicament. While the undershooting of the policy target and the looming spectre of deflation could very well merit a further increase in or extension of stimulus measures, such steps could lead to renewed criticism that, by financing public budgets, the European Central Bank is overstepping its mandate.

Developed Asia: linkage with developing East Asia holds the key to post-crisis recovery

Developed Asia—comprising Japan, Australia and New Zealand—experienced an unprecedented plunge in the level of its economic activities in the second quarter of 2020. While these countries could afford to implement unprecedented fiscal stimulus packages, it is the revival of their external demand—particularly from developing East Asia and notably from China—that will make recovery solid and sustainable. Indeed, Japan shares global supply chains for manufacturing with developing East Asia; East Asia is Australia's largest destination for commodity exports; and the recent growth in New Zealand's tourism sector has benefited from the visits of tourists from East Asia. For a post-crisis recovery to succeed, it is therefore crucial that developed Asia ensure the restoration of the value chains it has been sharing with developing East Asia.

Japan: exports are expected to lead the recovery

In Japan, real GDP is estimated to have contracted by 5.4 per cent in 2020 and is forecast to grow by 3.0 per cent in 2021. Despite the roll-out of an unprecedented stimulus package, including income transfers and employment subsidies, real GDP plunged in the second quarter, marking the third consecutive quarterly decline. Owing to stagnating domestic demand, household debt increased only slightly in the second quarter, to 345 trillion yen from 343 trillion yen in the previous quarter. In the same period, the debt of the non-financial sector showed a steep increase, from 1,754 trillion to 1,852 trillion yen, reflecting the utilization of emergency loan facilities. The third-quarter rebound was weak as households remained cautious when spending; and residential and corporate investments stayed subdued despite easing financing conditions. Although Japan was able to avoid a one-time surge in unemployment in the second quarter, the unemployment rate gradually rose to 3.0 per cent in September from 2.4 per cent in January. The fragile employment situation reflects weak prospects for corporate profits and wage growth; and domestic demand growth is projected to be mild. It is exports that are projected to lead the recovery as demand from the East Asian economies recovers.

Australia: the pace of recovery picked up towards the end of 2020

In Australia, real GDP, which is estimated to have contracted by 4.5 per cent in 2020 and will grow by 3.3 per cent in 2021, dipped substantially in the second quarter, reflecting the economic effects of the lockdown measures. The midyear recovery was relatively slow, due partly to another lockdown in the State of Victoria in August instituted in response to a second wave of pandemic outbreaks. While the unemployment rate has remained high, after jumping from 5.3 per cent in January to 7.5 per cent in July and decreasing only slightly to 7.0 per cent in October, the pace of recovery nevertheless picked up towards the end of the year. External demand for Australia's commodity exports is expected to lead growth in 2021.

New Zealand: the high-performing tourism sector was hit by the impact of border closures

In New Zealand, real GDP is estimated to have contracted by 6.1 per cent in 2020, with an expansion by 5.2 per cent expected in 2021. While lockdown measures instituted to contain community infection were successful in bringing down the number of COVID-19 outbreaks, the economy nonetheless came to a standstill in the second quarter with a plunge in domestic demand. The midyear recovery, on the other hand, was robust, with housing sales growing rapidly on the back of monetary easing. The recovery of exports has been weak, however, as strict border controls impacted the tourism sector, the main pillar of New Zealand's services exports. Also fragile is the employment situation: the unemployment rate jumped to 5.3 per cent in the third quarter from 4.0 per cent in the previous quarter.

Economies in transition

GDP Growth

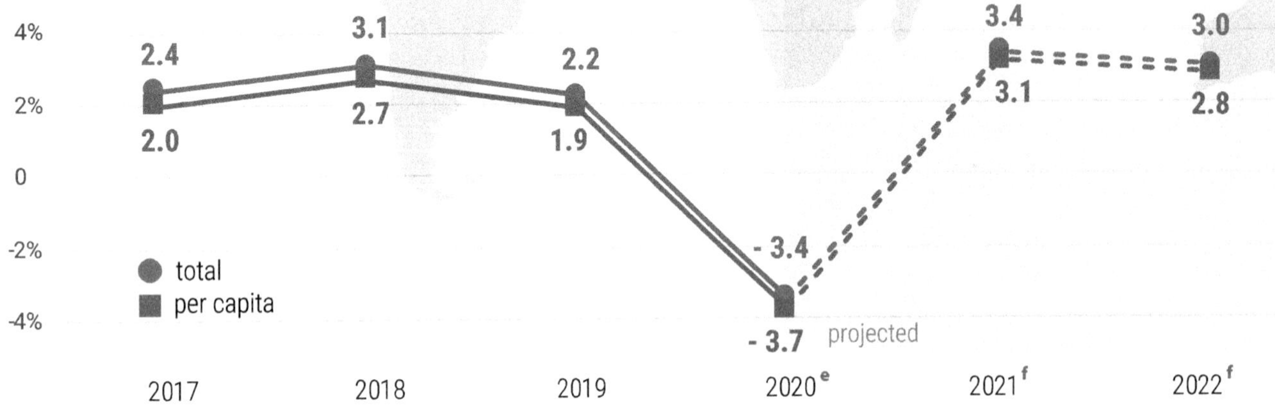

COVID-19 Cases per 100,000 people

by 1 January 2021

COVID-19 related deaths per 100,000

GDP per capita

2020

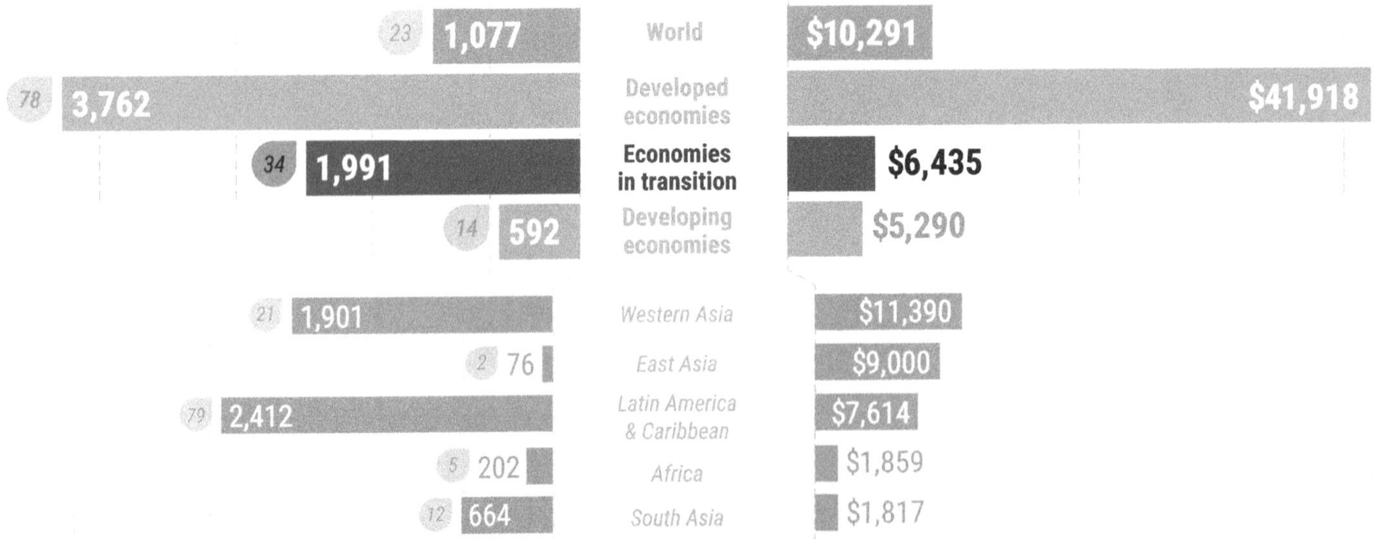

Note: The boundaries and names shown and the designations used on this map do not imply official endorsement or acceptance by the United Nations. The map represents countries and/or territories or parts thereof for which data is available and/or analysed in *World Economic Situation and Prospects 2021*. The shaded areas therefore do not necessarily overlap entirely with the delimitation of their frontiers or boundaries.

Aggregate data for Africa, excluding Libya.

e: 2020 estimates, **f:** 2021-22 forecasts.

Source for COVID-19 data: UNDESA calculations, based on data from Johns Hopkins University.

Economies in transition

- Both in the Commonwealth of Independent States and in South-Eastern Europe economic activities are unlikely to experience a quick recovery
- Lower commodity prices amplified the shock in the Commonwealth of Independent States
- Tourism-dependent countries in South-Eastern Europe were hit the hardest

Commonwealth of Independent States and Georgia: the pandemic has unleashed multiple shocks

The outbreak of the COVID-19 pandemic has unleashed multiple shocks in the Commonwealth of Independent States (CIS) and Georgia, having heavily depressed economic activity since the early part of the second quarter of 2020. The imposition of lockdowns and quarantine measures in the region, first introduced around April and then, after some loosening, reintroduced later in the year, caused far-reaching disruptions. Lower commodity prices, including for important non-oil commodities exported by the CIS countries (except for gold, whose higher price benefited gold exporters in Central Asia), exacerbated the contractionary effects of the pandemic (figure III.4). These shocks have been widespread across the region, resulting in declines in output in almost all countries. The magnitude of those declines has depended on a country's economic structure and its capacity to adopt offsetting measures.

The region's services sector has been particularly affected by the pandemic, with international tourism, a critical economic sector for some countries in the Caucasus and Central Asia, having been dealt a telling blow. Trade and transport disruptions in the region and reductions in levels of economic activity in the Russian Federation have led to a decrease in remittances and disrupted temporary migration flows, with a significant impact on small-

Figure III.4
Global prices of selected commodities exported by the CIS countries

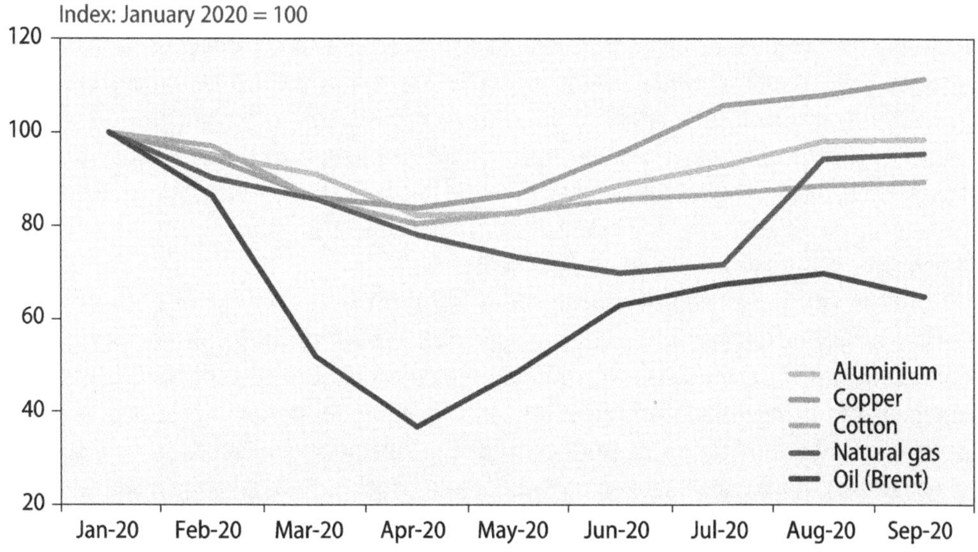

Source: UNCTAD and FRED (Federal Reserve Economic Data) database.

er economies in Central Asia. Although non-service sectors performed relatively better, oil production cuts under the OPEC+ agreement depressed industrial output in Azerbaijan, Kazakhstan and the Russian Federation. In addition, bad harvests contributed to poor economic performance in Azerbaijan and Ukraine. After expanding by 2.2 per cent in 2019, the aggregate GDP of CIS and Georgia is estimated to have shrunk by 3.4 per cent in 2020. Only a modest recovery is expected, with growth of 3.4 per cent for 2021 and 3 per cent for 2022.

Consumption has declined sharply and living standards have been deteriorating

Consumption in the region sharply contracted in 2020 as a result of the restrictions associated with the instituting of quarantines, higher unemployment and lower remittances, which led to a worsening of living standards, despite the provision of government support. While investment also contracted, it seems to have trailed behind the decline in consumption. In a number of countries, geopolitical tensions and internal conflicts in the second half of the year, including domestic political tensions in Belarus in the aftermath of presidential elections and the resumption of hostilities between Armenia and Azerbaijan as related to the conflict in Nagorno-Karabakh, contributed further to disruptions in economic activities and increased uncertainties.

The region's energy-importing countries saw deeper contractions in 2020

The economic contraction in 2020 was deeper in energy-importing countries, as the beneficial effect of lower oil prices on their economies was offset by multiple negative factors. The 2021 recovery in the region should, however, be supported by somewhat improved terms of trade and some breakthroughs in containment of the pandemic. The return to growth will neverthelesss be insufficient to compensate for the output losses in 2020 and investment—against a background of persistent economic headwinds—is expected to remain weak. Moreover, within a context marked by multiple risks and increased geopolitical tensions, growth projections are understandably subject to significant degrees of uncertainty. Exchange rate flexibility in most of the CIS countries has helped to offset the shocks, including that of lower energy prices in those energy-exporting countries—Kazakhstan, for example—where the devaluations have been particularly large. It has also helped to reduce the drain on reserves. However, the speed of exchange rate weakening constrained the implementation of policy options and prompted interventions designed to reduce volatility.

Some countries responded to the crisis by implementing large stimulus packages

Countries have reacted to the multiple shocks by implementing large stimulus packages, including an increase in health spending and social benefits. In addition, support—including through direct income transfers, utility subsidies and tax exemptions—has been directed towards individuals and sectors directly affected by containment measures, with small and medium-sized enterprises being a common target in this regard. The size of these programmes, which varies, has been determined largely by the availability of fiscal space. Energy-exporting countries have been able to tap into their sovereign wealth funds to finance increased spending; and in Kazakhstan, for example, the financing of the anti-crisis programme was equivalent to about 9 per cent of GDP.

Inflation remained for the most part contained, while labour-market conditions deteriorated

While inflation-related developments in 2020 in the CIS area have been generally benign, supply disruptions and currency depreciation have created upward pressures in some countries of Central Asia. In Kyrgyzstan, temporary price controls for food items were introduced to dampen inflation pressures; price controls for certain items and services, accompanied by food rationing, were continued in Turkmenistan; and to provide support to households, Kazakhstan capped utility prices. In Uzbekistan, inflation remains relatively elevated, reflecting the impact of past depreciation, but has declined as a result of weak demand and the postponement of utility price increases. By contrast, the impact of the rouble's weakness on prices has been limited in the Russian Federation. Despite support programmes, unemployment rates have increased throughout the region; and restrictions placed on mobility have contributed to the deterioration of labour markets in countries that rely on temporary migration, aggravating the situation in Central Asia.

Fiscal deficits are larger and public debt is higher

Fiscal deficits, which were modest in most CIS countries in 2019, have widened in 2020, owing to lower revenue and higher spending. In the Russian Federation, the central government budget balance will change from a surplus in 2019 to an estimated deficit of over 4 per cent in 2020, as a result of low energy revenues, declining economic activity and tax relief measures. The Government has borrowed in domestic financial markets and issued local-currency debt. Moreover, the stimulus packages enacted for 2020 and 2021 are together equivalent to about 7 per cent of GDP. To accommodate fiscal spending in 2020–2021 in an environment of low oil prices, some components of the fiscal rule have been temporarily relaxed and the application of certain articles of the Budget Code has been extended to 2021 in order to allow the Government to allocate funds for the financing of anti-crisis measures without amending the budget. Despite the country's massive international reserves and the relatively low public debt-to-GDP ratio (estimated at 13.7 per cent in June 2020), overall fiscal spending under the proposed 2021–2023 budget is likely to shrink in real terms, as the Government continues to prioritize fiscal stability. In Kazakhstan, previous fiscal consolidation plans have been postponed, while in Kyrgyzstan, border closures and the reduction of trade have directly impacted revenues, given the importance for that country of custom duties. Public debt ratios have increased sharply as a result of higher financing needs, output contraction and exchange rate depreciation. However, in energy-exporting countries, which can tap into their sovereign wealth funds (as noted above), these increases will be more limited.

Monetary conditions in the region have been relaxed

Monetary policy in CIS has been loosened throughout the year. In Kazakhstan, the depreciation of the tenge prompted the authorities, in March, to increase the key policy rate, but this hike was later fully unwound. In the Russian Federation, the key rate was cut by 200 basis points to a record low of 4.25 per cent. Amid concerns over exchange rate instability and the signs of a strengthening of economic activities, the authorities paused the loosening process in the second half of the year. In Ukraine, interest rates were cut from 15.5 to 6.0 per cent in the first half of the year, within a context of declining inflation. In the Republic of Moldova, in addition to interest rate cuts, there has been a relaxation of reserve requirements in order to increase liquidity and credit flows. Many countries have also introduced measures aimed at providing support to the banking sector, which has been asked to grant payments holidays and assist in debt restructuring.

Kyrgyzstan and Tajikistan are benefiting from the Debt Service Suspension Initiative

Current account balances will deteriorate in most countries in the region, owing to lower hydrocarbons exports, reduced remittances and reduced tourism revenue; and capital outflows have increased the need for balance-of-payments support in some countries. Although debt distress risks in the region are relatively low, some countries appear to be particularly vulnerable. Kyrgyzstan and Tajikistan have benefited from the G20 Debt Service Suspension Initiative, which has saved them the equivalent of 0.6–0.8 per cent of GDP in their 2020 debt servicing costs. Official financing is playing a critical role in covering the external funding requirements in most energy-importing countries. In June 2020, the Executive Board of the International Monetary Fund (IMF) approved a new standby programme for Ukraine (enabling an immediate disbursement of $2.1 billion), which was designed to address financing needs and advance reforms, and which could unlock access to further resources. While Belarus, Kazakhstan and Ukraine successfully issued international sovereign bonds, access of the CIS countries to external financing has generally become more difficult (box III.1) amid perceptions of the volatility of risk. Moreover, geopolitical tensions which arose in the second half of the year are further constraining financing options.

The economic outlook is marred by uncertainties and reduced policy space

The economic outlook for the region is uncertain, with downside risks predominating. The reintroduction of containment measures, should the outbreak of the pandemic lead to a further deterioration, would both inflict new damage in the realm of economic activities and undermine confidence. While the banking sector has remained stable over the course of the current period of turbulence, the deterioration of asset quality and high levels of dollarization in many countries will constrain lending and increase risks. In addition, geopolitical tensions have mounted and, in some cases, have spiralled into real conflict. Clearly, the COVID-19 crisis has exposed existing vulnerabilities in the region and reduced existing policy space.

Box III.1

External financing constraints and the impact of the COVID-19 crisis on the Commonwealth of Independent States and Georgia

The COVID-19 crisis has inflicted multiple shocks upon the economies of the Commonwealth of Independent States (CIS) and Georgia. It has negatively impacted foreign exchange earnings derived from commodity exports, tourism and remittances. Public financing needs related to funding the crisis response have increased, while revenues have slumped; consequently, access to external financing has become ever more critical for many of the countries in the region. However, external financing needs vary across the region, reflecting heterogeneity in economic structures and external trade composition. And for some countries, external financing needs were already large prior to the crisis.

Figure III.1.1

Share of public debt in foreign currency and public debt as percentage of GDP

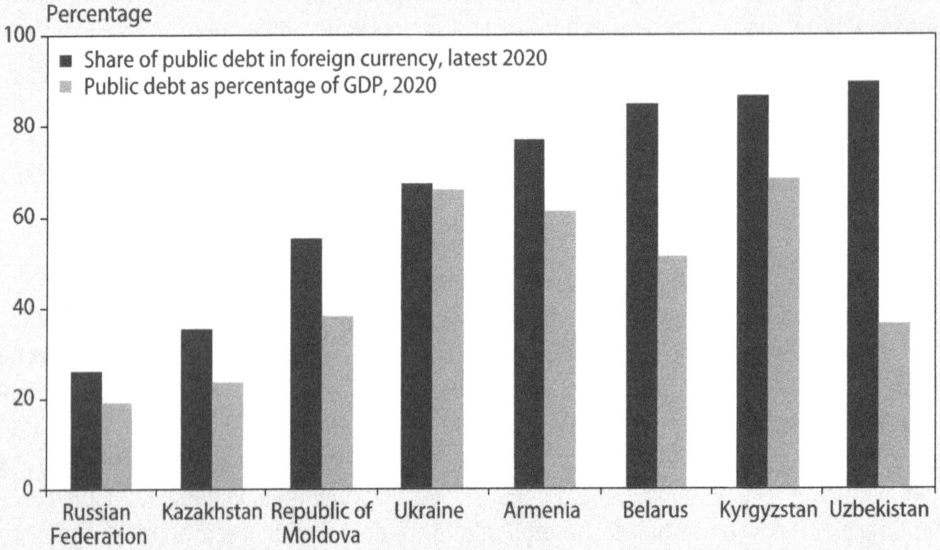

Sources: National Ministries of Finance; IMF projections, World Economic Outlook database, October 2020.

Note: Foreign debt is used as a proxy for foreign currency debt if other data is unavailable.

(*continued*)

Box III.1 (*continued*)

The energy-exporting countries entered the crisis with large amounts of foreign assets in their sovereign wealth funds and have been able to draw on these resources to partially finance growing budgetary imbalances and smooth exchange rate fluctuations. In Azerbaijan, Kazakhstan and the Russian Federation, those funds are substantially larger than their financing needs. Their public debt ratios are low, although they have increased during the crisis; and total external debt is also low, except for Kazakhstan where local subsidiaries' increased borrowing from their parent companies abroad has elevated private sector external debt in recent years. On the other hand, the introduction of sanctions for the Russian Federation starting in 2014 has significantly reduced the ability of public and private sector entities to borrow from international capital markets.

While the financing situation is less favourable in the region's energy-importing economies, there are nevertheless important differences among them in terms of their market access and liquidity positions. A common denominator in this crisis has been the reliance on official financing. All of these countries, except Belarus and Turkmenistan, have relied on official financing and received International Monetary Fund (IMF) emergency financing. The IMF also approved a new standby arrangement for Ukraine.

These new borrowings will further increase the already large share of external public debt owed to official creditors—both bilateral and multilateral. In Ukraine, commercial borrowing is more significant, which makes it stand out among energy importers; but even in this case, official creditors had accounted for 46 per cent of public and publicly guaranteed external debt by the end of September 2020. In recent years, several countries in the region have taken advantage of a favourable environment for the placement of government bonds in international capital markets, which included debut issues by Tajikistan (2017) and Uzbekistan (2019). In this regard, Georgia and Ukraine are likely to face additional financing constraints, as their international bonds are maturing in the immediate future. However, commercial borrowing has not fundamentally altered reliance on funding from bilateral and multilateral creditors, particularly on the part of the Central Asian countries. The growth of public debt in Kyrgyzstan, for example, is explained by increased bilateral official borrowing, despite the cancellation of debts to the Russian Federation in the aftermath of the 2014 crisis.

Overall, public and external debt has increased throughout the region in recent years. The growth of total external debt since the 2014 downturn has been driven by increased public liabilities, while the decline in borrowing costs has contributed to increased fiscal space in a few countries. In Ukraine, for example, interest payments fell to about 3 per cent of GDP in 2019, down from 4.2 per cent in 2015. This positive trend, however, is now being reversed.

Foreign currency reserves can help cushion growing external financing needs; and many energy-importing countries—including Armenia, the Republic of Moldova and Ukraine—have increased reserve holdings in recent years, amid an improving balance of payments. In contrast, in Belarus, international reserves remain precariously low. On the other hand, high gold prices have dampened the impact of the crisis on external finances in Uzbekistan and other countries with large gold holdings as part of total reserves.

The high share of foreign currency debt remains a major generator of vulnerability in the region, as countries are unable to tap financing in their own currency (figure III.1.1). While flexible exchange rates have contributed to a partial offset of the impact of declining sources of foreign income, improving competitiveness of exports and discouraging imports, currency depreciation has increased the relative debt burden, thus reducing further fiscal space. As high dollarization rates in energy-importing economies have amplified the destabilizing effect of exchange rate declines, reducing external risks would therefore require further efforts directed towards development of domestic capital markets and reduction of dollarization of those economies. Over the immediate horizon, the continued support of official creditors will be required to stave off reductions in public spending so that countries of the region can fully recover from the crisis, build back better and advance the 2030 Agenda for Sustainable Development.

Author: José Palacín (ECE)

South-Eastern Europe: standstill in tourism-related activities is dragging down economic performance

The subregion of South-Eastern Europe has displayed high rates of COVID-19 infection and has been affected by the repeated introduction of coercive social distancing measures, which has led to business closures and reduced consumer demand. Unemployment has increased from already high levels, reversing some of the improvements seen in previous years. The worsening economic situation in the European Union, the main destination for its exports and a source of investments and remittances, has depressed external demand and reduced income; and supply chain disruptions have dampened manufacturing production. However, as the external and health situations improve, growth is expected to return to the region.

The pandemic's impact in the subregion has varied

The impact of the pandemic on the countries of the subregion has varied. Serbia, with a relatively diversified economy, is likely to have seen only a modest contraction in GDP in 2020, at about 2 per cent, in part because of the implementation of a large fiscal programme (equivalent to 13 per cent of GDP), which contained the fall in output and prevented a sharp deterioration in the labour market. By contrast, the ability to implement expansionary policies designed to offset the contractionary effects of the crisis has been limited in countries with high public debt, including Albania and Montenegro, where tourism is an important contributor to overall output. Consequently, their economies are expected to have contracted by 6-11 per cent in 2020. The tourism industry's recovery will fall short of previous levels, which will exert a persistent dampening effect on economic activity in those two countries. In addition, the impact of government initiatives to support the economy through wages subsidies and credit guarantees, in particular in Albania and North Macedonia, has been limited because of the difficulties inherent in efforts to reach the informal sector.

To counteract the pandemic, the countries in the region increased health expenditures; but with lower fiscal revenues, this has resulted in widening fiscal deficits. After years of surpluses, Bosnia and Herzegovina recorded a fiscal deficit. In those countries with an independent monetary policy, namely, Albania and Serbia, the monetary authorities have cut policy interest rates to support economic activity. The policy interest rate was also cut in North Macedonia, where monetary policy is somewhat constrained by the pegging of the exchange rate to the euro.

Inflation has not been observed in the region

Inflationary pressures in the region have been absent, owing to weak demand and lower energy prices. Moreover, the noticeable deterioration of labour-market conditions in 2020 has represented a setback in the context of previous improvements.

The pandemic has exacerbated structural weaknesses

The subregion is confronting many adverse structural factors—including a challenging business environment, low productivity and the shrinking of its labour force due to population ageing and persistent outward migration—which will limit its recovery. EU accession, although not an immediate prospect, remains a critical anchor for policies and a source of financing. The aggregate GDP of South-Eastern Europe, after expanding by 3.5 per cent in 2019, is expected to have declined by 3.8 per cent in 2020, with a return to growth of 4 per cent expected in 2021 and 3.1 per cent in 2022.

Africa

GDP Growth

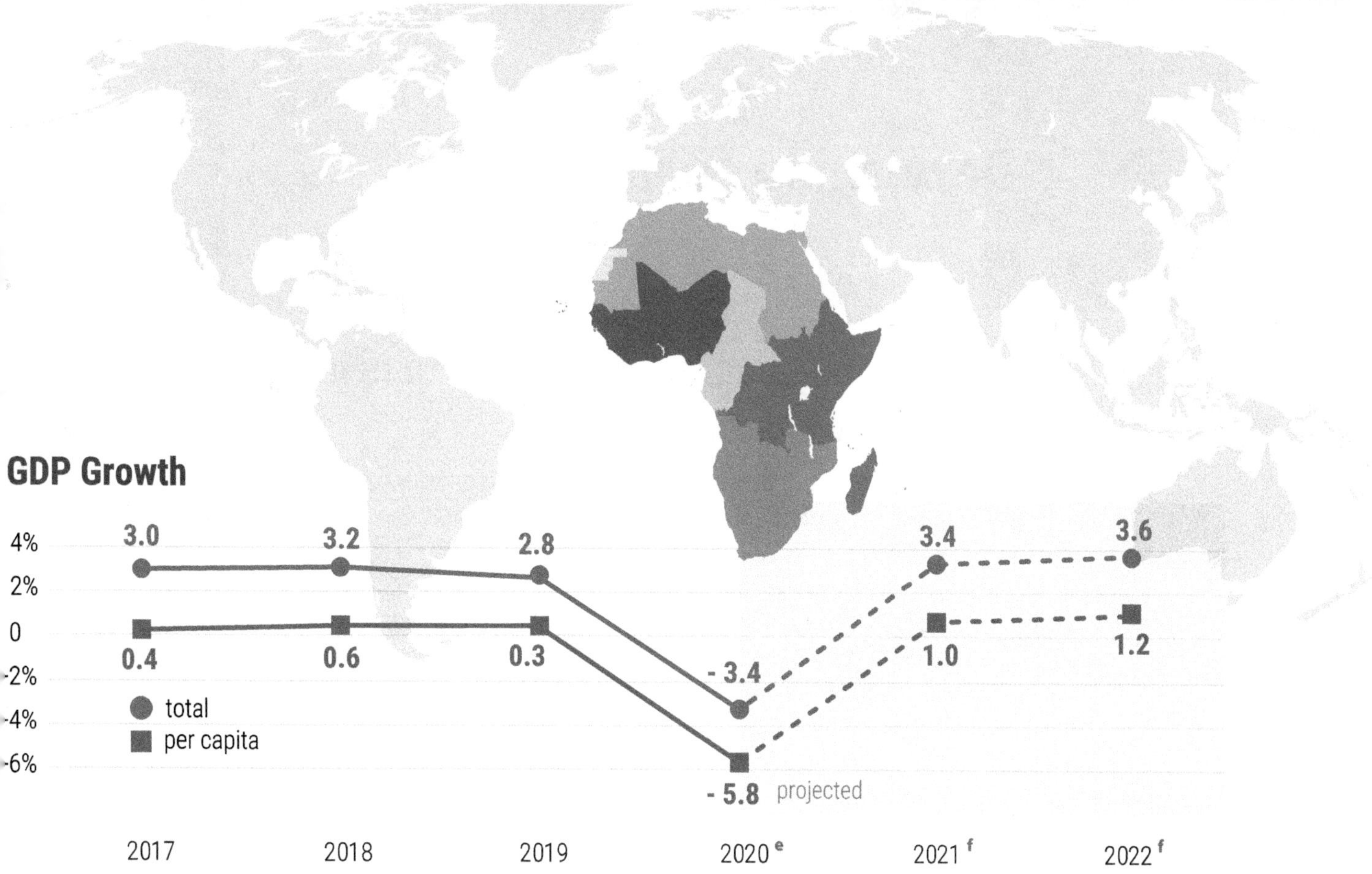

COVID-19 Cases per 100,000 people

by 1 January 2021

GDP per capita

2020

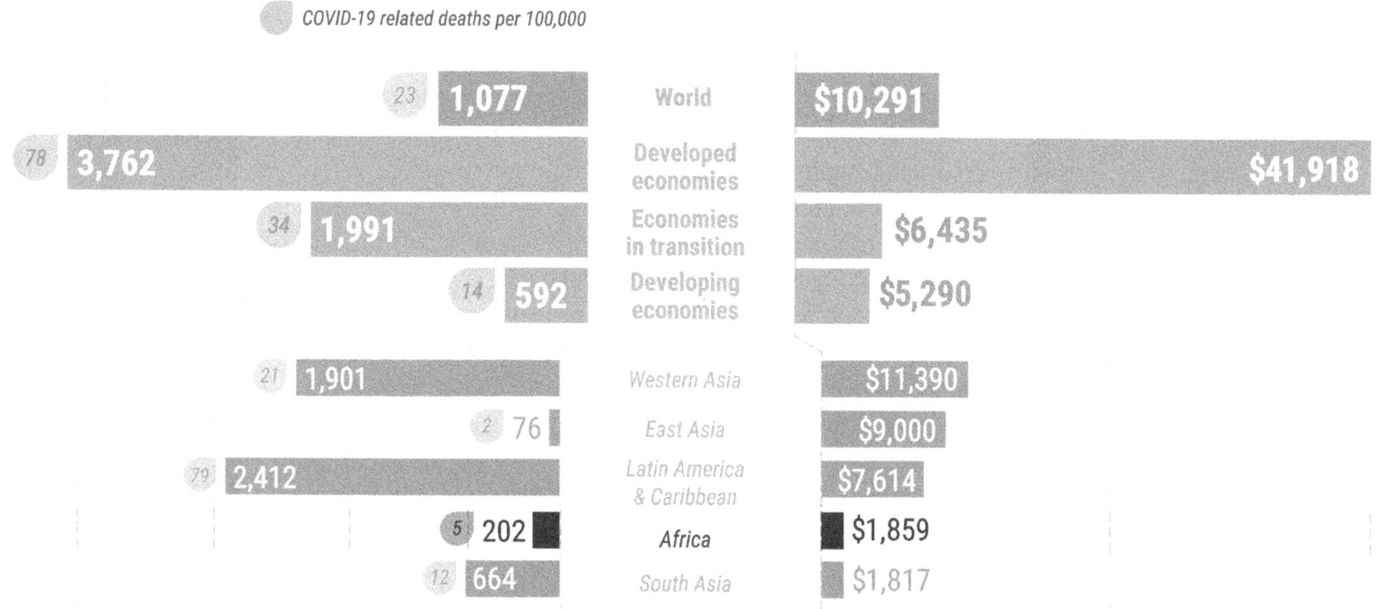

Note: The boundaries and names shown and the designations used on this map do not imply official endorsement or acceptance by the United Nations.

The map represents countries and/or territories or parts thereof for which data is available and/or analysed in *World Economic Situation and Prospects 2021*. The shaded areas therefore do not necessarily overlap entirely with the delimitation of their frontiers or boundaries.

Aggregate data for Africa, excluding Libya.

e: 2020 estimates, **f:** 2021-22 forecasts.

Source for COVID-19 data: UNDESA calculations, based on data from Johns Hopkins University.

Developing economies

Africa: a huge economic downturn is undermining development prospects

- The magnitude and unequal nature of the current crisis have resulted in an enormous setback to recent development gains, with impacts on unemployment, poverty and inequality
- After the largest economic contraction on record in 2020, there is only a feeble and uneven recovery projected for 2021, reflecting the region's limited policy space
- Forging the path towards a stronger and sustained recovery will require forceful policy actions and further multilateral support

An unprecedented economic downturn has occurred in 2020...

Africa is experiencing an unprecedented economic downturn with major adverse impacts on the long-term development of the continent. The lower external demand and lower commodity prices, the collapse of tourism and lower remittances—exacerbated through the institution of much-needed domestic lockdowns and other measures required to control the spread of the COVID-19 pandemic—have caused a severe and widespread deterioration of the economic situation. Also, more difficult financing conditions and rising public debt are exposing many countries to debt distress. Given its magnitude and unequal effects across population groups, the current crisis is causing a rise in unemployment, poverty and inequality which threatens to wipe out the development gains of recent decades. While African countries have acted quickly to limit the spread of COVID-19, most of them are nevertheless confronting enormous challenges as they strive to keep the pandemic under control and mobilize the financial resources needed to support health systems, protect vulnerable population groups and support the recovery.

...with prospects for only a moderate recovery in 2021

After a contraction of 3.4 per cent in 2020—the first in 27 years and the largest on record—Africa is projected to achieve a modest recovery, with regional GDP expanding by 3.4 per cent in 2021 (figure III.5) and 3.6 per cent in 2022. The achievement of the projected recovery is predicated on a recovery of domestic demand as generated through the relaxation of lockdown constraints and the pickup of exports and commodity prices. Still, many African countries will have to carefully manage policy priorities on the road to recovery, amid limited liquidity and elevated debt burdens. Should countries experience a spike in infections, saving lives and protecting livelihoods must remain the priority, with increased health spending and financial support to vulnerable groups. In countries where the pandemic has receded, emphasis should be placed on stimulating economic activities.

The recovery faces significant downside risks

The recovery faces downside risks, with the outlook being subject to high uncertainties over the progression of the pandemic at the local and global levels and the development of a vaccine, including its accessibility. New surges of the virus could force countries to reinstate lockdowns and other restrictive measures. So far, Africa continues to be the least

Figure III.5
Real GDP growth in Africa, by subregion

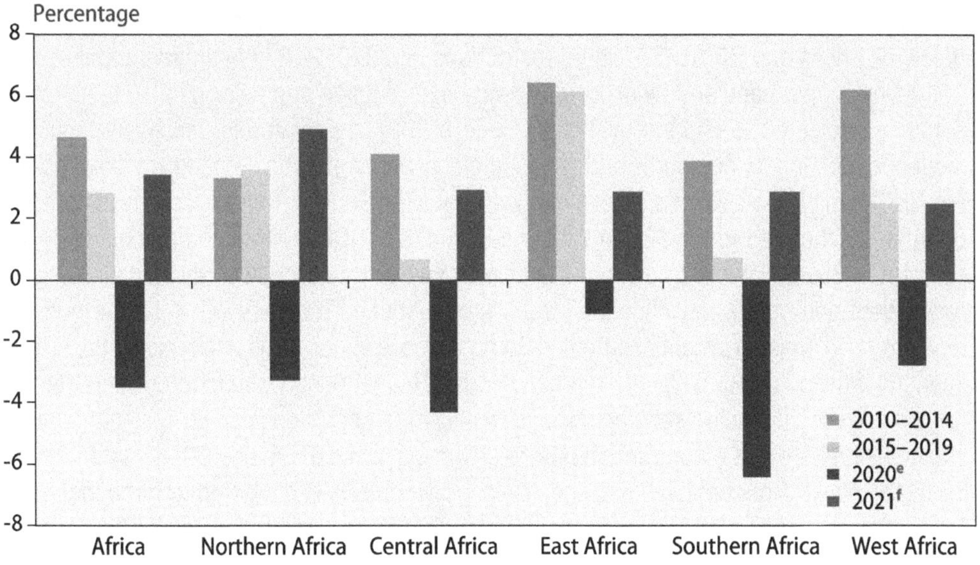

Source: UN DESA, based on projections and scenarios produced with the World Economic Forecasting Model (WEFM).

Note: Data for 2020 are estimations and data for 2021 are forecasts (**e** = estimate, **f** = forecast). Excludes Libya.

affected continent, with most cases occurring in Morocco and South Africa. At the time of writing, Africa accounts for only 3 per cent of confirmed cases (~2.5 million) and 3 per cent of reported COVID-19-related deaths (~59,000), while the continent accounts for 17 per cent of the world population. The incidence rate is highest in Cabo Verde, Libya, Morocco, South Africa and Tunisia, where tens of thousands of cumulative cases exist per million people. Given the renewed surges in several developed economies, African countries should take necessary measures to keep COVID-19 under control.

African countries must avert a painful debt crisis

The challenges related to external financing and high debt levels pose a major risk. The elevated public debt is limiting the capacity to boost spending at this critical juncture. At the same time, meagre growth prospects mean less capacity to sustain debt levels, as foreign reserves, remittances and capital flows falter and depreciations constrain the capacity to service foreign currency-denominated debt. In this regard, gross debt-to-GDP ratios are projected to have increased in 2020 by, on average, about 8 percentage points and by over 20 percentage points in the Congo, Seychelles, the Sudan, and Zambia. Indeed, six African countries are in debt distress (Mozambique, Republic of the Congo, São Tomé and Príncipe, Somalia, Sudan and Zimbabwe), while 14 other countries are at high risk (IMF, 2020d).

African countries need further support from the international community in averting a debt crisis, protracted low growth and a high-debt trap. A debt crisis would not just cause a brutal further deterioration of current conditions, making for a dire outlook, but also force painful fiscal adjustments, thereby worsening development prospects. In the absence of international assistance, some countries might find themselves facing extreme difficulties in their attempts to revive economic activity, which would make debt servicing more arduous. Against such a backdrop, social unrest and political tensions may easily escalate, which could in turn increase insecurity, violence, internal displacement, migration and food insecurity. Extreme weather events, such as floods and droughts, could also disrupt economic activities; and the La Niña phenomenon, in particular, is projected to create drier- than-normal conditions in East Africa and lead to increased rainfall in Southern Africa up until the first quarter of 2021.

Nigeria and South Africa face major economic challenges

Among the largest economies, Nigeria was dealt a severe blow by the twin shocks of low oil prices and COVID-19-related restrictions. In 2020, GDP is estimated to have contracted by 3.5 per cent, amid lockdowns, lower oil production and weak oil prices. Although output is projected to expand by 1.5 per cent in 2021, tighter foreign exchange liquidity, mounting inflationary pressures and subdued global and domestic demand are clouding the medium-term outlook. After a strict lockdown which led South Africa's economy to contract by what is estimated to have been 7.7 per cent in 2020, GDP is projected to expand by 3.3 per cent in 2021. However, it remains uncertain whether, amid power shortages, elevated public debt and policy challenges, a strong and sustained recovery will materialize in the medium-term. Raising potential output in South Africa is a step critical to tackling the strong impacts of the crisis on the labour market. In Egypt, higher fiscal expenditures supported by foreign currency financing secured through multilateral institutions and an easing monetary stance helped prevent a contraction on a yearly basis in 2020. Egypt's GDP is estimated to have grown by 0.2 per cent in 2020; and in 2021, GDP growth is projected to climb to 5.4 per cent, underpinned by a strong recovery of domestic demand and facilitated by the absence of severe balance-of-payments constraints.[1]

The crisis is severely impacting commodity- and tourism-dependent economies

The commodity-dependent economies are experiencing the full force of the crisis, and its impact has been exacerbated by the fall in the prices of commodities, especially oil. Algeria's GDP is projected to undergo an expansion of 5.2 per cent in 2021, underpinned by the recovery in crude oil production after a contraction of 7.7 per cent in 2020. Still, Algeria's fiscal position has weakened, and austerity measures planned by the government may hamper the recovery. A key challenge is the implementation of a reform agenda that can promote private investments. Angola's economic difficulties are continuing after a prolonged downturn, with GDP growth projected at only 1.2 per cent in 2021. There are also significant downside risks associated with the inability of recent macroeconomic policies and structural reforms to ensure external and fiscal sustainability.

In Central Africa, West Africa and Southern Africa, many oil and mineral exporters—the Central African Republic, the Congo, Equatorial Guinea, Namibia and Zimbabwe—face a bleak outlook. After its first contraction in almost three decades, in 2020, Cameroon's economy is projected to recover in 2021 underpinned by strengthened external and domestic demand. Risks are tilted towards the downside, however, owing to domestic political tensions and lingering conflict in English-speaking regions. Following a contraction of 0.5 per cent in 2020, the economy of Ethiopia, among agricultural exporters, is projected to expand by 2.3 per cent in 2021, which is well below the potential level of growth. While agricultural exports are showing resilience, the tourism sector's performance will likely remain restrained throughout 2021.

The crisis is severely impacting tourism-dependent economies, including Morocco and small island developing States such as Cabo Verde, Mauritius, São Tomé and Príncipe and Seychelles. As tourism accounts on average for more than 25 per cent of employment and 15 per cent of GDP in these countries, the effect on unemployment rates, poverty and inequality is clearly visible. Amid restrictions on international travel, potential tourists' fear

1 In terms of fiscal years, GDP growth is estimated at 3.5 per cent for FY 2020, and for FY 2021, the forecast is 2.1 per cent.

of contagion and renewed waves of infection worldwide, the outlook for these economies is bleak. In Morocco, GDP growth is projected at 5.6 per cent in 2021, after an estimated contraction of 7.1 per cent in 2020. In the short term, amid the shutdown of tourism and rising unemployment, economic activity will remain relatively subdued.

A major blow has been dealt to employment across the continent...

The crisis has dealt a major blow to labour markets; and in 2020, unemployment rates increased across the continent, especially in urban areas. The nature of its impact, however, has been heterogeneous, being dependent on the severity of the downturn and the stringency of containment measures. As the COVID-19 pandemic discouraged some workers from job seeking, the size of the labour force has also declined in large economies, such as Nigeria and South Africa, which can have longer-term consequences for potential growth and fiscal revenues. In South Africa, the number of employed persons declined significantly throughout 2020, with the unemployment rate climbing to a record-high of 30.8 per cent in the third quarter. In Nigeria, the unemployment rate had risen to 27.1 per cent by mid-2020. Notably, the number of Nigerians who are unemployed stands at about 21 million, which exceeds the figure for the population of any one of more than 30 countries on the continent.

...and the outlook for ending poverty, reducing inequality and other Sustainable Development Goals is worsening

The size and unequal impacts of the crisis are plunging millions into poverty and aggravating inequalities, which represents a major setback to gains reaped in the previous decades. The current job losses, disproportionally affecting women, youth and migrants in the informal sectors, are compounded by the lack of social protection systems. This being the case, countries that have recently made substantial progress on poverty reduction, such as Liberia, Mauritania, Rwanda and Sierra Leone, will likely witness years of development gains reversed or even erased.

The increase in a range of deprivations will also raise multidimensional poverty to levels observed a decade ago, on average, affecting education, health and other services such as sanitation, drinking water and electricity (United Nations Development Programme and Oxford Poverty and Human Development Initiative, 2020). For example, the crisis could affect measures such as years of schooling and school attendance in countries that were already relatively deprived (for example, Burkina Faso, Chad and the Niger). Maternal and child mortality, in addition to being directly affected by the COVID-19 pandemic, could be indirectly affected through the disruption of health systems, whose impacts may include lower rates of vaccination and regular immunization, and food deprivation.

Fiscal spending aimed at containing the impact of the crisis is on the rise...

African Governments have embarked on fiscal expansion to combat the impact of the crisis. However, given limited fiscal capacity, the responses are significantly more constrained than in the rest of the world. Indeed, the fiscal response in sub-Saharan Africa has amounted to only 3 per cent of GDP on average so far, compared with a figure for developed countries of about 7 per cent of GDP (IMF, 2020e). Most countries have opted for more immediate support in the form of additional spending and/or through the forgoing of fiscal revenue, entailing mostly non-health sector measures, although some (e.g., Chad, Namibia and South Africa) decided in favour of equity, loans and guarantee schemes, which have less immediate impact on fiscal balances but increase contingent liabilities.

...with fiscal deficits reaching double digits in a number of countries

Although Governments have implemented a wide array of measures, the delivery of assistance has been hampered by a chronic lack of safety nets which would allow a swifter allocation of resources to those most in need. On the other hand, certain digital methods—most notably mobile money transfers—have been effective in boosting social protection efforts, for example, in Burundi, Kenya, Lesotho, Malawi and the United Republic of Tanzania.

Africa's average fiscal deficit is estimated to have climbed to 10.7 per cent in 2020, from 4.9 per cent in 2019 (figure III.6). In the medium term, many countries will need both to implement reforms for creating fiscal space and to guarantee their sustainability by improving debt transparency and management, promoting efficiency of public spending and expanding the tax base.

Figure III.6
General government overall balance, selected African economies

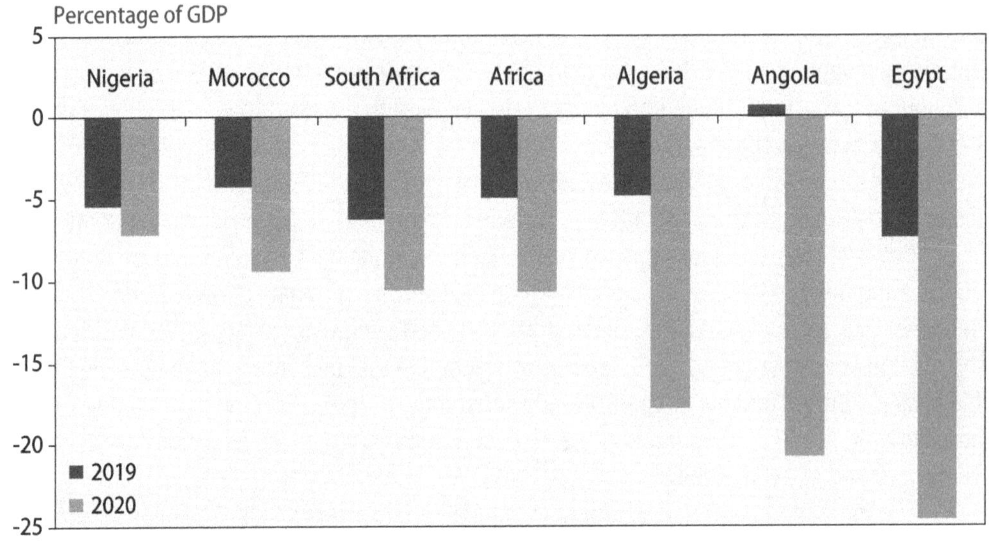

Source: UN DESA.
Note: Average for Africa excludes Libya.

Multilateral institutions have provided financial assistance, but more is needed

Multilateral institutions have been quick to provide financial assistance and debt relief. The IMF has extended $25 billion in assistance to African countries (representing 25 per cent of global financial assistance) and has provided debt service relief in the amount of almost $400 million (which represents 83 per cent of total debt service relief granted globally). For its part, the World Bank has pledged to deploy $50 billion for African countries over a 15-month period to cover operations ranging from expansion of virus testing and provision of medical equipment to the scaling up of social safety nets and support to farmers. In April 2020, the G20 finance ministers endorsed the Debt Service Suspension Initiative (DSSI), under which the world's poorest countries can postpone debt repayments due between 1 May 2020 and end of June 2021 (with the date possibly extended) and spread them over six years. Some countries—including Angola, the Congo, Djibouti, Mauritania and Mozambique—stand to save 1–2 per cent of GDP through participation in this initiative; and to date, 29 African countries have been benefiting from its implementation.

A debt moratorium will not suffice for the most indebted African countries

However, the expansion of private lenders has complicated debt relief efforts. In 2019, about 40 per cent of public and publicly guaranteed long-term external debt in sub-Saharan Africa was owed to private creditors, which have not yet begun to provide debt relief on equal terms. Rating agencies have made it clear that requests put forward by countries to private creditors for treatment on G20-comparable terms could lead to downgrades of those countries' credit rating. Strong action from Governments, citing force majeure, for example, could enforce comprehensive standstills (Rashid and Stiglitz, 2020). Yet, a debt moratorium will not suffice for the most indebted countries, and debt relief will be needed to avert defaults. In anticipation of such a need, the G20 reached an agreement, in principle, on a Common Framework for Debt Treatments, which it endorsed on 13 November, to facilitate debt restructuring on a case-by-case basis. This could represent a breakthrough under the international debt agenda. Ultimately, the current crisis not only calls for the creation of new liquidity initiatives (box III.2) but also presents an opportunity to establish a predictable, rules-based and comprehensive sovereign debt restructuring mechanism.

Aggressive monetary easing has been implemented amid contained inflationary pressures

Most African economies have sharply eased their monetary policies. In 2020, policy rates were cut in 25 countries as well as in the 14 member countries of the Central African Economic and Monetary Community (CEMAC) and the West African Economic and Monetary Union (WAEMU); other measures have included liquidity injections, moratoriums on debt repayments and restructuring of existing obligations. Cabo Verde, Guinea and Morocco also

Box III.2

Development financing through SDRs and the LSF—Options for policymakers

The COVID-19 pandemic has created financing challenges for numerous Governments in Africa saddled with high pre-COVID-19 debt levels and fiscal deficits, increasing borrowing costs, depreciating currencies and falling tax revenues (ECA, 2020). Africa's average debt-to-GDP ratio increased significantly, from 39.5 per cent of GDP in 2011 to an estimated 61.3 per cent of GDP in 2019.

Generally, borrowing costs are relatively high in Africa compared with developed and some emerging economies, as markets generally impose higher risk premiums on African economies. Estimates show that they pay about 2.9 percentage points more than their macroeconomic fundamentals would support (Olabisi and Stein, 2014), creating significant challenges for countries seeking to raise additional funding at reasonable cost. Furthermore, most African bonds are issued in dollars or in euros, which presents a high exchange rate risk for borrowing Governments if their currencies depreciate as a consequence of the COVID-19 pandemic.

These existing financing challenges have severely curtailed Africa's fiscal space for responding effectively to the pandemic, since even those economies that have access to international financial markets are finding it difficult to access liquidity on favourable terms. At the same time, the funds that have been freed by the G20 Debt Service Suspension Initiative for the poorest countries, and through International Monetary Fund (IMF) emergency funding for low- and middle-income countries, fall short of the vast amounts required to mitigate the effects of the crisis. More innovative financing measures are therefore needed to address both liquidity and solvency issues. Liquidity issues could be addressed through enhanced access to emergency funding facilities and new liquidity lines for the private sector in Africa, while solvency issues would require a more comprehensive temporary debt standstill as well as debt restructuring and reduction measures.

Special drawing rights

Access to special drawing rights (SDRs) can provide much-needed financing for many African countries. In April 2020, the IMF called on the G20 to support a new general allocation of SDRs which would benefit all countries. An alternative proposal is for developed economies to donate or lend unused portions of their existing SDR holdings to low- and middle-income countries that are in need of support. The combination of a new general allocation of SDRs with a mechanism for their subsequent reallocation to the countries most in need would further enhance the impact on liquidity.[a]

Under the IMF Articles of Agreement (articles XV and XVIII), any new general allocation of SDRs is distributed among member States in proportion to their quotas.[b] A new issuance of SDRs worth US$ 500 billion would therefore result in an allocation of US$ 11.9 billion for 51 African countries (excluding

a For further details on these two approaches in a global context, see, for example, United Nations (2020b).

b For further details regarding special drawing rights, see IMF (2020f).

(continued)

Box III.2 (*continued*)

Somalia, the Sudan and Zimbabwe) that account for a combined 2.381 per cent of IMF quotas—at no discernible cost. This is almost equivalent to the US$ 12.9 billion in debt relief offered through the Debt Service Suspension Initiative in 2020.

Alternatively, if all G20 countries were to lend or donate all of their existing unused SDRs (SDR 128.7 billion, equivalent to US$ 179.2 billion), this could go a long way towards helping African countries meet their immediate financing needs (estimated at $100 billion) (United Nations, ECA, 2020). Given the current interest rate of 0.5 per cent on SDR holdings, a voluntary redistribution of SDRs would entail a small cost for the giving country in the form of forfeited revenue. A case-by-case agreement on who is to bear this cost—the developed countries redistributing their SDRs or the developing countries receiving them—would be needed to facilitate the reallocation. For example, developed countries could levy charges, on a case-by-case basis, on lower-middle-income countries to help absorb the costs for low-income countries.

Joint proposal by ECA and PIMCO for a liquidity and sustainability facility

The liquidity problems facing economies across Africa have been exacerbated by high borrowing costs and a significant decline in capital flows. Some relief has been provided in the form of official sector debt moratoriums and standstill agreements. However, private sector debt, which has been mounting in Africa in recent years, has not benefited from such moratoriums and unlike other markets of developed countries, most COVID-impacted developing countries do not have access to central bank liquidity programmes with the ability to facilitate market functioning and help reduce financing costs. The establishment of a liquidity and sustainability facility, as proposed by ECA and PIMCO, would lead to an immediate reduction in borrowing costs for Governments in Africa and enhance their access to international capital markets and could also generate new investment interest from non-traditional investors. All risk would be borne by the private sector institutions accessing the facility, which could benefit official sector creditors and development finance institutions through its improvement of overall debt sustainability.[c]

Apart from pursuing its objective of raising the capital needed to address COVID-related needs and associated economic disruptions, the facility could also address the continent's debt problem. It is estimated that the facility could enable regional total savings in the amount of $39 billion-$56 billion over a five-year period, thereby significantly improving debt sustainability for vulnerable countries. The facility is designed for financing by central banks with hard currency reserves and would benefit for the most part vulnerable emerging market countries issuing bonds on the continent and even beyond, who face challenges related to market access and liquidity.[d]

c For further details, see the joint proposal of the Economic Commission for Africa and PIMCO regarding a liquidity and sustainability facility to improve market access for emerging market and other vulnerable sovereigns (United Nations, ECA, and PIMCO, 2020); and Songwe (2020).

d Joint proposal, p. 1, fourth bullet point.

Authors: Hopestone Kayiska Chavula and Christine Achieng Awiti (ECA)

reduced capital adequacy ratios and liquidity coverage ratios. While monetary policies will likely remain accommodative in the short-term, barring inflationary pressures, those policies should nonetheless balance supporting aggregate demand with preserving exchange rate stability, especially in case of a double-dip global recession and renewed financial turmoil.

In 2021 and 2022, aggregate inflation in Africa is projected to ease to 9.0 per cent and 6.4 per cent, respectively, as inflationary pressures decline at the same pace as the containment of the outbreak. Inflation is projected to remain elevated in only a handful of countries (e.g., South Sudan, the Sudan and Zimbabwe), amid macroeconomic imbalances coupled with deteriorating economic and financial conditions and the monetization of fiscal deficits. If renewed supply disruptions and financial turbulence were to emerge, the inflation outlook could worsen. In this regard, aggregate inflation trended upward in 2020 as a result of exchange rate depreciation in domestic currencies and food price inflation associated to supply disruptions in Nigeria, South Sudan, the Sudan and Zimbabwe.

There is an urgent need for a robust and sustained growth uplift

Africa needs a sustained revival of growth. In 2020, GDP per capita is estimated to have regressed to the level observed a decade ago (figure III.7), owing to the current crisis and the slowdown that has taken hold since the end of the commodity boom. While a focus on the short term is essential, African countries still need to lay the groundwork for a strong and inclusive development path in the medium term, which would entail the creation of decent and inclusive jobs at a large scale. As countries will be emerging from the crisis with higher levels of debt, a careful balance of policy priorities will be required to build resilience and boost productivity. This would include accelerating both implementation of the reform agenda to unlock growth opportunities and institutional changes to improve transparency and build trust in the rule of law, as well as forceful policy actions in the areas of technology adoption, climate resilience and domestic revenue mobilization. African countries should prioritize, in particular, the use and diffusion of digital technologies, supported by the expansion of affordable and universal digital infrastructure. In addition, an effective framework for the implementation of the African Continental Free Trade Area could become a major tool for promoting intra-African trade, food security and productivity.

Figure III.7
Real GDP per capita in Africa

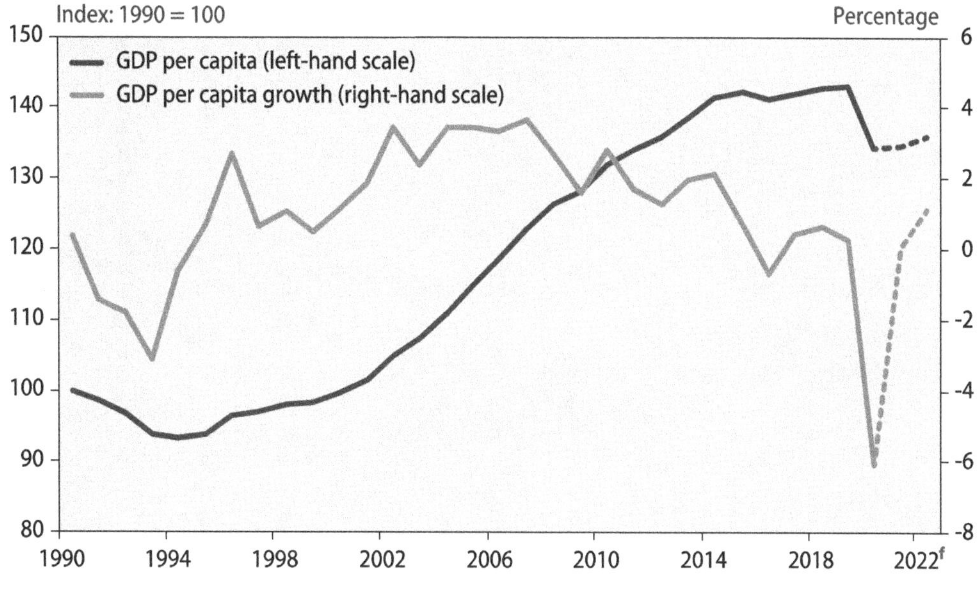

Source: UN DESA, based on projections and scenarios produced through the use of the World Economic Forecasting Model (WEFM).

Note: Data for 2020 are estimations and data for 2021 and 2022 are forecasts (**f** = forecast). Excludes Libya.

East Asia

GDP Growth

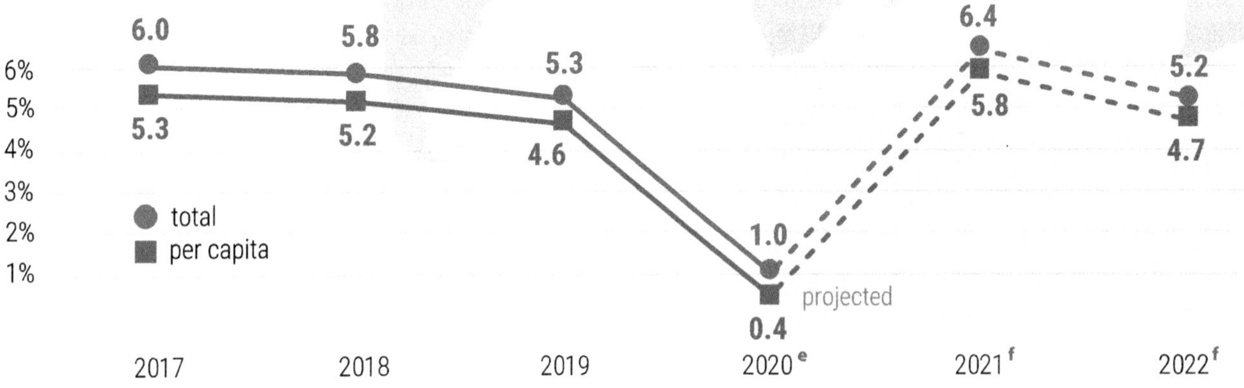

COVID-19 Cases per 100,000 people

by 1 January 2021

GDP per capita

2020

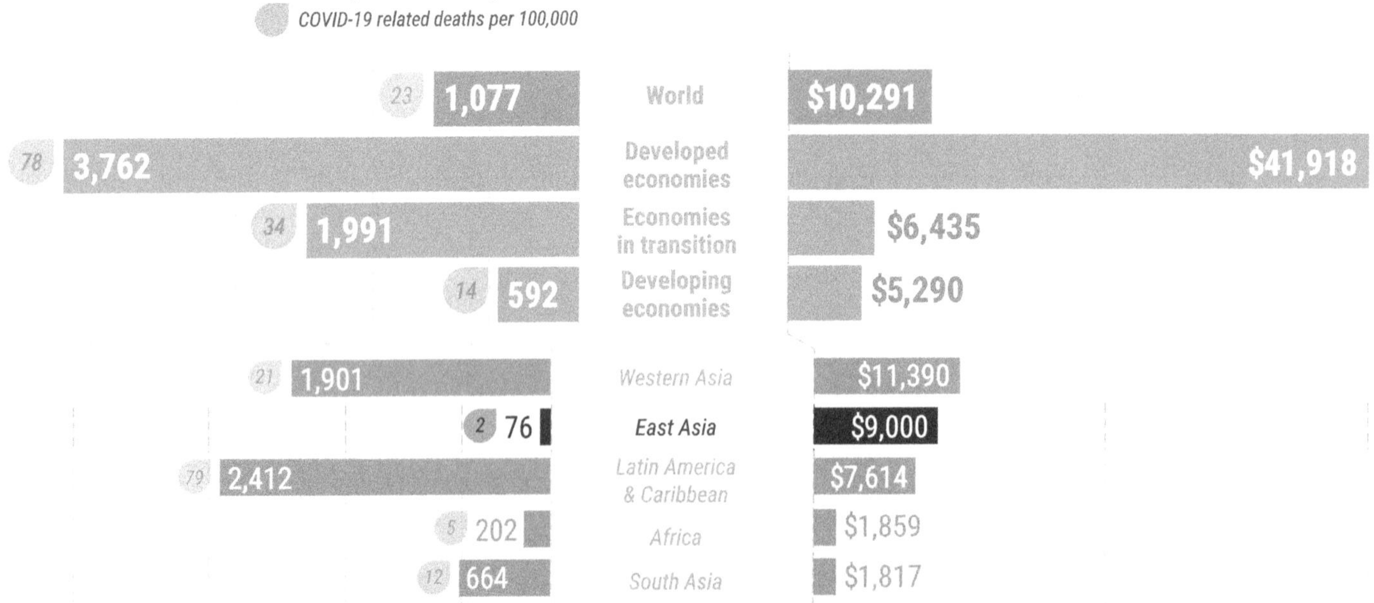

Note: The boundaries and names shown and the designations used on this map do not imply official endorsement or acceptance by the United Nations. The map represents countries and/or territories or parts thereof for which data is available and/or analysed in *World Economic Situation and Prospects 2021*. The shaded areas therefore do not necessarily overlap entirely with the delimitation of their frontiers or boundaries.

Aggregate data for Africa, excluding Libya.

e: 2020 estimates, **f:** 2021-22 forecasts.

Source for COVID-19 data: UNDESA calculations, based on data from Johns Hopkins University.

East Asia: growth is projected to rebound but downside risks are high

- The pandemic has set back the region's progress towards sustainable development
- Recovery in domestic demand needs to be supported by monetary and fiscal stimulus measures
- Key downside risks to the growth outlook stem from the potential for renewed lockdowns, rising trade tensions and persistent financial market volatility

East Asia's GDP growth decelerated sharply to 1.0 per cent in 2020, marking the region's weakest expansion since the Asian financial crisis (figure III.8). Measures designed to contain domestic outbreaks, including widespread restrictions on mobility and enforced business closures, significantly curtailed household spending and investment activities; and the region's investment prospects have been further dampened by heightened uncertainties and risk aversion. In many economies, however, the introduction of large policy stimulus packages provided some support to domestic demand during the year. On the external front, export volumes contracted owing to supply chain disruptions and weakened global economic activities. While, looking ahead, East Asia is projected to recover from a low base, with growth rebounding to 6.4 per cent in 2021, before moderating to 5.2 per cent in 2022, these growth projections are deeply contingent on the successful containment of the virus, both domestically and abroad. Indeed, with multiple waves of the pandemic threatening to trigger a renewal of lockdowns, downside risks to East Asia's growth outlook are high. Importantly, the pandemic has inflicted long-lasting socioeconomic damage on many parts of the region, with a disproportionate impact on the vulnerable segments of society.

Figure III.8
Real GDP growth in East Asia

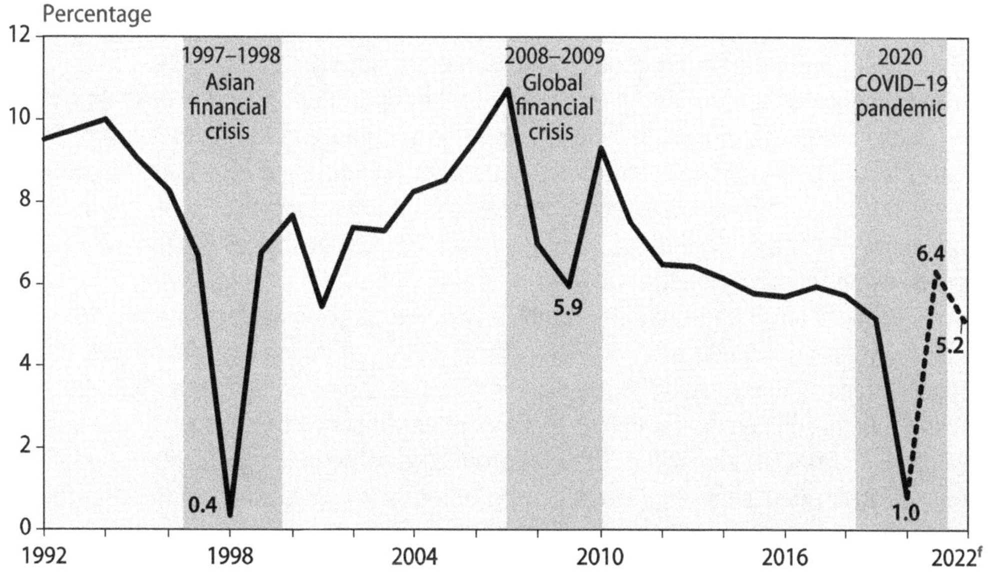

Source: UN DESA.

Note: Data for 2020 are estimations and data for 2021 and 2022 are forecasts (**f** = forecast).

Prospects for a recovery depend on the type and effectiveness of pandemic containment measures

The growth prospects for East Asia, compared with the prospects for other developing regions, suggest relatively greater resilience. With a large number of countries in the region successfully containing the virus, East Asia is likely to be the only developing region to observe positive growth in 2020. Nevertheless, the aggregate figures mask a wide divergence in the projected recovery paths of its different economies, with China being the main driver of the region's growth. For all countries, however, one of the major determinants of the strength of the short-term economic recovery will be the type and effectiveness of pandemic containment measures. Although it was the initial epicentre of the COVID-19 outbreak, China quickly contained the outbreak's spread, enabling a quick rebound in growth. In the South-East Asia subregion, most countries also imposed widespread social distancing restrictions, which resulted in sharp contractions in economic activity, particularly private consumption. However, while Singapore, Thailand, and Viet Nam flattened the curve relatively quickly and with shorter lockdowns, Indonesia, Myanmar and the Philippines are still struggling with high daily levels of new infections. In the latter group, a more prolonged period of limited mobility and weak sentiments will depress consumer spending and private investment, thus constraining the pace of recovery.

In contrast, the Republic of Korea and Taiwan Province of China did not impose large-scale social distancing regulations but, instead, utilized a strategy of extensive testing, contact tracing and targeted quarantines to control domestic outbreaks. As public confidence and domestic demand were less adversely impacted, these economies averted a severe economic downturn and had returned to a path of positive quarter-on-quarter growth by the third quarter. Indeed, the Asian Development Bank (2020) recently found that as compared with school and workplace closures, gathering bans, mass testing and contact tracing were associated with smaller output losses.

Growth prospects of the trade-dependent economies hinge on the strength of the global economic recovery

The pandemic's shock to global demand as well as its disruptions to production networks had a visible impact on East Asia's trade performance in 2020. Between January and October, nominal merchandise exports in the region contracted by 0.8 per cent compared with the same period in the previous year. However, the decline in East Asia's export performance was less severe than that of other developed and developing regions. For several East Asian economies, a surge in global demand for pandemic-related goods partially offset significantly weaker demand in other export sectors, such as commodities and automobiles. Economies that are deeply integrated into the region's electrical and electronic (E&E) production networks, including China, the Republic of Korea, and Taiwan Province of China, benefited from an increase in shipments of semiconductors, laptops and other work-from-home products. China also experienced a strong increase in exports of medical goods and protective equipment. As the effects of the pandemic subside, however, demand for these goods will eventually normalize.

Recent leading trade indicators, such as new export orders and business sentiments, point towards continued trade weakness ahead; and given strong external headwinds, the region's trade outlook is highly fragile. Several of East Asia's major trading partners, including many countries in Europe, could face a more prolonged period of lockdowns, which would weigh on their import demand. In 2020, trade tensions between China and the United States re-escalated, extending deeper into the areas of technology and telecommunication. While trade-related tensions between these two major economies could abate given the election of a new United States Administration, they are unlikely to dissipate completely considering the long-standing and complex nature of the issues under dispute.

The growth outlook for the East Asian economies will also be strongly influenced by their degree of reliance on other external sources of income, in particular tourism, remittances and commodities. Given the slow reopening of borders and cautious consumer behaviour, a swift rebound in international travel appears highly unlikely. This bleak outlook has severe implications for the growth prospects of the tourism-dependent economies in the region, given the importance of the tourism industry as a source of foreign exchange earnings, employment and income. Before the pandemic, international tourism receipts accounted for 18 per cent of GDP in Cambodia and 11 per cent of GDP in Thailand. The level of economic reliance on tourism is even higher in the Pacific island States. Indeed, in Fiji, Palau, Samoa and Vanuatu, international tourism receipts account for 17–32 per cent of GDP (figure III.9). Within these countries, the prolonged slump in tourist arrivals threatens the viability of many small and medium-sized enterprises, while at the same time affecting the livelihoods of low-skilled workers who depend on income derived from tourism-related industries.

The pandemic shock has severely impacted economies that rely heavily on other external sources of income, in particular tourism, remittances and commodities

Figure III.9
International tourism receipts in selected East Asian economies, 2019

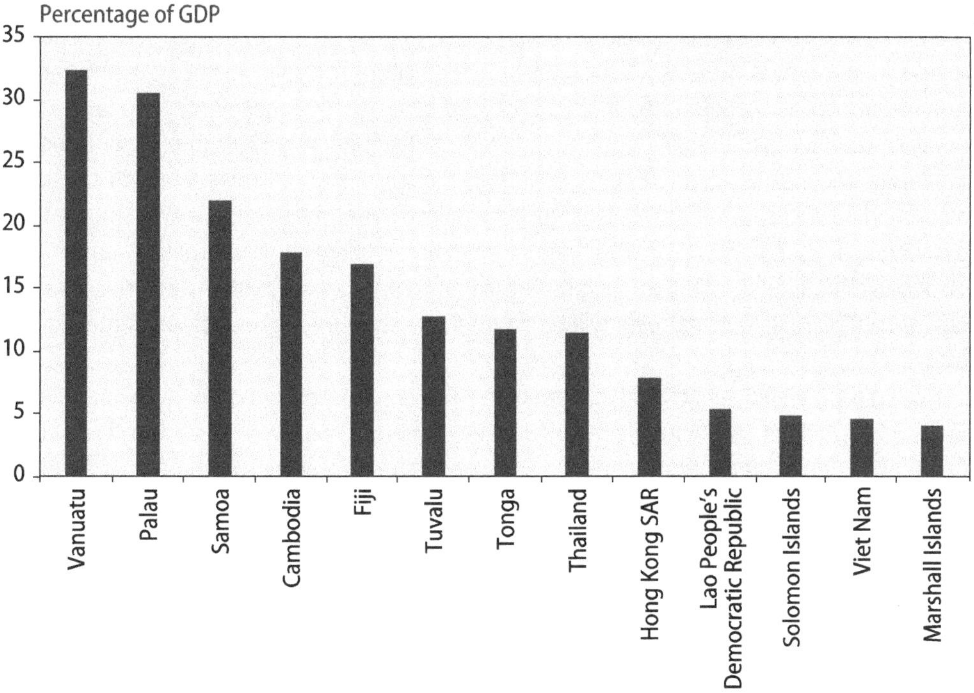

Source: UN World Tourism Organization.

The deterioration of global economic conditions will also hurt countries with a high reliance on remittance inflows. In the Philippines and Viet Nam, for example, remittances account for about 9 per cent and 6 per cent of GDP, respectively. However, from January to August 2020, the Philippines saw a contraction in remittance inflows by 2.6 per cent, a stark contrast to solid annual average growth in remittances of 4.1 per cent over the past five years. As migrant workers in host countries face employment losses and wage cuts, households in recipient countries could see a large decline in this major source of their income, which would constrain private consumption.

At the same time, the commodity-exporters, such as Brunei Darussalam, Indonesia, Mongolia and Timor-Leste, will confront strong headwinds arising from the renewed decline in global commodity prices. Not only will persistently low commodity prices hurt export revenues but they could also drive large capital outflows, exerting downward pressure on exchange rates. In addition, the collapse in commodity-related income will further weaken the fiscal positions of these economies, constraining the ability of their Governments to utilize additional fiscal stimulus measures to counter the pandemic and support domestic demand.

Growth will rebound in China, supported by stimulus measures

In China, early lockdown measures were successful in quickly containing the domestic spread of COVID-19, which enabled an economic recovery to unfold from the second quarter of 2020 onward. Following a deep GDP contraction of 6.8 per cent in the first quarter, growth picked up on the back of a rebound in industrial production and exports, as pandemic control measures were gradually removed. Growth was also supported by an increase in infrastructure investment as well as a modest revival in private consumption. Against this backdrop, the Chinese economy is likely to have expanded by 2.4 per cent in 2020, making it the only major economy in the world to have experienced positive growth in 2020.

Looking ahead, China's GDP growth is projected to increase to 7.2 per cent in 2021, before moderating to 5.8 per cent in 2022; but given the highly challenging environment, monetary and fiscal stimulus will remain in place over the outlook period. The economic recovery, however, is expected to be uneven across sectors. Public spending on infrastructure investment is likely to strengthen, supported by a rise in the issuance of local government special-purpose bonds. In contrast, private consumption is likely to recover at only a moderate pace, as weak sentiments constrain the willingness of consumers to purchase discretionary items. Also, amid elevated uncertainty over future income and employment prospects, household savings have risen to an estimated level of more than 35 per cent of disposable income. In addition, despite the initial strong revival in manufacturing production, growth in private investment will be dampened by the fragile outlook on domestic and external demand.

The region is subject to bouts of high volatility in international financial markets

Amid persistent uncertainty surrounding the duration and impact of the pandemic, financial markets in East Asia will remain subject to abrupt shifts in investor sentiment over the outlook period. In the first quarter of 2020, widespread COVID-19 outbreaks and sudden lockdowns across the world caused strong financial market turbulence and an increase in demand for safe-haven assets. Against this backdrop, the region experienced substantial portfolio outflows during the first quarter, reflected in large equity market declines and domestic currency depreciations. In Indonesia, the Philippines and Thailand, stock markets weakened by about 30 per cent compared with the previous quarter.

Financial market conditions in East Asia improved in the second quarter, as investor sentiments were supported by massive liquidity injections and unprecedented monetary stimulus measures taken by central banks, particularly in the developed economies. Moreover, financial markets began to stabilize as mobility restrictions and lockdown measures around the world were gradually eased. Nevertheless, the emergence of new waves of infections across the world in the latter part of the year continued to trigger periodic bouts of market volatility in the region.

Inflation will remain muted amid subdued domestic demand and low commodity prices

Inflationary pressures are expected to remain subdued in most East Asian economies, reflecting weak aggregate demand and low global commodity prices. In 2020, headline inflation remained below central bank targets in several countries and areas, including the

Republic of Korea, Taiwan Province of China and Thailand. Malaysia, Singapore and Thailand experienced deflation during the year amid a sharp contraction in economic activities. In contrast, inflation edged up in China and Viet Nam as an increase in domestic food prices more than offset conditions of weaker demand.

In most countries of the region, core inflation will remain low over the outlook period, amid a projected slow recovery in economic activity and soft labour-market conditions. Given renewed lockdowns in many parts of the world, disruptions to production and trade could result in supply shortages, thereby exerting upward pressure on product prices in the region. In addition, depreciation in domestic currencies due to heightened financial market volatility could drive up the cost of imported goods.

Monetary policy will remain expansionary, given the fragile economic outlook and elevated downside risks

The severe economic shock from the pandemic prompted swift monetary policy easing by central banks across the region (figure III.10). Some of the more aggressive interest rate cuts were seen in the Philippines, Mongolia, Myanmar and Viet Nam, where policy rates were reduced by between 175 and 300 basis points during the year. In the Republic of Korea and Thailand, interest rates were brought down to a record low of 0.5 per cent.

Alongside interest rate cuts, central banks in the region deployed a range of other policy tools aimed at stabilizing financial markets and supporting credit flows. These measures included lowering reserve requirement ratios, loosening countercyclical capital buffers and setting up special credit facilities. Several central banks also announced loan extensions and debt moratoriums to ease cash flow to households and businesses. For the first time, given the severity of the shock, central banks in Indonesia, the Philippines and the Republic of Korea introduced quantitative easing measures through the outright purchase of government bonds.

Amid a highly fragile growth outlook, monetary policy in East Asia is likely to remain expansionary, with further easing measures expected in parts of the region. However, given the existence of very low interest rates in many countries, central banks do not have much

Figure III.10
Interest rate cuts in selected East Asian economies, 2020

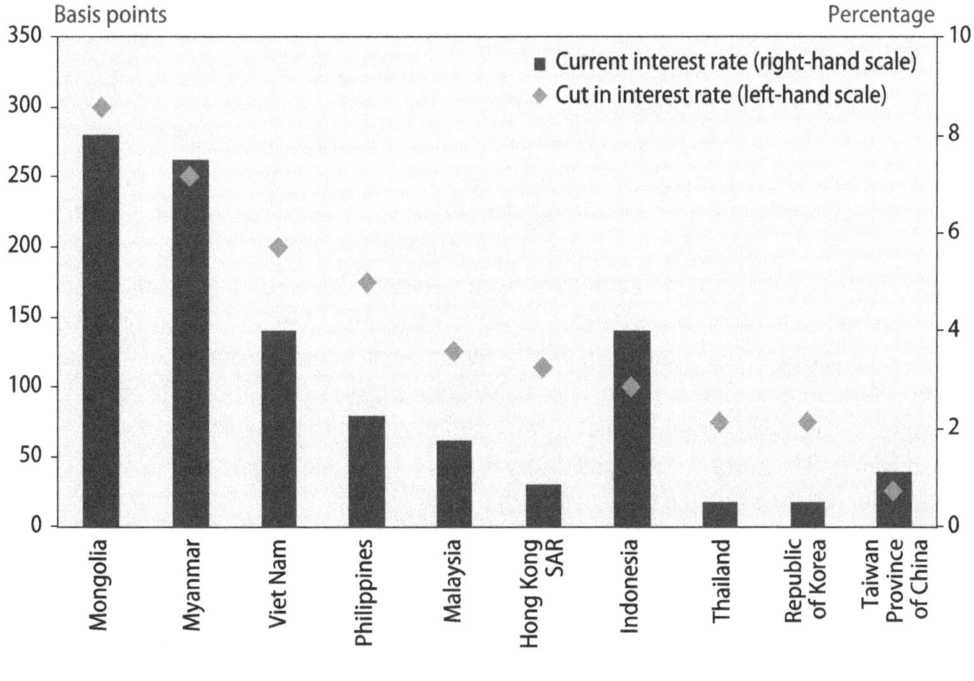

Source: National authorities.

space for embarking on further rate cuts, which may lead to more experimentation with unconventional monetary policy measures in the region. Hofman and Kamber (2020) caution, however, that pursuing unconventional monetary policies may entail risks for central banks that lack certain key preconditions for the conduct of such policies, for instance, credibility (p. 3). In addition, while a more prolonged period of low borrowing costs and high liquidity will provide some support to growth in the short term, it is likely to exacerbate financial vulnerabilities, particularly high indebtedness. It is worthy of note in this regard that household debt-to-GDP ratios in Hong Kong Special Administrative Region, Malaysia and the Republic of Korea have risen to above 80 per cent of GDP, exceeding those of several developed countries including Japan and the United States.

Fiscal stimulus measures have been critical in providing support to households and businesses

Policymakers across East Asia have rolled out large fiscal stimulus packages aimed at reducing the adverse health, economic and social consequences of the pandemic. The size of these packages have ranged from less than 2 per cent of GDP in countries such as Myanmar and the Lao People's Democratic Republic to about 20 per cent of GDP in Singapore. There were also differences among countries with respect to policy priority areas based on national circumstances. To ease cash flow for businesses, particularly small and medium-sized enterprises, the measures that were introduced included tax reliefs, soft loans that came with favourable interest rates and lending guarantees, as well as utilities and rental subsidies. Many countries, including Malaysia, Singapore and Thailand, also implemented wage subsidies to help firms retain employment. To support household incomes and consumer spending, countries in the region announced a range of measures including income tax cuts, cash transfers and the expansion of unemployment benefits. Looking ahead, fiscal policies in the region are likely to remain expansionary so as to aid economic recovery from the pandemic. In Indonesia, the Philippines and Thailand, public spending on infrastructure is likely to be an important driver of growth over the outlook period.

Downside risks to the region's growth outlook have intensified

While the prospects for an effective COVID-19 vaccine indicate that it is on the horizon, the East Asia region still faces multiple downside risks to its growth outlook. The occurrence of new waves of the pandemic before the successful development and distribution of the vaccine could lead to renewed lockdowns, which would in turn cause deeper and more prolonged economic slumps. On the financial front, stronger market turmoil could trigger a sharp tightening in credit conditions and large asset price declines, which would not only amplify the weaknesses in the real economy, but also exacerbate existing financial vulnerabilities, including high corporate and household debt.

The pandemic has intensified challenges to sustainable development in the region

The pandemic is threatening to reverse much of the progress made by the East Asian region in advancing its development agenda. Across the region, unemployment rates have risen to multi-year highs amid prolonged disruptions to economic activity. Importantly, job losses due to the pandemic have been disproportionately higher in the informal sector, where workers often earn low incomes and are vulnerable based on their employment conditions. Hence, countries characterized by a higher degree of informality are most at risk of experiencing significant setbacks to poverty eradication and a widening of inequality. In Cambodia, Indonesia and Myanmar, informality affects close to 90 per cent (or even more) of all workers (ILO, 2018). Given the high level of informality and a large digital divide, the share of workers that can work from home in South-East Asian and Pacific economies is much lower than the world average (ILO, 2020b).

The pandemic provides an opportunity for East Asian economies to reprioritize policies in order to enhance the region's resilience to future shocks. It is imperative for the region to improve social protection and public health emergency preparedness if it is to support the vulnerable segments of society. ESCAP (2019) estimates that to achieve the Sustainable Development Goals, the developing countries of Asia and the Pacific would need an additional annual investment of $1.5 trillion (or 5 per cent of GDP), including $669 billion for the provision of a social protection floor, targeted cash transfers for the poor, nutritious food, quality education and universal health-care systems.

Policymakers need to pursue recovery strategies that are greener and more inclusive and that promote a more resilient development path

As the effects of climate change on the region intensify, Governments will need to explicitly incorporate environmental sustainability into all policies going forward. This would entail, inter alia, accelerating green public investment, including in clean energy and climate-resilient infrastructure. Such investments have the potential to create jobs that are more secure, which would help to partially offset some of the job losses due to the pandemic.

GDP Growth

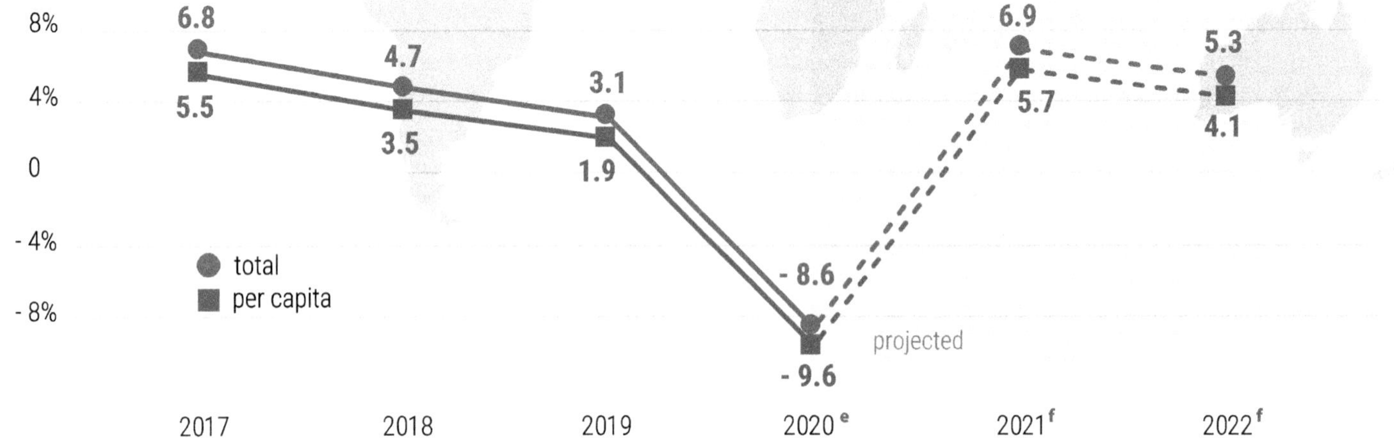

COVID-19 Cases per 100,000 people

by 1 January 2021

COVID-19 related deaths per 100,000

GDP per capita

2020

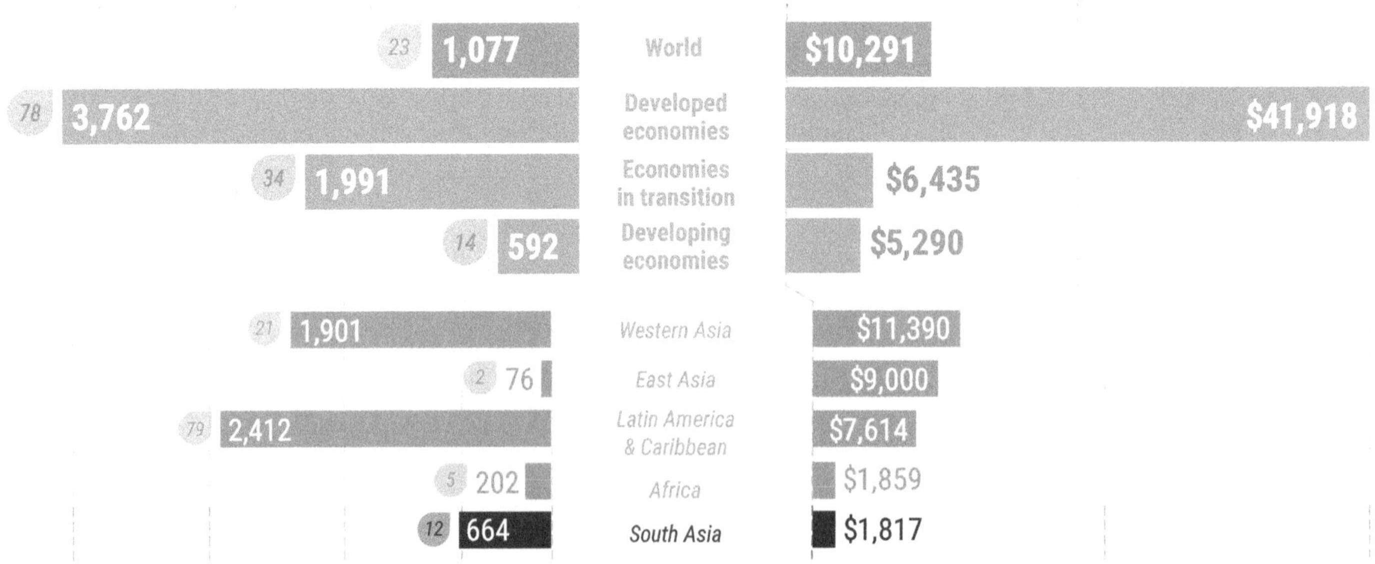

Note: The boundaries and names shown and the designations used on this map do not imply official endorsement or acceptance by the United Nations. The map represents countries and/or territories or parts thereof for which data is available and/or analysed in *World Economic Situation and Prospects 2021*. The shaded areas therefore do not necessarily overlap entirely with the delimitation of their frontiers or boundaries.

Aggregate data for Africa, excluding Libya.

e: 2020 estimates, **f:** 2021-22 forecasts.

Source for COVID-19 data: UNDESA calculations, based on data from Johns Hopkins University.

South Asia: this former champion will have to find its way back to growth

- The pandemic and resulting economic crisis have ravaged South Asia, the former growth champion, and turned it into the worst performing economic region
- Poverty has shot up and progress on many other Sustainable Development Goals has been reversed
- The long path to recovery will require structural reforms aimed at addressing South Asia's critical vulnerabilities

COVID-19 has hit an already vulnerable region...

Weak progress on achieving the Sustainable Development Goals—not least on ensuring the quality and accessibility of the public health infrastructure—has made South Asia a pandemic hotbed (United Nations, ESCAP, 2020). Before COVID-19 struck, the region was more or less on track towards achieving its targets on education (SDG 4) and energy (SDG 7) but was lagging behind with respect to access to drinking water and basic sanitation (SDG 6), ending hunger (SDG 2), reducing income inequality (SDG 10) and achieving gender equality (SDG 5), while in fact regressing in the area of peace, governance and institutions (SDG 16) (ibid.). Moreover, the region's public health infrastructure was in dire straits, with low levels of public health expenditure and few physicians, nurses, midwives and hospital beds per capita, as compared with both the global average and measures for other developing regions. This necessitated a rapid enforcement of lockdowns and other containment measures which were more stringent than those in other developing regions, even though caseloads and fatality were relatively moderate during the early months of the pandemic. The fact that, across South Asia, informal employment is the norm and social safety coverage minimal has aggravated the region's particular vulnerability to the unprecedented public health shock and limited the effectiveness of government response.

...and has left deep marks on every part of South Asia

The pandemic and the global economic crisis have consequently left deep marks on South Asia, turning this former growth champion into the worst performing region in 2020. Regional economic growth fell dramatically from 3.1 per cent in 2019 to -8.6 per cent in 2020, a far cry from the 5.1 per cent growth predicted in 2019. Without exception, all economies in the region have been badly hit by the crisis, whose impacts have been amplified and accelerated by existing vulnerabilities. Poorly organized labour markets and the absence of a reliable social safety net prevented Governments from implementing the effective restrictions needed to contain the spread of the pandemic, while fiscal constraints and limited economic diversification restricted Governments' manoeuvring space. In this regard, countries of the region compare unfavourably with other developing countries in Asia. Higher price inflation due to COVID-19-induced supply constraints limited the space required for monetary policy to make up for the shortfall. India's economic growth has fallen from 4.7 per cent in 2019 to -9.6 per cent in 2020,[2] as lockdowns and other containment efforts slashed domestic consumption without halting the spread of the disease, despite drastic fiscal and monetary stimulus. The Islamic Republic of Iran has suffered triply—from global sanctions, the sharp drop in oil prices and a fall in domestic consumption—which has deepened its

2 All growth figures for South Asia provided are on a calendar-year basis. For fiscal-year growth figures, please refer to the Statistical Annex.

already severe recession as evidenced by a growth contraction from -7.0 in 2019 to -13.3 per cent in 2020. Economic growth in Pakistan, which was already in the grip of an ongoing twin fiscal and balance-of-payments crisis, has fallen from 0.3 per cent in 2019 to -2.7 per cent in 2020. Maldives, meanwhile, took a brutal hit from the near standstill in international tourism, erasing more than a fifth of its output in 2020 compared with the previous year. Even Bangladesh, the fastest growing economy in the region, has seen economic growth fall, from 8.4 per cent in 2019 to 0.5 per cent in 2020, although this was cushioned somewhat by a recovery in trade and remittances in the second half of the year.

Perhaps even more worryingly, the crisis has devastated livelihoods across the region, reversing many years of progress on achieving the Sustainable Development Goals. As the population continued to grow in 2020, GDP per capita fell by nearly 10 per cent. Poverty is rising sharply and existing inequalities are widening. Nearly two out of five of 2020's new global poor are in South Asia. At the same time, it is the most vulnerable that have been hit hardest by the crisis. Women, for example, are significantly more likely to work in high-risk sectors and have been reported to suffer from increased domestic abuse during lockdowns; and children, especially those in poor households and in rural areas, suffer disproportionally from school closures, which could severely limit their lifetime earnings and increase their chances of ending up in poverty. Other vulnerable populations that have experienced a disproportional impact on their livelihood include slum dwellers, migrant workers and the elderly.

Recovery will be slow and uneven...

Economic growth in South Asia in 2021 will be insufficient, at 6.9 per cent, to make up for the losses of 2020, as pandemic hotspots re-emerge and, increasingly, the ability of Governments to deal with the multitude of challenges becomes exhausted. While trade, remittances and investment are expected to pick up in 2021, as much of the global economy moves towards recovery from the widespread lockdown, investment and domestic consumption in many South Asian countries will nevertheless remain subdued owing to the continuing threat of the pandemic and the scarring effects of the crisis. Regional economic growth for 2022 is forecast at 5.3 per cent, which would allow South Asia to finally exceed its 2019 economic output, albeit only marginally. On the other hand, South Asian countries that are relatively more exposed to global economic conditions, such as Bangladesh and Maldives with their high share of foreign trade and Nepal with its dependence on tourism and remittances, will enjoy a stronger rebound, of about 10 per cent growth in 2021. Other countries in the region will experience economic growth ranging from 3.1 per cent (Sri Lanka) to 7.3 per cent (India).

...and will remain subject to many risks

The recovery is subject, however, to significant risks. The forecasts assume effective containment of the virus in South Asia and the rest of the world including no further lockdowns in 2021, resurgence of global trade, and the effective continuation of fiscal stimulus and containment efforts in South Asia and other regions. Failure of any or all of these baseline assumptions to materialize could plunge the region deeper into crisis. Opportunities exist as well but they are less likely and would be less impactful than the downside risks. The development of new growth sectors, aided by targeted fiscal stimulus and the disruptive effects of the crisis, could propel South Asia's development trajectory and allow the region to make up lost ground much more quickly. A forceful global commitment to counter the negative consequences of the pandemic, particularly in developing countries, could also allow the region to build back better and stronger and regain its position as the global development champion.

But to grow back stronger, South Asian countries will need first to redouble their efforts to diversify their economies, while at the same time taking stock of global trends initiated by the crisis, such as reshoring of global value chains (GVCs) (box III.3) and a decreased appetite for contact-intensive services. Economic diversification is in fact low or minimal in many South Asian economies, with the near single-trade economies of Bangladesh (garments), the Islamic Republic of Iran (oil) and Maldives (tourism) especially exposed to external demand shocks (United Nations, 2020c). South Asian Governments should promote, in particular, the development of more complex, high-skills and high value added sectors that could reach a broader base of trade partners within and outside of South Asia or even the domestic market. Achieving resilience to external shocks should be among the most important considerations within the decision framework for policymakers in South Asia who are currently rethinking their industrial policies.

Policymakers in South Asia will need at the same time to strengthen their efforts to formalize labour markets and strengthen their social protection systems to dampen the impact of the crisis on the most vulnerable and improve macroeconomic resilience. Informal workers, accounting for over 80 per cent of workers in Bangladesh, India and Pakistan (International Labour Organization, 2020b), have indeed been far more exposed to loss of employment than formal workers during the crisis and South Asia's widespread informality has almost certainly magnified the impact of the pandemic (World Bank, 2020c). The COVID-19 fiscal response in South Asia has consisted of a vast ad hoc expansion of social assistance and direct cash transfers for the most needy but this kind of special support is neither sufficient nor sustainable. Policymakers in South Asia, taking stock of recent lessons, will therefore have to design their social protection systems with a view to rendering them more inclusive, especially for those in the informal sector, and more flexible and resilient.

However, they will need significantly more fiscal space to achieve all of these goals. While increased domestic revenue mobilization can make up for some of the shortfall, both bilateral and multilateral creditors will still need to adopt a concessionary stance to avert protracted debt crises in an already deeply wounded region. Indeed, several South Asian countries have run fiscal deficits of about 10 per cent of GDP in 2020 and government debt is forecast to grow significantly for most countries. Yet, fiscal austerity is not desirable until South Asian countries are back at or close to their economic growth potential, which might still take several years.

Box III.3

Global value chains in the aftermath of COVID-19: implications for Asia and the Pacific

While developing countries in the Asia-Pacific region continue to rely on global value chains (GVCs)[a] for sustained economic growth, structural transformation and poverty reduction, the feasibility of the GVC-led development model has come under scrutiny in recent years.

Persistent trade tensions, rising protectionism and a potential economic and technological "de-coupling" have cast a shadow over the future of GVCs. On the other hand, continuing deceleration in global trade implies that the "good old days" of fast growth fuelled by hyper-globalization may have truly peaked, even without factoring in the uncertainties brought about by automation and digitalization. Additionally, rising inequality and environmental damages call for new reflections on how to balance the economic, social and environmental objectives of GVC-led economic growth.

The COVID-19 outbreak has provided a new impetus for GVC adjustments, with an emphasis on GVC resilience and sovereign control over essential supplies for national security. These new considerations are likely to shift the focus from cost efficiency through lean inventories and just-in-time production towards resilience-building through shortened supply chains, greater redundancy in GVC configuration, larger buffer stocks of supplies, greater diversification to reduce overdependence, and digitalization for more efficient resilience management. Meanwhile, growing national security concerns are likely to trigger a further shift towards protectionism and onshoring, leaving less space for participation of developing countries in GVCs.

It is crucial for developing countries to anticipate these upcoming changes and recalibrate their related strategies and policies. In the Asia-Pacific region, three emerging trends can be anticipated. First, there will be a continuation of the shift in GVC diversification from China to established GVC hubs in neighbouring developing countries. Before COVID-19, such GVC reallocation was largely driven by rising production costs in China. Now, the need for both supplier diversification and less dependence

a GVCs break up production processes across countries, allowing them to engage in further specialization and participate in global production through the trade of components and other intermediate goods, instead of having to produce entire products by themselves.

Figure III.3.1

Global value chain (GVC) trade as share of GDP, 2005–2015

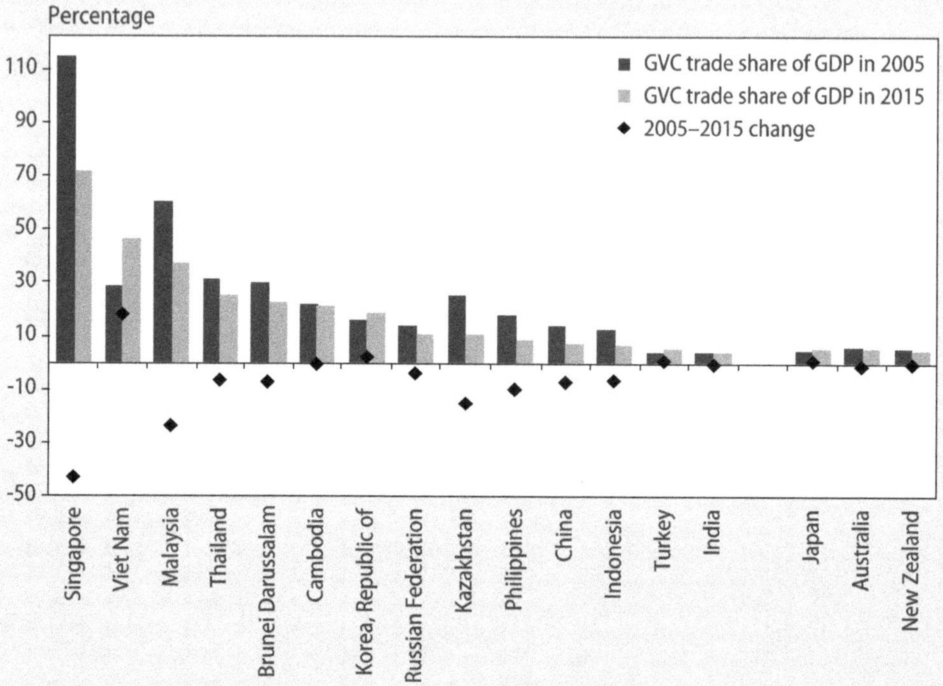

Source: ESCAP calculation, based on World Trade Organization, "Trade in value-added and global value chains" statistical profiles; and World Bank, World Development Indicators.

(continued)

Box III.3 (*continued*)

on a single country for essential intermediaries provides another motivation, potentially accelerating the process. However, the process will be gradual; and it is also more likely to benefit the more advanced members of the Association of Southeast Asian Nations in the ASEAN subregion, such as Indonesia, Malaysia, the Philippines, Thailand and Viet Nam, compared with the least developed country members of ASEAN[b] and developing countries in other parts of Asia, given the manufacturing-related advantages of the members of the first group (which are necessary for implementation of local sourcing and shortened supply chains) as well as their infrastructure and institutions.

Second, rising protectionism and ongoing trade tensions, coupled with continued deceleration in global trade and economic growth, imply intensified competition for GVC investment and less space for future GVC expansion. Under such a scenario, labour's share in GVC profits could be further squeezed. The least developed countries of the Asia-Pacific region that are hoping to leverage GVCs as an engine for development, such as Bangladesh and Cambodia, may feel both increasingly compelled to divert scarce public revenues or assets[c] to GVC investments and increasingly challenged to meet the rising social-environmental standards demanded by end consumers in the advanced economies.

Last but not least, the weaker potential of GVCs to boost growth and growing public awareness of long-term social-environmental challenges would put a greater onus on policymakers to balance the demands associated with the economic, social and environmental pillars of development. Although important for economic growth and transformation, GVCs are unlikely to generate double-digit gross domestic product (GDP) growth in the near future. Within a context of lower expectations for improvements in income, the traditional GDP-centric development thinking in the Asia-Pacific region will be challenged, with social-environmental concerns becoming more urgent.

While there is no silver bullet, two strategies could help Asia-Pacific developing countries better address these challenges. First, Asia-Pacific countries should continue promoting regional integration and regional value chains. As the Asia-Pacific region is the biggest economic block and market worldwide and possesses mature and advanced regional value chains, a more integrated regional economy would help offset many of the GVC deceleration shocks from outside. Second, Asia-Pacific countries should accelerate domestic economic reforms and transformation. Between 2005 and 2015, GVC trade as a share of GDP stagnated or decreased in most countries of the region (figure III.3.1), indicating that countries may find it increasingly difficult to rely on GVCs as a main vehicle for growth thrusts. Instead, more emphasis should be placed on maximizing the catalysing effect of GVC participation for sustained productivity improvement in the domestic economy.

b Cambodia, Lao People's Democratic Republic and Myanmar.

c Such as land or resources.

Author: Zheng Jian (ESCAP), with a contribution by Witada Anukoonwattaka (ESCAP)

Western Asia

GDP Growth

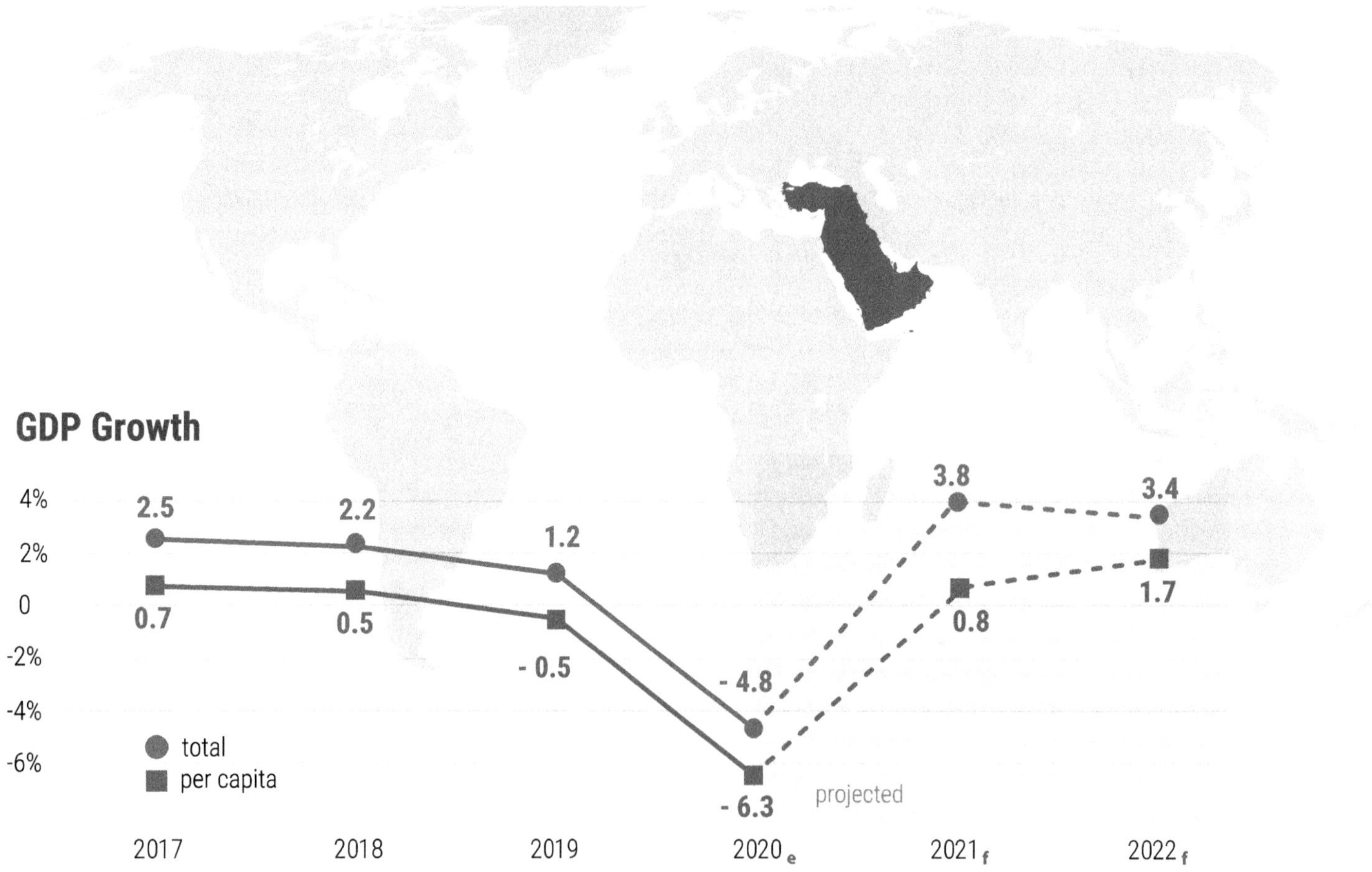

COVID-19 Cases per 100,000 people

by 1 January 2021

GDP per capita

2020

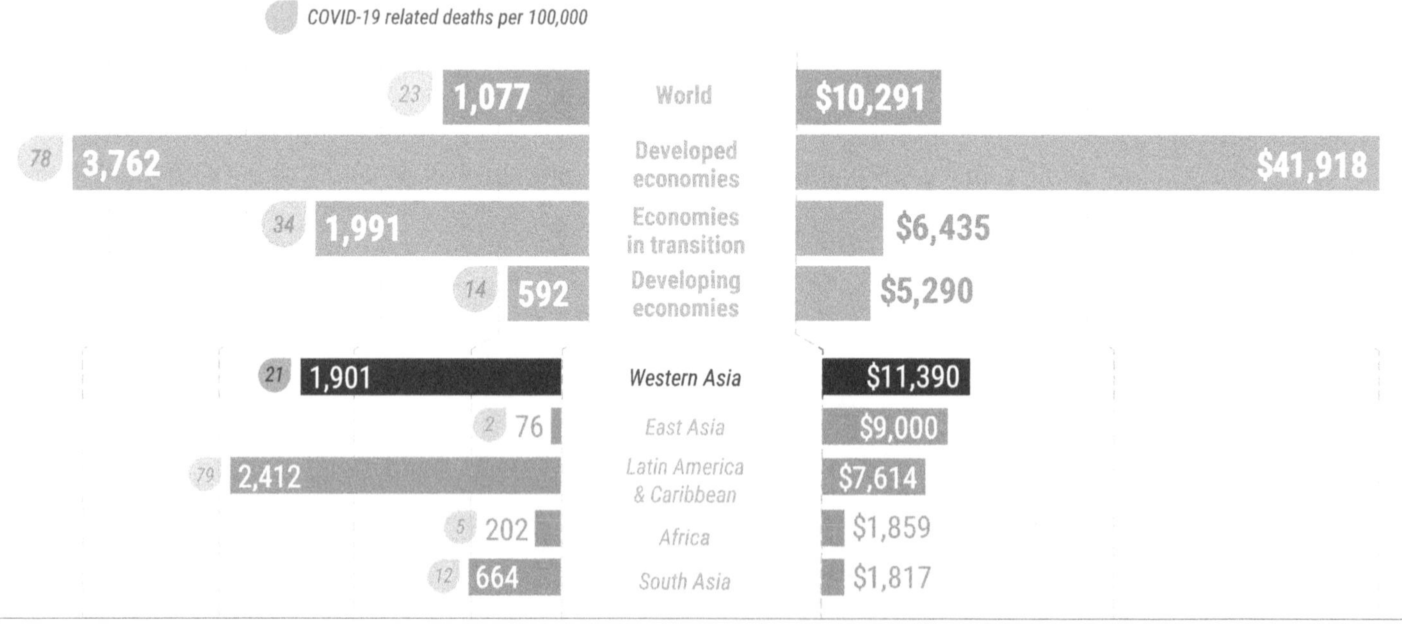

Note: The boundaries and names shown and the designations used on this map do not imply official endorsement or acceptance by the United Nations. The map represents countries and/or territories or parts thereof for which data is available and/or analysed in *World Economic Situation and Prospects 2021*. The shaded areas therefore do not necessarily overlap entirely with the delimitation of their frontiers or boundaries.

Aggregate data for Africa, excluding Libya.

e: 2020 estimates, **f:** 2021-22 forecasts.

Source for COVID-19 data: UNDESA calculations, based on data from Johns Hopkins University.

Western Asia: deteriorating fiscal positions cloud post-crisis recovery prospects

- The region faces plunging domestic and external demand.
- The midyear recovery in 2020 was weak given the region's excessive dependence on energy and tourism.
- Fiscal space has shrunk, except for a few high-income countries in the region, which clouds post-crisis recovery prospects.

Western Asia, on average, is estimated to have contracted by 4.8 per cent in 2020 and a slow recovery with growth of 3.8 per cent is expected in 2021. The COVID-19 pandemic and mitigation measures for the ensuing public health emergencies stalled economic activities in the region. Early in the second half of the year, those emergency measures were gradually relaxed; this, however, rendered several countries in the region susceptible to a second wave of outbreaks. Consequently, Western Asia's midyear rebound was weak. The pandemic's impact was felt most acutely in the region's high-performing tourism sector, and that impact led to a significant weakening of accommodation, transport, and wholesale and retail trade services. Only a few sectors—telecommunications and financial services—have managed to maintain positive growth.[3]

Heavy suffering has been inflicted on the energy sector

The energy sector, the main driver of the region's growth and government revenues, suffered significant contractions. In compliance with the Organization of the Petroleum Exporting Countries (OPEC)-led crude oil production quota, the region's major oil exporters cut crude oil production substantially. For example, crude oil production was cut by 6 per cent in Saudi Arabia and by 14 per cent in Iraq. Despite the production cuts, however, oil prices remained 35 per cent lower than the 2019 average, as global energy demand failed to recover completely from the shock of the initial shutdowns. Government revenues of the Member States of the Gulf Cooperation Council (GCC)[4] are estimated to have declined by 54 per cent on average and that of Iraq is estimated to have declined by 69 per cent (United Nations, ESCWA, 2020a).

Fiscal positions have deteriorated rapidly

Nevertheless, the GCC countries utilized their available fiscal space to implement stimulus packages of an estimated size of $194 billion to combat the current crisis (United Nations, ESCWA, 2020a). Other countries in the region, however—particularly Iraq, Jordan, Lebanon, the Syrian Arab Republic and Yemen—were not able to take countercyclical economic measures to deal with their overstretched health expenditures. The fiscal space of Iraq, despite its being the world's fifth-largest crude oil producer, contracted sharply as oil revenues were estimated to have declined by 69 per cent. In view of this general deterioration of fiscal positions (figure III.11), Governments attempted to diversify revenue sources. Saudi Arabia, for example, hiked the value added tax (VAT) rate in July from 5 to 15 per cent. However, most countries—including Saudi Arabia—became more dependent on debt to finance growing fiscal outlays.

3 See annex table A.3 for GDP estimates and forecasts for individual countries.

4 Bahrain, Kuwait, Oman, Qatar, Saudi Arabia and the United Arab Emirates.

Figure III.11

Fiscal position and public debt as a percentage of GDP in selected ESCWA countries

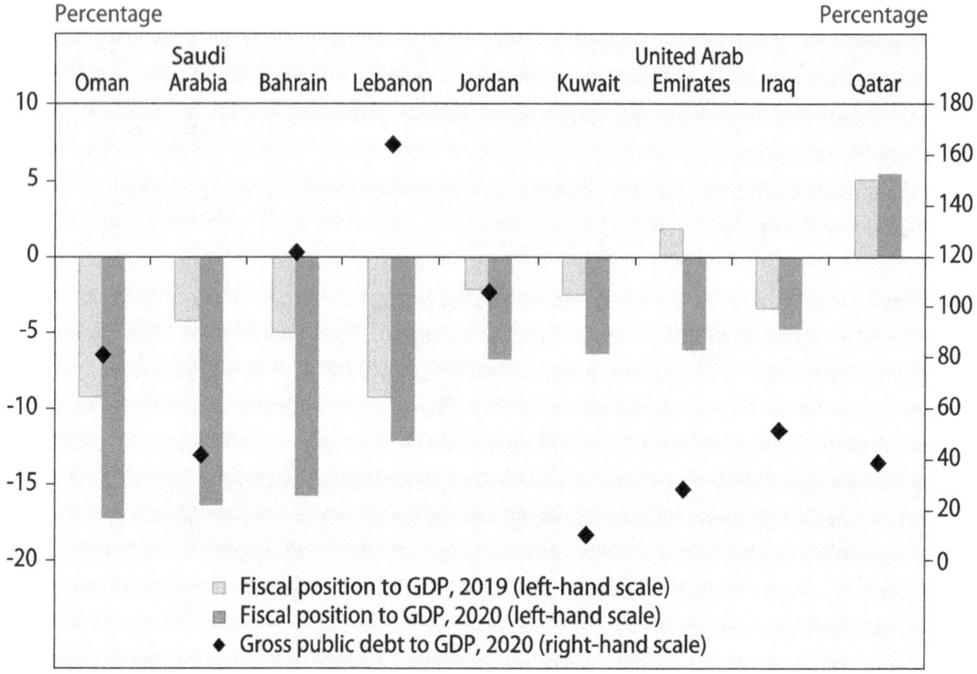

Source: United Nations, ESCWA, Survey of Economic and Social Developments in the Arab Region, 2019–2020 (forthcoming).

Conflicts and political instability are exacerbating the dire economic situation

Iraq, Lebanon, the Syrian Arab Republic, Yemen and the State of Palestine continue to endure conflicts, political instability and tense geopolitical situations. Despite the international community's appeal for a global ceasefire during the pandemic, continuing hostilities have made the region more prone to humanitarian crises. In Lebanon, the situation swiftly became dire owing to the rapid deterioration of living standards and rising poverty (box III.4).

The midyear rebound in Israel has been substantially weak

In Israel, the renewed lockdown in September instituted to contain the spread of the pandemic's second wave dented the midyear rebound, despite the Government's large-scale fiscal stimulus. In Turkey, despite an early reopening of the borders for tourists, third-quarter tourism revenue plunged by 71 per cent, compared with the same period in 2019. In addition, continuing high inflation due to a rapid depreciation of the Turkish lira has eroded real household income.

There has been a jump in the unemployment rate

Except for a few oil exporting high-income economies, the employment situation in Western Asia, was already dire before the onset of the pandemic, owing partly to ongoing armed conflicts and displacements. Along with the plunge in economic activities, job losses mounted in the second quarter of 2020. For Saudi nationals, the unemployment rate jumped to 15.4 per cent, from 11.8 per cent in the first quarter; and in Jordan, it surged to 23 per cent from 19.3 per cent in the first quarter.

Recovery prospects are highly uncertain

Economic recovery in the region will depend on global energy demand, international tourism and the extent of the recovery of domestic demand on the back of fiscal support measures. Both global energy demand and international tourism are projected to recover slowly, and to reach pre-crisis levels only after 2022. Domestic demand is projected to recover to a certain extent with the stabilization of the pandemic situation; still, without additional fiscal support, it is projected to remain below the pre-crisis level. As there are no

Box III.4
Overlapping crises in Lebanon: rising poverty, urgent needs for reform and significant regional fallout

Before the tragic explosion at the port of Beirut on 4 August 2020, Lebanon was already undergoing one of the most severe economic crises in the modern period of its history. The crisis began in autumn 2019, when the banks imposed limits on the withdrawal of dollars from Lebanese accounts in order to prevent a bank run and assure an adequate supply of dollars. Unfortunately, owing to the inability of the government to pursue economic reforms and reduce twin deficits and a massive government debt burden of more than 150 per cent of GDP, the Central Bank of Lebanon could not provide the supply of dollars needed to maintain the pegged exchange rate. This led to a further exacerbation of the economic crisis, fuelling protests where protesters called for the abolishment of the sectarian power-sharing system and the overthrow of the political elite. The COVID-19 pandemic and lockdowns initiated to contain the disease further aggravated the crisis; and the explosion at the port of Beirut only added fuel to the public discontent in Lebanese society which was already at high levels.

The Rapid Damage and Needs Assessment conducted by the World Bank in cooperation with the European Union and the United Nations in August estimates that, besides exacting a heavy human toll, the explosion has inflicted significant economic damage in the short run stemming from (a) the destruction of physical capital stock, resulting in up to 0.4 and 0.6 percentage point declines in the growth rate of real GDP in 2020 and 2021, respectively; and (b) an increase of trade costs stemming directly from the destruction of port facilities, resulting in an additional loss of 0.4 and 1.3 percentage points of GDP growth in 2020 and 2021, respectively (World Bank, European Union and United Nations, 2020).

These impacts are further deepening the double-digit contraction in real GDP growth resulting from the pre-existing economic and financial crisis and the repercussions of COVID-19. Moreover, the explosion will have important social repercussions. Before the explosion, general and extreme poverty rates as measured at the thresholds of $14 per day (2011 PPP) and $8.5 per day (2011 PPP) were at 45 per cent and 23 per cent, respectively. The headcount poverty rate is expected to have jumped from 28 per cent in 2019 to 55 per cent in May 2020, with a corresponding increase in the extreme poverty rate from 8 to 23 per cent. This would bring the total number of poor in the Lebanese population to 1.1 million and 2.7 million for the lower and upper poverty lines (as referred to above), respectively. The figure of $2.7 million poor represents an increase of 1.3 million from the figure under the reference growth scenario for 2020 (pre-COVID-19 and pre-explosion). The corresponding rise in the number of extreme poor would be 750,000 (ESCWA, 2020b).

The crisis does, however, present a unique opportunity to implement a number of required policy and social reforms, which would include:

1. Establishment of a national solidarity fund to tackle the country's humanitarian crisis and close the poverty gap. For this purpose, Lebanon should mobilize its own substantial resources, based on a fair system of shared responsibility. Currently, Lebanon has lower tax revenues as a share of GDP than other countries at a similar level of income (figure III.4.1). To reduce poverty, progressive income taxation should be introduced and taxes increased and this should be accompanied by political will and strong institutional capacity so as to ensure societal solidarity.
2. Bolstering of food and health security and social protection, which urgently requires the support of the international community.
3. Enactment of necessary economic governance reforms, limits on rent-seeking activities and enhancement of transparency and accountability. Greater transparency with respect to income and wealth would allow the ministries of finance and social affairs as well as related institutions to improve poverty-targeting practices.

While the political and economic crisis is deeply rooted in Lebanon, it will nevertheless exert significant pressure on the entire Arab world. The most important impact will be on the Syrian Arab

(*continued*)

Box III.4 (*continued*)

Figure III.4.1

GDP per capita vs. tax revenues as a percentage of GDP (latest available year)

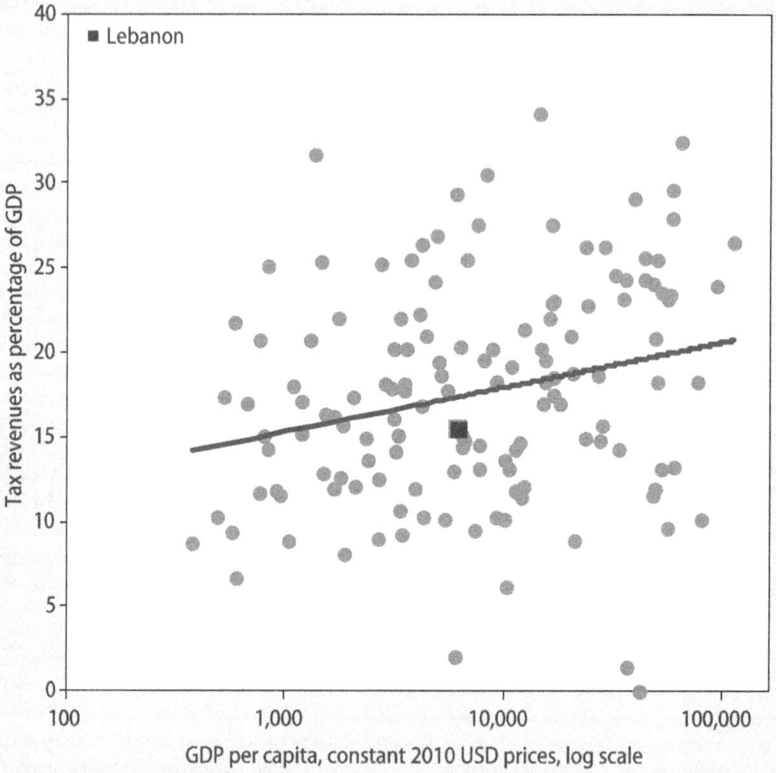

Source: World Bank, World Development Indicators database.

Republic, as the economies of both countries are deeply intertwined. Indeed, many Syrians have been affected by the informal capital controls, as they parked their savings in Lebanese banks. The crisis has also had a profound impact on the approximately 1.5 million Syrian refugees residing in Lebanon who, as a result of losing their jobs, have been unable to provide remittances to their families. Despite various obstacles, some evidence regarding return migration to the Syrian Arab Republic has emerged (Center for Operational Analysis and Research (COAR), 2019). At the same time, the current crisis will also accelerate the process through which the location of the Arab world's financial hub has been shifting to Dubai. This would extinguish Lebanon's aspirations towards building a modern economy based on financial and information technology services.

Authors: Hedi Bchir, Jan Gaska and Ahmed Moummi (ESCWA)

prospects for improvement in public revenue over 2021 and 2022, the region's high-income countries are likely to depend to a greater extent on debt financing. However, without international financial support, the current situation would likely compel the region's middle- and low-income countries to curtail or roll back fiscal support measures that could impede their economic recovery.

Latin America & Caribbean

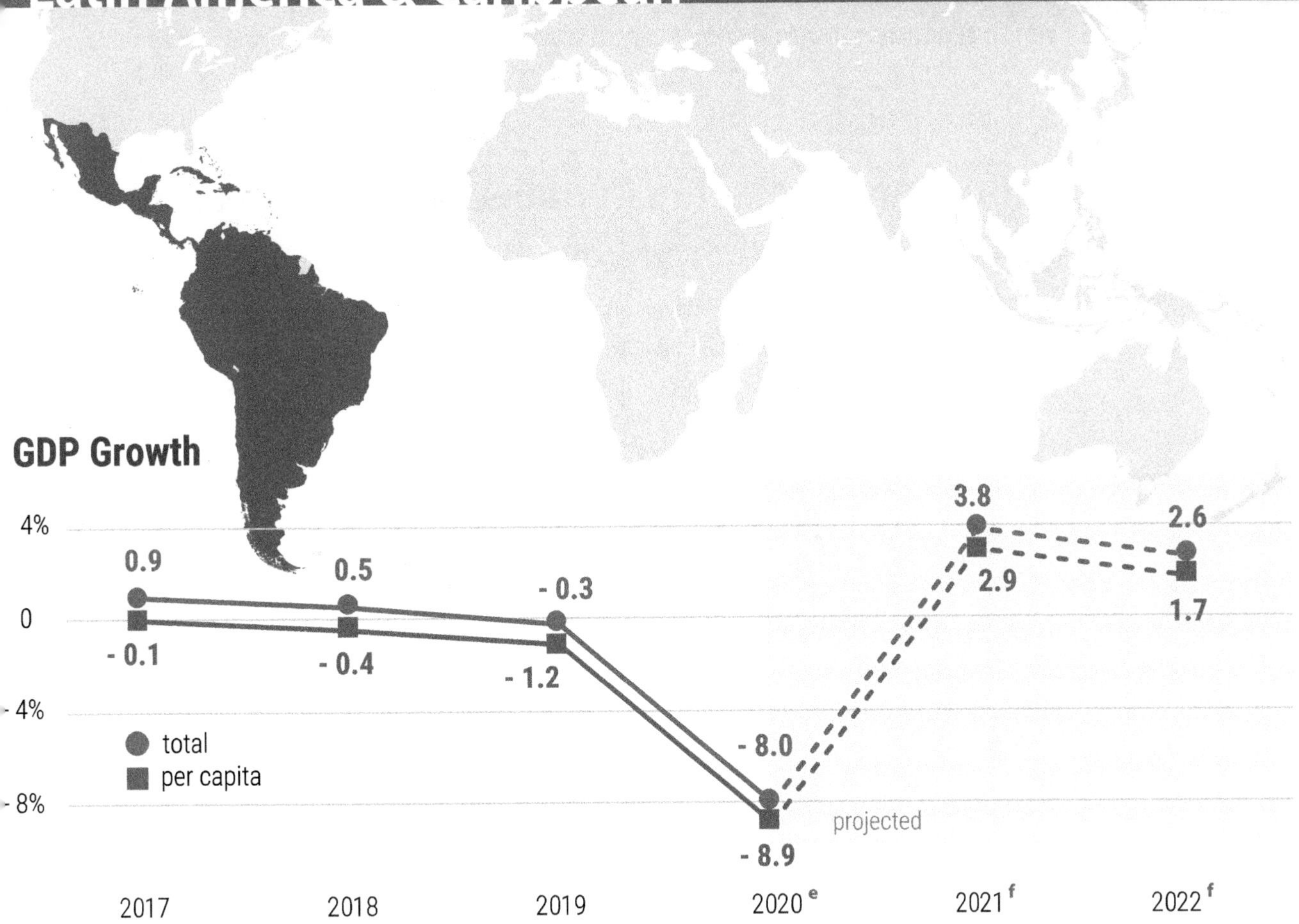

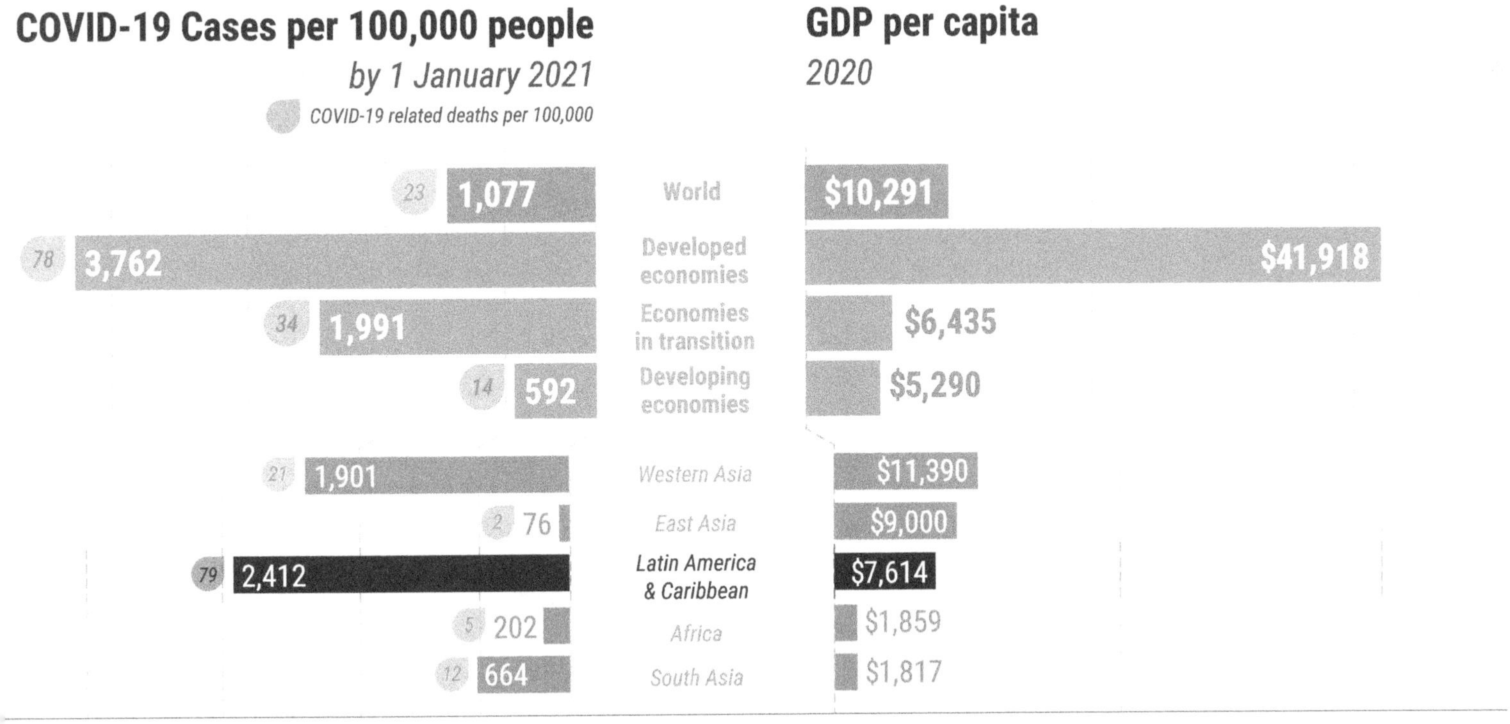

Note: The boundaries and names shown and the designations used on this map do not imply official endorsement or acceptance by the United Nations.

The map represents countries and/or territories or parts thereof for which data is available and/or analysed in *World Economic Situation and Prospects 2021*. The shaded areas therefore do not necessarily overlap entirely with the delimitation of their frontiers or boundaries.

Aggregate data for Africa, excluding Libya.

e: 2020 estimates, **f:** 2021-22 forecasts.

Source for COVID-19 data: UNDESA calculations, based on data from Johns Hopkins University.

Latin America and the Caribbean: the recovery from a historic recession will be uneven and fragile

- The pandemic has wreaked havoc on the region's economy, exacerbating deep-rooted inequalities and pushing millions into poverty
- Continued monetary and fiscal support are critical for the recovery even as policy space is constrained
- The crisis offers an opportunity to redefine the social contract and embrace a new development model

The region has suffered a devastating health and economic crisis

The COVID-19 pandemic has ravaged Latin America and the Caribbean, exacting a heavy human toll and inflicting massive economic damages. Although most countries implemented early and strict containment measures, the region has become an epicentre of the pandemic and now has one of the world's highest per capita mortality rates. The health crisis has been accompanied by an economic downturn of historic proportions, which follows several years of disappointing growth. Real GDP is estimated to have declined by 8 per cent in 2020 as prolonged national lockdowns, weaker merchandise exports and a collapse in tourism undermined economic activities. Amid a drastic contraction in employment, an estimated 45 million people in the region have been pushed into poverty, wiping out all progress made over the past 15 years (United Nations, ECLAC, 2020c). Moreover, the crisis has been responsible for further setbacks to achievement of the Sustainable Development Goals by exacerbating deep-rooted structural inequalities, for example, between formal and informal workers and women and men. Despite severe fiscal constraints, many of the region's Governments have adopted substantial stimulus packages in response to the pandemic. This support, along with monetary easing, a gradual lifting of restrictions and a pickup in global economic activity, has prompted a modest recovery starting in the second half of 2020. Regional growth is forecast at 3.8 per cent in 2021, before moderating to 2.6 per cent in 2022, while aggregate output is expected to reach its pre-crisis level only by the end of 2023. The recovery will likely remain fragile and uneven, with outlook risks tilted towards the downside. Indeed, a resurgence of infection rates could lead to a renewed tightening of containment measures. At the same time, several countries in the region face significant political risks and the possibility of a debt crisis.

Lockdowns have caused massive employment and income losses, aggravating disparities

The pandemic disrupted economic activities in Latin America and the Caribbean at a time when many countries were already engaged in a struggle against severe economic difficulties. Stagnant growth, weak investment and limited macroeconomic policy space made the region highly vulnerable to a global shock. National lockdowns and movement restrictions have led to massive employment and income losses, aggravating long-standing disparities. According to estimates of ECLAC and ILO (2020), 47 million workers in Latin America and the Caribbean lost their jobs in the first half of 2020. Working hours dropped by about 21 per cent during the first nine months, while labour income fell by 19 per cent (ILO, 2020b). Job losses have been particularly severe in the informal sector, where most occupations are contact-intensive; and women, young people and workers with low education, who make up the bulk of employment in sectors such as retail and hospitality, were disproportionately affected. Countries where informal work is widespread and where Governments implemented stringent and lengthy lockdowns have experienced the largest employment shocks. In

Peru, for example, the employment rate declined by a staggering 38 per cent in the second quarter, as the country experienced one of the region's largest output contractions.

The job and income losses have caused sharp declines in household spending, with private consumption expenditure estimated to have contracted by about 9 per cent at the regional level in 2020. As movement restrictions are gradually easing, labour markets have started to improve and this trend is expected to continue in 2021. While employment gains, especially in some of the hardest-hit countries, are expected to lift household spending and buttress the recovery, some of the damage to labour markets (through, for example, departure of women from the workforce) will not be quickly reversed and will leave lasting scars.

Investment will recover from a deep slump but only slowly

Investment activities across the region have taken a severe—and most likely prolonged—hit from the pandemic. Amid falling consumer demand, temporary business closures and heightened uncertainties, firms have rolled back planned investment. Gross fixed capital formation declined by an estimated 13 per cent in 2020, dwarfing the drop experienced in 2009. According to estimates of the United Nations Conference on Trade and Development (UNCTAD) (2020b), foreign direct investment (FDI) flows to the region may have fallen by up to 50 per cent, with the travel and leisure and oil sectors recording the largest losses. While investment bounced back quickly following the global financial crisis, a fast recovery seems unlikely this time around. Uncertainties over the regional and global outlook, coupled with lingering effects of the crisis such as elevated unemployment and increased fiscal pressures, are expected to weigh on capital spending over the coming year. According to the baseline projections, gross fixed capital formation in the region will increase by about 7 per cent in 2021 and by only 3 per cent in 2022.

Recoveries in exports, commodity prices and remittances are providing some measure of uplift

The domestic shock from the undermining of economic activities has been compounded by a rapidly deteriorating external environment as the global economy fell into recession. Many of the region's economies are highly dependent on external inflows, most notably from commodity exports, personal remittances and tourism (figure III.12). Merchandise exports and commodity prices plummeted in the first half of 2020 but have since been recovering, which can be attributed mostly to a strong rebound in industrial activity and import demand from China. During the first eight months of 2020, the level of exports of Latin America and the Caribbean was about 6 per cent lower than one year ago. Unlike oil prices, which remain well below the pre-pandemic level, prices of metals and agricultural commodities have recouped their losses. Further moderate gains are expected for 2021, which should support the recovery in major commodity exporters. Brazil, Chile and Peru appear to be best positioned to gain from a continued rebound in China. Remittance flows to the region have also pulled back from the lows during the second quarter and are likely to be at a level for the year similar to that in 2019, which has helped to mitigate the shock experienced by remittance-dependent Central American countries. Tourism flows, by contrast, have remained at a standstill, leading to sharp contractions in economic activities in Caribbean countries; but given a gradual improvement in international tourism flows in the coming years, most Caribbean countries should expect a recovery from a low base.

Monetary policy is expected to remain extraordinarily accommodative

Across the region, Governments have responded forcefully to limit the socioeconomic fallout from the crisis, preserve financial stability and boost recovery. Central banks have eased monetary policy and provided liquidity to the financial system; and in many countries, policy rates have been cut to record low levels. These measures have supported credit flows to the private sector, reduced market stress and contributed to a general improvement in financial conditions. After a spike in risk aversion triggered massive capital outflows from the region in early 2020, the situation improved in the subsequent quarters. However, given

Figure III.12

Contribution of commodity exports, personal remittances and tourism to GDP, 2016–2018 average

Percentage

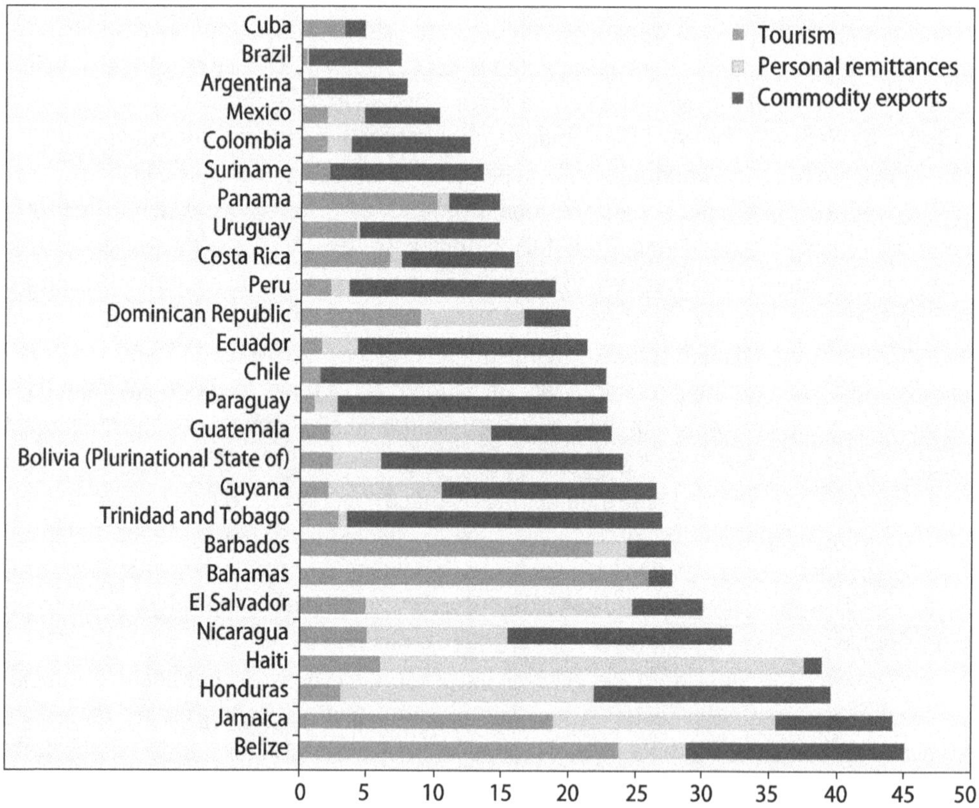

Sources: UN DESA, based on World Bank, World Development Indicators; UNWTO; and UNCTAD.

Note: Personal remittance data is not available for the Bahamas and Cuba.

considerable global uncertainties and the subdued outlook for Latin America and the Caribbean, capital flows will likely have a rocky period ahead. In view of subdued inflationary pressures—mainly due to the persistence of economic slack—monetary policy is set to remain extraordinarily accommodative in the coming years.

Fiscal support remains critical for recovery

Large-scale fiscal policy stimulus has been critical in strengthening health-care systems and providing lifelines to firms and households. Although many countries entered the pandemic with sizeable fiscal deficits and high public debt levels, Governments deployed considerable resources to combat the economic shock. Brazil, Chile and Peru introduced the largest packages in the region in terms of direct support through additional expenditure and forgone revenue. The total fiscal stimulus packages in these three countries, including loans, equity injections and government guarantees, are estimated to have amounted to 10–15 per cent of GDP. In this regard, Brazil's fiscal response stands out, as it provided sizeable support for households and workers, which helped boost the country's recovery during the second half of 2020. By contrast, Mexico's fiscal response has been relatively timid, as the Government focused on public finance sustainability even as economic activity collapsed; and in many Caribbean economies, government responses were constrained by a lack of fiscal space. Going forward, Governments must balance the need for further fiscal

Box III.5
Challenges for fiscal policy in Latin America and the Caribbean during the post-pandemic period

The unfolding COVID-19 crisis has triggered an economic and social collapse of historic proportions in Latin America and the Caribbean and it is projected that a return to pre-crisis levels of economic activity will take from two to three years. The region, like so many others, is witnessing the destruction of its productive capacities and increases in unemployment, poverty and inequality and will bear the scars of the collapse well into the future. In this context, the role of the public sector and active fiscal policy will be crucial as Governments support recovery efforts and seek to build back better. The post-pandemic period will provide an opportunity for the countries of the region to embark on a different development path, one that is in line with the objectives of the 2030 Agenda for Sustainable Development, and to move in the direction of establishing welfare States and introducing universal social protection schemes.

Despite the strain on public accounts induced by the crisis—with average central government gross public debt projected to increase by 9.3 percentage points of gross domestic product (GDP) and to reach 55.3 per cent of GDP in 2020—fiscal austerity is not an option and would inflict unnecessary social and economic harm. Active fiscal policies should link the short term (covering the emergency period) with the medium and long terms by gearing public spending, tax policies and regulations towards achieving the goals of stimulating economic activities and building back better. These goals will require policies that boost aggregate demand, while placing an emphasis on supporting household consumption, encouraging investment, reducing inequalities, protecting the environment and laying the foundations for sustainable development. To the extent that these policies revived the economy and improved the prospects for post-pandemic growth, they would also increase the likelihood that countries could meet their fiscal commitments despite the prevailing constraints.

Creating the space necessary to maintain active fiscal policies hinges critically on the mobilization of both domestic and external resources. With tax evasion and avoidance as well as illicit financial flows endemic in the region, there is substantial room at the national level to enhance the State's revenue-raising capacity. The Economic Commission for Latin America and the Caribbean (ECLAC) (2020b) estimates that countries in Latin America lost a combined US$ 325 billion in 2018, equivalent to 6.1 per cent of GDP, owing to income tax and value added tax non-compliance. Tax expenditures—i.e., revenue losses resulting from the granting of various forms of tax advantages—are widely used and entail significant forgone revenues, averaging 3.7 per cent of GDP between 2015 and 2019 (ibid.). The region's tax intake is low and skewed towards regressive indirect taxes. Moreover, the fact that direct taxation on income—particularly personal income—and on property is especially weak deprives countries of revenues and leaves tax systems with little leverage for reducing income and wealth inequalities. There are also opportunities to bolster taxation of other tax bases, such as those related to the digital economy, and to levy corrective taxes related to the environment and public health. At the same time, given the importance of fiscal policy as a development tool, it is critical that the efficiency, effectiveness and equity of public interventions be enhanced. Further, the resources mobilized need to be channelled towards investments that reduce inequality and foster growth.

Efforts at the national level must be supplemented by greater access to external finance on favourable terms, whether it be on international markets or through international financial institutions. To this end, the international community should take steps to create additional liquidity for low- and middle-income countries, for example, through issuance of special drawing rights (SDRs), along with implementation of mechanisms that allow for the transfer of SDRs between countries. Other measures could include additional funding for multilateral lending institutions and promotion of closer cooperation between central banks. International cooperation should play a fundamental role in coordinating debt service suspensions and the creation of an international mechanism for the restructuring of sovereign debt.

(*continued*)

Box III.5 (*continued*)

The fund to alleviate COVID-19 economics (FACE) is a concrete example of this type of innovative mechanism conceived to unleash the potential for greater international cooperation in providing assistance during the period of recovery from the COVID-19 pandemic. As described in a proposal put forward by the President of Costa Rica in September 2020 within the framework of the seventy-fifth session of the General Assembly, the objective of the FACE initiative would be to mitigate the social and economic impact of the pandemic and contribute to a sustainable recovery. Under the initiative, the distribution of global liquidity to developing countries would be improved through the provision of concessional financing to those countries with a repayment period of 50 years and interest rates close to zero. Importantly, the allocation criteria of the fund—which would hold US$ 516 billion in resources, to be channelled through multilateral banks—would not incorporate conditionalities.

Source: Economic Survey of Latin America and the Caribbean: Main Conditioning Factors of Fiscal and Monetary Policies in the Post-COVID-19 Era.

support to buttress a fragile recovery against increased pressure for fiscal consolidation. Box III.5 discusses the region's fiscal challenges in the post-pandemic period.

Threat of another lost decade has prompted calls for a new development model

Although Latin America and the Caribbean is projected to see a moderate recovery in 2021 and 2022, the danger of another lost decade—in terms of both economic growth and development progress—is looming large. Judging by the experience of previous crises, there are likely to be significant long-term damages to potential output. Prolonged school closures, challenges associated with remote learning activities and persistently high unemployment are expected to have a negative effect on human capital accumulation (Di Gropello, 2020). This could exacerbate skills shortages, which have been a severe constraint in many countries. In addition, corporate and public investment will likely be hampered by heightened uncertainties, sluggish household demand and needs for fiscal consolidation, which could, in turn, further stifle innovation and productivity growth. In this context, an increasingly fragmented and uncertain global trade environment could generate external headwinds to exports and growth. Against this challenging backdrop, ECLAC has called for a new development model which centres on a radical transformation of production and consumption patterns, with investment redirected towards productivity, environmental stewardship, employment and social inclusion (United Nations, ECLAC, 2020b; OECD, 2020a).

Statistical annex

Data sources, country classifications and aggregation methodology

The statistical annex contains a set of data that the *World Economic Situation and Prospects* (*WESP*) employs to delineate trends in various dimensions of the world economy.

Data sources

The annex was prepared by the Economic Analysis and Policy Division (EAPD) of the Department of Economic and Social Affairs of the United Nations Secretariat (UN DESA). It is based on information obtained from the Statistics Division and the Population Division of UN DESA, as well as from the five United Nations regional commissions, the United Nations Conference on Trade and Development (UNCTAD), the International Monetary Fund (IMF), the World Bank, the Organization for Economic Cooperation and Development (OECD), Eurostat and national sources. Estimates for 2020 and forecasts for 2021 and 2022 were made by EAPD in consultation with the regional commissions and UNCTAD, guided partly by the World Economic Forecasting Model (WEFM) of EAPD.[1] Longer-term projections are based on a technical model-based extension of the WEFM.

Data presented in the WESP may differ from those published by other organizations for several reasons, including differences in timing, sample composition and aggregation methods. Historical data may differ from those in previous editions of the WESP because of updating and changes in the availability of data for individual countries.

Country classifications

For analytical purposes, the WESP classifies all countries of the world into one of three broad categories: developed economies, economies in transition and developing economies.[2] The composition of these analytical groupings, specified in tables A, B and C, is intended to reflect basic economic country conditions, and are not strictly aligned with the regional classifications defined by the Statistics Division of UN DESA known as M49.[3] Table A.4 reports estimates for regional GDP growth according to the M49 definitions for comparison. Several countries (in particular the economies in transition) have characteristics that could place them in more than one category; however, for purposes of analysis, the groupings have been made mutually exclusive. Within each broad category, some subgroups are defined based either on geographical location or on ad hoc criteria, such as the subgroup of "major developed economies", which is based on the membership of the Group of Seven.

In parts of the analysis, a distinction is made between fuel exporters and fuel importers. An economy is classified as a fuel exporter if the share of fuel exports in its total merchandise exports is greater than 20 per cent and the level of fuel exports is at least 20 per cent higher than that of the country's fuel imports (table D). This criterion is drawn from the share of fuel exports in the total value of world merchandise trade. Fuels include coal, oil and natural gas.

1 See Altshuler and others (2016).

2 These analytical groupings are not strictly aligned with geographical groupings of Developed Regions and Developing Regions designated by the Statistics Division of UN DESA.

3 Full details of the M49 standard can be found on the Statistics Division website at https://unstats.un.org/unsd/methodology/m49.

For other parts of the analysis, countries have been classified by their level of development as measured by per capita gross national income (GNI). Accordingly, countries have been grouped as high-income, upper-middle-income, lower-middle-income and low-income (table E). To maintain compatibility with similar classifications used elsewhere, the threshold levels of GNI per capita are those established by the World Bank. Countries with less than $1,036 GNI per capita are classified as low-income countries, those with between $1,036 and $4,045 as lower-middle-income countries, those with between $4,046 and $12,535 as upper-middle-income countries, and those with incomes of more than $12,535 as high-income countries. GNI per capita in dollar terms is estimated using the World Bank Atlas method,[4] and the classification in table E is based on data for 2019.

The list of the least developed countries (LDCs) is determined by the United Nations Economic and Social Council and, ultimately, by the General Assembly, on the basis of recommendations made by the Committee for Development Policy. The basic criteria for inclusion require that certain thresholds be met with regard to per capita GNI, a human assets index and an economic vulnerability index.[5] As of December 2020, there were 46 LDCs (table F).

The WESP also makes reference to the group of heavily indebted poor countries (HIPCs), which are considered by the World Bank and IMF as part of their debt-relief initiative (the Enhanced HIPC Initiative).[6] In December 2018, there were 39 HIPCs (table G).

Aggregation methodology

Aggregate data are either sums or weighted averages of individual country data. Unless otherwise indicated, multi-year averages of growth rates are expressed as compound annual percentage rates of change. The convention followed is to omit the base year in a multi-year growth rate. For example, the 10-year average growth rate for the decade of the 2000s would be identified as the average annual growth rate for the period from 2001 to 2010.

The WESP utilizes market exchange rate conversions of national data in order to aggregate output of individual countries into regional and global totals. The growth of output in each group of countries is calculated from the sum of gross domestic product (GDP) of individual countries measured at 2015 prices and exchange rates. This method supplies a reasonable set of aggregate growth rates for a period of about 15 years, centred on 2015.

The exchange rate-based aggregation method differs from the one mainly applied by the IMF for their estimates of world and regional economic growth, which is based on purchasing power parity (PPP) weights. Over the past two decades, the growth of world gross product (WGP) on the basis of the exchange rate-based approach has been below that based on PPP weights. This is because developing countries, in the aggregate, have seen significantly higher economic growth than the rest of the world in the 1990s and 2000s and the share in WGP of these countries is larger under PPP measurements than under market exchange rates. Table I.1 in Chapter I reports world output growth with PPP weights as a comparator.

4 See http://data.worldbank.org/about/country-classifications.

5 *Handbook on the Least Developed Country Category: Inclusion, Graduation and Special Support Measures* (United Nations publication, Sales No. E.18.II.A.1). Available at https://www.un.org/development/desa/dpad/wp-content/uploads/sites/45/2018CDPhandbook.pdf.

6 International Monetary Fund, Debt Relief Under the Heavily Indebted Poor Countries (HIPC) Initiative. Available at https://www.worldbank.org/en/topic/debt/brief/hipc.

Table A
Developed economies

Northern America	Europe: European Union	Europe: Other Europe	Major developed economies (G7)
Canada	Austria[a]	Iceland	Canada
United States	Belgium[a]	Norway	France
	Bulgaria	Switzerland	Germany
	Croatia	United Kingdom[b]	Italy
	Cyprus[a]		Japan
	Czechia		United Kingdom
	Denmark		United States
	Estonia[a]		
	Finland[a]		
	France[a]		
	Germany[a]		
	Greece[a]		
	Hungary		
	Ireland[a]		
	Italy[a]		
Developed Asia and Pacific	Latvia[a]		
Australia	Lithuania[a]		
Japan	Luxembourg[a]		
New Zealand	Malta[a]		
	Netherlands[a]		
	Poland		
	Portugal[a]		
	Romania		
	Slovakia[a]		
	Slovenia[a]		
	Spain[a]		
	Sweden		

a Member of euro area.

b The United Kingdom withdrew from the EU on 31 January 2020 and is therefore excluded from all EU aggregations.

Table B
Economies in transition

South-Eastern Europe	Commonwealth of Independent States and Georgia[a]	
Albania	Armenia	Republic of Moldova
Bosnia and Herzegovina	Azerbaijan	Russian Federation
Montenegro	Belarus	Tajikistan
North Macedonia	Georgia[a]	Turkmenistan
Serbia	Kazakhstan	Ukraine[b]
	Kyrgyzstan	Uzbekistan

a Georgia officially left the Commonwealth of Independent States on 18 August 2009. However, its performance is discussed in the context of this group of countries for reasons of geographic proximity and similarities in economic structure.

b Starting in 2010, data for the Ukraine excludes the temporarily occupied territory of the Autonomous Republic of Crimea and Sevastopol.

Table C
Developing economies by region[a]

Africa

North Africa
- Algeria
- Egypt
- Libya
- Mauritania
- Morocco
- Sudan
- Tunisia

Central Africa
- Cameroon
- Central African Republic
- Chad
- Congo
- Equatorial Guinea
- Gabon
- Sao Tome and Prinicipe

East Africa
- Burundi
- Comoros
- Democratic Republic of the Congo
- Djibouti
- Eritrea
- Ethiopia
- Kenya
- Madagascar
- Rwanda
- Somalia
- South Sudan
- Uganda
- United Republic of Tanzania

Southern Africa
- Angola
- Botswana
- Eswatini
- Lesotho
- Malawi
- Mauritius
- Mozambique
- Namibia
- South Africa
- Zambia
- Zimbabwe

West Africa
- Benin
- Burkina Faso
- Cabo Verde
- Côte d'Ivoire
- Gambia
- Ghana
- Guinea
- Guinea-Bissau
- Liberia
- Mali
- Niger
- Nigeria
- Senegal
- Sierra Leone
- Togo

Asia

East Asia[b]
- Brunei Darussalam
- Cambodia
- China
- Democratic People's Republic of Korea
- Fiji
- Hong Kong SAR[c]
- Indonesia
- Kiribati
- Lao People's Democratic Republic
- Malaysia
- Mongolia
- Myanmar
- Papua New Guinea
- Philippines
- Republic of Korea
- Samoa
- Singapore
- Solomon Islands
- Taiwan Province of China
- Thailand
- Timor-Leste
- Vanuatu
- Viet Nam

South Asia
- Afghanistan
- Bangladesh
- Bhutan
- India
- Iran (Islamic Republic of)
- Maldives
- Nepal
- Pakistan
- Sri Lanka

Western Asia
- Bahrain
- Iraq
- Israel
- Jordan
- Kuwait
- Lebanon
- Oman
- Qatar
- Saudi Arabia
- State of Palestine
- Syrian Arab Republic
- Turkey
- United Arab Emirates
- Yemen

Latin America and the Caribbean

Caribbean
- Bahamas
- Barbados
- Belize
- Guyana
- Jamaica
- Suriname
- Trinidad and Tobago

Mexico and Central America
- Costa Rica
- Cuba
- Dominican Republic
- El Salvador
- Guatemala
- Haiti
- Honduras
- Mexico
- Nicaragua
- Panama

South America
- Argentina
- Bolivia (Plurinational State of)
- Brazil
- Chile
- Colombia
- Ecuador
- Paraguay
- Peru
- Uruguay
- Venezuela (Bolivarian Republic of)

a Economies systematically monitored for the World Economic Situation and Prospects report. These analytical groupings differ from the geographical aggregations defined according to M49.

b Throughout the report the term 'East Asia' is used in reference to this set of developing countries, and excludes Japan.

c Special Administrative Region of China.

Table D
Fuel-exporting countries

		Developing countries			
Developed countries	**Economies in transition**	Latin America and the Caribbean	Africa	East Asia	South Asia
Australia Norway	Azerbaijan Kazakhstan Russian Federation Turkmenistan	Bolivia (Plurinational State of) Colombia Ecuador Trinidad and Tobago Venezuela (Bolivarian Republic of)	Algeria Angola Cameroon Chad Congo Equatorial Guinea Gabon Libya Mozambique Nigeria	Brunei Darussalam Democratic People's Republic of Korea Indonesia Mongolia Papua New Guinea	Iran (Islamic Republic of) **Western Asia** Bahrain Iraq Kuwait Oman Qatar Saudi Arabia United Arab Emirates Yemen

Source: UN DESA, based on data from UNCTAD.

Table E
Economies by per capita GNI in June 2020[a]

High-income		Upper-middle-income		Lower-middle-income	
Australia	Latvia	Albania	Iraq	Algeria[b]	Mauritania
Austria	Lithuania	Argentina	Jamaica	Angola	Mongolia
Bahamas	Luxembourg	Armenia	Jordan	Bangladesh	Morocco
Bahrain	Malta	Azerbaijan	Kazakhstan	Benin[c]	Myanmar
Barbados	Mauritius[c]	Belarus	Lebanon	Bhutan	Nepal[c]
Belgium	Netherlands	Belize	Libya	Bolivia (Plurinational State of)	Nicaragua
Brunei Darussalam	New Zealand	Bosnia and Herzegovina	Malaysia	Cabo Verde	Nigeria
Canada	Norway	Botswana	Maldives	Cambodia	Pakistan
Chile	Oman	Brazil	Mexico	Cameroon	Papua New Guinea
Croatia	Panama	Bulgaria	Montenegro	Comoros	Philippines
Cyprus	Poland	China	Namibia	Congo	Republic of Moldova
Czechia	Portugal	Colombia	North Macedonia	Côte d'Ivoire	Sao Tome and Principe
Denmark	Qatar	Costa Rica	Paraguay	Djibouti	Senegal
Estonia	Republic of Korea	Cuba	Peru	Egypt	Solomon Islands
Finland	Romania[c]	Dominican Republic	Russian Federation	El Salvador	Sri Lanka[b]
France	Saudi Arabia	Ecuador	Samoa	Eswatini	State of Palestine
Germany	Singapore	Equatorial Guinea	Serbia	Ghana	Timor-Leste
Greece	Slovakia	Fiji	South Africa	Honduras	Tunisia
Hong Kong SAR[d]	Slovenia	Gabon	Suriname	India	Ukraine
Hungary	Spain	Georgia	Thailand	Kenya	United Republic of Tanzania[c]
Iceland	Sweden	Guatemala	Turkey	Kiribati	Uzbekistan
Ireland	Switzerland	Guyana	Turkmenistan	Kyrgyzstan	Vanuatu
Israel	Taiwan Province of China	Indonesia[c]	Venezuela (Bolivarian Republic of)	Lao People's Democratic Republic	Viet Nam
Italy	Trinidad and Tobago	Iran (Islamic Republic of)		Lesotho	Zambia
Japan	United Arab Emirates				Zimbabwe
Kuwait	United Kingdom				
	United States				
	Uruguay				

Low-income			
Afghanistan	Democratic Republic of the Congo	Madagascar	Sudan[b]
Burkina Faso	Eritrea	Malawi	Syrian Arab Republic
Burundi	Ethiopia	Mali	Tajikistan
Central African Republic	Gambia	Mozambique	Togo
Chad	Guinea	Niger	Uganda
Democratic People's Republic of Korea	Guinea-Bissau	Rwanda	Yemen
	Haiti	Sierra Leone	
	Liberia	Somalia	
		South Sudan	

Source: World Bank, Country classification by income (https://datahelpdesk.worldbank.org/knowledgebase/articles/906519).

a Economies systematically monitored for the World Economic Situation and Prospects report, based on World Bank country classifications by income.
b Indicates the country has been shifted downward by one category from previous year's classification.
c Indicates the country has been shifted upward by one category from previous year's classification.
d Special Administrative Region of China.

Table F
Least developed countries *(as of December 2020)*

Africa		East Asia	South Asia	Western Asia	Latin America and the Caribbean
Angola	Malawi	Cambodia	Afghanistan	Yemen	Haiti
Benin	Mali	Kiribati	Bangladesh		
Burkina Faso	Mauritania	Lao People's Democratic Republic	Bhutan		
Burundi	Mozambique	Myanmar	Nepal		
Central African Republic	Niger	Solomon Islands			
Chad	Rwanda	Timor Leste			
Comoros	Sao Tome and Principe	Tuvalu[a]			
Democratic Republic of the Congo	Senegal				
Djibouti	Sierra Leone				
Eritrea	Somalia				
Ethiopia	South Sudan				
Gambia	Sudan				
Guinea	Togo				
Guinea-Bissau	Uganda				
Lesotho	United Republic of Tanzania				
Liberia	Zambia				
Madagascar					

Source: UN DESA (https://www.un.org/development/desa/dpad/wp-content/uploads/sites/45/publication/ldc_list.pdf).
a Economies not systematically monitored for the World Economic Situation and Prospects report.

Table G
Heavily indebted poor countries *(as of March 2020)*

Post-completion point HIPCs[a]		Pre-decision point HIPCs[b]
Afghanistan	Haiti	Eritrea
Benin	Honduras	Sudan
Bolivia	Liberia	
Burkina Faso	Madagascar	
Burundi	Malawi	
Cameroon	Mali	
Central African Republic	Mauritania	
Chad	Mozambique	
Comoros	Nicaragua	
Congo	Niger	
Côte D'Ivoire	Rwanda	
Democratic Republic of the Congo	Sao Tome and Principe	
Ethiopia	Senegal	
Gambia	Sierra Leone	
Ghana	Somalia	
Guinea	Togo	
Guinea-Bissau	Uganda	
Guyana	United Republic of Tanzania	
	Zambia	

Source: The World Bank and the International Monetary Fund (https://www.worldbank.org/en/topic/debt/brief/hipc).
a Countries that have qualified for irrevocable debt relief under the HIPC Initiative.
b Countries that are potentially eligible and may wish to avail themselves of the HIPC Initiative or the Multilateral Debt Relief Initiative (MDRI).

Table H
Small island developing States

United Nations members		Non-UN members/Associate members of the Regional Commissions[a]
Antigua and Barbuda[a]	Marshall Islands[a]	American Samoa
Bahamas	Mauritius	Anguilla
Bahrain	Nauru[a]	Aruba
Barbados	Palau[a]	Bermuda
Belize	Papua New Guinea	British Virgin Islands
Cabo Verde	Saint Kitts and Nevis[a]	Cayman Islands
Comoros	Saint Lucia[a]	Commonwealth of Northern Marianas
Cuba	Saint Vincent and the Grenadines[a]	Cook Islands
Dominica[a]	Samoa	Curaçao
Dominican Republic	Sao Tome and Príncipe	French Polynesia
Federated States of Micronesia[a]	Seychelles[a]	Guadeloupe
Fiji	Singapore	Guam
Grenada[a]	Solomon Islands	Martinique
Guinea-Bissau	Suriname	Montserrat
Guyana	Timor-Leste	New Caledonia
Haiti	Tonga[a]	Niue
Jamaica	Trinidad and Tobago	Puerto Rico
Kiribati	Tuvalu[a]	Sint Maarten
Maldives	Vanuatu	Turks and Caicos Islands
		U.S. Virgin Islands

Source: UN DESA (https://sustainabledevelopment.un.org/topics/sids/list).
a Economies not systematically monitored for the World Economic Situation and Prospects report.

Table I
Landlocked developing countries

Landlocked developing countries		
Afghanistan	Ethiopia	North Macedonia
Armenia	Kazakhstan	Paraguay
Azerbaijan	Kyrgystan	Republic of Moldova
Bhutan	Lao People's Democratic Republic	Rwanda
Bolivia (Plurinational State of)	Lesotho	South Sudan
Botswana	Malawi	Tajikistan
Burkina Faso	Mali	Turkmenistan
Burundi	Mongolia	Uganda
Central African Republic	Nepal	Uzbekistan
Chad	Niger	Zambia
Eswatini		Zimbabwe

Source: UN-OHRLLS (http://unohrlls.org/about-lldcs/country-profiles/).

Table J
International Organization for Standardization of Country Codes

ISO Code	Country	ISO Code	Country	ISO Code	Country	ISO Code	Country
AFG	Afghanistan	DZA	Algeria	LBN	Lebanon	ROU	Romania
AGO	Angola	ECU	Ecuador	LBR	Liberia	RUS	Russian Federation
AIA	Anguilla	EGY	Egypt	LBY	Libya	RWA	Rwanda
ALB	Albania	ERI	Eritrea	LCA	Saint Lucia	SAU	Saudi Arabia
AND	Andorra	ESP	Spain	LIE	Liechtenstein	SDN	Sudan
ARE	United Arab Emirates	EST	Estonia	LKA	Sri Lanka	SEN	Senegal
ARG	Argentina	ETH	Ethiopia	LSO	Lesotho	SGP	Singapore
ARM	Armenia	FIN	Finland	LTU	Lithuania	SLB	Solomon Islands
ATG	Antigua and Barbuda	FJI	Fiji	LUX	Luxembourg	SLE	Sierra Leone
AUS	Australia	FRA	France	LVA	Latvia	SLV	El Salvador
AUT	Austria	FSM	Micronesia (Federated States of)	MAR	Morocco	SMR	San Marino
AZE	Azerbaijan	GAB	Gabon	MCO	Monaco	SOM	Somalia
BDI	Burundi	GBR	United Kingdom of Great Britain and Northern Ireland	MDA	Republic of Moldova	SRB	Serbia
BEL	Belgium	GEO	Georgia	MDG	Madagascar	SSD	South Sudan
BEN	Benin	GHA	Ghana	MDV	Maldives	STP	Sao Tome and Principe
BFA	Burkina Faso	GIN	Guinea	MEX	Mexico	SUR	Suriname
BGD	Bangladesh	GMB	Gambia	MHL	Marshall Islands	SVK	Slovakia
BGR	Bulgaria	GNB	Guinea-Bissau	MKD	North Macedonia	SVN	Slovenia
BHR	Bahrain	GNQ	Equatorial Guinea	MLI	Mali	SWE	Sweden
BHS	Bahamas	GRC	Greece	MLT	Malta	SWZ	Eswatini
BIH	Bosnia and Herzegovina	GRD	Grenada	MMR	Myanmar	SYC	Seychelles
BLR	Belarus	GTM	Guatemala	MNE	Montenegro	SYR	Syrian Arab Republic
BLZ	Belize	GUY	Guyana	MNG	Mongolia	TCD	Chad
BOL	Bolivia (Plurinational State of)	HND	Honduras	MOZ	Mozambique	TGO	Togo
BRA	Brazil	HRV	Croatia	MRT	Mauritania	THA	Thailand
BRB	Barbados	HTI	Haiti	MSR	Montserrat	TJK	Tajikistan
BRN	Brunei Darussalam	HUN	Hungary	MUS	Mauritius	TKM	Turkmenistan
BTN	Bhutan	IDN	Indonesia	MWI	Malawi	TLS	Timor-Leste
BWA	Botswana	IND	India	MYS	Malaysia	TON	Tonga
CAF	Central African Republic	IRL	Ireland	NAM	Namibia	TTO	Trinidad and Tobago
CAN	Canada	IRN	Iran (Islamic Republic of)	NER	Niger	TUN	Tunisia
CHE	Switzerland	IRQ	Iraq	NGA	Nigeria	TUR	Turkey
CHL	Chile	ISL	Iceland	NIC	Nicaragua	TUV	Tuvalu
CHN	China	ISR	Israel	NLD	Netherlands	TZA	United Republic of Tanzania
CIV	Côte D'Ivoire	ITA	Italy	NOR	Norway	UGA	Uganda
CMR	Cameroon	JAM	Jamaica	NPL	Nepal	UKR	Ukraine
COD	Democratic Republic of the Congo	JOR	Jordan	NRU	Nauru	URY	Uruguay
COG	Congo	JPN	Japan	NZL	New Zealand	USA	United States of America
COL	Colombia	KAZ	Kazakhstan	OMN	Oman	UZB	Uzbekistan
COM	Comoros	KEN	Kenya	PAK	Pakistan	VCT	Saint Vincent and the Grenadines
CPV	Cabo Verde	KGZ	Kyrgyzstan	PAN	Panama	VEN	Venezuela (Bolivarian Republic of)
CRI	Costa Rica	KHM	Cambodia	PER	Peru	VNM	Viet Nam
CUB	Cuba	KIR	Kiribati	PHL	Philippines	VUT	Vanuatu
CYP	Cyprus	KNA	Saint Kitts and Nevis	PLW	Palau	WSM	Samoa
CZE	Czechia	KOR	Republic of Korea	PNG	Papua New Guinea	YEM	Yemen
DEU	Germany	KWT	Kuwait	POL	Poland	ZAF	South Africa
DJI	Djibouti	LAO	Lao People's Democratic Republic	PRK	Democratic People's Republic of Korea	ZMB	Zambia
DMA	Dominica			PRT	Portugal	ZWE	Zimbabwe
DNK	Denmark			PRY	Paraguay		
DOM	Dominican Republic			PSE	State of Palestine		
				QAT	Qatar		

Annex tables

Table A.1
Developed economies: rates of growth of real GDP

Annual percentage change

	1998–2012[a]	2013	2014	2015	2016	2017	2018	2019	2020[b]	2021[c]	2022[c]
Developed economies	**1.9**	**1.3**	**2.0**	**2.4**	**1.7**	**2.5**	**2.3**	**1.7**	**-5.6**	**4.0**	**2.5**
United States	2.3	1.8	2.5	3.1	1.7	2.3	3.0	2.2	-3.9	3.4	2.7
Canada	2.5	2.3	2.9	0.7	1.0	3.2	2.0	1.7	-5.6	3.8	2.3
Japan	0.6	1.9	0.4	1.1	0.6	2.2	0.2	0.7	-5.4	3.0	1.8
Australia	3.3	2.1	2.6	2.3	2.8	2.5	2.8	1.8	-4.5	3.3	2.7
New Zealand	2.7	2.2	3.2	4.1	4.2	3.8	3.1	2.3	-6.1	5.2	3.3
European Union	**1.7**	**0.3**	**1.8**	**2.3**	**2.0**	**2.6**	**1.9**	**1.5**	**-7.8**	**5.2**	**2.6**
Austria	2.0	0.0	0.7	1.0	2.1	2.5	2.4	1.6	-6.7	3.8	2.5
Belgium	1.9	0.5	1.6	2.0	1.5	1.9	1.5	1.4	-7.9	4.8	2.0
Bulgaria	3.2	0.3	1.9	4.0	3.8	3.5	3.1	3.4	-4.2	3.9	3.3
Croatia	1.8	-0.6	-0.1	2.5	3.4	3.2	2.6	2.9	-8.0	4.5	2.6
Cyprus	3.1	-6.5	-1.9	3.4	6.7	4.4	4.0	3.3	-7.6	3.1	2.6
Czechia	2.5	0.0	2.3	5.4	2.5	5.2	3.2	2.3	-6.8	4.2	2.9
Denmark	1.2	0.9	1.6	2.3	3.2	2.0	2.4	2.3	-4.3	3.8	3.3
Estonia	3.9	1.3	3.0	1.8	3.2	5.5	4.4	5.0	-3.5	3.0	2.0
Finland	2.3	-0.9	-0.4	0.5	2.8	3.3	1.5	1.1	-3.8	2.3	1.4
France	1.7	0.6	1.0	1.1	1.1	2.3	1.8	1.5	-9.2	6.3	3.3
Germany	1.3	0.4	2.2	1.5	2.2	2.6	1.3	0.6	-5.8	4.1	2.0
Greece	0.7	-3.2	0.7	-0.4	-0.2	1.5	1.9	1.9	-8.4	3.2	2.9
Hungary	2.2	2.0	4.2	3.8	2.2	4.3	5.1	4.9	-5.8	4.5	3.4
Ireland	3.8	1.2	8.6	25.2	2.0	9.1	8.5	5.6	-4.7	3.3	2.7
Italy	0.5	-1.8	0.0	0.8	1.3	1.7	0.8	0.3	-10.2	5.9	2.6
Latvia	4.2	2.3	1.9	3.3	1.8	3.8	4.3	2.2	-4.3	4.8	4.5
Lithuania	4.2	3.6	3.5	2.0	2.6	4.2	3.6	3.9	-1.9	3.0	2.2
Luxembourg	3.4	3.7	4.3	4.3	4.6	1.8	3.1	2.3	-5.4	4.7	1.8
Malta	2.8	5.4	7.7	9.6	3.8	8.1	5.1	4.9	-6.5	4.3	2.5
Netherlands	1.9	-0.1	1.4	2.0	2.2	2.9	2.4	1.7	-5.9	4.4	1.9
Poland	4.0	1.4	3.3	3.8	3.1	4.9	5.3	4.1	-3.6	4.1	3.4
Portugal	0.9	-0.9	0.8	1.8	2.0	3.5	2.6	2.2	-9.1	4.8	2.9
Romania	3.1	3.5	3.4	3.9	4.8	7.1	4.4	4.1	-5.0	4.5	3.6
Slovakia	3.9	0.7	2.8	4.8	2.1	3.0	3.9	2.4	-8.0	6.7	3.9
Slovenia	2.5	-1.0	2.8	2.2	3.1	4.8	4.3	3.2	-6.8	5.4	3.5
Spain	2.1	-1.4	1.4	3.8	3.0	2.9	2.4	2.0	-11.8	6.3	4.0
Sweden	2.5	1.2	2.7	4.5	2.1	2.6	2.0	1.3	-3.8	2.7	2.4
Other Europe	**1.9**	**1.6**	**2.3**	**1.6**	**1.6**	**2.0**	**2.3**	**1.2**	**-4.1**	**3.5**	**1.9**
Iceland	3.0	4.1	2.1	4.7	6.6	4.5	3.9	1.9	-8.5	4.2	3.6
Norway	1.8	1.0	2.0	2.0	1.1	2.3	1.3	1.2	-3.4	2.9	2.5
Switzerland	2.0	1.9	2.4	1.3	1.7	1.8	2.8	1.2	-4.4	3.9	1.5
United Kingdom[d]	2.0	2.1	2.6	2.4	1.9	1.9	1.3	1.5	-9.5	6.8	2.0
Memorandum items											
Northern America	2.3	1.9	2.6	2.9	1.7	2.4	2.9	2.1	-4.0	3.4	2.7
Developed Asia and Pacific	1.1	2.0	0.9	1.5	1.1	2.3	0.8	1.0	-5.2	3.1	2.0
Europe	1.7	0.4	1.8	2.3	2.0	2.6	2.0	1.5	-7.6	5.1	2.5
Major developed economies	1.8	1.5	2.0	2.2	1.5	2.3	2.1	1.6	-5.5	4.0	2.5
Euro area	1.5	-0.2	1.4	2.1	1.9	2.6	1.8	1.3	-7.9	5.0	2.6

Source: UN DESA, based on data of the United Nations Statistics Division and individual national resources.

Note: Regional aggregates calculated at 2015 prices and exchange rates.

a Average percentage change.

b Partly estimated.

c Baseline scenario forecasts, based in part on UN DESA World Economic Forecasting Model.

d The United Kingdom withdrew from the EU on 31 January 2020 and is therefore excluded from all EU aggregations.

Table A.2
Economies in transition: rates of growth of real GDP

Annual percentage change

	1998–2012[a]	2013	2014	2015	2016	2017	2018	2019	2020[b]	2021[c]	2022[c]
Economies in transition	**4.8**	**2.6**	**1.2**	**-1.2**	**0.8**	**2.4**	**3.1**	**2.2**	**-3.4**	**3.4**	**3.0**
South-Eastern Europe	**3.7**	**2.6**	**0.2**	**2.4**	**3.2**	**2.5**	**4.1**	**3.5**	**-3.8**	**4.0**	**3.1**
Albania	5.9	1.0	1.8	2.2	3.3	3.8	4.1	2.2	-6.1	4.8	3.5
Bosnia and Herzegovina	4.4	2.4	1.2	3.1	3.1	3.2	3.7	2.6	-4.5	3.0	3.3
Montenegro	2.9	3.5	1.8	3.4	2.9	4.7	5.1	4.1	-10.8	5.9	3.0
North Macedonia	2.9	2.9	3.6	3.8	2.9	1.0	2.7	3.6	-5.8	5.2	3.0
Serbia	3.2	3.0	-1.6	1.8	3.4	2.0	4.5	4.2	-1.6	3.8	3.0
Commonwealth of Independent States and Georgia[d]	**4.8**	**2.6**	**1.2**	**-1.4**	**0.7**	**2.4**	**3.0**	**2.2**	**-3.4**	**3.4**	**3.0**
Commonwealth of Independent States and Georgia – net fuel exporters	**4.8**	**2.5**	**1.4**	**-1.3**	**0.3**	**2.2**	**2.8**	**1.8**	**-3.6**	**3.2**	**2.7**
Azerbaijan	11.7	5.8	2.8	1.1	-3.1	0.1	1.4	2.2	-3.9	2.0	2.0
Kazakhstan	7.1	6.0	4.2	1.2	1.1	4.1	4.1	4.5	-2.6	3.8	4.0
Russian Federation	4.4	1.8	0.7	-2.0	0.2	1.8	2.5	1.3	-4.0	3.0	2.4
Turkmenistan	8.8	10.2	10.3	6.5	6.2	6.5	6.2	3.0	5.6	6.0	6.0
Commonwealth of Independent States and Georgia – net fuel importers	**4.9**	**2.9**	**0.4**	**-1.8**	**2.7**	**3.7**	**4.3**	**4.0**	**-2.7**	**4.4**	**4.3**
Armenia	7.3	3.3	3.6	3.2	0.2	7.5	5.2	7.6	-6.9	4.0	5.4
Belarus	6.6	1.0	1.7	-3.8	-2.5	2.5	3.2	1.2	-1.5	2.0	2.0
Georgia[d]	5.6	3.6	4.4	3.0	2.9	4.8	4.8	5.1	-5.2	4.2	4.0
Kyrgyzstan	3.9	10.9	4.0	3.9	4.3	4.7	3.5	4.5	-7.5	4.8	4.5
Republic of Moldova	3.2	9.0	5.0	-0.3	4.4	4.7	4.3	3.5	-5.6	3.8	3.5
Tajikistan	7.2	7.4	6.7	6.0	6.9	7.1	7.1	7.5	3.0	6.0	4.0
Ukraine[e]	3.2	0.0	-6.6	-9.8	2.4	2.5	3.4	3.2	-5.6	4.5	4.0
Uzbekistan	6.5	7.6	7.2	7.4	6.1	4.5	5.5	5.6	0.5	5.6	6.0

Source: UN DESA, based on data of the United Nations Statistics Division and individual national sources.
Note: Regional aggregates calculated at 2015 prices and exchange rates.
a Average percentage change.
b Partly estimated.
c Baseline scenario forecasts, based in part on UN DESA World Economic Forecasting Model.
d Georgia officially left the Commonwealth of Independent States on 18 August 2009. However, its performance is discussed in the context of this group of countries for reasons of geographic proximity and similarities in economic structure.
e Data for the Ukraine excludes the temporarily occupied territory of the Autonomous Republic of Crimea and Sevastopol.

Table A.3
Developing economies: rates of growth of real GDP

Annual percentage change

	1998–2012[a]	2013	2014	2015	2016	2017	2018	2019	2020[b]	2021[c]	2022[c]
Developing countries[d]	**5.6**	**5.0**	**4.7**	**4.4**	**4.2**	**4.7**	**4.3**	**3.6**	**-2.5**	**5.7**	**4.6**
Africa	**4.7**	**1.1**	**3.2**	**2.6**	**1.8**	**3.4**	**3.4**	**2.9**	**-4.2**	**3.8**	**3.7**
Northern Africa	**4.2**	**-6.4**	**-0.8**	**1.9**	**2.9**	**5.0**	**4.1**	**3.1**	**-5.6**	**6.0**	**4.4**
Algeria	3.8	2.8	3.8	3.7	3.2	1.3	1.4	0.7	-7.7	5.2	4.2
Egypt[e]	4.6	2.2	2.9	4.4	4.3	4.2	5.3	5.6	3.5	2.1	3.7
Libya	2.7	-52.1	-50.1	-45.5	-16.1	64.0	17.9	9.9	-68.9	92.8	18.1
Mauritania	4.8	4.2	4.3	5.4	1.3	3.5	2.1	2.4	-2.9	1.9	2.2
Morocco	4.8	4.9	4.0	4.5	1.1	4.2	3.1	2.5	-7.1	5.6	2.9
Sudan[e]	...	5.6	6.9	3.7	3.9	7.4	-2.3	-2.5	-3.4	3.8	3.7
Tunisia	4.1	2.3	2.4	1.2	1.1	1.9	2.5	1.0	-7.2	5.3	3.2
East Africa	**5.0**	**7.9**	**7.7**	**6.5**	**5.5**	**5.5**	**6.7**	**6.5**	**-0.7**	**3.0**	**4.1**
Burundi	2.9	4.9	4.2	-0.4	3.2	4.2	0.1	1.8	-3.3	3.0	3.2
Comoros	1.9	8.9	3.9	2.0	2.8	5.6	3.8	3.2	-1.9	2.9	3.0
Democratic Republic of the Congo	3.1	8.5	9.5	6.9	2.4	3.7	5.8	4.4	-2.2	3.5	4.0
Djibouti	6.2	13.4	7.1	7.7	6.9	5.1	5.6	7.5	-1.0	4.5	5.0
Eritrea	1.2	4.6	2.9	2.6	1.9	5.0	4.2	3.8	-2.5	4.1	3.0
Ethiopia	8.1	10.4	10.3	9.0	8.5	8.1	7.9	8.3	-0.5	2.3	4.2
Kenya	4.0	5.9	5.4	5.7	5.9	4.8	6.3	5.4	-0.4	3.0	4.0
Madagascar	2.9	2.3	3.3	3.1	4.0	3.9	3.2	4.4	-2.6	3.0	2.8
Rwanda	8.2	4.7	6.2	8.9	6.0	4.0	8.6	9.4	1.1	4.5	6.0
Somalia	2.8	2.6	3.7	2.7	4.9	2.3	3.1	2.9	-3.7	2.7	3.1
South Sudan	0.3	29.9	21.7	3.4	0.3	-0.7	3.4	11.3	-7.2	2.0	2.2
Uganda	7.2	4.7	4.5	5.7	2.6	4.9	8.9	4.9	-0.5	4.1	4.8
United Republic of Tanzania	6.1	6.8	6.7	6.2	6.9	6.8	7.0	7.0	1.5	3.0	4.0
Central Africa	**5.1**	**-0.6**	**4.8**	**-0.3**	**0.0**	**0.0**	**1.5**	**1.9**	**-4.3**	**2.9**	**3.6**
Cameroon	4.0	5.4	5.9	5.7	4.6	3.5	4.1	3.9	-2.5	3.4	4.1
Central African Republic	2.1	-36.7	1.0	4.8	4.5	4.3	4.3	3.0	-2.0	2.8	4.3
Chad	9.1	-6.9	3.8	4.6	-2.7	-2.4	2.4	3.0	-3.4	4.8	5.5
Congo	5.2	-2.5	9.7	-13.2	-2.8	-3.1	1.0	-0.9	-8.8	1.6	3.3
Equatorial Guinea	14.6	-4.1	0.4	-9.1	-8.8	-5.7	-6.4	-5.6	-8.0	0.3	-0.6
Gabon	0.9	5.6	4.3	3.9	2.1	0.5	1.2	3.6	-4.0	2.9	3.7
Sao Tome and Principe	4.3	4.8	6.5	3.9	4.2	3.8	2.9	1.3	-7.1	4.7	5.0
West Africa	**5.9**	**6.8**	**6.0**	**3.0**	**0.3**	**2.6**	**3.2**	**3.3**	**-2.7**	**2.5**	**3.7**
Benin	4.1	6.9	6.5	6.5	5.0	5.8	6.5	6.4	0.2	3.7	5.1
Burkina Faso	5.8	5.8	4.3	3.9	6.0	6.2	6.7	5.7	-1.6	4.7	5.5
Cabo Verde	5.6	0.8	0.6	1.0	4.7	3.7	4.5	5.7	-8.4	3.4	4.9
Côte D'Ivoire	1.4	9.3	8.8	8.8	8.0	7.7	7.4	6.9	0.7	6.5	7.2
Gambia	3.3	2.9	-1.4	4.1	1.9	4.8	6.5	6.0	-4.0	4.8	5.3
Ghana	6.2	7.3	2.9	2.2	3.4	8.1	6.3	6.5	-0.6	4.1	4.0
Guinea	3.5	3.9	3.7	3.8	10.8	13.4	5.8	5.6	0.0	5.5	6.5
Guinea-Bissau	1.6	3.3	1.0	6.1	6.3	5.9	3.8	4.6	-2.5	2.6	3.6
Liberia	9.4	4.6	5.2	0.0	-1.6	2.5	1.2	-2.5	-3.0	2.1	4.1
Mali	9.0	7.0	7.8	7.5	8.9	6.7	6.8	6.6	-2.1	2.8	4.3

Table A.3
Developing economies: rates of growth of real GDP *(continued)*

Annual percentage change

	1998–2012[a]	2013	2014	2015	2016	2017	2018	2019	2020[b]	2021[c]	2022[c]
Niger	4.9	5.3	7.5	4.3	5.7	5.0	7.0	5.8	-2.0	4.5	8.3
Nigeria	6.5	6.7	6.3	2.7	-1.6	0.8	1.9	2.2	-3.5	1.5	2.8
Senegal	4.1	3.9	4.1	6.4	6.4	7.4	6.4	5.2	-1.3	5.0	6.0
Sierra Leone	6.9	20.7	4.6	-20.5	6.3	3.8	4.6	5.1	-3.0	2.6	4.1
Togo	2.3	6.1	5.9	5.7	5.6	3.8	4.9	5.3	-1.8	3.8	4.5
Southern Africa	**4.1**	**3.5**	**3.0**	**1.5**	**0.2**	**1.5**	**0.8**	**-0.2**	**-6.4**	**2.9**	**2.6**
Angola	7.3	5.0	4.8	0.9	-2.6	-0.1	-2.0	-1.5	-3.0	1.2	2.6
Botswana	4.2	11.3	4.1	-1.7	4.3	2.9	4.5	3.0	-8.5	4.5	4.2
Eswatini	3.2	3.9	0.9	2.3	1.3	2.0	2.4	1.0	-3.3	0.9	2.3
Lesotho	3.6	1.8	3.1	1.6	3.6	-0.9	1.2	1.2	-3.0	2.1	2.8
Malawi	3.8	6.3	6.2	3.3	2.7	5.2	3.9	5.2	0.2	2.4	2.7
Mauritius	4.3	3.4	3.7	3.6	3.8	3.8	3.8	3.6	-12.0	8.5	3.0
Mozambique	7.8	7.0	7.4	6.7	3.8	3.7	3.4	2.3	-1.3	2.3	3.0
Namibia	4.4	5.6	6.4	6.1	1.1	-0.9	-0.1	-1.4	-4.6	2.5	2.6
South Africa	3.1	2.5	1.8	1.2	0.4	1.4	0.8	0.2	-7.7	3.3	2.4
Zambia	6.4	5.1	4.7	2.9	3.8	3.5	4.0	1.4	-3.5	2.2	2.7
Zimbabwe	3.2	2.0	2.4	1.8	0.8	4.7	4.8	-8.3	-9.8	2.5	3.1
Africa - net fuel exporters	**5.3**	**-3.5**	**1.4**	**0.6**	**-0.9**	**1.8**	**1.8**	**1.7**	**-6.5**	**3.4**	**3.5**
Africa - net fuel importers	**4.3**	**4.4**	**4.3**	**3.9**	**3.4**	**4.3**	**4.3**	**3.5**	**-3.0**	**4.0**	**3.9**
East and South Asia	**7.1**	**6.3**	**6.3**	**6.0**	**6.2**	**6.2**	**5.6**	**4.9**	**-0.5**	**6.5**	**5.2**
East Asia	**7.5**	**6.6**	**6.3**	**5.9**	**5.8**	**6.0**	**5.8**	**5.3**	**1.0**	**6.4**	**5.2**
Brunei Darussalam	1.6	-2.1	-2.5	-0.4	-2.5	1.3	0.1	3.9	1.2	2.6	3.0
Cambodia	8.0	7.4	7.1	7.0	6.9	7.0	7.5	7.1	-1.4	4.8	5.5
China	9.8	7.8	7.3	6.9	6.7	6.8	6.6	6.1	2.4	7.2	5.8
Democratic People's Republic of Korea	1.3	1.1	1.0	-1.1	3.9	-3.5	-4.1	-1.3	-4.5	2.5	1.5
Fiji	1.9	4.7	5.6	4.7	2.5	5.4	3.5	0.5	-16.2	9.6	3.2
Hong Kong SAR[f]	3.4	3.1	2.8	2.4	2.2	3.8	3.0	-1.2	-6.0	4.2	2.2
Indonesia	3.7	5.6	5.0	4.9	5.0	5.1	5.2	5.0	-1.6	5.2	4.6
Kiribati	1.6	4.3	-0.6	10.3	1.1	4.3	2.3	2.3	-8.5	6.5	5.0
Lao People's Democratic Republic	7.0	8.0	7.6	7.3	7.0	6.9	6.2	4.7	0.5	5.2	5.8
Malaysia	4.2	4.7	6.0	5.1	4.4	5.8	4.8	4.3	-4.8	6.6	4.2
Mongolia	6.8	11.6	7.9	2.4	2.0	5.4	7.0	4.9	-2.8	5.2	5.6
Myanmar[e]	10.8	8.4	8.0	7.0	5.9	6.8	6.2	6.5	2.3	6.5	6.4
Papua New Guinea	3.1	3.8	13.5	9.5	4.1	3.5	-0.8	5.6	-1.9	3.8	4.7
Philippines	4.3	7.1	6.1	6.1	6.9	6.7	6.2	5.9	-8.8	6.2	6.0
Republic of Korea	4.4	3.3	3.2	3.1	3.0	2.9	2.8	2.2	-0.7	2.8	2.2
Samoa	2.6	0.8	2.6	6.7	3.7	-0.6	0.7	2.3	-3.4	2.7	3.3
Singapore	5.4	4.8	3.9	3.0	3.2	4.3	3.4	0.7	-6.5	5.2	3.0
Solomon Islands	2.9	3.0	2.2	2.5	3.2	3.7	3.9	3.2	-5.5	4.8	3.3
Taiwan Province of China	4.3	2.5	4.7	1.5	2.2	3.3	2.7	2.7	1.5	3.0	2.6
Thailand	3.6	2.7	1.0	3.1	3.4	4.0	4.1	2.4	-6.6	4.0	3.8
Timor-Leste	7.3	-11.1	-25.9	20.6	0.7	-9.2	2.8	3.1	-6.5	3.0	3.5
Vanuatu	2.9	2.0	2.3	0.2	3.5	4.4	2.8	2.8	-8.5	4.6	3.1

Table A.3
Developing economies: rates of growth of real GDP *(continued)*

Annual percentage change

	1998–2012[a]	2013	2014	2015	2016	2017	2018	2019	2020[b]	2021[c]	2022[c]
Viet Nam	6.5	5.4	6.0	6.7	6.2	6.8	7.1	7.0	3.4	7.8	7.1
South Asia	**5.6**	**4.8**	**6.3**	**6.3**	**8.0**	**6.8**	**4.7**	**3.1**	**-8.6**	**6.9**	**5.3**
Afghanistan[e]	7.8	6.5	3.1	-1.8	3.6	7.1	-1.7	3.0	-3.8	4.4	4.5
Bangladesh[e]	5.8	6.0	6.1	6.6	7.1	7.3	7.9	8.2	4.3	5.1	7.6
Bhutan	8.2	2.1	4.0	6.6	8.1	4.7	3.0	5.3	0.0	3.5	5.2
India[e]	6.5	6.4	7.4	8.0	8.3	7.0	6.1	4.2	-5.7	7.0	5.6
Iran (Islamic Republic of)[e]	3.2	-0.2	4.6	-1.3	13.4	3.8	-5.4	-6.5	-9.6	4.6	3.1
Maldives	5.1	7.3	7.3	2.9	6.3	7.2	8.1	7.0	-20.4	9.9	6.2
Nepal[e]	4.1	4.1	6.0	3.3	0.6	8.2	6.7	7.0	-0.5	-0.1	8.0
Pakistan[e]	4.0	4.7	4.7	5.5	5.6	5.8	3.3	0.5	-1.2	0.5	3.5
Sri Lanka	5.6	3.4	5.0	5.0	4.5	3.6	3.3	2.3	-4.2	3.1	2.7
East and South Asia – net fuel exporters	**3.5**	**3.0**	**4.6**	**3.3**	**6.4**	**5.1**	**2.4**	**1.4**	**-4.8**	**5.1**	**4.2**
East and South Asia – net fuel importers	**7.5**	**6.6**	**6.4**	**6.2**	**6.1**	**6.2**	**5.9**	**5.2**	**-0.2**	**6.6**	**5.3**
Western Asia	**4.3**	**4.9**	**3.3**	**3.7**	**3.3**	**2.5**	**2.2**	**1.2**	**-4.8**	**3.8**	**3.4**
Western Asia – net fuel exporters	**4.6**	**3.9**	**2.7**	**3.0**	**3.3**	**-0.4**	**1.7**	**1.0**	**-6.1**	**3.7**	**2.8**
Bahrain	5.1	5.4	4.4	2.9	3.6	3.7	2.5	1.8	-6.5	3.5	2.7
Iraq	6.4	7.6	0.2	2.6	13.8	-3.8	0.9	4.4	-11.1	5.4	5.0
Kuwait	4.6	1.1	0.5	0.6	2.9	-4.7	1.2	0.4	-5.6	4.9	3.1
Oman	3.3	5.1	1.4	4.7	5.1	0.3	0.9	-0.8	-6.6	2.9	2.9
Qatar	11.4	4.4	4.0	3.7	2.1	1.6	1.5	-0.2	-4.1	3.9	2.8
Saudi Arabia	3.6	2.7	3.7	4.1	1.7	-0.7	2.4	0.3	-5.7	3.2	2.2
United Arab Emirates	4.5	5.1	4.3	5.1	3.1	2.4	1.2	1.7	-5.2	3.7	2.8
Yemen	3.2	3.6	-10.6	-30.5	-14.6	-10.0	-1.3	1.6	-5.2	-1.1	1.0
Western Asia – net fuel importers	**4.0**	**6.1**	**4.1**	**4.5**	**3.3**	**6.0**	**2.8**	**1.3**	**-3.4**	**4.0**	**4.0**
Israel	3.7	4.3	4.2	2.1	3.8	3.6	3.6	3.4	-5.7	3.6	3.1
Jordan	5.2	2.4	3.4	2.6	2.1	2.1	1.9	2.0	-5.4	4.2	2.1
Lebanon	4.3	3.8	2.5	0.2	1.5	0.9	-1.9	-6.5	-31.2	14.0	9.2
State of Palestine	4.9	4.7	-0.2	3.7	8.9	1.4	1.2	0.9	-7.9	3.3	2.1
Syrian Arab Republic	2.4	-23.9	-18.2	-7.7	-5.6	-0.8	0.4	2.8	-7.4	4.5	3.9
Turkey	4.2	8.5	4.9	6.1	3.3	7.5	3.0	0.9	-1.0	3.8	4.2
Latin America and the Caribbean[g]	**3.0**	**2.8**	**1.0**	**0.1**	**-1.2**	**0.9**	**0.5**	**-0.3**	**-8.0**	**3.8**	**2.6**
South America	**3.1**	**3.2**	**0.2**	**-1.3**	**-3.0**	**0.3**	**-0.3**	**-0.7**	**-7.9**	**3.8**	**2.7**
Argentina	2.6	2.4	-2.5	2.7	-2.1	2.7	-2.5	-2.1	-10.5	4.9	2.5
Bolivia (Plurinational State of)	3.8	6.8	5.5	4.9	4.3	4.2	4.2	2.2	-8.0	5.1	3.0
Brazil	3.1	3.0	0.5	-3.5	-3.3	1.1	1.1	1.4	-5.3	3.2	2.2
Chile	4.0	4.0	1.8	2.3	1.7	1.3	4.0	1.1	-6.0	5.0	3.0
Colombia	3.4	4.6	4.7	3.0	2.1	1.4	2.6	3.3	-7.0	5.0	3.4
Ecuador	3.6	4.9	3.8	0.1	-1.2	2.4	1.4	0.1	-9.0	1.0	2.0
Paraguay	3.5	8.4	4.9	3.1	4.3	5.0	3.7	0.0	-1.6	3.5	3.2
Peru	4.8	5.9	2.4	3.3	4.0	2.5	4.0	2.2	-12.9	9.0	4.0
Uruguay	2.6	4.6	3.2	0.4	1.7	2.6	1.6	0.2	-4.5	4.0	2.1

Table A.3
Developing economies: rates of growth of real GDP *(continued)*

Annual percentage change

	1998–2012[a]	2013	2014	2015	2016	2017	2018	2019	2020[b]	2021[c]	2022[c]
Venezuela (Bolivarian Republic of)	2.6	1.3	-3.9	-6.2	-17.0	-15.7	-19.5	-28.0	-30.0	-7.0	7.8
Mexico and Central America	**2.7**	**1.9**	**3.1**	**3.6**	**3.1**	**2.4**	**2.4**	**0.6**	**-8.3**	**3.8**	**2.4**
Costa Rica	4.5	2.3	3.5	3.6	4.2	3.4	2.7	2.1	-4.8	3.0	2.5
Cuba	4.7	2.7	1.0	4.4	0.5	1.8	2.2	0.5	-8.5	3.0	1.5
Dominican Republic	4.9	4.9	7.6	7.0	6.6	4.6	7.0	5.1	-5.5	5.0	4.2
El Salvador	2.3	2.2	1.7	2.4	2.5	2.3	2.5	2.4	-8.6	3.5	2.2
Guatemala	3.5	3.7	4.2	4.1	3.1	2.8	3.1	3.8	-2.5	3.5	2.9
Haiti[e]	1.0	4.2	2.8	1.2	1.5	1.2	1.5	0.7	-2.0	-1.8	1.8
Honduras	3.7	2.8	3.1	3.8	3.9	4.8	3.7	2.7	-8.0	4.5	2.6
Mexico	2.3	1.4	2.8	3.3	2.9	2.1	2.0	-0.1	-9.0	3.8	2.2
Nicaragua	3.8	4.9	4.8	4.8	4.6	4.7	-3.8	-3.9	-4.0	1.3	1.7
Panama	6.2	6.9	5.1	5.7	5.0	5.3	3.7	3.0	-11.0	5.5	3.8
Caribbean	**2.7**	**0.7**	**0.2**	**1.1**	**-2.2**	**-0.2**	**1.8**	**0.4**	**-7.8**	**3.8**	**2.8**
Bahamas	1.6	-3.0	0.7	0.6	0.4	0.1	1.6	1.8	-14.5	4.5	3.3
Barbados	0.9	-1.4	-0.2	2.2	2.3	-0.2	-0.6	-0.1	-16.0	6.0	2.9
Belize	4.5	0.9	3.7	3.4	-0.6	1.4	3.0	0.3	-15.5	7.5	3.0
Guyana	2.3	5.0	3.9	3.1	3.4	2.2	4.1	5.4	30.9	8.1	8.5
Jamaica	0.5	0.5	0.7	0.9	1.4	1.0	1.7	0.9	-9.0	2.0	2.0
Suriname	4.0	2.9	0.3	-3.4	-5.6	1.7	1.9	0.3	-10.1	2.0	2.4
Trinidad and Tobago	5.6	2.0	-1.0	1.8	-6.5	-1.9	1.9	-1.2	-6.8	3.3	1.7
Latin America and the Caribbean – net fuel exporters	**3.1**	**3.1**	**0.4**	**-1.5**	**-6.8**	**-5.0**	**-5.1**	**-6.5**	**-12.5**	**2.1**	**3.8**
Latin America and the Caribbean – net fuel importers	**3.0**	**2.8**	**1.1**	**0.4**	**-0.2**	**1.9**	**1.4**	**0.6**	**-7.4**	**4.0**	**2.4**
Memorandum items:											
Least developed countries	5.9	5.9	5.5	3.7	4.0	5.1	5.1	4.8	-1.3	4.9	4.6
Africa (excluding Libya)	4.9	4.6	4.8	3.3	1.9	3.0	3.2	2.8	-3.4	3.4	3.6
Northern Africa (excluding Libya)	4.5	3.1	3.9	4.1	3.3	3.8	3.7	2.9	-3.3	4.9	4.1
East Asia (excluding China)	4.3	4.1	4.1	3.7	3.8	4.2	4.0	3.2	-2.4	4.4	3.6
South Asia (excluding India)	4.2	2.1	4.7	3.3	7.5	5.4	1.1	-0.3	-6.1	5.9	3.9
Western Asia (excluding Israel and Turkey)	4.6	3.3	2.4	2.8	3.2	-0.3	1.6	0.9	-6.7	3.9	2.9
Arab States[h]	4.4	0.1	1.4	2.5	3.1	1.3	2.4	1.6	-6.4	4.6	3.4
Landlocked developing economies	6.3	6.7	5.7	3.7	3.4	4.6	4.9	4.3	-2.4	4.1	4.4
Small island developing economies	4.6	3.9	3.6	3.7	2.7	3.4	3.3	1.5	-6.8	4.7	3.0

Source: UN DESA, based on data of the United Nations Statistics Division and individual national sources.

Note: Regional aggregates calculated at 2015 prices and exchange rates.

a Average percentage change.

b Partly estimated.

c Baseline scenario forecasts, based in part on UN DESA World Economic Forecasting Model.

d Covering countries that account for 98 per cent of the population of all developing countries.

e Fiscal-year basis.

f Special Administrative Region of China.

g Figures for Latin America and the Caribbean for 2020–2021 were provided by UN/ECLAC.

h Currently includes data for Algeria, Bahrain, Comoros, Djibouti, Egypt, Iraq, Jordan, Kuwait, Lebanon, Libya, Mauritania, Morocco, Oman, Qatar, Saudi Arabia, Somalia, Sudan, Syrian Arab Republic, Tunisia, United Arab Emirates, and Yemen.

Table A.4
Growth of world output and gross domestic product by SDG regions

Annual percentage change

	2018	2019	2020[a]	2021[b]	2022[b]
World	**3.1**	**2.5**	**-4.3**	**4.7**	**3.4**
Developed regions	**2.3**	**1.7**	**-5.6**	**4.0**	**2.5**
Developing regions	**4.3**	**3.6**	**-2.4**	**5.7**	**4.6**
Africa	**3.4**	**2.9**	**-4.2**	**3.8**	**3.7**
Northern Africa	4.1	3.1	-5.7	6.0	4.4
Eastern Africa	6.3	5.0	-1.4	3.0	3.9
Middle Africa	0.6	0.8	-3.3	2.2	3.2
Southern Africa	0.9	0.2	-7.6	3.3	2.5
Western Africa	3.2	3.3	-2.7	2.5	3.7
Americas	**2.4**	**1.6**	**-4.8**	**3.5**	**2.7**
Northern America	2.9	2.1	-4.0	3.4	2.7
Latin America and the Caribbean	0.5	-0.3	-8.0	3.8	2.6
Caribbean	3.7	2.0	-7.5	3.8	2.7
Central America	2.1	0.3	-8.5	3.8	2.3
South America	-0.3	-0.7	-7.8	3.8	2.7
Asia	4.5	3.9	-1.9	5.8	4.6
Central Asia	4.8	4.7	-0.7	4.7	4.8
Eastern Asia	4.7	4.4	0.3	5.9	4.7
Southern Asia	4.7	3.1	-8.6	6.9	5.3
South-eastern Asia	5.1	4.3	-3.7	5.6	4.7
Western Asia	2.2	1.2	-6.1	3.8	3.3
Europe	**2.0**	**1.5**	**-7.3**	**4.9**	**2.5**
Eastern Europe	3.5	2.5	-4.5	3.7	2.9
Northern Europe	2.0	1.8	-7.3	5.3	2.2
Southern Europe	1.6	1.2	-10.3	5.7	3.1
Western Europe	1.7	1.1	-6.9	4.8	2.3
Oceania	**2.8**	**1.9**	**-4.7**	**3.6**	**2.8**

Sources: UN DESA, based on data of the United Nations Statistics Division and UN DESA forecasts.

Notes: Regional aggregates in this table follow geographic regions defined under the Standard Country or Area Codes for Statistical Use (known as M49) and are not strictly comparable to those in the WESP. Full details on the M49 standard can be found on the United Nations Statistics Division website at https://unstats.un.org/unsd/methodology/m49. Calculated at 2015 prices and exchange rates.

Figures are based on the countries actively monitored for the World Economic Situation and Prospects report.

a Partly estimated.

b Baseline scenario forecasts, based in part on UN DESA World Economic Forecasting Model.

Table A.5
Developed economies: consumer price inflation

Annual percentage change[a]

	2012	2013	2014	2015	2016	2017	2018	2019	2020[b]	2021[c]	2022[c]
Developed economies	**2.0**	**1.4**	**1.4**	**0.3**	**0.8**	**1.8**	**2.0**	**1.5**	**0.9**	**1.4**	**1.4**
United States	2.1	1.5	1.6	0.1	1.3	2.1	2.4	1.8	1.3	1.9	1.6
Canada	1.5	0.9	1.9	1.1	1.4	1.6	2.3	1.9	0.8	1.3	1.7
Japan	-0.1	0.3	2.8	0.8	-0.1	0.5	1.0	0.5	0.4	0.4	1.0
Australia	1.7	2.5	2.5	1.5	1.3	2.0	1.9	1.6	-0.8	0.2	1.2
New Zealand	1.0	1.1	1.2	0.3	0.6	1.8	1.6	1.6	1.2	1.4	1.7
European Union	**2.5**	**1.4**	**0.4**	**0.2**	**0.2**	**1.5**	**1.8**	**1.4**	**0.6**	**1.2**	**1.3**
Austria	2.6	2.1	1.5	0.8	1.0	2.2	2.1	1.5	1.2	1.5	1.5
Belgium	2.6	1.2	0.5	0.6	1.8	2.2	2.3	1.2	0.5	0.9	1.0
Bulgaria	2.4	0.4	-1.6	-1.1	-1.3	1.2	2.6	2.4	1.8	2.6	2.0
Croatia	3.4	2.3	0.2	-0.3	-0.6	1.3	1.5	0.8	0.3	1.0	1.9
Cyprus	3.1	0.4	-0.3	-1.5	-1.2	0.7	0.8	0.5	-0.2	1.0	1.2
Czechia	3.6	1.3	0.5	0.2	0.7	2.4	1.9	2.6	3.1	2.6	2.6
Denmark	2.4	0.5	0.4	0.2	0.0	1.1	0.7	0.7	0.2	0.2	1.1
Estonia	4.2	3.2	0.5	0.1	0.8	3.7	3.4	2.3	-0.9	2.9	2.0
Finland	3.2	2.2	1.2	-0.2	0.4	0.8	1.2	1.1	0.3	1.2	1.6
France	2.2	1.0	0.6	0.1	0.3	1.2	2.1	1.3	0.6	1.3	1.1
Germany	2.1	1.6	0.7	0.7	0.4	1.7	1.9	1.4	0.4	1.1	1.4
Greece	1.0	-0.9	-1.4	-1.1	0.0	1.1	0.8	0.5	-0.8	1.0	1.2
Hungary	5.7	1.7	0.0	0.1	0.4	2.4	2.9	3.4	3.6	2.7	2.6
Ireland	1.8	0.5	0.3	0.0	-0.2	0.3	0.7	0.9	0.8	1.0	1.2
Italy	3.3	1.3	0.2	0.1	-0.1	1.4	1.2	0.7	0.1	1.2	1.2
Latvia	2.3	0.0	0.7	0.2	0.1	2.9	2.6	2.7	0.7	1.6	1.7
Lithuania	3.2	1.2	0.2	-0.7	0.7	3.7	2.5	2.2	1.3	1.3	1.2
Luxembourg	2.9	1.7	0.7	0.1	0.0	2.1	2.0	1.7	0.2	1.1	1.3
Malta	3.2	1.0	0.8	1.2	0.9	1.3	1.7	1.5	0.3	1.1	1.3
Netherlands	2.8	2.6	0.3	0.2	0.1	1.3	1.6	2.7	0.7	1.1	1.2
Poland	3.6	0.8	0.1	-0.7	-0.2	1.6	1.2	2.1	3.0	2.4	2.1
Portugal	2.8	0.4	-0.2	0.5	0.6	1.6	1.2	0.3	0.0	0.4	1.1
Romania	3.4	3.2	1.4	-0.4	-1.1	1.1	4.1	3.9	2.5	2.5	2.5
Slovakia	3.7	1.5	-0.1	-0.3	-0.5	1.4	2.5	2.8	1.9	2.0	1.9
Slovenia	2.8	1.9	0.4	-0.8	-0.1	1.6	1.9	1.7	0.3	1.6	1.8
Spain	2.4	1.5	-0.2	-0.6	-0.3	2.0	1.7	0.8	0.0	0.9	0.6
Sweden	0.9	0.4	0.2	0.7	1.1	1.9	2.0	1.7	1.0	1.1	1.2
Other European countries	**2.0**	**2.0**	**1.3**	**0.1**	**0.8**	**2.2**	**2.2**	**1.6**	**0.9**	**0.7**	**1.3**
Iceland	6.0	4.1	1.0	0.3	0.8	-1.6	0.7	2.0	3.7	2.7	2.8
Norway	0.3	2.0	1.9	2.0	3.9	1.8	3.0	2.3	1.8	2.4	2.7
Switzerland	-0.7	0.1	0.0	-0.8	-0.5	0.6	0.9	0.4	-1.0	-0.3	0.5
United Kingdom[d]	2.9	2.5	1.5	0.0	0.7	2.7	2.4	1.8	1.3	0.7	1.4
Memorandum items:											
Northern America	2.0	1.4	1.6	0.2	1.3	2.1	2.4	1.8	1.3	1.8	1.6
Developed Asia and Pacific	0.4	0.8	2.7	0.9	0.2	0.8	1.2	0.8	0.1	0.4	1.0
Europe	2.4	1.5	0.6	0.2	0.4	1.7	1.9	1.4	0.7	1.1	1.3
Major developed economies	1.9	1.4	1.5	0.3	0.8	1.8	2.1	1.5	1.0	1.4	1.4
Euro area	2.5	1.4	0.4	0.2	0.3	1.5	1.7	1.3	0.4	1.1	1.2

Sources: UN DESA, based on OECD *Main Economic Indicators*; Eurostat; and individual national sources.

a Data for country groups are weighted averages, where weights for each year are based on 2015 GDP in United States dollars.

b Partly estimated.

c Baseline scenario forecasts, based on UN DESA World Economic Forecasting Model.

d The United Kingdom withdrew from the EU on 31 January 2020 and is therefore excluded from all EU aggregations.

Table A.6
Economies in transition: consumer price inflation

Annual percentage change[a]

	2012	2013	2014	2015	2016	2017	2018	2019	2020[b]	2021[c]	2022[c]
Economies in transition	**6.6**	**6.6**	**7.7**	**14.6**	**8.0**	**5.4**	**4.4**	**5.0**	**4.1**	**4.9**	**4.3**
South-Eastern Europe	**4.7**	**4.5**	**1.1**	**0.9**	**0.5**	**2.5**	**2.0**	**1.3**	**0.9**	**1.5**	**1.6**
Albania	2.0	1.9	1.6	1.9	1.3	2.0	2.0	1.4	1.6	1.7	1.6
Bosnia and Herzegovina	2.1	-0.1	-0.9	-1.0	-1.6	0.8	1.4	0.6	-0.5	1.0	1.0
Montenegro	4.1	2.2	-0.7	1.5	-0.3	2.4	2.6	0.4	-0.4	1.0	1.9
North Macedonia	1.8	2.7	0.0	0.1	0.2	2.1	2.3	0.7	0.7	0.8	0.9
Serbia	7.3	7.7	2.3	1.5	1.3	3.4	2.0	1.9	1.5	2.0	2.0
Commonwealth of Independent States and Georgia[d]	**6.7**	**6.7**	**8.0**	**15.2**	**8.3**	**5.5**	**4.5**	**5.1**	**4.3**	**5.1**	**4.4**
Commonwealth of Independent States and Georgia – net fuel exporters	**5.0**	**6.5**	**7.4**	**13.9**	**8.0**	**4.5**	**3.5**	**4.5**	**3.8**	**4.7**	**4.2**
Azerbaijan	1.1	2.4	1.4	4.0	12.4	12.9	2.3	2.6	3.1	3.2	3.5
Kazakhstan	5.2	5.9	6.8	6.7	14.4	7.4	6.0	5.2	6.3	5.8	5.2
Russian Federation	5.1	6.8	7.8	15.5	7.0	3.7	2.9	4.5	3.3	4.5	4.0
Turkmenistan	5.3	6.8	6.0	7.4	3.6	8.0	13.3	5.1	12.1	8.3	8.2
Commonwealth of Independent States and Georgia – net fuel importers	**16.2**	**7.7**	**11.1**	**22.2**	**10.0**	**10.9**	**10.2**	**8.7**	**6.9**	**7.0**	**5.8**
Armenia	2.6	5.8	3.0	3.7	-1.4	1.0	2.5	1.4	1.6	2.0	2.2
Belarus	59.2	18.3	18.1	13.5	11.8	6.0	4.9	5.6	5.6	4.3	3.7
Georgia[d]	-0.9	-0.5	3.1	4.0	2.1	6.0	2.6	4.9	4.8	3.9	4.1
Kyrgyzstan	2.8	6.6	7.5	6.5	0.4	3.2	1.5	1.1	5.3	5.3	2.8
Republic of Moldova	4.5	4.6	5.1	9.7	6.4	6.6	3.0	4.8	4.1	4.3	4.1
Tajikistan	5.8	5.0	6.1	5.7	6.0	7.3	3.8	7.8	8.4	7.2	6.6
Ukraine[e]	0.6	-0.2	12.1	48.7	13.9	14.4	11.0	7.9	3.1	5.7	3.9
Uzbekistan[f]	11.9	11.7	9.1	8.5	8.8	13.9	17.5	14.5	13.4	11.7	10.5

Sources: UN DESA, based on data of the United Nations Statistics Divisio and individual national sources.

Note: Regional aggregates calculated at 2015 prices and exchange rates.

a Average percentage change.

b Partly estimated.

c Baseline scenario forecasts, based in part on the UN DESA World Economic Forecasting Model.

d Georgia officially left the Commonwealth of Independent States on 18 August 2009. However, its performance is discussed in the context of this group of countries for reasons of geographic proximity and similarities in economic structure.

e Data for Ukraine excludes the temporarily occupied territory of the Autonomous Republic of Crimea and Sevastopol.

f Based on 2019 criteria, Uzbekistan is considered a net fuel importer.

Table A.7
Developing economies: consumer price inflation

Annual percentage change[a]

	2012	2013	2014	2015	2016	2017	2018	2019	2020[b]	2021[c]	2022[c]
Developing countries by region[d]	**4.9**	**4.9**	**4.2**	**3.8**	**4.7**	**4.1**	**4.7**	**5.5**	**5.9**	**4.7**	**3.8**
Africa	**9.7**	**7.5**	**7.3**	**7.4**	**13.0**	**15.1**	**11.3**	**11.0**	**14.5**	**9.0**	**6.4**
Northern Africa	**9.5**	**9.5**	**9.5**	**7.8**	**10.6**	**19.0**	**14.9**	**10.5**	**18.1**	**12.1**	**8.6**
Algeria	8.9	3.3	2.9	4.4	5.8	5.9	3.5	2.4	1.9	3.3	3.9
Egypt	7.1	9.5	10.1	9.8	14.3	29.5	14.4	9.4	5.1	6.5	7.8
Libya	6.1	2.6	2.4	9.0	25.9	25.8	13.6	-2.1	3.3	4.6	5.5
Mauritania	4.9	4.1	3.5	0.5	1.4	2.3	3.0	2.3	2.2	2.7	2.9
Morocco	1.3	1.9	0.4	1.6	1.6	0.8	1.8	0.3	0.7	1.1	1.2
Sudan	35.6	36.5	36.9	16.9	17.8	32.4	63.3	51.0	140.7	73.5	31.9
Tunisia	4.6	5.3	4.6	4.4	3.6	5.3	7.3	6.7	5.4	4.0	4.4
East Africa	**15.6**	**5.4**	**5.2**	**8.5**	**22.5**	**19.5**	**12.9**	**8.9**	**14.2**	**15.6**	**14.6**
Burundi	18.2	7.9	4.4	5.5	5.6	16.1	-2.8	-0.7	8.1	5.9	7.7
Comoros	6.3	-4.3	0.0	0.9	0.8	0.1	1.7	3.3	2.5	2.5	3.1
Democratic Republic of the Congo	9.7	0.8	1.2	0.7	2.9	35.8	29.3	4.8	35.9	48.5	47.5
Djibouti	3.7	2.7	1.3	-0.8	2.7	0.6	0.1	3.3	1.6	3.0	3.6
Eritrea	4.8	5.9	10.0	28.5	-5.6	-13.3	-14.4	-16.4	4.2	5.3	5.8
Ethiopia	23.4	7.5	6.9	9.6	6.6	10.7	13.8	15.8	21.5	19.7	16.7
Kenya	9.4	5.7	6.9	6.6	6.3	8.0	4.7	5.2	4.8	6.6	7.1
Madagascar	5.7	5.8	6.1	7.4	6.0	8.6	8.6	5.6	4.0	4.7	4.2
Rwanda	10.3	5.9	2.3	2.5	7.2	8.3	-0.3	3.4	8.2	6.8	6.1
Somalia	-1.9	-3.2	-5.6	-5.6	-0.6	0.9	1.9	4.2	3.9	2.7	3.0
South Sudan	45.1	0.0	1.7	52.8	379.8	187.9	83.5	51.2	36.1	28.5	22.3
Uganda	12.7	4.9	3.1	5.4	5.4	5.6	2.6	2.9	4.3	5.3	5.9
United Republic of Tanzania	16.0	7.9	6.1	5.6	5.2	5.3	3.5	3.5	4.0	4.5	4.5
Central Africa	**3.9**	**2.0**	**3.1**	**3.0**	**1.3**	**0.8**	**2.2**	**1.8**	**6.4**	**10.1**	**11.8**
Cameroon	2.7	2.1	1.8	2.7	0.9	0.6	1.1	2.5	-0.9	-1.7	-1.7
Central African Republic	5.8	1.5	25.3	37.1	4.9	4.2	1.6	2.7	1.7	2.4	2.8
Chad	7.5	0.2	1.7	4.4	-0.8	-1.5	4.3	-1.0	2.9	6.2	7.6
Congo	5.0	4.6	0.9	3.2	3.2	0.5	1.2	2.2	16.4	26.4	31.0
Equatorial Guinea	3.7	2.9	4.3	1.7	1.4	0.7	1.3	1.2	11.9	18.9	21.4
Gabon	2.7	0.5	4.7	-0.3	2.1	2.7	4.7	2.5	12.5	19.1	21.6
Sao Tome and Principe	10.6	8.1	7.0	5.3	5.4	5.7	7.9	8.4	4.8	4.1	3.5
West Africa	**10.3**	**7.6**	**7.3**	**8.4**	**13.3**	**13.8**	**10.1**	**9.2**	**1.2**	**-2.0**	**-2.8**
Benin	6.7	0.4	-0.5	0.2	-0.8	1.8	0.8	-0.9	-2.0	-0.6	0.5
Burkina Faso	3.8	0.5	-0.3	0.7	0.4	1.5	2.0	-3.2	0.3	3.2	3.8
Cabo Verde	2.5	1.5	-0.2	0.1	-1.4	0.8	1.3	1.1	-3.6	-2.7	-1.4
Côte D'Ivoire	1.3	2.6	0.4	1.3	0.7	0.7	0.4	-1.1	-1.6	-0.5	0.6
Gambia	4.3	5.7	5.9	6.8	7.2	8.0	6.5	7.1	0.6	-1.9	-2.5
Ghana	7.1	11.7	15.5	17.1	17.5	12.4	7.8	7.2	8.5	10.2	10.6
Guinea	15.2	11.9	7.1	10.8	8.2	8.9	9.8	9.5	1.6	-0.4	-0.5
Guinea-Bissau	2.1	1.2	-1.5	1.5	2.7	-0.2	0.4	0.2	-5.0	-6.5	-6.3
Liberia	6.8	7.6	9.9	7.7	8.8	12.4	23.6	27.0	-13.6	-30.4	-36.2
Mali	5.3	-0.6	0.9	1.5	-1.8	1.8	0.3	-1.7	-8.8	-11.2	-10.9
Niger	0.5	2.3	-0.9	-0.6	1.7	2.8	3.0	-2.5	0.7	3.6	5.4

Table A.7
Developing economies: consumer price inflation *(continued)*

Annual percentage change[a]

	2012	2013	2014	2015	2016	2017	2018	2019	2020[b]	2021[c]	2022[c]
Nigeria	12.2	8.5	8.1	9.0	15.7	16.5	12.1	11.4	1.0	-3.5	-4.8
Senegal	1.4	0.7	-1.1	0.1	0.8	1.3	0.5	1.8	0.5	2.4	3.2
Sierra Leone	6.6	5.5	4.6	6.7	10.9	18.2	16.0	14.8	13.1	12.7	12.4
Togo	2.6	1.8	0.2	2.6	1.3	-1.0	0.9	0.7	-0.6	0.9	1.7
Southern Africa	**6.8**	**6.5**	**6.2**	**5.8**	**12.6**	**11.1**	**8.2**	**16.3**	**27.1**	**14.3**	**9.5**
Angola	10.3	8.8	7.3	10.3	32.4	31.7	20.2	17.1	23.0	18.7	14.6
Botswana	7.5	5.9	4.4	3.1	2.8	3.3	3.2	2.8	1.9	2.6	3.2
Eswatini	8.9	5.6	5.7	5.0	7.8	6.2	4.8	2.6	4.6	5.0	4.0
Lesotho	6.1	4.9	5.4	3.2	6.6	4.4	4.8	5.2	4.6	5.0	4.0
Malawi	21.3	27.3	23.8	21.9	21.7	11.5	12.4	9.4	10.4	10.8	9.9
Mauritius	3.9	3.5	3.2	1.3	1.0	3.7	3.2	0.4	2.4	4.0	4.5
Mozambique	2.6	4.3	2.6	3.6	17.4	15.1	3.9	2.8	3.9	4.8	3.8
Namibia	6.7	5.6	5.4	3.4	6.7	6.1	4.3	3.7	2.3	3.0	3.7
South Africa	5.7	5.8	6.1	4.5	6.6	5.2	4.5	4.1	4.5	6.2	6.0
Zambia	6.6	7.0	7.8	10.1	17.9	6.6	7.5	9.2	14.6	12.7	10.7
Zimbabwe	3.7	1.6	-0.2	-2.4	-1.6	0.9	10.6	255.3	499.6	152.0	50.4
Africa – net fuel exporters	**10.3**	**6.8**	**6.3**	**7.6**	**14.9**	**15.2**	**10.5**	**9.2**	**4.7**	**2.4**	**1.4**
Africa – net fuel importers	**9.3**	**7.9**	**8.0**	**7.3**	**11.8**	**15.0**	**11.8**	**12.1**	**20.6**	**13.1**	**9.5**
East and South Asia	**4.2**	**4.5**	**3.1**	**2.3**	**2.4**	**2.1**	**2.8**	**4.0**	**3.8**	**3.1**	**2.8**
East Asia	**2.8**	**2.7**	**2.2**	**1.5**	**1.9**	**1.8**	**2.1**	**2.5**	**2.5**	**2.1**	**1.8**
Brunei Darussalam	0.1	0.4	-0.2	-0.5	-0.3	-1.3	1.0	-0.4	1.0	1.0	1.2
Cambodia	2.9	2.9	3.9	1.2	3.0	2.9	2.5	1.9	2.0	2.1	2.2
Democratic People's Republic of Korea	2.6	2.6	1.9	1.4	2.0	1.6	2.1	2.9	3.1	2.1	1.8
China	4.0	1.6	3.7	3.1	-0.6	7.2	2.3	0.3	0.3	2.6	3.3
Fiji	3.4	2.9	0.5	1.4	3.9	3.3	4.1	1.8	-2.0	2.3	2.6
Hong Kong SAR[e]	4.1	4.3	4.4	3.0	2.4	1.5	2.4	2.9	1.7	2.3	2.4
Indonesia	4.0	6.4	6.4	6.4	3.5	3.8	3.3	2.8	2.6	2.9	2.9
Kiribati	-3.0	-1.5	2.1	0.6	1.9	0.4	0.6	-1.9	3.5	7.3	8.8
Lao People's Democratic Republic	4.3	6.4	4.1	1.3	1.6	0.8	2.0	3.3	5.5	4.1	3.3
Malaysia	1.7	2.1	3.1	2.1	2.1	3.9	0.9	0.7	-1.0	2.1	2.3
Mongolia	14.3	10.5	12.3	5.7	0.7	4.3	6.8	7.3	4.6	6.4	6.0
Myanmar	1.5	5.6	5.0	9.5	6.9	4.6	6.9	8.8	5.4	5.2	4.9
Papua New Guinea	4.5	5.0	5.2	6.0	6.7	5.4	4.7	3.6	3.2	3.4	5.1
Philippines	3.0	2.6	3.6	0.7	1.3	2.9	5.2	2.5	1.1	2.1	2.8
Republic of Korea	2.2	1.3	1.3	0.7	1.0	1.9	1.5	0.4	1.1	1.4	1.4
Samoa	2.0	0.6	-0.4	0.7	1.3	1.7	4.2	1.0	3.0	4.9	5.8
Singapore	4.6	2.4	1.0	-0.5	-0.5	0.6	0.4	0.6	-0.3	1.5	1.8
Solomon Islands	5.9	5.4	5.2	-0.6	0.5	0.5	3.5	1.6	1.0	1.2	1.4
Taiwan Province of China	1.9	0.8	1.2	-0.3	1.4	0.6	1.4	0.6	0.1	1.1	1.2
Thailand	3.0	2.2	1.9	-0.9	0.2	0.7	1.1	0.7	-0.8	0.9	1.4
Timor-Leste	11.8	11.1	0.7	0.6	-1.3	0.6	2.6	0.1	0.8	1.9	2.0
Vanuatu	1.3	1.5	0.8	2.5	0.8	3.1	2.3	2.8	3.2	3.9	3.3
Viet Nam	9.1	6.6	4.1	0.6	2.7	3.5	3.5	2.8	3.3	3.7	3.1

Table A.7
Developing economies: consumer price inflation *(continued)*

Annual percentage change[a]

	2012	2013	2014	2015	2016	2017	2018	2019	2020[b]	2021[c]	2022[c]
South Asia	**11.4**	**13.5**	**7.7**	**6.4**	**5.2**	**3.7**	**6.5**	**11.7**	**10.5**	**8.7**	**7.7**
Afghanistan	6.4	7.4	4.7	-0.7	4.4	5.0	0.6	2.3	5.4	4.7	5.1
Bangladesh	6.2	7.5	7.0	6.2	5.5	5.7	5.5	5.6	5.7	6.2	6.1
Bhutan	10.9	7.0	8.3	4.5	3.2	5.0	2.7	2.7	6.0	4.6	4.3
India	9.3	10.9	6.4	5.9	4.9	2.5	4.9	7.7	8.0	6.6	7.2
Iran (Islamic Republic of)	27.3	36.6	16.6	12.5	7.2	8.0	18.0	39.9	29.5	20.6	10.3
Maldives	10.9	3.8	2.1	1.0	0.5	2.8	-0.1	1.3	2.2	7.5	9.8
Nepal	9.5	9.0	8.4	7.9	8.8	3.6	4.1	5.6	5.0	8.2	8.2
Pakistan	9.7	7.7	7.2	2.5	3.8	4.1	5.1	10.6	9.8	11.0	10.6
Sri Lanka	7.5	6.9	3.2	3.8	4.0	7.7	2.1	3.5	2.4	4.8	3.7
East and South Asia – net fuel exporters	**11.0**	**15.3**	**9.4**	**8.1**	**4.6**	**5.1**	**7.7**	**13.9**	**10.6**	**8.2**	**5.2**
East and South Asia – net fuel importers	**3.7**	**3.7**	**2.6**	**1.9**	**2.3**	**1.9**	**2.4**	**3.2**	**3.3**	**2.8**	**2.6**
Western Asia	**4.9**	**4.6**	**4.3**	**3.8**	**3.8**	**4.1**	**6.5**	**4.2**	**5.9**	**4.5**	**3.8**
Net fuel exporters	**2.8**	**2.7**	**2.5**	**2.4**	**2.3**	**0.9**	**2.4**	**-1.1**	**1.2**	**2.3**	**1.7**
Bahrain	2.8	3.3	2.6	1.8	2.8	1.4	2.1	1.0	-2.3	1.2	1.7
Iraq	6.1	1.9	2.2	1.4	1.4	0.2	0.4	-0.2	0.5	0.9	1.2
Kuwait	3.3	2.7	2.9	3.3	3.2	1.9	0.6	1.1	1.9	2.7	2.1
Oman	2.9	1.0	1.0	0.1	1.1	1.6	0.9	0.1	-0.6	1.6	1.5
Qatar	2.3	3.2	3.3	1.8	2.7	0.4	0.3	-0.5	-2.4	1.2	0.9
Saudi Arabia	2.9	3.5	2.2	1.2	2.1	-0.8	2.5	-2.1	3.5	3.0	1.1
United Arab Emirates	0.7	1.1	2.3	4.1	1.6	2.0	3.1	-1.9	-1.6	1.5	2.2
Yemen	9.9	11.0	8.1	22.0	21.3	30.4	27.6	10.0	12.1	15.5	17.7
Net fuel importers	**7.4**	**6.9**	**6.6**	**5.5**	**5.7**	**8.1**	**11.6**	**10.8**	**11.7**	**7.2**	**6.4**
Israel	1.7	1.6	0.5	-0.6	-0.5	0.2	0.8	0.8	-0.6	0.0	0.8
Jordan	4.5	4.8	2.9	-0.9	-0.8	3.3	4.5	0.8	0.3	1.2	2.4
Lebanon	6.6	4.8	1.9	-3.7	-0.8	4.3	6.1	3.0	74.1	23.9	7.7
State of Palestine	2.8	1.7	1.7	1.4	-0.2	0.2	-0.2	1.6	-0.9	1.5	1.3
Syrian Arab Republic	36.5	82.3	22.6	38.4	47.7	18.1	0.9	13.0	41.7	33.9	19.6
Turkey	9.0	7.5	8.9	7.7	7.7	11.1	16.3	15.2	12.4	8.5	8.3
Latin America and the Caribbean[d]	**5.3**	**5.3**	**7.0**	**7.7**	**10.1**	**6.7**	**7.6**	**9.8**	**9.8**	**8.6**	**6.5**
South America[d]	**5.8**	**6.1**	**8.5**	**10.1**	**13.7**	**7.6**	**9.1**	**12.9**	**12.4**	**10.2**	**7.6**
Argentina	10.0	10.6	21.4	21.5	40.5	25.7	34.2	53.3	47.1	34.1	22.2
Bolivia (Plurinational State of)	4.5	5.8	5.8	4.1	3.6	2.8	2.3	1.9	0.5	1.9	2.4
Brazil	5.4	6.2	6.3	9.0	8.7	3.4	3.7	3.7	4.4	5.0	4.4
Chile	3.0	1.9	4.7	4.3	3.8	2.2	2.4	2.2	4.4	3.5	2.9
Colombia	3.2	2.0	2.9	5.0	7.5	4.3	3.2	3.6	5.3	5.3	4.6
Ecuador	5.1	2.7	3.6	4.0	1.7	0.4	-0.2	0.3	-0.2	0.2	0.8
Paraguay	3.7	2.7	5.0	3.1	4.1	3.6	4.0	2.8	1.7	3.0	3.3
Peru	3.7	2.8	3.2	3.6	3.6	2.8	1.3	2.1	1.7	2.8	2.8
Uruguay	8.1	8.6	8.9	8.7	9.6	6.2	7.6	7.9	10.8	9.7	9.1
Venezuela (Bolivarian Republic of)	21.1	40.6	62.2	121.7	254.9	438.1	65374.1	...	...	...	...

Table A.7
Developing economies: consumer price inflation *(continued)*

Annual percentage change[a]

	2012	2013	2014	2015	2016	2017	2018	2019	2020[b]	2021[c]	2022[c]
Mexico and Central America	**4.0**	**3.8**	**3.8**	**2.6**	**2.5**	**5.1**	**4.4**	**3.4**	**4.5**	**5.2**	**4.4**
Costa Rica	4.5	5.2	4.5	0.9	0.0	1.6	2.2	2.1	0.4	1.4	2.1
Cuba	1.9	0.6	1.1	4.9	-0.5	-1.1	1.9	2.0	0.4	1.7	2.1
Dominican Republic	3.7	4.8	3.0	0.8	1.6	3.3	3.6	2.3	4.6	4.9	3.9
El Salvador	1.7	0.8	1.1	-0.7	0.6	1.0	1.1	0.1	-0.5	0.2	0.6
Guatemala	3.8	4.3	3.4	2.4	4.4	4.4	3.8	3.7	2.1	3.4	3.9
Haiti	6.3	5.9	4.6	9.0	13.8	14.7	14.0	19.8	25.5	23.7	19.7
Honduras	5.2	5.2	6.1	3.2	2.7	3.9	4.3	4.4	2.7	3.5	3.7
Mexico	4.1	3.8	4.0	2.8	2.8	6.0	4.9	3.6	5.3	6.0	5.0
Nicaragua	7.5	7.1	6.0	3.9	3.4	4.0	4.8	6.1	4.2	4.6	4.5
Panama	5.7	4.0	2.6	0.1	0.7	0.9	0.8	-0.3	-1.1	-0.4	0.4
Caribbean	**6.3**	**4.5**	**4.6**	**3.3**	**5.6**	**4.0**	**2.4**	**2.5**	**3.8**	**3.4**	**3.1**
Bahamas	2.0	0.3	1.2	1.9	-0.3	1.5	2.3	2.5	0.5	1.0	1.2
Barbados	4.5	1.8	1.9	-1.1	1.1	4.7	3.7	4.1	4.9	4.3	4.0
Belize	1.4	0.5	1.0	-0.7	0.7	1.1	0.3	0.2	-0.8	0.7	0.8
Guyana	2.4	2.1	0.6	-1.0	0.8	1.9	1.2	2.1	-0.4	0.8	2.3
Jamaica	6.9	9.4	8.3	3.7	2.3	4.4	3.7	4.2	5.6	5.3	4.9
Suriname	5.0	1.9	3.4	6.9	53.0	21.5	6.9	4.4	27.4	19.7	13.5
Trinidad and Tobago	9.3	5.2	5.7	4.6	3.1	1.9	1.0	1.0	0.5	0.8	1.1
Latin America and the Caribbean – net fuel exporters	**4.0**	**2.6**	**3.4**	**4.7**	**5.7**	**3.2**	**2.3**	**2.6**	**3.5**	**3.7**	**3.4**
Latin America and the Caribbean – net fuel importers	**5.4**	**5.6**	**7.4**	**8.0**	**10.6**	**7.1**	**8.1**	**10.5**	**10.4**	**9.0**	**6.8**
Memorandum items:											
Least developed countries	11.5	9.0	8.2	8.4	15.6	15.5	14.8	11.7	21.4	15.9	11.6
East Asia (excluding China)	3.2	2.9	2.9	1.8	1.7	2.2	2.1	1.4	1.1	1.9	2.1
South Asia (excluding India)	15.6	19.0	10.5	7.4	5.6	6.3	9.9	20.2	15.9	13.1	8.8
Western Asia (excluding Israel and Turkey)	3.3	3.7	2.7	2.6	2.7	1.2	2.5	-0.8	3.7	3.3	2.1
Arab States[f]	5.2	5.5	4.8	4.2	5.1	6.7	6.3	2.7	8.1	6.0	4.1
Landlocked developing economies	8.5	6.1	5.7	6.7	14.4	10.3	8.3	13.3	20.7	11.2	7.9
Small island developing States	4.3	2.9	2.0	1.3	1.1	1.5	1.7	1.6	1.2	2.6	2.7

Sources: UN DESA, based on data of the United Nations Statistics Division, individual national sources and UN DESA forecasts.
a Data for country groups are weighted averages, where weights for each year are based on 2015 GDP in United States dollars.
b Partly estimated.
c Baseline scenario forecasts, based in part on UN DESA World Economic Forecasting Model.
d Regional aggregates exclude Venezuela (Bolivarian Republic of).
e Special Administrative Region of China.
f Includes data for Algeria, Bahrain, Comoros, Djibouti, Egypt, Iraq, Jordan, Kuwait, Lebanon, Libya, Mauritania, Morocco, Oman, Qatar, Saudi Arabia, Somalia, Sudan, Syrian Arab Republic, Tunisia, United Arab Emirates, and Yemen.

Table A.8

Selected economies: real effective exchange rates, broad measurement[a, b]

	2011	2012	2013	2014	2015	2016	2017	2018	2019	2020[c]
Developed economies										
Australia	99.4	100.0	94.8	90.1	81.1	81.8	84.7	81.4	77.6	75.1
Austria	101.1	100.0	101.7	103.2	101.1	102.6	103.6	104.7	103.7	105.0
Belgium	102.2	100.0	101.2	101.2	97.5	100.0	101.5	103.3	101.7	102.4
Bulgaria	101.8	100.0	99.9	99.6	96.9	96.7	96.6	100.2	100.0	103.5
Canada	100.8	100.0	96.4	90.3	81.2	79.4	80.8	80.0	79.0	77.2
Croatia	101.5	100.0	100.7	100.4	98.6	99.6	99.8	101.3	100.0	98.1
Czechia	102.5	100.0	97.4	92.2	91.4	93.8	96.8	100.8	101.0	101.8
Denmark	102.9	100.0	100.6	101.5	97.3	98.3	98.6	99.7	97.8	98.7
Finland	102.3	100.0	102.3	104.8	101.9	103.2	102.3	104.4	102.9	104.0
France	103.1	100.0	101.1	101.2	96.2	97.5	98.0	99.7	98.2	99.1
Germany	103.2	100.0	102.0	102.6	98.2	99.8	100.6	102.4	100.8	101.7
Greece	105.2	100.0	99.3	98.0	92.1	93.6	94.5	93.4	90.4	89.9
Hungary	101.7	100.0	98.4	95.0	92.5	93.1	94.3	93.5	92.4	88.9
Ireland	104.9	100.0	101.5	100.5	92.7	93.9	94.2	95.0	92.4	93.3
Italy	102.0	100.0	101.6	101.7	97.0	98.1	98.7	99.5	97.0	97.5
Japan	101.6	100.0	80.1	75.2	69.9	78.7	74.9	74.4	76.3	77.4
Netherlands	102.6	100.0	102.8	102.8	98.3	99.6	99.9	101.2	101.0	102.4
New Zealand	97.9	100.0	102.4	105.1	96.1	97.3	99.2	94.0	92.1	90.5
Norway	101.0	100.0	97.9	92.7	84.9	86.1	86.8	87.5	85.6	79.9
Poland	102.2	100.0	100.0	101.1	98.4	94.9	96.9	97.5	96.3	96.3
Portugal	101.9	100.0	100.0	99.3	96.8	98.7	98.9	98.3	96.7	97.4
Romania	99.7	100.0	101.1	101.8	99.8	100.0	99.1	100.4	101.0	103.2
Slovakia	105.9	100.0	103.6	105.0	102.5	101.3	99.1	101.1	100.6	102.7
Spain	102.8	100.0	101.6	101.0	95.9	96.8	98.5	98.2	96.0	96.3
Sweden	100.3	100.0	101.3	96.3	91.1	91.8	90.9	86.7	83.4	85.7
Switzerland	104.3	100.0	98.5	99.1	104.6	102.7	100.9	97.9	98.5	101.8
United Kingdom	96.3	100.0	98.7	105.5	110.3	98.5	93.7	95.3	94.7	95.2
United States	97.8	100.0	100.1	101.9	112.9	117.7	118.5	111.9	113.9	114.8
Economies in transition										
Azerbaijan	96.7	100.0	99.7	103.5	95.5	70.1	71.0	72.6	75.5	78.4
Belarus	104.3	100.0	107.8	119.5	110.1	101.5	99.3	97.8	99.9	91.1
Kazakhstan	96.1	100.0	100.6	93.5	93.4	71.0	76.8	75.9	72.6	72.1
Russian Federation	98.3	100.0	100.2	90.0	74.3	74.4	86.7	79.5	81.5	75.7
Ukraine[d]	98.0	100.0	96.4	73.9	69.9	70.1	73.6	78.0	89.4	89.1
Developing economies										
Algeria	95.5	100.0	98.0	99.8	94.9	93.6	94.7	90.7	92.8	89.1
Argentina	99.2	100.0	90.9	74.3	87.6	77.7	85.6	59.8	53.1	55.6
Bangladesh	103.7	100.0	110.7	118.6	135.3	143.2	144.8	142.7	150.1	156.5
Brazil	111.8	100.0	94.5	92.4	75.5	80.2	89.8	73.7	70.8	55.1
Chile	98.4	100.0	98.9	89.6	87.1	88.5	92.3	91.2	85.7	78.6
China	96.1	100.0	103.8	106.5	114.3	109.1	106.4	106.5	104.8	106.1

Table A.8
Selected economies: real effective exchange rates, broad measurement[a, b] *(continued)*

	2011	2012	2013	2014	2015	2016	2017	2018	2019	2020[c]
Developing economies *(continued)*										
Colombia	95.4	100.0	96.3	91.4	74.1	72.8	79.3	68.4	62.2	55.3
Dominican Republic	100.3	100.0	96.8	94.7	96.3	96.6	95.5	86.1	83.8	77.8
Egypt	94.8	100.0	94.2	101.0	111.3	98.2	69.3	78.1	91.6	99.6
Ethiopia	85.2	100.0	99.9	99.7	108.2	109.7	106.8	108.7	119.6	118.7
Guatemala	98.4	100.0	102.0	106.4	114.4	121.9	130.0	124.5	124.9	126.5
Hong Kong SAR[e]	98.2	100.0	101.9	105.0	112.2	117.4	117.2	115.2	119.7	121.6
India	105.9	100.0	99.4	101.1	107.4	108.6	112.9	107.9	112.7	115.0
Indonesia	104.6	100.0	95.1	89.1	89.9	94.1	95.5	90.0	93.5	93.2
Iran, Islamic Republic of	90.7	100.0	88.6	72.7	76.6	78.1	77.4	72.8	87.4	59.8
Israel	105.8	100.0	106.2	107.3	105.8	107.8	112.6	110.9	113.2	115.7
Korea, Republic of	101.4	100.0	103.3	108.6	107.5	106.4	109.7	110.7	105.1	103.3
Kuwait	99.0	100.0	100.7	101.9	104.8	108.0	107.9	105.9	106.8	106.5
Malaysia	101.1	100.0	99.3	98.6	89.7	86.6	85.3	89.0	87.4	84.9
Mexico	103.3	100.0	105.6	104.3	92.4	80.2	82.4	81.1	83.0	74.3
Morocco	102.4	100.0	101.5	102.1	101.8	104.1	103.4	104.2	104.4	105.0
Nigeria	89.6	100.0	106.7	113.9	110.4	98.0	91.6	99.6	111.5	106.1
Pakistan	99.6	100.0	97.2	103.7	109.5	112.8	114.4	101.1	91.5	91.9
Peru	93.1	100.0	98.8	96.7	95.1	94.2	97.9	93.8	94.9	92.8
Philippines	96.2	100.0	102.0	100.9	105.0	101.7	96.9	94.5	98.8	102.9
Qatar	97.7	100.0	103.7	106.3	115.6	118.5	117.0	113.7	113.9	110.5
Saudi Arabia	97.3	100.0	102.9	104.4	112.2	114.7	111.4	111.3	109.6	112.5
Singapore	95.7	100.0	101.7	101.2	99.0	98.2	97.0	96.2	96.0	93.3
South Africa	106.6	100.0	88.9	83.7	81.1	76.5	85.7	86.8	81.0	67.8
Sri Lanka	107.4	100.0	104.3	105.5	110.3	107.8	108.3	100.2	93.8	91.6
Taiwan Province of China	100.8	100.0	100.1	98.6	99.0	98.9	104.2	103.4	101.6	105.1
Thailand	100.3	100.0	103.7	100.0	100.0	97.0	100.1	103.4	108.8	106.4
Turkey	97.2	100.0	98.7	94.4	92.2	91.0	80.8	68.5	67.8	63.7
United Arab Erirates	100.2	100.0	101.0	103.5	113.2	115.2	115.4	117.3	114.0	112.9
Uruguay	96.5	100.0	106.8	103.3	104.7	106.9	117.9	103.7	97.0	90.1
Viet Nam	94.2	100.0	104.9	107.4	111.9	114.4	113.6	112.9	114.8	117.4

Source: UN DESA, Bank for International Settlements, IMF International Financial Statistics.

a 2012=100.

b CPI-based indices. The real effective exchange rate gauges the effect on international price competitiveness of currency changes and inflation differentials. A rise in the index implies a fall in competitiveness and vice versa.

c Average for the first ten months.

d Data for Ukraine excludes the temporarily occupied territory of the Autonomous Republic of Crimea and Sevastopol.

e Special Administrative Region of China.

Table A.9
Free market commodity price indices

Index: Year 2015=100

	Non-fuel commodities							
	Food	Tropical beverages	Vegetable oilseeds and oils	Agricultural raw materials	Minerals and metals	All groups	All groups excluding fuels	Fuels
2011	135	144	151	177	164	182	158	198
2012	127	112	152	143	153	177	145	197
2013	120	90	136	131	138	170	131	194
2014	118	111	123	115	121	157	119	180
2015	100	100	100	100	100	100	100	100
2016	104	97	107	100	105	91	104	83
2017	103	94	106	105	116	106	110	104
2018	96	86	100	103	118	123	109	132
2019	98	81	93	99	125	114	112	116
2017								
I	109	99	109	114	117	107	113	104
II	105	93	104	103	112	101	108	97
III	100	93	107	102	118	104	110	100
IV	97	90	106	101	119	113	110	115
2018								
I	100	90	107	105	124	120	114	124
II	100	90	106	105	121	126	112	135
III	92	80	95	102	113	126	104	140
IV	94	82	92	100	114	121	105	131
2019								
I	96	79	94	101	120	115	109	119
II	97	79	89	101	123	117	110	121
III	98	80	92	97	130	112	114	110
IV	102	87	98	97	127	113	114	112
2020								
I	103	87	99	97	129	101	116	91
II	99	83	92	91	134	82	116	61
III	100	84	101	95	154	98	128	79

Source: UNCTAD, *Monthly Commodity Price Bulletin*; UN DESA

Table A.10
World oil supply and demand

	2012	2013	2014	2015	2016	2017	2018	2019	2020[a]
World oil supply[b,c] *(millions of barrels per day)*	**89.0**	**89.3**	**91.7**	**94.3**	**94.7**	**95.5**	**98.2**	**97.1**	**94.2**
Developed economies	17.0	18.1	20.1	21.4	21.0	22.0	24.7	26.5	25.6
Economies in transition	13.7	13.9	14.0	14.1	14.3	14.4	14.7	15.0	13.5
Developing economies	56.2	55.1	55.3	56.6	57.1	56.8	56.5	53.3	52.7
OPEC	37.5	37.7	37.7	39.1	39.6	39.5	39.5	36.7	32.6
Non-OPEC	18.7	17.4	17.6	17.6	17.5	17.2	16.9	16.5	20.1
Processing gains[d]	2.1	2.2	2.2	2.2	2.3	2.3	2.3	2.4	2.4
Global biofuels[e]	1.9	2.0	2.2	2.3	2.4	2.4	2.6	2.8	2.8
World total demand[f]	**90.7**	**92.0**	**93.2**	**95.0**	**96.1**	**97.9**	**99.2**	**100.5**	**92.1**
Oil prices *(dollars per barrel)*									
OPEC basket[g]	109.5	105.9	96.3	49.5	40.8	52.4	69.8	64.1	40.5
Brent oil	112.0	108.9	98.9	52.3	43.7	54.2	71.2	64.3	41.2

Source: UN DESA, International Energy Agency; U.S. Energy Information Administration; and OPEC.

a Partly estimated.

b Including global biofuels, crude oil, condensates, natural gas liquids (NGLs), oil from non-conventional sources and other sources of supply.

c Totals may not add up because of rounding.

d Net volumetric gains and losses in the refining process and marine transportation losses.

e Global biofuels comprise all world biofuel production including fuel ethanol from Brazil and the United States.

f Measured as deliveries from refineries and primary stocks, comprises inland deliveries, international marine bunkers, refinery fuel, crude for direct burning.

g As of 6 March 2020, The basket price excludes the Ecuadorean crude "Oriente".

Table A.11

World trade:[a] Changes in value and volume of exports and imports, by major country group

Annual percentage change

	2012	2013	2014	2015	2016	2017	2018	2019	2020[b]	2021[c]	2022[c]
Dollar value of exports											
World	**1.6**	**2.7**	**1.7**	**-11.0**	**-2.1**	**10.0**	**9.3**	**-0.1**	**-4.7**	**10.5**	**5.5**
Developed economies	**-1.6**	**3.3**	**3.2**	**-9.6**	**0.3**	**8.7**	**8.6**	**-1.2**	**-2.7**	**11.4**	**5.0**
Northern America	3.5	3.2	3.9	-6.2	-1.9	6.8	6.4	-0.5	-13.7	16.6	4.8
Europe	-3.1	4.8	3.2	-10.5	0.7	9.1	9.6	-1.6	-0.4	10.5	5.0
Developed Asia and Pacific	-2.3	-6.6	1.8	-11.7	3.4	10.5	6.9	-0.8	6.7	7.9	5.1
Economies in transition	**3.2**	**-0.6**	**-5.7**	**-28.7**	**-11.7**	**21.5**	**20.6**	**-1.7**	**-10.6**	**9.4**	**5.2**
South-Eastern Europe	-6.1	15.3	4.1	-9.9	9.2	15.1	16.6	6.7	-6.7	10.0	5.2
Commonwealth of Independent States and Georgia[d]	3.6	-1.1	-6.1	-29.5	-12.8	22.0	20.8	-2.2	-10.9	9.3	5.2
Developing economies	**5.6**	**2.3**	**0.6**	**-11.2**	**-4.6**	**11.0**	**9.3**	**1.6**	**-6.9**	**9.3**	**6.3**
Latin America and the Caribbean	2.1	-0.2	-4.0	-12.8	-2.9	9.7	7.4	-0.9	-12.4	9.2	3.1
Africa	8.0	-10.2	-3.5	-28.0	-8.1	16.2	14.0	14.8	-13.7	12.2	7.4
East Asia	5.2	5.0	4.0	-5.8	-5.1	10.2	8.6	-0.7	-0.3	7.5	6.4
South Asia	0.9	3.2	-4.4	-9.1	2.3	13.3	5.6	1.5	-20.5	25.7	8.4
Western Asia	11.3	0.7	-3.6	-23.7	-5.8	13.1	14.1	8.5	-19.5	9.1	7.1
Dollar value of imports											
World	**1.2**	**2.8**	**2.1**	**-9.8**	**-2.9**	**9.8**	**9.4**	**-0.7**	**-4.3**	**9.8**	**5.5**
Developed economies	**-2.0**	**1.6**	**3.0**	**-9.8**	**-0.5**	**8.7**	**9.3**	**-1.1**	**-1.4**	**10.1**	**4.9**
Northern America	3.0	0.1	3.4	-4.1	-2.1	7.0	6.8	-0.5	-9.7	12.6	4.7
Europe	-5.3	3.6	3.0	-11.1	0.9	9.4	10.3	-1.1	0.2	9.8	5.1
Developed Asia and Pacific	5.3	-5.4	1.7	-16.9	-4.5	9.5	9.7	-3.3	12.6	5.7	4.2
Economies in transition	**8.5**	**3.3**	**-9.1**	**-28.3**	**-4.8**	**19.3**	**8.8**	**12.9**	**-14.4**	**10.0**	**5.4**
South-Eastern Europe	-6.6	4.9	4.0	-13.8	5.4	14.6	16.7	6.2	-8.5	7.5	3.9
Commonwealth of Independent States and Georgia[d]	9.6	3.2	-9.9	-29.3	-5.7	19.8	8.0	13.6	-15.0	10.2	5.5
Developing economies	**5.4**	**4.2**	**2.0**	**-8.2**	**-5.9**	**10.8**	**9.5**	**-1.1**	**-7.5**	**9.3**	**6.5**
Latin America and the Caribbean	5.9	4.8	-0.1	2.5	-18.2	6.4	5.4	-2.8	-10.3	10.8	4.6
Africa	3.3	5.7	1.6	-16.9	-7.1	3.7	12.2	13.5	-4.5	7.9	5.4
East Asia	5.1	4.8	2.9	-9.8	-3.2	12.4	12.3	-1.2	-5.5	7.2	6.7
South Asia	6.0	-3.6	-3.9	-7.6	1.0	17.9	6.3	-4.8	-27.8	31.4	8.1
Western Asia	7.5	5.6	4.6	-8.6	-5.7	7.9	2.1	-4.6	-2.0	7.3	6.6
Volume of exports											
World	**4.2**	**2.6**	**3.9**	**2.9**	**2.4**	**5.8**	**3.9**	**0.9**	**-7.7**	**7.5**	**3.8**
Developed economies	**2.2**	**2.8**	**4.4**	**4.6**	**2.7**	**5.0**	**3.3**	**1.9**	**-10.6**	**9.1**	**3.5**
Northern America	3.3	3.4	4.6	0.9	0.5	3.5	3.0	0.1	-12.3	13.7	3.0
Europe	2.0	2.7	3.9	6.1	3.5	5.3	3.4	2.8	-9.5	8.1	3.6
Developed Asia and Pacific	1.3	1.9	8.5	3.9	2.9	6.1	3.4	0.2	-13.9	5.4	4.1
Economies in transition	**1.2**	**2.5**	**-0.9**	**1.8**	**3.2**	**5.3**	**5.7**	**0.5**	**-6.2**	**6.5**	**4.5**
South-Eastern Europe	1.7	11.4	5.3	8.3	10.7	9.7	8.7	5.7	-9.2	6.4	4.0

Table A.11

World trade[a]: Changes in value and volume of exports and imports by major country group *(continued)*

Annual percentage change

	2012	2013	2014	2015	2016	2017	2018	2019	2020[b]	2021[c]	2022[c]
Commonwealth of Independent States and Georgia[d]	1.2	2.1	-1.1	1.5	2.8	5.1	5.5	0.2	-6.0	6.5	4.6
Developing economies	**7.0**	**2.4**	**3.5**	**0.9**	**1.9**	**6.8**	**4.6**	**-0.3**	**-4.1**	**5.7**	**4.2**
Latin America and the Caribbean	3.0	1.1	1.3	4.7	1.8	3.7	3.6	0.4	-7.7	8.4	2.3
Africa	33.3	-25.2	-8.1	-4.5	3.8	13.7	4.9	1.6	-10.4	8.4	4.3
East Asia	4.9	6.8	5.8	1.0	1.3	7.5	4.5	-0.7	-0.1	3.5	4.1
South Asia	3.1	4.3	3.0	-1.5	6.6	5.8	5.5	-0.7	-18.8	24.1	6.9
Western Asia	8.4	1.8	1.1	0.5	1.5	3.8	5.5	-0.1	-9.1	4.8	4.4
Volume of imports											
World	**3.3**	**3.1**	**3.1**	**2.0**	**1.6**	**5.7**	**4.4**	**1.0**	**-7.4**	**6.5**	**3.7**
Developed economies	**1.0**	**2.1**	**4.6**	**5.6**	**3.1**	**4.8**	**3.7**	**2.5**	**-8.4**	**7.1**	**3.2**
Northern America	2.9	1.6	4.6	4.4	1.4	4.6	3.9	1.0	-10.5	9.5	3.0
Europe	-0.6	2.4	4.4	7.0	4.5	4.9	3.5	3.7	-8.8	6.8	3.4
Developed Asia and Pacific	5.4	2.0	5.7	1.1	-0.9	4.6	3.9	-0.9	0.7	1.6	2.2
Economies in transition	**9.2**	**2.8**	**-6.3**	**-16.7**	**-0.3**	**12.8**	**4.9**	**6.3**	**-10.7**	**7.3**	**3.9**
South-Eastern Europe	-0.1	3.0	6.5	3.5	7.9	9.7	9.2	5.2	-9.9	4.9	2.4
Commonwealth of Independent States and Georgia[d]	9.8	2.8	-7.1	-18.2	-1.0	13.1	4.5	6.4	-10.8	7.5	4.0
Developing economies	**5.9**	**4.2**	**2.0**	**-1.2**	**-0.1**	**6.6**	**5.3**	**-1.3**	**-5.8**	**5.6**	**4.4**
Latin America and the Caribbean	9.3	-0.4	-4.6	-6.3	-10.9	1.6	4.7	-1.9	-10.2	6.9	2.6
Africa	4.1	7.1	-2.3	-3.9	-0.5	5.0	4.3	5.2	-1.9	4.7	3.8
East Asia	5.0	7.1	5.0	1.3	3.3	7.7	6.5	-1.9	-3.4	3.4	4.7
South Asia	2.9	-5.9	-1.4	-3.9	2.5	13.6	7.3	-1.8	-23.7	25.5	5.7
Western Asia	7.7	5.6	4.6	-1.3	-2.5	4.2	-0.5	-1.7	-1.5	3.9	4.4

Source: UN DESA.

a Includes goods and services.

b Partly estimated.

c Baseline scenario forecasts, based in part on UN DESA World Economic Forecasting Model.

d Georgia officially left the Commonwealth of Independent States on 18 August 2009. However, its performance is discussed in the context of this group of countries for reasons of geographic proximity and similarities in economic structure.

Table A.12
Balance of payments on current accounts, by country or country group, summary table

Billions of dollars

	2011	2012	2013	2014	2015	2016	2017	2018	2019	2020[a]
Developed economies	**-223.3**	**-141.1**	**31.7**	**3.3**	**25.6**	**133.3**	**225.2**	**125.3**	**90.3**	**57.5**
Japan	129.8	59.7	45.9	36.8	136.4	197.9	203.5	176.6	184.3	143.5
United States	-455.3	-418.1	-336.9	-367.8	-407.4	-394.9	-365.3	-449.7	-480.2	-441.7
Europe	202.1	356.2	437.9	427.3	413.1	422.9	475.1	479.7	420.4	366.8
Europe excluding the United Kingdon	248.9	449.1	570.6	572.0	556.8	563.8	568.2	590.4	533.9	420.8
Other Europe[b]	68.7	42.2	2.0	-28.9	-35.3	-56.8	-30.2	-20.9	-14.2	16.1
Economies in transition	**98.7**	**58.9**	**12.6**	**52.7**	**48.9**	**-2.4**	**15.4**	**105.8**	**46.6**	**-1.4**
South-Eastern Europe	-8.4	-8.4	-5.6	-6.0	-3.8	-3.9	-5.0	-5.2	-6.6	-7.1
Commonwealth of Independent States and Georgia[c]	108.9	69.2	19.2	60.5	54.5	3.4	21.7	112.2	54.1	7.4
Developing economies	**520.3**	**511.6**	**372.8**	**388.8**	**189.9**	**188.9**	**299.3**	**185.4**	**285.6**	**170.4**
Net fuel exporters	463.1	422.9	349.5	201.1	-166.2	-111.6	28.1	137.0	31.3	-131.3
Net fuel importers	57.2	88.7	23.3	187.7	356.1	300.5	271.3	48.4	254.3	301.7
Latin America and the Caribbean	**-112.9**	**-148.4**	**-172.6**	**-185.5**	**-171.7**	**-99.3**	**-85.7**	**-129.5**	**-89.3**	**-19.8**
Net fuel exporters	10.9	-3.5	-2.5	-11.1	-37.0	-17.7	-2.3	-6.3	-8.7	-16.2
Net fuel importers	-123.9	-144.9	-170.1	-174.4	-134.7	-81.6	-83.4	-123.1	-80.6	-3.6
Africa	**-9.0**	**-45.4**	**-63.3**	**-90.0**	**-143.3**	**-115.1**	**-85.7**	**-82.7**	**-103.5**	**-120.5**
Net fuel exporters	40.1	34.8	15.6	-25.1	-72.8	-45.9	-21.4	-15.2	-37.1	-51.0
Net fuel importers	-49.1	-80.2	-78.9	-64.9	-70.5	-69.2	-64.3	-67.5	-66.4	-69.5
Western Asia	**270.9**	**336.6**	**284.6**	**200.8**	**-72.8**	**-85.6**	**-3.1**	**126.1**	**103.6**	**-64.7**
Net fuel exporters	351.0	399.8	348.4	243.6	-47.4	-53.4	45.1	157.4	96.8	-48.6
Net fuel importers	-80.1	-63.2	-63.8	-42.8	-25.5	-32.2	-48.2	-31.3	6.9	-16.1
East and South Asia	**290.2**	**274.4**	**289.5**	**434.6**	**555.5**	**473.5**	**408.7**	**180.1**	**327.7**	**375.1**
Net fuel exporters	61.1	-8.2	-12.0	-6.3	-9.0	5.4	6.7	1.1	-19.6	-15.5
Net fuel importers	229.1	282.6	301.4	440.9	564.5	468.1	402.0	179.0	347.3	390.6
World residual[d]	**395.7**	**429.4**	**417.0**	**444.8**	**264.4**	**319.7**	**540.0**	**416.6**	**422.5**	**226.5**

Source: International Monetary Fund (IMF), World Economic Outlook database, October 2020.

a Partly estimated.

b Other Europe consists of Iceland, Norway, Switzerland and the United Kingdom (Table A).

c Georgia officially left the Commonwealth of Independent States on 18 August 2009. However, its performance is discussed in the context of this group of countries for reasons of geographic proximity and similarities in economic structure.

d Statistical discrepancy.

Other notes: Africa includes South Sudan; West Asia excludes Palestine; and East Asia excludes Democratic People's Republic of Korea.

Table A.13
Net ODA from major sources, by type

Donor group or country	Growth rate of ODA (2016 prices and exchange rates)					ODA as a percentage of GNI	Total ODA (millions of dollars)	Percentage distribution of ODA by type, 2019			
								Bilateral	Multilateral		
	1998–2008	2008–2016	2017	2018	2019	2019	2019	Total	Total (United Nations & other)	United Nations	Other
Total DAC countries	**5.6**	**4.9**	**-0.2**	**-2.2**	**0.3**	**0.29**	**147680**	**71.0**	**29.0**	**4.9**	**24.2**
Total EU	**5.3**	**4.8**	**0.1**	**-0.4**	**-1.1**	**0.47**	**84079**	**64.1**	**35.9**	**5.3**	**30.6**
Austria	7.8	4.7	-25.8	-12.4	9.1	0.28	1227	36.2	63.8	3.2	60.6
Belgium	6.5	6.3	-7.9	0.6	-2.3	0.42	2211	53.4	46.6	6.9	39.8
Denmark	0.3	0.2	0.2	-0.2	2.5	0.71	2534	69.3	30.7	09.0	21.7
Finland	6.6	7.4	-0.4	-15.1	20.1	0.42	1144	52.1	47.9	13.8	34.1
France[a]	1.0	3.5	15.0	7.4	-3.1	0.43	11980	62.3	37.7	4.0	33.7
Germany	5.0	4.1	-1.9	-3.4	-2.8	0.61	24122	76.7	23.3	2.9	20.3
Greece	8.5	6.5	-16.9	-12.0	32.5	0.18	368	38.8	61.2	3.3	57.9
Ireland	13.2	10.6	1.3	5.7	4.5	0.31	935	56.9	43.1	10.2	32.8
Italy	8.0	-1.0	12.2	-17.6	-2.7	0.23	4733	38.5	61.5	3.4	58.1
Luxembourg	8.9	7.1	4.6	4.0	2.7	1.05	474	73.3	26.7	7.4	19.2
Netherlands	3.3	2.5	-3.3	5.8	-3.3	0.59	5292	65.9	34.1	9.6	24.5
Portugal	3.0	1.3	7.2	-4.2	-7.4	0.15	344	25.3	74.7	4.1	70.6
Spain	10.5	9.4	-41.3	-4.4	6.7	0.19	2662	29.6	70.4	3.3	67.0
Sweden	6.5	7.8	11.2	7.3	-8.2	0.96	5205	66.6	33.4	13.5	19.9
United Kingdom[b]	4.9	4.2	-13.2	4.1	-2.5	0.22	2949	77.4	22.6	3.4	19.2
Australia	2.9	3.1	4.6	5.8	-2.0	0.26	4535	67.0	33.0	6.5	26.5
Canada	-0.1	-3.0	13.7	-13.5	13.5	0.22	11639	64.2	35.8	4.5	31.3
Japan	4.7	4.2	-4.7	25.7	3.4	0.28	559	81.6	18.4	8.4	10.1
New Zealand	3.0	3.8	-10.8	-4.0	9.9	1.03	4298	77.1	22.9	9.9	12.9
Norway	3.9	5.0	-11.6	-2.5	0.6	0.44	3089	76.9	23.1	7.0	16.1
Switzerland	8.4	8.5	3.1	1.8	1.8	0.70	19343	66.6	33.4	5.2	28.2
United States	10.6	9.1	-1.0	-5.0	-1.5	0.16	33889	88.2	11.8	2.9	8.8

Source: UN DESA, based on OECD/DAC online database, available from http://www.oecd-ilibrary.org/statistics.

a Excluding flows from France to the Overseas Departments, namely Guadeloupe, French Guiana, Martinique and Réunion.

b The United Kingdom was still a member of the EU during the period covered in this table and is therefore included in the EU aggregations. The country withdrew from the EU at the end of January 2020.

Table A.14
Total net ODA flows from OECD Development Assistance Committee countries, by type

	Net disbursements at current prices and exchange rates (billions of dollars)									
	2010	2011	2012	2013	2014	2015	2016	2017	2018	2019
Official Development Assistance	**128.5**	**135.1**	**127.0**	**134.8**	**137.5**	**131.6**	**144.9**	**147.2**	**150.1**	**147.7**
Bilateral official development assistance	**90.6**	**94.8**	**88.5**	**93.5**	**94.8**	**94.2**	**103.1**	**105.6**	**105.2**	**104.8**
in the form of:										
Technical cooperation	18.6	18.0	18.2	16.9	17.3	14.9	15.7	16.5	15.8	...
Humanitarian aid	9.3	9.7	8.5	10.5	13.1	13.4	14.4	16.1	16.0	...
Debt forgiveness	4.2	6.3	3.3	6.1	1.4	0.3	2.1	0.4	0.3	...
Bilateral loans	3.8	1.9	2.6	1.4	5.3	6.0	5.8	6.6	6.2	...
Contributions to multilateral institutions[a]	**37.8**	**40.3**	**38.6**	**41.4**	**42.7**	**37.3**	**41.8**	**41.6**	**44.8**	**42.9**
of which are:										
UN agencies	6.5	6.5	6.6	6.9	6.8	6.1	5.9	6.2	6.6	7.2
EU institutions	13.7	13.8	12.0	12.8	13.3	11.9	13.8	13.9	15.2	15.4
World Bank	8.8	10.2	8.6	9.4	9.8	8.6	8.8	8.2	11.3	9.6
Regional development banks	3.2	4.1	3.9	3.9	4.0	3.2	4.6	4.2	4.2	4.1
Others	4.9	4.4	6.4	7.2	7.5	6.7	7.8	8.1	6.3	...
Memorandum item										
Bilateral ODA to least developed countries	0.1	-1.8	0.7	-0.8	0.5	1.2	1.2	2.2	2.5	...

Source: UN DESA, based on OECD/DAC online database, available from http://www.oecd.org/dac/stats/idsonline.
a Grants and capital subscriptions. Does not include concessional lending to multilateral agencies.

Table A.15
Commitments and net flows of financial resources, by selected multilateral institutions

Billions of dollars

	2010	2011	2012	2013	2014	2015	2016	2017	2018	2019
Resource commitments[a]	**245.4**	**163.8**	**189.8**	**130.8**	**185.0**	**119.9**	**245.4**	**256.7**	**224.8**	**225.0**
Financial institutions, excluding International Monetary Fund (IMF)	**119.6**	**106.8**	**96.5**	**98.8**	**99.2**	**99.9**	**106.9**	**108.0**	**114.6**	**129.3**
Regional development banks[b]	46.2	46.9	43.0	45.8	41.1	46.9	49.8	54.0	56.0	59.8
World Bank Group[c]	73.4	59.9	53.5	53.0	58.1	53.0	57.0	54.0	58.6	69.5
International Bank for Reconstruction and Development (IBRD)	44.2	26.7	20.6	15.2	18.6	23.5	29.7	22.6	23.0	28.0
International Development Association (IDA)	14.6	16.3	14.8	16.3	22.2	19.0	16.2	19.5	24.0	30.4
International Financial Corporation (IFC)[d]	14.6	16.9	9.2	11.0	10.0	10.5	11.1	11.9	11.6	11.1
International Fund for Agricultural Development (IFAD)	0.8	1.0	1.0	0.8	0.7	1.3	0.8	1.3	1.3	1.7
International Monetary Fund (IMF)	**114.1**	**45.7**	**82.5**	**19.6**	**72.7**	**6.2**	**123.9**	**132.9**	**89.9**	**75.6**
United Nations operational agencies[e]	**11.6**	**11.3**	**10.8**	**12.4**	**13.1**	**13.7**	**14.7**	**15.8**	**20.4**	**20.1**
Net flows	**64.6**	**78.7**	**35.1**	**8.8**	**-5.1**	**17.7**	**32.2**	**36.3**	**82.6**	**62.8**
Financial institutions, excluding IMF	**27.2**	**38.0**	**26.3**	**22.2**	**25.0**	**35.5**	**33.8**	**36.6**	**46.8**	**49.4**
Regional development banks[b]	9.9	10.5	8.6	5.7	11.2	15.4	14.2	13.1	14.2	15.2
World Bank Group[c]	17.2	27.6	17.7	16.5	13.8	20.1	19.6	23.6	32.7	34.2
International Bank for Reconstruction and Development (IBRD)	8.3	17.2	8.0	7.8	6.4	9.0	10.0	13.2	17.4	17.4
International Development Association (IDA)	7.0	9.1	7.8	7.0	7.4	9.9	8.8	8.8	14.7	15.3
International Financial Corporation (IFC)	1.9	1.2	1.9	1.6	0.1	1.3	0.8	1.6	0.6	1.6
International Fund for Agricultural Development (IFAD)	0.2	0.3	0.3	0.2	0.2	0.2	0.2	0.3	0.3	0.3
International Monetary Fund (IMF)	**37.4**	**40.7**	**8.9**	**-13.4**	**-30.1**	**-17.9**	**-1.5**	**-0.4**	**35.8**	**13.4**

Source: Annual reports of the relevant multilateral institutions, various issues.

a Loans, grants, technical assistance and equity participation, as appropriate; all data are on a calendar-year basis.

b African Development Bank (AfDB), Asian Development Bank (ADB), Caribbean Development Bank (CDB), European Bank for Reconstruction and Development (EBRD), Inter-American Development Bank (IaDB) and the International Fund for Agricultural Development (IFAD).

c Data is for fiscal year.

d Effective 2012, data does not include short-term finance.

e United Nations Development Programme (UNDP), United Nations Population Fund (UNFPA), United Nations Children's Fund (UNICEF), and the World Food Programme (WFP).

Bibliography

A

Afonso, Helena, and Sebastian Vergara (2021, forthcoming). The impact of COVID-19: Does inequality matter? UN DESA Policy Brief.

African Development Bank Group (2020). The African Development Bank Group's Covid-19 Rapid Response Facility (CRF). 21 April.

Ahmad, Nadim, and Annalisa Primi (2017). From domestic to regional to global: factory Africa and factory Latin America? In *Global Value Chain Development Report 2017: Measuring and Analyzing the Impact of GVCs on Economic Development*. Chap. 3. Washington, DC: World Bank.

Akinci, Ozge, and Jane Olmsted-Rumsey (2015). How effective are macroprudential policies? an empirical investigation. Board of Governors of the Federal Reserve System (FRB) International Finance Discussion Paper, No. 1136. May. Washington, DC.

Altavilla, Carlo, and others (2020). *The Great Lockdown: Pandemic Response Policies and Bank Lending Conditions. ECB Working Paper*, No. 2465 (September). Available at www.ecb.europa.eu/pub/pdf/scpwps/ecb.wp2465~c0502b9e88.en.pdf.

Altshuler, Clive, and others (2016). The World Economic Forecasting Model at the United Nations. New York: United Nations, Department of Economic and Social Affairs. Available at https://www.un.org/development/desa/dpad/wpcontent/uploads/sites/45/publication/2016_Apr_WorldEconomicForecastingModel.pdf.

Aman, Mohammad Adil, Mohd Sadiq Salman and Ali P. Yunus (2020). COVID-19 and its impact on environment: improved pollution levels during the lockdown period – a case from Ahmedabad, India. *Remote Sensing Applications: Society and Environment*, vol. 20: 100382.

Andersson, Fredrik N.G., and Lars Jonung (2020). Don't do it again! the Swedish experience with negative central bank rates in 2015-2019. VoxEU, CEPR policy portal. 8 May. Available at https://voxeu.org/article/swedish-experience-negative-central-bank-rates.

Anner, Mark (2020). Leveraging desperation: apparel brands' purchasing practices during Covid-19. Center for Global Workers' Rights (CGWR) research report. University Park, Pennsylvania: Penn State College of the Liberal Arts.

Anukoonwattaka, Witada, and Mia Mikic (2020). Beyond the COVID-19 pandemic: coping with the "new normal" in supply chains. ESCAP policy brief. Available at https://www.unescap.org/sites/default/files/Policy_brief_supply_chain.pdf.

Araujo, Juliana, and others (2020). *Effects of Macroprudential Policy: Evidence from Over 6,000 Estimates. IMF Working Paper*, No. 20/67. May. International Monetary Fund.

Arnold, Carrie (2020). Pandemic speeds largest test yet of universal basic income. *Nature*. 10 July.

Arslan, Yavuz, Mathias Drehmann and Boris Hofmann (2020). Central bank bond purchases in emerging market economies. *BIS Bulletin*, No. 20 (2 June). Bank for International Settlements. Available at www.bis.org/publ/bisbull20.pdf.

Asian Development Bank (2020). *Asian Development Outlook 2020 Update: Wellness in Worrying Times*. Manila. September.

AstraZeneca (2020). AZD1222 vaccine met primary efficacy endpoint in preventing COVID-19. News release. 23 November. Available at www.astrazeneca.com/content/dam/az/media-centre-docs/press-releases/2020/AZD1222-HLR-RNS.pdf.

Australian Bureau of Statistics (2020). A series of unprecedented events: the June quarter 2020. Australian Statistician's Analytical Series. 14 September. Available at www.abs.gov.au/articles/series-unprecedented-events-june-quarter-2020.

Autor, David H., David Dorn and Gordon H. Hanson (2013). The China Syndrome: local labour market effects of import competition in the United States. *American Economic Review*, vol. 103, No. 6 (October), pp. 2121-2168. Available at https://pubs.aeaweb.org/doi/pdfplus/10.1257/aer.103.6.2121.

B

Balchin, Neil, and others (2016). Trade in services and economic transformation. London: Overseas Development Institute. November.

Baldwin, Richard (2019). *The Globotics Upheaval: Globalization, Robotics, and the Future of Work*. New York: Oxford University Press.

Baldwin, Richard, and Rebecca Freeman (2020). Supply chain contagion waves: thinking ahead on manufacturing "contagion and reinfection" from the COVID concussion. VoxEU, CEPR policy portal. 1 April. Available at https://voxeu.org/article/covid-concussion-and-supply-chain-contagion-waves.

Baldwin, Richard, and Rikard Forslid (2020). Globotics and development: when manufacturing is jobless and services are tradable. *NBER Working Paper*, No. 26731. Cambridge, Massachusetts: National Bureau of Economic Research. February. Available at https://www.nber.org/system/files/working_papers/w26731/w26731.pdf.

Banga, Karishma, and others (2020). *Africa Trade and Covid19: The Supply Chain Dimension*. ODI and African Trade Policy Centre working paper, No. 586. August. Available at www.odi.org/sites/odi.org.uk/files/resource-documents/africa_trade-covid-19_web_1.pdf.

Bangladesh, Ministry of Finance, Economic Relations Division (2020). Inputs of national focal points of LDCs in the Asia-Pacific on response to COVID-19 and way forward: Bangladesh context. 30 September.

Bank for International Settlements (BIS) (2020). *Annual Economic Report: June 2020*. Available at www.bis.org/publ/arpdf/ar2020e.pdf.

Bhagwati, Jagdish, Pravin Krishna and Arvind Panagariya, (2014). The world trade system: trends and challenges. Columbia University Working Paper. Available at www.columbia.edu/~jb38/papers/pdf/paper1-the_world_trading_system.pdf.

Blanchard, Olivier J., and Daniel Leigh (2013). Growth forecast errors and fiscal multipliers. *American Economic Review*, vol. 103, No. 3 (May), pp. 117–120.

Bulow, Jeremy, and others (2020). The debt pandemic: new steps are needed to improve sovereign debt workouts. *Finance and Development* (September). International Monetary Fund. Available at www.imf.org/external/pubs/ft/fandd/2020/09/debt-pandemic-reinhart-rogoff-bulow-trebesch.htm.

Burke, Marshall (2020). COVID-19 reduces economic activity, which reduces pollution, which saves lives. Global Food, Environment and Economic Dynamics (G-FEED) website. Posted on 8 March.

C

Catalano, Michele, Lorenzo Forni and Emilia Pezzolla (2020). Climate-change adaptation: the role of fiscal policy. *Resource and Energy Economics*, vol. 59, issue C (February).

Center for Operational Analysis and Research (COAR) (2019). Two countries, one crisis: the impact of Lebanon's upheaval on Syria. 21 December. Available at https://coar-global.org/2019/12/21/two-countries-one-crisis-the-impact-of-lebanons-upheaval-on-syria/.

Central Bank News (2020). Easier or tighter? CentralBankNews.info (website). Available at www.centralbanknews.info/p/eas.html. Accessed on 3 January 2021.

Charumilind, Sarun, and others (2020). When will the COVID-19 pandemic end? McKinsey and Company. 23 November. Available at www.mckinsey.com/industries/healthcare-systems-and-services/our-insights/when-will-the-covid-19-pandemic-end.

Clifford, Catherine (2020). This free cash plan would pay you $1,320 per month and wouldn't cost the government a cent. CNBC.com. 14 January. Available at www.cnbc.com/2020/01/14/budget-neutral-universal-basic-income-plan-would-pay-1320-per-month.html.

Cowley, Stacy, and Ella Koeze (2020). 1 percent of P.P.P. borrowers got over one-quarter of the loan money. *New York Times*, 2 December.

D

de Bolle, Monica, and Jeromin Zettelmeyer (2019). *Measuring the Rise of Economic Nationalism.* PIIE working paper, No. 19-15. Washington, DC: Peterson Institute for International Economics. August.

Del Prete, Davide, and others (2016). Global agro-food value chains: new evidence from SSA. Rome: Food and Agriculture Organization of the United Nations. May. Rome.

Dellink, Rob, and others (2017). *International Trade Consequences of Climate Change.* OECD Trade and Environment Working Paper, No. 2017/01.

Di Comite, Francesco, Antonella Nocco and Gianluca Orefice (2018). Trade liberalization and the wage gap: the role of vertical linkages and fixed costs. *Review of World Economics*, vol. 154 (4 August), pp. 75–115. Available at https://link.springer.com/article/10.1007/s10290-017-0293-1.

Di Gropello, Emanuela (2020). The costs of COVID-19 in education in Latin America: acting now to protect the future of our children. World Bank *Education for Global Development* blog. 7 October. Available at https://blogs.worldbank.org/education/costs-covid-19-education-latin-america-acting-now-protect-future-our-children.

Dossche, Maarten, and Stylianos Zlatanos (2020). COVID-19 and the increase in household savings: precautionary or forced? *ECB Economic Bulletin*, No. 6/2020. Available at www.ecb.europa.eu/pub/economic-bulletin/focus/2020/html/ecb.ebbox202006_05~d36f12a192.en.html.

Duke Global Health Innovation Center (2020). Launch and Scale Speedometer: COVID-19. Durham, North Carolina. Available at https://launchandscalefaster.org/COVID-19.

E

Elgar, Frank J., Anna Stefaniak and Michael J.A. Wohl (2020). The trouble with trust: time-series analysis of social capital, income inequality, and COVID-19 deaths in 84 countries. *Social Science and Medicine*, vol. 263 (October), 113365.

European Central Bank (2020). Household sector report 2020 Q2. Available at https://sdw.ecb.europa.eu/servlet/desis?node=1000004962.

European Commission (2018). WTO modernisation. Concept paper. Available at https://trade.ec.europa.eu/doclib/docs/2018/september/tradoc_157331.pdf.

European Parliament (2020). *Trade Related Aspects of a Carbon Border Adjustment Mechanism: A Legal Assessment*. Briefing requested by the European Parliament Committee on International Trade. 19 August.

European Parliamentary Research Service (2017). EU single market: boosting growth and jobs in the EU. November.

Eurostat (2020). Data browser (beta version). Household saving rate. Online data code: TEINA500.

Evenett, Simon J. (2020). What's next for protectionism? watch out for state largesse, especially export incentives. In *COVID-19 and Trade Policy: Why Turning Inward Won't Work*, Richard E. Baldwin and Simon J. Evenett, eds. Chap. 13. London: CEPR Press. Available at https://voxeu.org/system/files/epublication/Covid-19_and_Trade_Policy.pdf.

Evenett, Simon J., and Johannes Fritz (2020). *Collateral Damage: Cross-Border Fallout from Pandemic Policy Overdrive*. 26th Global Trade Alert Report. Available at www.globaltradealert.org/reports/download/60.

Evenett, Simon J., and Richard Baldwin (2020). *Revitalising Multilateralism: Pragmatic Ideas for the New WTO Director-General*. London: CEPR Press. Available at https://voxeu.org/system/files/epublication/Revising_Multilateralism.pdf.

F

Fatas, Antonio (2019). *Are the Current "Automatic Stabilisers" in the Euro Area Member States Sufficient to Smooth Economic Cycles?* European Parliament in-depth analysis. May.

Food and Agriculture Organization of the United Nations (2020). *Food Price Monitoring and Analysis (FPMA) Bulletin*, No. 9. 10 November.

Foster, Christopher, and Shamel Azmeh (2020). Latecomer economies and national digital policy: an industrial policy perspective. *Journal of Development Studies*, vol. 56, No. 7, pp. 1247-1262.

Frederick, Stacey, and Jack Daly (2020). Global value chain lens can inform responses to bolster tourism industry in developing countries. Trade for Development News website, managed by Enhanced Integrated Framework (EIF). 20 October. Available at https://trade4devnews.enhancedif.org/en/op-ed/global-value-chain-lens-can-inform-responses-bolster-tourism-industry-developing-countries.

Furceri, Davide, and others (2020). Will Covid-19 affect inequality? evidence from past pandemics. *Covid Economics*, No. 12 (1 May), pp. 138-157. CEPR Press.

G

Gallagher, Kevin P. (2010). Policy space to prevent and mitigate financial crises in trade and investment agreements. G-24 Discussion Paper, No. 58. May. UNCTAD/GDS/MDP/G24/2010/1. Available at https://unctad.org/system/files/official-document/gdsmdpg2420101_en.pdf.

Garrett, Thomas A. (2009). War and pestilence as labor market shocks: U.S. manufacturing wage growth 1914-1919. *Economic Enquiry*, vol. 47, No. 4 (October), pp. 711-725.

Giani, Paolo, and others (2020). Short-term and long-term health impacts of air pollution reductions from COVID-19 lockdowns in China and Europe: a modelling study. *Lancet Planetary Health*, vol. 4, No. 10 (1 October), pp. E474-E482.

Gouel, Christophe, and David Laborde (2018). The crucial role of international trade in adaptation to climate change. *NBER Working Paper*, No. 25221. Cambridge, Massachusetts: National Bureau of Economic Research.

Greenville, Jared, Kentaro Kawasaki and Marie-Agnes Jouanjean (2019). Employment in agriculture and food trade: assessing the role of GVCs. *OECD Food, Agriculture and Fisheries Paper*, No. 124. Paris: Organization for Economic Cooperation and Development. Available at http://dx.doi.org/10.1787/5ed3b181-en.

H

Hacker, Jacob S. (2018). Economic security (chap. 8). In *For Good Measure: Advancing Research on Well-being Metrics Beyond GDP*, Joseph E. Stiglitz, Jean-Paul Fitoussi and Martine Durand, eds.. Paris: OECD.

Hanefeld, Johanna, and Richard Smith (2019). The upside of trade in health services. *BMJ*, vol. 365, No. 2208 (28 May).

Hasdell, Rebecca (2020). What we know about Universal Basic Income: a cross-synthesis of reviews. Stanford, California: Basic Income Lab. July. Available at https://basicincome.stanford.edu/uploads/Umbrella%20Review%20BI_final.pdf.

Heimberger, Philipp (2020). Potential output, EU fiscal surveillance and the COVID-19 shock. *Intereconomics*, vol. 55, No. 3, pp. 167–174.

Hoekman, Bernard, and Ben Shepherd (2020). The future of global trade. Background paper prepared for *World Economic Situation and Prospects 2021*.

Hoekman, Bernard, and Charles Sabel (2019). Open plurilateral agreements, international regulatory cooperation and the WTO. *EUI RSCAS Working Paper*, No. *2019*/10. Fiesole, Italy: European University Institute. Available at https://cadmus.eui.eu/bitstream/handle/1814/60905/RSCAS_2019_10.pdf?sequence=1&isAllowed=y.

Hoekman, Bernard, and Douglas Nelson (2020). Rethinking international subsidy rules. Bertelsmann working paper. 17 March. Gütersloh, Germany: Bertelsmann Stiftung. Available at www.bertelsmann-stiftung.de/fileadmin/files/user_upload/MT_Rethinking_Subsidy_Rules_2020_EN.pdf.

Hofman, David, and Gunes Kamber (2020). Unconventional monetary policy in emerging market and developing economies. Special Series on COVID-19. Note produced by the International Monetary Fund Monetary and Capital Markets Department. 23 September.

Hollweg, Claire H., and others (2014). *Sticky Feet: How Labor Market Frictions Shape the Impact of International Trade on Jobs and Wages.* Directions in Development report, No. 88890. Washington, DC: World Bank. Available at http://documents1.worldbank.org/curated/en/820801468156898298/pdf/Sticky-feet-how-labor-market-frictions-shape-the-impact-of-international-trade-on-jobs-and-wages.pdf.

Hoynes, Hilary, and Rothstein, Jesse (2020). Universal basic income in the United States and advanced countries. *Annual Review of Economics*, vol. 11, pp. 929–958.

I

Igan, Deniz, Divya Kirti and Soledad Martinez Peria (2020). The disconnect between financial markets and the real economy. Special Notes Series on COVID-19 (26 August). International Monetary Fund.

Ignatenko, Anna, Faezeh Raei and Borislava Mircheva (2019). *Global Value Chains: What are the Benefits and Why Do Countries Participate? IMF Working Paper*, No. 19/18. Washington DC: International Monetary Fund. Available at www.imf.org/en/Publications/WP/Issues/2019/01/18/Global-Value-Chains-What-are-the-Benefits-and-Why-Do-Countries-Participate-46505

Institute of International Finance (2020). Global Debt Monitor (16 July). Sharp spike in debt ratios. Available at www.iif.com/Portals/0/Files/content/Research/Global Debt Monitor_July2020.pdf.

Inter-American Development Bank (2020). IDB Group approves record $21.6 billion in lending in 2020. News release. 21 December.

International Energy Agency (2020). *Electricity Market Report – December 2020.* Paris.

International Labour Organization (2017). *World Social Protection Report 2017–19: Universal Social Protection to Achieve the Sustainable Development Goals.* Geneva: International Labour Office.

__________ (2018). *World Employment and Social Outlook: Trends 2018.* Geneva: International Labour Office. Available at https://www.ilo.org/global/research/global-reports/weso/2018/WCMS_615594/lang--en/index.htm.

__________ (2020). ILO Monitor: COVID-19 and the world of work, 6th ed. Updated estimates and analysis. 23 September.

__________ (2020a). Labour overview in times of COVID-19: impact on the labour market and income in Latin America and the Caribbean. Technical note, 2nd ed. Available at https://www.ilo.org/wcmsp5/groups/public/---americas/---ro-lima/documents/publication/wcms_756697.pdf. (Note: The analysis is based on nine countries, which account for more than 80 per cent of the region's economically active population.)

__________(2020b). Statistics on the informal economy. Indicator: Informal employment and informal sector as a percent of employment by sex. ILOSTAT database. Available at https://ilostat.ilo.org/topics/informality/.

__________(2020c). Working from home: estimating the worldwide potential. ILO policy brief. April. Available at www.ilo.org/wcmsp5/groups/public/---ed_protect/---protrav/---travail/documents/briefingnote/wcms_743447.pdf.

International Monetary Fund (2020a). *Fiscal Monitor: Policies for the Recovery – October 2020*. Washington, DC.

__________(2020b). Fiscal rules, escape clauses, and large shocks. Special series on fiscal policies to respond to COVID-19. Available at www.imf.org/~/media/Files/Publications/covid19-special-notes/enspecial-series-on-covid19fiscal-rules-escape-clauses-and-large-shocks.ashx.

__________(2020c). *Global Financial Stability Report: Bridge to Recovery – October 2020*. Washington, DC.

__________(2020d). List of LIC DSAs for PRGT-eligible countries as of December 31, 2020. Available at www.imf.org/external/Pubs/ft/dsa/DSAlist.pdf.

__________(2020e). *Regional Economic Outlook: Sub-Saharan Africa – A Difficult Road to Recovery*. Washington, DC. 20 October. Available at www.imf.org/en/Publications/REO/Issues/2020/10/20/Regional-Economic-Outlook-October-2020-Sub-Saharan-Africa-A-Difficult-Road-to-Recovery-49787.

__________(2020f). Special drawing right (SDR). Factsheet. 24 March. Available at https://www.imf.org/en/About/Factsheets/Sheets/2016/08/01/14/51/Special-Drawing-Right-SDR.

__________(2020g). *World Economic Outlook: A Long and Difficult Ascent - October 2020*. Washington, DC.

Ismail, Yasmin (2020). E-commerce in the World Trade Organization: history and latest developments under the Joint Statement. Briefing note. International Institute for Sustainable Development and CUTS International, Geneva. January.

J

Japan, Cabinet Office (2020). Quarterly estimates of household disposable income and household saving ratio.

K

Khomsi, K., and others (2020). COVID-19 national lockdown in Morocco: impacts on air quality and public health. *One Health*, vol. 11 (20 December), 100200.

Kozul-Wright, Richard (2020). Covid-19 crisis: how South-South cooperation can support economic recovery. UNCTAD website. 3 June. Available at https://unctad.org/news/covid-19-crisis-how-south-south-cooperation-can-support-economic-recovery.

L

Lee, Keun, Franco Malerba and Annalisa Primi (2020). The fourth industrial revolution, changing global value chains and industrial upgrading in emerging economies. *Journal of Economic Policy Reform*, vol. 23, No. 4, pp. 359-370. Available at https://eiufabc.files.wordpress.com/2020/09/lee_malerba_primi_2020.pdf.

Lee, Minsoo, Ruben Carlo Asuncion and Jungsuk Kim (2015). Effectiveness of macroprudential policies in developing Asia: an empirical analysis. *ADB Economics Working Paper*, No. 439. July. Manila: Asian Development Bank.

Lodefalk, Magnus (2015). Tear down the trade-policy silos! or how the servicification of manufacturing makes divides in trade policymaking irrelevant. VoxEU, CEPR policy portal. 16 January. Available at https://voxeu.org/article/servicification-manufacturing-and-trade-policy.

Long, Heather (2020). Nearly 8 million Americans have fallen into poverty since the summer. *Washington Post*, 16 December.

M

McKinsey Global Institute (2016). *Digital Globalization: The New Era of Global Flows*. March.

__________ (2017). *Jobs Lost, Jobs Gained: Workforce Transitions in a Time of Automation*. December. Available at www.mckinsey.com/~/media/McKinsey/Industries/Public%20and%20Social%20Sector/Our%20Insights/What%20the%20future%20of%20work%20will%20mean%20for%20jobs%20skills%20and%20wages/MGI-Jobs-Lost-Jobs-Gained-Report-December-6-2017.pdf.

__________ (2020). *Risk, Resilience, and Rebalancing in Global Value Chains*. Authors: Susan Lund and others. August.

McNeill, Desmond, and others (2017). Trade and investment agreements: implications for health protection. *Journal of World Trade*, vol. 51, No. 1 (February), pp. 159-182. Available at www.researchgate.net/profile/Pepita_Barlow2/publication/316609740_Trade_and_investment_agreements_Implications_for_health_protection/links/5c0647bd299bf169ae307c11/Trade-and-investment-agreements-Implications-for-health-protection.pdf.

Miroudot, Sébastien, and Håkan Nordström (2020). Made in the world? global value chains in the midst of rising protectionism. *Review of Industrial Organization*, vol. 57, No. 2 (September), pp. 195-222.

Moderna (2020). Moderna announces the European Commission's approval of advance purchase agreement for initial 80 million doses of mRNA vaccine against COVID-19 (mRNA-1273). Press release. 25 November.

N

Neumann, Frederic, and Abanti Bhaumik (2020). Who, where, what? mapping Asian supply chains. HSBC Global Research. Hong Kong SAR: Hongkong and Shanghai Banking Corporation Limited. 22 July.

Nordahl, Helene (2014). Social inequality in chronic disease outcomes. *Danish Medical Journal*, vol. 61, No. 11 (November), B4943.

O

Olabisi, Michael, and Howard Stein (2015). Sovereign bond issues: do African countries pay more to borrow? *Journal of African Trade*, vol. 2: Nos. 1-2 (December), pp. 87-109.

Organization for Economic Cooperation and Development (2015). *OECD Digital Economy Outlook 2015*. Paris.

__________(2020a). COVID-19 in Latin America and the Caribbean: regional socio-economic implications and policy priorities. Policy note. Updated 8 December. Available at https://read.oecd-ilibrary.org/view/?ref=129_129904-k3xp17fqbl&title=COVID-19-in-Latin-America-and-the-Caribbean-Regional-socio-economic-implications-and-policy-priorities.

__________(2020b). Global value chains in agriculture. Agriculture Policy Brief. February. Available at https://issuu.com/oecd.publishing/docs/global_value_chains_in_agriculture

__________(2020c). *OECD Employment Outlook 2020: Worker Security and the COVID-19 Crisis*. Paris.

Ortiz, Isabel, and others (2020). Universal social protection floors: Costing estimates and affordability in 57 lower income countries. ESS Working Paper No. 58. Geneva: International Labour Organization, Social Protection Department. Available at https://www.social-protection.org/gimi/RessourcePDF.action?id=54915.

Oxfam International (2020). World on the brink of a "hunger pandemic": coronavirus threatens to push millions into starvation.

P

Patel, Priyank Pravin, Sayoni Mondal and Krishna Gopal Ghosh (2020). Some respite for India's dirtiest river? examining the Yamuna's water quality at Delhi during the COVID-19 lockdown period. *Science of The Total Environment*, vol. 744 (20 November), 140851.

Pfizer (2020). Pfizer and Biontech to supply Canada with their BNT162 MRNA-based vaccine candidate. Press release. 5 August.

Pickett, Kate E., and Richard G. Wilkinson (2015). Income inequality and health: a causal review. *Social Science and Medicine*, vol. 128, issue C (March), pp. 316-326.

Powell, Jerome H. (2020). New economic challenges and the Fed's monetary policy review. Speech delivered on 27 August at the economic policy symposium on "Navigating the decade ahead: implications for monetary policy", sponsored by the Federal Reserve Bank of Kansas City, Jackson Hole, Wyoming (via webcast). Available at www.federalreserve.gov/newsevents/speech/powell20200827a.htm.

R

Roidt, Mario, and others (2020). Unlocking the impacts of COVID-19 lockdowns: changes in thermal electricity generation water footprint and virtual water trade in Europe. *Environmental Science and Technology Letters*, vol. 7, No. 9, pp. 683–689.

Rutter, Paul D., and others (2012). Socio-economic disparities in mortality due to pandemic influenza in England. *International Journal of Public Health*, vol. 57, No. 4 (August), pp. 745-750.

S

Schlegl, Matthias, Christoph Trebesch and Mark L.J. Wright (2019). *The Seniority Structure of Sovereign Debt. NBER Working Paper*, No. 25793. Cambridge, Massachusetts: National Bureau of Economic Research. May.

Scudellari, Megan (2020). How the pandemic might play out in 2021 and beyond. *Nature*, 5 August.

Seric, Adnan, and Yee Siong Tong (2019). What are global value chains and why do they matter? UNIDO Industrial Analytics Platform at unido.org. August. Available at https://iap.unido.org/articles/what-are-global-value-chains-and-why-do-they-matter.

Shepherd, Ben (forthcoming). Come undone: tariffs, trade wars, and cross-border production sharing. Working paper, in progress.

Shih, Willy C. (2020). Global supply chains in a post-pandemic world. *Harvard Business Review*, September-October issue. Available at https://hbr.org/2020/09/global-supply-chains-in-a-post-pandemic-world.

Shiller, Robert J. (2020). People fear a market crash more than they have in years. *New York Times*, 23 October.

Slotman, Julian Rodrick (2020). The long-term impact of COVID-19 on poverty. UN DESA policy brief, No. 86. New York: Department of Economic and Social Affairs of the United Nations Secretariat.

Songwe, Vera (2020). Africa needs its own "repo" market: G20 central banks should spur recovery from the crisis by backing a new lending vehicle. *Financial Times*, 25 June. Available at www.ft.com/content/c784b7f5-6a07-4500-bb4a-da4f95f891f8.

Sostero, Matteo, and others (2020). *Teleworkability and the COVID-19 Crisis: A New Digital Divide?* JRC Working Paper on Labour, Education and Technology, No. 2020/05. Seville, Spain: European Commission, Joint Research Centre.

Ståhl, Christian, and Ellen MacEachen (2020). Universal Basic Income as a policy response to COVID-19 and precarious employment: potential impacts on rehabilitation and return-to-work. *Journal of Occupational Rehabilitation*, Editorial. 20 August. Available at https://link.springer.com/article/10.1007/s10926-020-09923-w.

Statistics Canada (2020). Gross domestic product, income and expenditure, second quarter 2020. 28 August.

Stelitano, Laura, and others (2020). The digital divide and COVID-19: teachers' perceptions of inequities in students' Internet access and participation in remote learning. Data note: Insights from the American Educator Panels. Rand Corporation. Available at https://doi.org/10.7249/RRA134-3.

Stiglitz, Joseph, and Hamid Rashid (2020). Averting catastrophic debt crises in developing countries: extraordinary challenges call for extraordinary measures. Centre for Economic Policy Research (CEPR) Policy Insight No. 104. July . Available at https://cepr.org/active/publications/policy_insights/viewpi.php?pino=104.

T

Thangavelu, Shandre M., Wenxiao Wang and Sothea Oum (2018). Servicification in global value chains: comparative analysis of selected Asian countries with OECD. *World Economy*, vol. 41, No. 11, pp 3045-3070. Available at https://digital.library.adelaide.edu.au/dspace/bitstream/2440/116864/3/hdl_116864.pdf.

Trommer, Silke (2017). The WTO in an era of preferential trade agreements: thick and thin institutions in global trade governance. *World Trade Review*, vol. 16, No. 3, pp. 501-526.

U

United Kingdom of Great Britain and Northern Ireland, Office for National Statistics (2020a). Coronavirus and its impact on the UK institutional sector accounts: quarter 2 (Apr to June) 2020. 30 September.

_________(2020b). Households (S.14). Households' savings ratio (per cent): current price: £m: SA. Release date: 30 September. Available at www.ons.gov.uk/economy/grossdomesticproductgdp/timeseries/dgd8/ukea.

United Nations (2016). *World Economic and Social Survey 2016: Climate Change Resilience - An Opportunity for Reducing Inequalities*. Sales No. E.16.II.C.1.

_________(2018). *World Economic and Social Survey 2018: Frontier Technologies for Sustainable Development*. Sales No. E.18.II.C.1. Available at www.un.org/development/desa/dpad/wp-content/uploads/sites/45/publication/WESS2018_full_web.pdf.

_________(2020a). COVID-19 and transforming tourism. Policy brief. August.

_________(2020b). Report of the Secretary-General on the international financial system and development. A/75/268. 28 July. Available at https://undocs.org/A/75/268.

_________(2020c). *World Economic Situation and Prospects 2020*. Sales No. E.20.II.C.1.

United Nations Children's Fund (2020). COVID-19: at least a third of the world's schoolchildren unable to access remote learning during school closures, new report says. Press release. 26 August.

United Nations Conference on Trade and Development (2015). *Global Value Chains and South-South Trade: Economic Cooperation and Integration among Developing Countries*. October.UNCTAD/GDS/ECIDC/2015/1. Available at: https://unctad.org/system/files/official-document/gdsecidc2015d1_en.pdf.

_________(2017). *Services and Structural Transformation for Development*, Mina Mashayekhi and Bruno Antunes, eds. UNCTAD/DITC/TNCD/2017/2.

_________(2018). *Trade and Development Report 2018: Power, Platforms and the Free Trade Delusion*. Sales No. E.18.II.D.7. Available at https://unctad.org/system/files/official-document/tdr2018_en.pdf.

_________(2019). *Trade Policies for Combating Inequality: Equal Opportunities to Firms, Workers and Countries*. Sales No. E.19.II.D.21. Available at https://unctad.org/system/files/official-document/ditctab2019d6_en.pdf.

_________(2020). *Trade and Development Report 2020: From Global Pandemic to Prosperity for All - Avoiding Another Lost Decade*. Sales No. E.20.II.D.30.

_________(2020a). Estimates of global e-commerce 2018. UNCTAD technical note on ICT for development, No. 15. Available at https://unctad.org/system/files/official-document/tn_unctad_ict4d15_en.pdf.

_________(2020b). *World Investment Report 2020: International Production Beyond the Pandemic*. Sales No. E.20.II.D.23.

_________(forthcoming a). Services value-added in exports: policies for development.

_________(forthcoming b). Guidebook on the methodology for the measurement of services value-added in exports.

__________, Trade and Development Board (2020). Report of the Multi-year Expert Meeting on Trade, Services and Development on its eighth session. 13 October. TD/B/C.I/MEM.4/24.

United Nations Development Programme, and Oxford Poverty and Human Development Initiative (2020). Charting pathways out of multidimensional poverty: achieving the SDGs. Available at http://hdr.undp.org/sites/default/files/2020_mpi_report_en.pdf.

United Nations Industrial Development Organization (2015). *Industrial Development Report 2016: The Role of Technology and Innovation in Inclusive and Sustainable Industrial Development*. Sales No. E.15.II.B.47.

United Nations, Department of Economic and Social Affairs (2020). World Economic Situation and Prospects: August 2020 briefing, No. 140. Available at www.un.org/development/desa/dpad/publication/world-economic-situation-and-prospects-august-2020-briefing-no-140/.

United Nations, Economic and Social Commission for Asia and the Pacific (2019). *Economic and Social Survey of Asia and the Pacific 2019: Ambitions Beyond Growth*. Sales No. E.19.II.F.6.

__________(2020). COVID-19 and South Asia: national strategies and subregional cooperation for accelerating sustainable and resilient recovery.

United Nations, Economic and Social Commission for Western Asia (2020a). COVID-19 stimulus tracker. Available at http://covdata.unescwa.org/RPT/qualitative.aspx.

__________(2020b). Poverty in Lebanon: solidarity is vital to address the impact of multiple overlapping shocks. ESCWA/2020/Policy Brief.15. Available at www.unescwa.org/sites/www.unescwa.org/files/20-00268_pb15_beirut-explosion-rising-poverty-en.pdf.

__________(forthcoming). *Survey of Economic and Social Developments in the Arab Region, 2019-2020.*

United Nations, Economic Commission for Africa (2020). Making special drawing rights work for COVID-19 economic relief. ECA Policy Brief. Available at www.uneca.org/publications/eca-policy-brief-making-special-drawing-rights-work-covid-19-economic-relief.

__________, and PIMCO (2020). Joint proposal of the Economic Commission for Africa and PIMCO on a liquidity and sustainability facility to improve market access for emerging market and other vulnerable sovereigns. September.

United Nations, Economic Commission for Latin America and the Caribbean (2020a). *Building a New Future: Transformative Recovery with Equality and Sustainability.* Sales No. E.20.II.G.14.

__________(2020b). *Economic Survey of Latin America and the Caribbean: Main Conditioning Factors of Fiscal and Monetary Policies in the Post-COVID-19 Era.* Sales No. E.20.II.G.2.

__________(2020c). Political and social compacts for equality and sustainable development in Latin America and the Caribbean in the post-COVID-19 recovery. COVID-19 special report, No. 8. 15 October.

__________, and International Labour Organization (2020). Employment situation in Latin America and the Caribbean: employment trends in an unprecedented crisis - policy challenges. LC/TS.2020/128.

United Nations, Inter-agency Task Force on Financing for Development (2020). *Financing for Sustainable Development Report 2020.* Sales No. E.20.I.4. Available at https://developmentfinance.un.org/sites/developmentfinance.un.org/files/FSDR_2020.pdf.

United States Department of Commerce, Bureau of Economic Analysis (2020) Gross domestic product, third quarter 2020 (advance estimate). Table 8.

Usher, Ann Danaiya (2020). South Africa and India push for COVID-19 patents ban. *Lancet*, vol. 396, No. 10265 (5 December), pp. 1790-1791.

W

Wang, Zhi, Shang-Jin Wei and Kunfu Zhu (2013). *Quantifying International Production Sharing at the Bilateral and Sector Levels. NBER Working Paper*, No. 19677. Cambridge, Massachusetts: National Bureau of Economic Research.

Weill, Joakim A., and others (2020). Social distancing responses to COVID-19 emergency declarations strongly differentiated by income. *Proceedings of the National Academy of Sciences of the United States of America (PNAS)*, vol. 117, No. 33 (18 August), pp. 19658-19660.

World Bank (2020). *International Debt Statistics 2021.* Washington, DC.

__________(2020a). *Africa's Pulse*, vol. 22 (October). *Charting the Road to Recovery.* Authors: Albert G. Zeufack and others. Washington, DC.

__________(2020b). *Commodity Markets Outlook: Persistence of Commodity Shocks.* October. Available at https://openknowledge.worldbank.org/bitstream/handle/10986/34621/CMO-October-2020.pdf.

__________(2020c). *South Asia Economic Focus, Fall 2020: Beaten or Broken? - Informality and COVID-19.* Washington, DC. Available at https://openknowledge.worldbank.org/bitstream/handle/10986/34517/9781464816406.pdf?sequence=7&isAllowed=y.

__________(2020d). *World Development Report 2020: Trading for Development in the Age of Global Value Chains.* Washington, DC.

World Bank, European Union and United Nations (2020). *Beirut Rapid Damage and Needs Assessment.* August.

World Food Programme (2020). World Food Programme to assist largest number of hungry people ever, as coronavirus devastates poor nations. News release. 29 June.

World Tourism Organization (2019). *The Future of Work and Skills Development in Tourism.* Policy paper. Madrid. October. Available at www.e-unwto.org/doi/book/10.18111/9789284421213.

__________(2020a). *UNWTO Briefing Note:Tourism and COVID-19*, No. 1 (June). How are countries supporting tourism recovery?

__________(2020b). *UNTWO Briefing Note: Tourism and COVID-19*, No. 2 (June). Tourism in SIDS: the challenge of sustaining livelihoods in times of COVID-19. Available at www.e-unwto.org/doi/book/10.18111/9789284421916.

__________(2020c). *UNWTO Briefing Note: Tourism and Covid-19*, No. 3 (September). Understanding domestic tourism and seizing its opportunities. Available at www.e-unwto.org/doi/book/10.18111/9789284422111.

__________(2020d). *UNWTO Recommendations on Tourism and Rural Development: A Guide to Making Tourism an Effective Tool for Rural Development*. September. Available at www.e-unwto.org/doi/book/10.18111/9789284422173.

__________(2020e). *UNWTO World Tourism Barometer*, vol. 18, No. 6 (October). Available at https://doi.org/10.18111/wtobarometereng.

World Trade Organization (2019a). *Global Value Chain Development Report 2019: Technological Innovation, Supply Chain Trade, and Workers in a Globalized World*. Geneva. Available at http://documents1.worldbank.org/curated/en/384161555079173489/pdf/Global-Value-Chain-Development-Report-2019-Technological-Innovation-Supply-Chain-Trade-and-Workers-in-a-Globalized-World.pdf.

__________(2019b). *World Trade Report 2019: The Future of Services Trade*. Geneva. Available at www.wto.org/english/res_e/booksp_e/00_wtr19_e.pdf.

__________(2020a). Export prohibitions and restrictions. Information note. 23 April. Available at www.wto.org/english/tratop_e/covid19_e/export_prohibitions_report_e.pdf.

__________(2020b). Market access for products and services of export interest to least developed countries.Note by the Secretariat. WT/COMTD/LDC/W/68. 23 October.

__________(2020c). New initiatives launched to intensify WTO work on trade and the environment. 17 November. Available at www.wto.org/english/news_e/news20_e/envir_17nov20_e.htm.

__________(2020d). WTO to host first Trade for Peace Week. 25 November. Available at www.wto.org/english/news_e/news20_e/acc_25nov20_e.htm.

__________, Subcommittee on Least Developed Countries (2019). Market access for products and services of export interest to least developed countries. Note by the secretariat. WT/COMTD/LDC/W/67. 15 October.

Z

Zahler, Andrés, Leonardo Iacovone and Aaditya Mattoo (2014). Trade and innovation in services: evidence from a developing economy. *World Economy*, vol. 37, No. 7 (July), pp. 953-979.

Zimmer, Carl, Jonathan Corum and Sui-Lee Wee (2021). Coronavirus Vaccine Tracker. *New York Times*. Updated 6 January.

New Edition

GCSE Business Studies

David Butler

Oxford University Press

Contents

Preface

This book is for students preparing for the GCSE examination in Business Studies and will also be useful for related courses such as GNVQ. The text has taken account of the National Criteria for Business Studies and all SCAA approved Business Studies syllabuses. The text and exercises have been trialled with a mixed ability group of GCSE Business Studies students in a comprehensive school. This new edition retains the structure of the first edition but takes account of developments in business and new ideas in business studies.

The approach, wherever possible, is student centred and places emphasis on the development of key concepts through case studies and exercises. After a brief introductory section, the student is first introduced to basic business ideas through the small firm. This approach has proved to be successful as the student can more easily identify with the small business unit in the early stages of the course. Many of these ideas are then developed in relation to the large firm in Section III, while new concepts are also introduced. The final section of the book deals with wider issues and looks at the relationship between the State and business activity. A concluding unit considers the most recent changes affecting business activity.

The teaching aims are clearly identified at the start of each unit and there is a summary of key words and ideas at the end of each unit. Apart from the activities, questions, and exercises within the body of the text, there are test questions at the end of each unit as well as suggestions for coursework assignments. The questions are designed to test understanding of ideas rather than factual recall and are structured for the full ability range.

The main body of the text is targeted at average-ability students and there has been a deliberate effort to avoid the use of too much unnecessary jargon. The book does also contain all that is required by the most able students in order to obtain the highest possible grades. Some sections of the book are marked as 'extension' sections where the ideas are regarded as more difficult or not essential to the 'core' needs of most syllabuses. Extension questions have been included at the end of each unit in order to test the more able student.

Section

1 An introduction to business

unit 1 The nature and purpose of business activity

Aims

At the end of this unit you should understand:

- What is meant by business activity.
- The terms producer, consumer, goods and services.
- The aims and objectives of businesses.
- What is meant by profit.
- The chain of production and added value.
- The primary, secondary and tertiary sectors of the economy.
- The factors of production.
- Planned, market and mixed economies.

What is business activity?

In this book business activity includes all organisations where people work to produce goods or services for consumers. Goods are any items such as cars, washing machines, chocolate etc. Services are any work undertaken for customers such as hairdressing, insurance, health care etc. A consumer is anyone who buys goods and services – so we are all consumers. A business may also be a consumer. For example, a clothing business might buy zips from a business producing fasteners.

Business activity includes the smallest organisations, such as an artist working from home, through to the largest multi-national corporations such as Ford and Coca-Cola. Business activity also includes services provided by the Government such as the National Health Service and services provided by local government such as schools and by charities such as Oxfam.

Exercise

For each picture on the next page name a good or service associated with the illustration. For example, the aircraft is a good and travel provided by British Airways is a service.

GOODS	SERVICES
1 Aircraft	1 Airtravel provided by BA
2	2
3	3